Social Skills Across the Life Span

Social Skills Across the Life Span

Theory, Assessment, and Intervention

Edited by

Douglas W. Nangle
Cynthia A. Erdley
Rebecca A. Schwartz-Mette

ELSEVIER

ACADEMIC PRESS
An imprint of Elsevier

Academic Press is an imprint of Elsevier
125 London Wall, London EC2Y 5AS, United Kingdom
525 B Street, Suite 1650, San Diego, CA 92101, United States
50 Hampshire Street, 5th Floor, Cambridge, MA 02139, United States
The Boulevard, Langford Lane, Kidlington, Oxford OX5 1GB, United Kingdom

Library of Congress Cataloging-in-Publication Data
A catalog record for this book is available from the Library of Congress

British Library Cataloguing-in-Publication Data
A catalogue record for this book is available from the British Library

ISBN 978-0-12-817752-5

For information on all Academic Press publications
visit our website at https://www.elsevier.com/books-and-journals

Publisher: Nikki P. Levy
Editorial Project Manager: Barbara L. Makinster
Production Project Manager: Viswanathan Sreejith
Cover Designer: Matthew Limbert

Typeset by SPi Global, India

Contents

9. The Fast Track Friendship Group program

Karen L. Bierman

10. The *PATHS* curriculum: Thirty-five years and counting

Carol A. Kusché

Contributors

Numbers in parenthesis indicate the pages on which the authors' contributions begin.

Tandra T. Allen (295), Center for BrainHealth®, The University of Texas at Dallas, Dallas, TX, United States

Laura A. Andrews (3,115), University of Maine, Orono, ME, United States

Lara Ashmore (295), Center for BrainHealth®, The University of Texas at Dallas, Dallas, TX, United States

Karen L. Bierman (181), The Pennsylvania State University, University Park, PA, United States

Julia Browne (329), Center of Excellence for Psychosocial and Systemic Research, Massachusetts General Hospital; Harvard Medical School, Boston, MA, United States

Michelle L. Buffie (115), University of Maine, Orono, ME, United States

Sandra Bond Chapman (295), Center for BrainHealth®, The University of Texas at Dallas, Dallas, TX, United States

Lori G. Cook (295), Center for BrainHealth®, The University of Texas at Dallas, Dallas, TX, United States

Robert J. Coplan (165), Carleton University, Ottawa, ON, Canada

James A. Courtney (91), Monash University, Melbourne, VIC, Australia

Samantha Coyle (237), Montclair State University, Montclair, NJ, United States

Cynthia A. Erdley (25,69), University of Maine, Orono, ME, United States

Elissa R. Failes (139), Wichita State University, Wichita, KS, United States

Eliot Fearey (47), University of Maine, Orono, ME, United States

Sarah Fischer (91), University of Nebraska-Lincoln, Lincoln, NE, United States

Shelly Gordon (295), Center for BrainHealth®, The University of Texas at Dallas, Dallas, TX, United States

Samantha J. Gregus (139), Wichita State University, Wichita, KS, United States

Rachel L. Grover (3,115), Loyola University Maryland, Baltimore, MD, United States

Raegan Harrington (139), University of Maine, Orono, ME, United States

Kate A. Helbig (221), University of South Dakota, Vermillion, SD, United States

Jennifer Holloway (311), National University of Ireland Galway, Galway, Ireland

Melissa S. Jankowski (69), University of Maine, Orono, ME, United States

Kimberly E. Kamper-DeMarco (47), State University of New York Buffalo State College, Buffalo, NY, United States

Julie Newman Kingery (25), Hobart and William Smith Colleges, Geneva, NY, United States

Carol A. Kusché (201,277), Seattle Psychoanalytic Society and Institute; University of Washington; PATHS® Training LLC; Institute for Emotional & Social Competence (IESC), Seattle, WA, United States

Julian B.R. Kusché (277), Institute for Emotional & Social Competence (IESC), Seattle, WA, United States

Elizabeth Laugeson (255), University of California, Los Angeles Semel Institute for Neuroscience and Human Behavior, Los Angeles, CA, United States

Hannah R. Lawrence (47), University of Maine, Orono, ME, United States

Helena Lydon (311), National University of Ireland Galway, Galway, Ireland

Anna-Lisa Mackey (277), Institute for Emotional & Social Competence (IESC), Seattle, WA; PATHS® Program LLC, Avondale, AZ, United States

Farah Mahmud (237), Montclair State University, Montclair, NJ, United States

Carrie Masia Warner (237), Montclair State University, Montclair, NJ; Nathan Kline Institute for Psychiatric Research, Orangeburg, NY, United States

Emily Moulton (255), University of California, Los Angeles Semel Institute for Neuroscience and Human Behavior, Los Angeles, CA, United States

Kim T. Mueser (329), Center for Psychiatric Rehabilitation, Boston University, Boston, MA, United States

Douglas W. Nangle (3,115), University of Maine, Orono, ME, United States

Peter J. Norton (91), Monash University, Melbourne, VIC, Australia

Sarah I. Pratt (329), The Geisel School of Medicine at Dartmouth, Concord, NH, United States

Keith C. Radley (221), University of Utah, Salt Lake City, UT, United States

Elizabeth Ramirez (139), Wichita State University, Wichita, KS, United States

Emily Scarpulla (25), University of Maine, Orono, ME, United States

Rebecca A. Schwartz-Mette (47,139), University of Maine, Orono, ME, United States

Jessica Shankman (47), University of Maine, Orono, ME, United States

William Spaulding (91), University of Nebraska-Lincoln, Lincoln, NE, United States

Aaron Tate (295), Center for BrainHealth®, The University of Texas at Dallas, Dallas, TX, United States

Edith Walsh (311), National University of Ireland Galway, Galway, Ireland

Cody Weeks (237), Montclair State University, Montclair, NJ, United States

Phoebe Welcome (139), University of Maine, Orono, ME, United States

Preface

Now more than ever, the importance of social interactions in determining psychological adjustment has been recognized by the helping professions. We live in a time in which we are racing to find effective treatments for autism spectrum disorder, tracking social centers of the brain with neuroimaging techniques, and employing virtual reality to help people improve their social interactions, and yet the last truly comprehensive social skills books were published decades ago. In that span of time, the field has become more fragmented, with increasing specialization and available resources restricted to particular populations. This book fills that gap by providing state-of-the-art, in-depth, and comprehensive coverage of social skills theory, assessment, and intervention. Unlike existing resources, this book addresses the full life-span, early childhood through older adulthood. Designed for a wide audience that includes academics, clinicians, and graduate students within the disciplines of psychology, education, counseling, applied development, and social work, this volume is divided into three major sections.

The first section is devoted to theory and includes foundational reviews of the definitions of social competence, normative social development, and links to adjustment and psychopathology. The second section covers overarching assessment and treatment considerations with separate chapters for youth and adults. The third section provides cutting-edge coverage of particular evidence-based interventions. It features standalone chapters describing many of the most renowned social skills training programs for young children, adolescents, and adults with more normative functioning levels, such as universal socioemotional learning and workplace skills interventions, as well as more clinical concerns, such as shyness and social anxiety, conduct problems and aggression, and autism spectrum disorders and schizophrenia. An added feature of these intervention chapters is their standard format that includes rich details about program implementation along with reviews of the evidence base.

Douglas W. Nangle, Cynthia A. Erdley, and
Rebecca A. Schwartz-Mette

Part I

Theory

Chapter 1

Defining social skills

Rachel L. Grover[a], Douglas W. Nangle[b], Michelle Buffie[b], and Laura A. Andrews[b]
[a]*Loyola University Maryland, Baltimore, MD, United States,* [b]*University of Maine, Orono, ME, United States*

We wish we could start this book with a widely agreed upon definition of social skills. At first glance, such a definition would seem intuitive. Even a quick internet search reveals that social skills are the "skills we use to communicate and interact with each other" ("What Are Social Skills," 2019). Although this definition is essentially correct, a deeper review of the literature on social skills uncovers important nuances regarding level of skill (e.g., micro or macro, verbal or nonverbal), degree of consideration of person factors (e.g., social goals, diversity factors), as well as attention to situation factors. For example, the construct can encompass molecular skills like eye contact and vocal tone, as well as more molar and flexible sets of skills like social problem solving (SPS). In addition, appropriate social skills depend on social goals (e.g., being popular versus being well liked), cultural/ethnic norms (e.g., amount of appropriate eye contact or personal space), and the context of that particular social situation (e.g., maintaining a conversation during an interview versus with a friend), thus effectively blurring the clarity of the easily accessed web definition. Further contributing to the complexity of the construct is recent research supporting the inclusion of emotion regulation (e.g., emotion modulation) and neuropsychological abilities (e.g., attention) as essential skills that influence social functioning. Thus, although understandable, the absence of a universal definition likely contributes to empirical inaccuracy (at worst) or vague understanding (at best). Therefore, a synthesis of the various existing global definitions and models is warranted, and we set out to do just that in this chapter. Starting with an overview of the various definitions of social skills and social competence, we move on to review prominent models that address both. Next, we distill these major models, extracting four core target areas: communication skills, emotion regulation skills, cognitive skills, and problem-solving skills. Finally, each target area is reviewed with attention to its importance to adjustment and intervention across the lifespan.

The terms social skills and social competence are often used interchangeably, when they actually represent related, but distinct constructs. Social skills

Social Skills Across the Life Span. https://doi.org/10.1016/B978-0-12-817752-5.00001-9

are typically defined in relation to social competence and are commonly thought of as the requisite skills that enable effective social responding. In his seminal review, McFall (1982) states that while *competence* is a general evaluative process, *skills* are needed to perform competently. For example, a new driver is deemed competent upon passing the driver's test, but it is the specific driving skills (e.g., use of turn signals, ability to parallel park, knowledge of laws) that contribute to the competent performance. Thus, social competence is determined by social evaluations (e.g., being well-liked, getting a job, getting married), whereas social skills (e.g., smiling, being assertive, negotiating conflict) help us to get there. Before we undertake the challenge of defining social skills, we must first wrestle with the more global social competence construct.

It is hard to define social skills, because it is difficult to define social competence. From a large list of definitions of social competence ranging across several decades, Nangle, Grover, Holleb, Cassano, and Fales (2010) identified a few common themes. Specifically, most of the existing definitions refer to effectiveness, focus on the behavior of the individual (rather than the dyad or group), and consider the influence of the situational context. McFall's (1982) definition contains all three of these themes: "quality or adequacy (*effectiveness*) of a person's overall performance (*individual behavior*) in a particular task (*situational context*)" (p. 12). Reaching farther back, White (1959) defined competence as an "effective interaction with the environment" (p. 297). Subsequent definitions of social competence echo this early conceptualization while focusing more specifically on the social domain. For example, Goldfried and D'Zurilla (1969) defined social competence as "the effectiveness or adequacy with which an individual is capable of responding to various problematic situations" (p. 161). Two decades later, Taylor and Asher (1984) described social competence as "the formulation and adoption of personal goals that are appropriate and adaptive to specific social situations and implementing effective behavior strategies for achieving goals" (p. 57).

Despite the common threads connecting these various definitions, what constitutes socially competent behavior remains somewhat difficult to determine, mainly because competent responding is relative and dependent on several contextual factors. One powerful contextual influence is the situation; social competence likely looks very different when comparing behavior at a cocktail party versus a committee meeting. Asher and McDonald (2009) recommend condensing the likely limitless possible social situations to those that have similar meaning and functionality and then researching those social situations that are critical to social functioning. For example, Dodge and colleagues found that peer group entry is related to both peer acceptance and sociometric status, and interventions focused on peer group entry skills may help social functioning (Dodge, Schlundt, Schocken, & Delugach, 1983). What is considered competent also depends on the social goals of the individual. For instance, Cillessen and Bellmore (2011) reported that preferred children often endorse communal goals and use prosocial behaviors to reach those goals, whereas popular children endorse agentic goals and tend to use a mix of prosocial and domineering or aggressive strategies to reach those goals. Diversity factors like culture, ethnicity, and gender also influence what is considered socially competent behavior. In fact, Han and Thomas (2010) state that culture may be the most important determinant of what is considered socially competent as culture influences both expectations and values placed on behavior. In addition, research suggests that different cultures and ethnic groups vary on appropriate levels of eye contact, personal space, touch, gestures, and facial expression (Norton, Washington, Peters, & Hayes, 2010).

As social competence is relative, so are the social skills required to be socially competent. Social skills are the component abilities needed to be competent in a specific social situation. We can probably agree that the social situations of having a conversation with a friend and resolving a conflict with a romantic partner, require different sets of social skills, with some likely overlap. Definitions of social skills reflect this context relativity. For example, Gresham and Elliott (1984) define social skills as those interpersonal behaviors that result in positive responses and avoid negative responses. Earlier conceptualizations of social skill focus solely on observable microbehaviors (e.g., turn taking, rate of interaction, eye gaze), while more recent definitions focus on macrobehaviors such as problem-solving ability and include complementary cognitive (e.g., response selection) and emotional processes (e.g., anxiety regulation; Matson & Burns, 2017). Social skills also encompass both verbal and nonverbal expressions. Importantly, social skills are often seen as more directly changeable than social competence, and are therefore considered to be the primary target for intervention (Little, Swangler, & Akin-Little, 2017).

Part of the difficulty in defining social competence and social skills emerges from the multiple ways the two constructs are assessed. Cavell (1990) organized these measurement attempts into three main areas: products of social functioning, requisite skills of social functioning, and actual social functioning. Products of social functioning, which map onto what we think of as social competence, include such global achievements as employment, a stable romantic relationship, and peer acceptance. In contrast, assessment of the requisite skills of social functioning focuses on specific social skills (e.g., problem identification) considered essential for competent responding. Cavell groups these social skills assessments into three types: encoding skills (e.g., perception of task, attributions), decision skills (e.g., response selection, self-efficacy), and enactment skills (e.g., execution of plan, monitoring, emotional regulation). Assessment measures in the third area, measures of actual social functioning, connect the social skill and social competence constructs by assessing effective social performance within specific social contexts. For example, this approach may include those prosocial behaviors associated with sociometric status, or those social skills needed for empirically identified key social situations (like peer entry tasks as mentioned earlier). As one can imagine, such varied assessment approaches yield varied results. In fact, Cavell (1990) posits that much of the noncongruence among measures that purport to assess social skills may be explained by the fact that the measures are actually assessing functionally different constructs.

Models of social skills and social competence

Getting from this theoretical morass to something more useful in the applied sense requires some work. In the following content, we hope to bring some clarity by reviewing and synthesizing some of the major models of social competence and social skills. In contrast to the definitions presented, the models provide more detailed conceptualizations that act as a guide for assessment, intervention, and research. Each of the models summarized later takes a slightly different perspective; considered together, they deepen our understanding of the constructs. The definitional models describe social skills and competence and map the relations among the constructs. The situational models turn our attention to the identification of critical situations and prompt thinking about the social skills needed for specific situations. The process models facilitate our understanding of how different social skills may function together as part of a system. Finally, the skill sets models bring a holistic view of the large range of related skills that work in concert to enable competent social interactions.

Definitional models

The late 1970s and early 1980s was a boom time for research on social skills and social skills training. This proliferation prompted several researchers to propose models of the important terms and how they may be related. These definitional models continue to serve an important role as they build consensus, which aids theory and research development and guides assessment and intervention efforts. In fact, Rose-Krasnor (1997) argued that it makes sense to focus primarily on the conceptual level due to the highly idiosyncratic nature of the social context (e.g., developmental stage, culture, gender, social goals). At the same time, the definitional models leave some important questions unanswered. Specifically, these models do not classify particular critical social situations or identify certain necessary skills or skill sets.

McFall (1982) and Dodge and Murphy (1984) were some of the first to publish definitional models. McFall focused on three primary related concepts: social skills and social competence (discussed earlier) and social tasks. McFall used the term social task to refer to an "organizing and directing force on behavior" and provided the examples of "having a conversation" and "developing an intimate relationship" (p. 14–15). Social tasks likely have sublevels of behavior; for example, "making a friend" might include "finding people with similar interests," and "initiating a shared social activity." Ideally, social competence is evaluated based on behavioral criteria established for a specific social task. Thus, to evaluate the competence of a person's behavior, one must first understand the demands of the task. McFall recommended empirically identifying those social tasks that are the most "relevant and critical" (p. 19) to social functioning. Like McFall, Dodge and Murphy (1984) asserted that social competence is based on an evaluation by relevant others (e.g., peer acceptance), and that social behavior must be evaluated in the context of specific situations, or social tasks. Dodge and Murphy (1984) theorized that the third essential concept was social information processing (SIP) skills, or a system of interpreting a situation, deciding on a response, and acting on that response, a process that is further explored in the process models section below.

Building on these early models, Cavell's (1990) Tri-Component Model of Social Competence is an integrative model of three hierarchical concepts. *Social adjustment*, or the ability to meet appropriate social goals (e.g., employment, relationship status, peer acceptance), is at the top of the hierarchy. Cavell's model echoes the importance of context at this level and notes that these social goals are determined by societal and cultural norms, as well as developmental stage. For example, peer acceptance may be of critical importance during childhood while romantic relationship status may be more important during late adolescence and early adulthood. One step down Cavell's ladder is *social performance*, or the ability of an individual to manage social situations in a way that meets "socially valid criteria" (p. 118). Like other theorists, Cavell agreed that social performance is best assessed in the context of specific social tasks and stressed the importance of considering social validity, or the need to take into account social significance (i.e., societal value of the social behavior), as well as social importance (i.e., link to relevant social outcomes) in assessing social performance (Gresham, 1986). Not surprisingly, the third level is *social skills*, or the specific abilities that facilitate competent performance. Cavell noted that social skills refer to molecular skills (e.g., eye gaze, conversational turn taking), or sequences of skills (e.g., problem solving) and encompass cognitive (e.g., attributions) and emotional (e.g., emotion regulation) processes. Social skills are viewed as an integral aspect of social competence, but they are not seen as the root of all social competence. As such, assessment and intervention should take place at all levels.

Rose-Krasnor's (1997) three-level Prism Model of Social Competence nicely complements and expands on Cavell's model. The top, or *Theoretical Level*, is global social competence defined as effective interaction that meets developmental needs. Social competence is viewed as transactional, meaning that it is evaluated by the reactions of others, as well as situation dependent. Like Cavell (1990), Rose-Krasnor stressed that gender, culture, and developmental stage all influence what is considered socially competent. Contributing further nuance, Rose-Krasnor added that social competence also depends on the individual's goals for the specific social situation. The *Index Level* represents specific indicators of social competence (e.g., sociometric status, relationship quality, social self-efficacy). These indices are organized into two groups: Self (focus on individual needs and perspectives; e.g., self-efficacy) and Other (focus on social connectedness; e.g., sociometric status, friendship quality). These sides represent the balance between autonomy and interdependence; social competence is viewed as being able to manage one's own needs while also maintaining relationships with others. Other theorists support the importance of this balance. Cillessen and Bellmore (2011) describe social competence as having two main components: the ability to be prosocial and cooperative, as well as the ability to achieve individual social goals. Rose-Krasnor further segmented these domains to represent different social contexts or situations.

Finally, the base of Rose-Krasnor's prism is the *Skills Level*, which comprises the social, behavioral, emotional, cognitive, and motivational building blocks of social competence. The Skills Level is considered foundational as these skills likely impact the indices in the level above. For instance, Rose-Krasnor pointed out that an individual can be effective at meeting his or her social goals, but the types of goals may impact larger social indices. Think back to the preferred and popular children researched by Cillessen and Bellmore (2011). Each group has its own motivation context that results in different outcomes: the preferred children are generally well liked, whereas the perceived popular children are rated as socially savvy leaders but are not always universally liked.

Models identifying key situations

Several definitions of social skills and social competence emphasize the importance of the situation; however, few suggest ways to assess the importance of specific situations. In contrast, Goldfried and D'Zurilla's (1969) Behavior-Analytic Model for Assessing Competence identifies a highly situational, five-step process for operationalizing and assessing competence. Integral to their definition of social competence is that an effective response "alters the situation so that it is no longer problematical, and at the same time produces a maximum of other positive consequences and a minimum of negative ones (p. 158)." This definition suggests that it is possible to assess the *degree* of competence by weighing potential positive and negative consequences for each behavioral response within a specific situation. Thus, there can be several different ways to respond to a situation, and these responses can be rated as inferior, average, or superior levels of competence. The Behavioral-Analytic Model is unique in that it "builds in" ecological validity by polling the target population regarding critical situations and possible responses. In addition, most definitions of social competence recognize an evaluative component in determining effectiveness, and this approach incorporates expert raters' judgments of the degree of competence of possible responses. Once clear criteria for competence have been established, individual responses can be reliably rated, thus facilitating measurement in research and/or intervention. Regarding weaknesses, the model relies heavily on consensus: Critical situations are those that are rated by the group as difficult and common, and expert judges' ratings are averaged or discussed to reach consensus. Thus, it is possible that innovative or particularly creative responses may be difficult to rate. In addition, the model is exclusively focused on assessment of competence; this model essentially generates an outcome measure, and does not attend to the underlying skills, goals, and motivations that may facilitate competence.

The Behavioral-Analytic Model comprises five steps that clearly outline a systematic strategy to operationalize and then assess competence in specific populations and in specific situations. The first entails a thorough situational analysis, or identification of the critical situations with which the target population must cope. The situations that best determine competence are those that occur with some frequency and that are perceived as challenging, or those that require active, purposeful problem solving. This taxonomy of critical situations may be collected through behavioral observation, self-monitoring (e.g., diary studies), surveys, or identification through significant others (e.g., parents, teachers, romantic partner). Once a list of key situations is collected, the next step is response enumeration, or the amassing of the range of potential responses to each situation. The third step is response evaluation or determining the effectiveness of each response. Goldfried and D'Zurilla recommend having these judgments made by significant others (e.g., those that have contact or expertise with the target group). Consistent with their view of competence, these judges rate each response using the following definition of effectiveness: those responses that are "likely to resolve the problematic nature of the situation and avoid possible negative consequences" (p. 166). At this point, the list of critical situations, possible responses, and effectiveness of each response serves as the criteria for assessing competence. In fact, the final steps in this process are measure development and measure evaluation. Ideally, competence would be assessed through direct behavioral observation in a sampling of critical situations; however, role play, imaginal role play, or self-monitoring are additional options.

Process models

Several theorists believe that intervention at a *process* level will be more fruitful than at the molecular skill level. Trower (1982) explained that the central social skill is the ability to generate appropriate behavior that matches both the individual's goals and the demands of the situation. In this vein, both the generative model of social skills (Trower, 1982) and the SIP model (Crick & Dodge, 1994; Dodge & Murphy, 1984) focus on the cognitive process of socially competent responding. These models make an important contribution in that they describe how several social skills may work together in a functional system. As such, they offer specific potential areas for assessment and intervention. On the other hand, they give only cursory attention to other, noncognitive factors that may affect competent responding (e.g., emotion regulation).

Trower (1982) described three key processes in his Generative Model of Social Skills. First, the model begins with attending to both external (e.g., environment, social cues), as well as internal events (e.g., attitudes). Individuals process the incoming information by comparing it to their existing social schema or scripts. This internal schema provides useful information on social norms and rules of behavior in similar situations. The next phase involves self-monitoring of actual performance in the situation. The third step is the comparison of the performance to goals and standards of behavior. If the outcome of the social situation matches the goals, then the process continues. If there is a mismatch, then the individual will likely either withdraw from the situation or try a different behavioral response. Learning occurs during this process with the formation of new cognitive schemas. Trower (1982) viewed these steps as a feedback loop that repeats over and over during social interactions.

Dodge and colleagues' (Crick & Dodge, 1994; Dodge & Murphy, 1984) SIP model describes a five-step cognitive process of social responding. The first step involves decoding important social cues and requires the ability to notice relevant social information. The second step is the interpretation of those cues. For example, a stranger may bump a person's coffee cup while passing on a sidewalk. This bumped person will use both relevant social cues (e.g., facial expression, gestures, degree of crowding on sidewalk) and personal memory (e.g., scanning of past similar situations) to determine the intent of the stranger (e.g., accidental or hostile). The third step involves a response search process, or the rapid recall and evaluation of potential responses to the situation. The fourth step is response decision or the selection of the best choice from the internal list of potential responses. The final step is response enactment, or actually performing the selected response. To be effective, the individual must monitor the outcome of this response and be able to adapt the response if needed. Dodge and colleagues posited that SIP occurs in a larger context of the demands of the specific social task, the individual's social goals, and memories of past experiences, all of which can influence the decisions made at each step. Deficits can occur at any one of the steps, or at multiple levels. In addition, much like other definitions of social competence, the evaluative judgment of relevant others determines whether the chosen behavior is socially competent.

Skill sets models

The final type of model to consider are those that identify core social skill sets associated with socially competent responding. It should be noted that social skills are always contextual, and even the skill sets models assume that there is an agreed upon goal of social performance. Overall, the skills set models serve an important function as they list specific areas for assessment and intervention. Additional research is needed to determine the skill sets that are most critical to social functioning. In one of the earliest skill sets models, McFall (1982) described three systems of social skills: physiological, cognitive, and overt motor behavior. In McFall's conceptualization, physiological skills include sensory processes, as well as those related to biological regulation and control. Cognitive skills are best thought of in the context of information processing (as described in the previous process models section). In addition, McFall points to verbal and nonverbal motor skills as an essential aspect of social skills.

Subsequent models added and expanded the three areas highlighted by McFall (1982). For example, Felner, Lease, and Phillips (1990) reviewed the social skills literature and created a quadripartite model to represent the key aspects of social skills. Like McFall (1982), Felner and colleagues identified behavioral skills (those necessary to negotiate specific social situations), as well as cognitive skills, as essential social skills. Felner and colleagues added to McFall's original framework by stating that essential cognitive skills also include cultural information about social norms and decision-making ability. Echoing and expanding McFall's physiological regulation, Felner et al. discussed the importance of emotion regulation and emotion competence, which includes both the management of strong negative emotions (e.g., anxiety, anger) and the fostering of positive emotional attachment bonds. Finally, Felner and colleagues added that motivation and expectancy sets also influence our behavior. Thus, social skills depend on the desire to enact appropriate behavior and the expectation that one can enact the behavior.

Over time, and with additional research, the key skill sets models became more inclusive, dynamic, and more contextual. Spence (2003) proposed a model of socially skilled responding that addresses behavioral (e.g., ability to perform skills), cognitive (e.g., interpersonal problem solving skills, information processing, maladaptive thinking styles), emotional (e.g., affect regulation), and environmental factors (e.g., contingencies for social behavior, opportunities to learn skills from others). Spence's model is noteworthy in its inclusion of specific environmental influences that may contribute to social skills. Importantly, deficits can occur in one or more areas, meaning that assessment of multiple skill areas may be needed to design an effective intervention. A recent integrative chapter distilled the literature on social skills to three similar target areas: behavioral (e.g., molecular social skills, including turn taking and eye contact), cognitive (e.g., perspective taking, attributions), and emotional (e.g., emotional knowledge and regulation; Milligan, Sibalis, Morgan, & Phillips, 2017). However, Milligan and colleagues incorporated the increased knowledge of neuropsychological factors that influence social skill, including attention control, executive functioning, processing speed, and visual-spatial processing. Milligan and colleagues also noted that skills in each area likely interact with those of other areas, in a dynamic process.

Distillation of core skills targets

In this final section, we distill the definitions and models to four social skills target areas: communication, cognition, emotion, and problem-solving skills. These four social skills areas were selected based on their links to models and their common inclusion in social skills interventions. For each, we provide a definition, summarize related research, and discuss intervention programs that target that skill set. See Tables 1–4 for an overview of the skills and example applications of those skills.

TABLE 1 Communication skills.

Definition	The process through which the behavior of one individual influences the behavior of another individual (Buck & VanLear, 2002)
Relevant skills	*Use of language*: the incorporation of a variety of forms of language into conversation, including greeting others (e.g., saying hello or good bye), gathering and providing information (e.g., asking questions, making statements or declarations), negotiating conflict (e.g., clarifying intentions, recognizing others' reactions, apologizing), and making requests (e.g., asking for favors, managing potential conflict, initiating or ending interactions) *Adjustment of language*: adjusting the content of the interaction based on individual factors of the receiver, such as age, setting, or type of relationships (e.g., speaking differently to an adolescent than a toddler) *Conversation skills*: following the rules of conversation in order to initiate and maintain the interaction, including taking verbal turns (e.g., allowing the other individual in the conversation dyad to speak), understanding assumed or implied knowledge (e.g., consideration of the context and type of relationship), alerting the receiver to the topic and changes in the topic (e.g., introducing the topic at the beginning of the interaction and providing cues or transitions throughout the interaction), and incorporating nonverbal communications (e.g., eye contact, posture, proxemics, or facial expressions)
Sample interventions that target communication skills	Program for the education and enrichment of relational skills (PEERS, for young adults; Laugeson, 2017) Skillstreaming (for children and adolescents; McGinnis, 2011a, 2011b)

TABLE 2 Emotion regulation skills.

Definition	An individual's efforts to influence the type, strength, timing, and expression of their emotional experience (Gross, Richards, & John, 2006)
Relevant skills	*Situation selection*: choosing situations that will minimize negative and/or maximize positive emotion (e.g., selecting a "family-friendly" restaurant when dining out with a toddler) *Situation modification*: attempts to modify the current situation to change emotional impact (e.g., planning to walk with a friend to the first day of school) *Attentional deployment*: altering the focus of attention to modify emotional experience (e.g., gaze aversion, distraction, shifting concentration; focusing on the other people at the party instead of an ex) *Cognitive change*: altering cognitive appraisal of the situation (e.g., "Rollercoasters are exciting!") or the ability to cope with the situation (e.g., "I have ridden other rides and enjoyed them") *Response modulation*: directly regulating the emotional response (e.g., medication, exercise, relaxation) or emotional expression (e.g., hiding anxiety during a presentation or first date)
Sample interventions	Secret agent society (for youth with autism; Beaumont & Sofronoff, 2013) Emotional competence intervention (for adults; Nelis et al., 2011)

TABLE 3 Cognitive skills.

Definition	An individual's knowledge and interpretation of social situations, as well as basic neuropsychological processes (Milligan et al., 2017)
Relevant skills	*Informational knowledge*: applying knowledge and schemas about social situations from prior learning to understand behavioral expectations and roles (e.g., remaining seated during class and listening quietly while the teacher is speaking) *Informational processing*: making attributions about the causes of events and others' behaviors from social cues to organize behavioral responses (e.g., "My mom has not talked to me in several days. She might be angry and hurt from our last disagreement, so I will call and apologize") *Perspective taking*: identifying the emotions, beliefs, and desires of others' and recognizing that these may differ from one's own. (e.g., "I do not enjoy sporting events, but going to the hockey game is important to my boyfriend and he is looking forward to attending together") *Neuropsychological processing*: basic cognitive functions contributing to social information processing and social responding (e.g., focusing attention on a conversation, processing social information rapidly, using decision making and problem solving to respond)
Sample interventions	Second step program (for typically developing youth; Committee for Children, 2011) Seaver-NETT (for children with autism spectrum disorder; Soorya et al., 2015) Social effectiveness therapy (SET; for children and adults with social anxiety; Turner, Beidel, Cooley, Woody, & Messer, 1994)

TABLE 4 Social problem-solving skills.

Definition	The process through which individuals identify effective and adaptive responses to problems in everyday living (D'Zurilla & Goldfried, 1971)
Relevant skills	*Problem definition and formulation*: gathering all information relevant to the problem and formulating a clear idea of the source and extent of the issue *Generation of alternatives*: brainstorming several different possible responses regardless of the effectiveness or adaptiveness of each *Decision making*: consideration of the positive and negative consequences of each solution in light of the individual's personal goals and greater social context *Solution implementation and verification*: enacting the solution and evaluating the success or failure of the solution in achieving the desired outcome and consequences
Sample interventions that target social problem-solving skills	Problem-solving therapy (Nezu, Nezu, & Perri, 1989) Tools for getting along (Daunic et al., 2012)

Communication skills

Communication skills are central to interpersonal interactions and social relationships. In general, communication occurs when a message from one individual (i.e., the "sender") influences the behavior of another individual (i.e., the "receiver;" Buck & VanLear, 2002). Communication includes both verbal and nonverbal components that interact to facilitate mutual understanding between the sender and the receiver. Verbal communication primarily includes the use of language, whereas nonverbal communication includes voice qualities such as rate, tone, or intonation patterns; eye contact; gestures; body language or posture; proxemics (i.e., the use and understanding of space); and facial expressions (Duncan, 1969).

Social communication skills include using language in a variety of ways, adjusting language based on the receiver, and following the rules of conversation (MacDonald & Gillette, 1984). Breaking this down, specific skills involved in language use might include greeting others, gathering and providing information, negotiating conflict, and making requests. Adjusting language based on the receiver functions to enhance mutual understanding and might include changes made in response to age, setting, or type of relationship (e.g., close friend versus coworker). Notably, skills specific to following the rules of conversation are a critical aspect of communication. These skills include initiating and maintaining a conversation, taking verbal turns, understanding assumed or implied knowledge, alerting the receiver to the topic and changes in topic, and incorporating nonverbal communication into the interaction (MacDonald & Gillette, 1984). In addition, nonverbal expression contributes to the communication of emotions, engagement in the social interaction, and the transmission of underlying or indirect messages (Duncan, 1969). Nonverbals can serve to enhance or replace the verbally communicated message depending on the context of the interaction.

Communication skills deficits have serious implications. When communication skills are low in quality or effectiveness, intended messages can be distorted, resulting in conflict between individuals (Erozkan, 2013). In addition, communication deficits are associated with lower social competence (Bierman & Furman, 1984). As further evidence of their negative impact, communication deficits are central to several disorders included in the DSM-5 [American Psychiatric Association (APA), 2013]. For example, social (pragmatic) communication disorder is characterized by persistent difficulty in verbal and nonverbal social communication. Individuals with this disorder often struggle with basic conversation skills such as greeting or sharing information, verbal turn taking, and understanding the combination of both verbal and nonverbal messages. Other developmental disorders are associated with similar deficits in social communication skills. Autism spectrum disorder (ASD), for instance, is characterized by deficits in initiating and maintaining conversations, nonverbal communication skills, and adjusting social communication to context (APA, 2013).

Communication skills are a common module in social skills training programs. These interventions often use techniques such as didactic instruction, modeling, and coaching to help teach and rehearse skills across contexts (Elliott & Gresham, 1993). The commonly used Skillstreaming series for children and adolescents with social skills deficits includes several communication skills modules (McGinnis, 2011a, 2011b). Although communication skills are included in social skills interventions across a variety of problem areas, they feature prominently in those targeting ASD. Communication targets of these interventions include vocal repetition of syllables, receptive and expressive identification of language, communication initiation, responding to questions, or greeting peers. For example, the PEERS curriculum for young adults with social challenges, particularly ASD, includes skills such as entering and exiting a conversation, incorporating humor, and using electronic communication (Laugeson, 2017).

Emotion regulation

Imagine being asked to do a particularly unpleasant task at work or chore at home. How one manages emotions in that situation will likely impact work or family relationships. Indeed, several of the models presented here discuss the impact that emotion regulation can have on social competence and social skills. Emotion regulation refers to an individual's efforts to influence the type, strength, timing, and expression of his or her emotional experience (Gross et al., 2006). These efforts may be completed automatically or be conscious and purposeful. Antecedent-focused strategies aim to change the emotion response *before* it happens. For example, an individual might alter his or her thoughts about a situation (cognitive change), avoid a situation or person that elicits strong emotion (situation selection), or focus attention on more pleasant aspects of a situation (attentional deployment). Response-focused strategies target emotional responses that are already in full swing and are referred to as response modulation strategies. For example, an individual might try to suppress the emotional experience or change the behavioral expression of the emotion. Research on emotion regulation in young children tends to be focused on external emotion regulation as mediated (primarily) by parents, whereas the research on adults tends to be focused more on intrapersonal and independent regulation (Hofmann & Doan, 2018). For both children and adults, effective emotion regulation is linked to a variety of positive outcomes.

Positive and negative emotions occur frequently as a part of everyday life, and theorists recognized early on that regulation of strong emotional responses is necessary for adaptive social functioning (Gross et al., 2006). Emotion dysregulation could negatively impact either or both the acquisition or performance of social skills, and thereby influence the presence or quality of social relationships. Existing research underscores this assertion as several studies report positive associations between emotion regulation and social outcomes in both children and adults (e.g., Perry, Dollar, Calkins, Keane, & Shanahan, 2018; Trevisan, Tafreshi, Slaney, Yager, & Iarocci, 2018). Interestingly, the relationship between emotion regulation and functioning in social relationships may be bidirectional. A recent longitudinal study of young adolescents found that having a reciprocal friendship at baseline predicted lower usage of the anger management strategies of verbal or relational aggression and ignoring approximately 1 year later (von Salisch & Zeman, 2018). The positive relation between emotion regulation and social outcomes is also present in clinical samples across the lifespan. For example, associations between emotion regulation and social functioning are present in those with attention deficit hyperactivity disorder (ADHD), ASD, and depression (e.g., Bunford, Evans, & Langberg, 2018; Goldsmith & Kelley, 2018; Marroquin & Nolen-Hoeksema, 2015).

The growing evidence for the connection between emotion regulation and social outcomes coincides with the increased presence of emotion regulation interventions designed to impact social outcomes. For example, Nelis et al. (2011) designed a brief emotion competence training (18 h) for use with college students that yielded increases in social functioning (e.g., quality of relationships, perceived social support) at postassessment. In addition, emotion regulation components are often present in social skills interventions. For example, the secret agent society (SAS) is a 10-week social-emotional skills intervention designed for use with children with ASD (Beaumont & Sofronoff, 2013). Along with cognitive and behavioral components, children practice emotion recognition and regulation skills by playing an at-home computer game. The PATHS curriculum, an intervention aimed to increase social skills in youth with conduct problems, also incorporates emotion understanding and regulation elements (Greenberg, Kusche, Cook, & Quamma, 1995).

Cognitive skills

As the process and skills set models suggest, several cognitive factors contribute to social competence. Cognitive social skills refer to the knowledge, thoughts, and reasoning involved in social interactions. For example, informational knowledge helps individuals understand and make predictions about the role of each person and what actions may be required in a specific social context. A child understands the need to take turns and follow the rules while playing a game, and adults can draw from previous experiences to understand the different expectations for casual gatherings with friends versus formal business meetings. SIP (as described earlier) is another essential cognitive skill. SIP involves several steps, including encoding of social cues, interpretation of those cues, clarification of social goals, response construction, response decision, and behavioral enactment (Crick & Dodge, 1994). Attributions or beliefs about events and others also influence social behavior. For example, youth who are frequently rejected by peers are more likely to make hostile attributions of negative intent to the neutral behavior of their peers and then respond aggressively (Crick & Dodge, 1994).

Additional cognitive skills that impact social functioning include theory of mind (ToM), which influences the interpretation or understanding of others' emotions and behaviors. ToM reflects the ability to attribute various mental states (i.e., beliefs, desires, emotions) to others and recognize that these mental states may differ from one's own (Milligan, Astington, & Dack, 2007). For example, adults can recognize and make inferences about why their partner appears sad, allowing them to respond effectively with prosocial behaviors.

Social cognitive information processing is also influenced by basic neuropsychological abilities involving aspects of attention, processing speed, executive functions, and visual-spatial processing (Milligan et al., 2017). Neurodevelopmental disorders characterized by deficits in basic cognitive functions can disrupt effective social skill acquisition and performance. For example, individuals with ADHD have difficulty sustaining attention, inhibiting behavioral urges, and understanding and completing complex activities. These deficits can make it difficult for children with ADHD to engage in cooperative play or group learning activities and for adults to focus and take turns during lengthy conversations. Individuals with specific learning disorders or traumatic brain injuries are also likely to have cognitive functioning deficits that contribute to difficulties with SIP and effective social responding (Milligan et al., 2017).

Cognitive social skills are integral for socioemotional wellbeing across the lifespan (Masten, Burt, & Coatsworth, 2006). Cognitive skills assist children and adults with understanding and interpreting social information and selecting and performing behavioral responses successfully to support the development and maintenance of relationships. Deficits in cognitive social skills are associated with a range of behavioral or emotional disorders that are likely to contribute to significant social and emotional problems for children and adults alike. For example, emotional disorders, such as social anxiety and depression, are characterized by cognitive biases and negative schemas that influence SIP. As more attention is given to negative information and negative attributions about peer behaviors, this likely contributes to more negative social interactions (Reid, Salmon, & Lovibond, 2006). Individuals with deficits in basic neuropsychological abilities, such as those seen in ADHD, also struggle to make and sustain friendships, complete school or occupational work, and are at greater risk for other internalizing and externalizing problems (Wehmeier, Schacht, & Barkley, 2010).

Interventions with cognitive social skills are designed for typically developing youth and adults, as well as diverse populations of individuals with specific disorders and social challenges. One such intervention program targeting social cognitive skills for typically developing youth in the educational setting is the second step program (Committee for Children, 2011). Through didactic instruction, skills practice, and reinforcement, children learn to focus their attention with self-talk, develop perspective taking and ToM with empathy, and adjust unhelpful thinking. Other interventions are designed for individuals with a range of disorders and associated deficits or challenges. For example, the social effectiveness therapy (SET) program is a multicomponent program for adults with social anxiety disorder (Turner et al., 1994). Individuals with social anxiety tend to have negative beliefs or expectations about social situations, interpret social situations as dangerous, and overestimate the likelihood and cost of possible negative outcomes (Heimberg, Brozovich, & Rapee, 2010). To address these challenges and support social participation and effective performance of social skills in the presence of anxiety, SET provides group instruction in social skills and individualized exposure for anxiety-inducing situations specific to each adult. In recent years, many social skills programs have been designed for children and adults with ASD and include training in cognitive skills. One such program is Seaver-NETT (nonverbal communication, emotion recognition, and theory of mind training), a modular cognitive-behavioral group intervention for children ages 4–12 years (Soorya et al., 2015). Children are introduced to ToM with the phrase "I think, you think" and practice ToM skills using activities, picture books, idioms, and metaphors.

Social problem-solving skills

Several models of social competence reviewed earlier refer to the ability to adapt and respond to a variety of social situations. SPS is the process by which individuals identify effective and adaptive responses to problems in everyday living (D'Zurilla & Nezu, 1990). Problems are real-word dilemmas (social or otherwise) that may involve personal, interpersonal, or broader social issues, for example losing a job, navigating a conflict with a peer, or experiencing discrimination. When problems arise that do not have a readily apparent solution, individuals use SPS skills to generate solutions that maximize positive consequences and minimize negative consequences. The net outcome of consequences is a key component to this process, as many problems that arise may have several effective solutions; however, the individual needs to consider personal goals and the social context, as well as both short- and long-term outcomes, to identify the most adaptive solution.

SPS begins with a general problem orientation, which refers to an individual's typical attitude or schema that is activated in response to problems (D'Zurilla & Nezu, 1990). An adaptive, or positive problem orientation involves the ability to recognize problems, the acceptance of problems as an inherent aspect of daily life, the belief in one's ability to solve the problem, and the use of adaptive solution response tendencies (Maydeu-Olivares & D'Zurilla, 1996). In contrast, a maladaptive, or negative problem orientation, involves the perception of problems as unsolvable, doubt in one's ability to solve the problem, and frustration or intolerance when confronted with a problem. In addition to a general problem orientation, specific skills that comprise the process of SPS include: (a) problem definition and formulation, (b) generation of alternatives, (c) decision making, and (d) solution implementation and verification (D'Zurilla & Goldfried, 1971).

These components are not necessarily a sequential process, but often overlap or repeat until a solution is successful.

Deficits in the process of SPS have important implications for adjustment across the lifespan. Difficulty in effective SPS has been found to impact adaptive functioning in children (Stewart & Rubin, 1995), emerging adults (D'Zurilla & Sheedy, 1991), and older adults (Kant, D'Zurilla, & Maydeu-Olivares, 1997). In older adults, SPS was found to be an important mediating variable between everyday problems and psychological distress. SPS deficits have been connected to both internalizing and externalizing symptoms (Bell & D'Zurilla, 2009), as well as multiple forms of psychopathology, particularly depression and anxiety (Anderson, Goddard, & Powell, 2011). Disorders that impair executive functioning, such as ADHD, and social cognition, such as ASD, are more likely to be associated with deficits in SPS (Bernard-Opitz, Sriram, & Nakhoda-Sapuan, 2001; Matthys, Cuperus, & Van Engeland, 1999).

Perhaps the most widespread intervention developed to target deficits in SPS is problem-solving therapy (Nezu et al., 1989). Psychoeducation, cognitive restructuring, and behavioral interventions are utilized in order to help the individual understand environmental triggers and negative emotions, boost adaptive self-efficacy, and actively build skills associated with SPS. Another program focused on SPS skills is Tools for Getting Along (Daunic et al., 2012), a universally delivered intervention for youth struggling with anger. This program uses direct instruction, modeling, and skill generalization to teach proactive problem-solving techniques that help to prevent conflict. In addition to SPS-focused interventions, SPS skill training is embedded within a wide range of social skills interventions for diverse populations. Meta-analyses have demonstrated that interventions that target specific skills sets, such as SPS, are more effective in reducing symptoms and corresponding distress than general skill interventions (e.g., Quinn, Kavale, Mathur, Rutherford Jr, & Forness, 1999).

Conclusions

In this chapter, we synthesized the various definitions of social skills and social competence, analyzed several types of models that address the two concepts, and distilled the information into four core target areas. There are several "take-home points" from this process. First, the definition of social skills is a bit of a moving target. Even the simplest of definitions, that social skills are the requisite abilities needed to perform competently in social situations, becomes much more complex once we consider both person and situation factors. "Competent" social performance depends on the evaluation of the other (e.g., peer acceptance), the social goals of the actor (e.g., to lead or to follow in a group of peers), and the needs and norms of the particular social situation (e.g., party versus conference). In addition, contextual factors like developmental stage and time period (not addressed in any of the current models) may influence the social behaviors that are considered competent. Diversity factors, including ethnicity and culture, also affect our understanding of social competence (despite being mentioned in only two of the models; i.e., Cavell, 1990; Rose-Krasnor, 1997). At an applied level, clinicians need to consider all of these aspects when selecting the appropriate social skills to target. Second, there is no perfect, all-encompassing model of social functioning. Instead, we have several types of models that all serve important functions. The variety of models reminds us of the importance of considering several layers and perspectives when we think about social skills. Third, the core skill areas of communication skills, emotion regulation, cognitive skills, and social problem-solving emerged due to their prominence in both theory and practice. Clinicians looking to grow their tool kit by adding social skill interventions are encouraged to focus on these areas. Finally, we are excited about future work in this area. New comprehensive models based on additional empirical data would be useful as would research on how different skill sets work together. A closer examination of diversity contextual factors and how they influence social skills and social competence is needed. Also, it will be interesting to see how our conceptualization of social skills expands to include more electronic social interaction.

References

American Psychiatric Association. (2013). *Diagnostic and statistical manual of mental disorders* (5th ed.). Washington, DC, US: Author.

Anderson, R. J., Goddard, L., & Powell, J. H. (2011). Social problem-solving and depressive symptom vulnerability: The importance of real-life problem-solving performance. *Cognitive Therapy and Research, 35*, 48–56.

Asher, S. R., & McDonald, K. L. (2009). The behavioral basis of acceptance, rejection, and perceived popularity. In K. H. Rubin, W. M. Bukowski, & B. Laursen (Eds.), *Handbook of peer interactions, relationships, and groups* (pp. 232–248). New York, NY, USA: Guildford.

Bell, A. C., & D'Zurilla, T. J. (2009). The influence of social problem-solving ability on the relationship between daily stress and adjustment. *Cognitive Therapy and Research, 33*, 439–448.

Bernard-Opitz, V., Sriram, N., & Nakhoda-Sapuan, S. (2001). Enhancing social problem solving in children with autism and normal children through computer-assisted instruction. *Journal of Autism and Developmental Disorders, 31*, 377–384.

Beaumont, R., & Sofronoff, K. (2013). Multimodal intervention for social skills training in students with high functioning ASD: The secret agent society. In A. Scarpa, S. W. White, & T. Attwood (Eds.), *CBT for children and adolescents with high functioning autism spectrum disorders* (pp. 147–170). New York, NY, US: Guildford Press.

Bierman, K. L., & Furman, W. (1984). The effects of social skills training and peer involvement on the social adjustment of preadolescents. *Child Development, 55*, 151–162.

Buck, R., & VanLear, C. A. (2002). Verbal and nonverbal communication: Distinguishing symbolic, spontaneous, and pseudo-spontaneous nonverbal behavior. *Journal of Communication, 52*, 522–541.

Bunford, N., Evans, S. W., & Langberg, J. M. (2018). Emotion dysregulation is associated with social impairment among adolescents with ADHD. *Journal of Attention Disorders, 22*, 66–82. https://doi.org/10.1177/1087054714527793.

Cavell, T. A. (1990). Social adjustment, social performance, and social skills: A tri-component model of social competence. *Journal of Clinical Child Psychology, 19*, 111–122.

Cillessen, A. H. N., & Bellmore, A. D. (2011). Social skills and social competence in interactions with peers. In P. K. Smith & C. H. Hart (Eds.), *The Wiley Blackwell handbook of childhood social development* (2nd ed., pp. 393–412). Hoboken, NJ: Wiley-Blackwell.

Committee for Children. (2011). *Second step: Skills for social and academic success*. Seattle, WA: Author.

Crick, N. R., & Dodge, K. A. (1994). A review and reformulation of social information-processing mechanisms in children's social adjustment. *Psychological Bulletin, 115*(1), 74–101. https://doi.org/10.1037//0033-2909.115.1.74.

Daunic, A. P., Smith, S. W., Garvan, C. W., Barber, B. R., Becker, M. K., Peters, C. D., … Naranjo, A. H. (2012). Reducing developmental risk for emotional/behavioral problems: A randomized controlled trial examining the tools for getting along curriculum. *Journal of School Psychology, 50*, 149–166. https://doi.org/10.1016/j.jsp.2011.09.003.

Dodge, K. A., Schlundt, D. C., Schocken, I., & Delugach, J. D. (1983). Social competence and children's sociometric status: The role of peer group entry strategies. *Merrill-Palmer Quarterly, 29*, 309–336.

Dodge, K. A., & Murphy, R. R. (1984). The assessment of social competence in adolescents. In P. Karoly & J. Steffen (Eds.), *Adolescent behavior disorders: Foundations and contemporary concerns, advances in child behavioral analysis and therapy* (pp. 61–96). Lexington, MA: Lexington Books.

Duncan, S., Jr. (1969). Nonverbal communication. *Psychological Bulletin, 72*, 118–137.

D'Zurilla, T. J., & Goldfried, M. R. (1971). Problem solving and behavior modification. *Journal of Abnormal Psychology, 78*, 107–126.

D'Zurilla, T. J., & Nezu, A. M. (1990). Development and preliminary evaluation of the Social Problem-Solving Inventory. *Psychological Assessment: A Journal of Consulting and Clinical Psychology, 2*, 156–163.

D'Zurilla, T. J., & Sheedy, C. F. (1991). Relation between social problem-solving ability and subsequent level of psychological stress in college students. *Journal of Personality and Social Psychology, 61*, 841–846.

Elliott, S. N., & Gresham, F. M. (1993). Social skills interventions for children. *Behavior Modification, 17*, 287–313.

Erozkan, A. (2013). The effect of communication skills and interpersonal problem solving skills on social self-efficacy. *Educational Sciences: Theory and Practice, 13*, 739–745.

Felner, R. D., Lease, A. M., & Phillips, R. S. C. (1990). Social competence and the language of adequacy as a subject matter for psychology: A quadripartite trilevel framework. In T. P. Gullota, G. R. Adams, & R. Montemayor (Eds.), *The development of social competence in adolescence* (pp. 245–264). Beverly Hills, CA: Sage.

Goldfried, M. R., & D'Zurilla, T. J. (1969). A behavioral-analytic model for assessing competence. In C. Spielberger (Ed.), *Vol. 1. Current topics in clinical and community psychology* (pp. 151–196). New York: Academic.

Goldsmith, S. F., & Kelley, E. (2018). Associations between emotion regulation and social impairment in children and adolescents with autism spectrum disorder. *Journal of Autism and Developmental Disorders, 48*, 2164–2173. https://doi.org/10.1007/s10803-018-3483-3.

Greenberg, M. T., Kusche, C. A., Cook, E. T., & Quamma, J. P. (1995). Promoting emotional competence in school-aged children: The effects of the PATHS curriculum. *Development and Psychopathology, 7*, 117–136. https://doi.org/10.1017/s0954579400006374.

Gresham, F. M. (1986). Conceptual issues in the assessment of social competence in children. In P. S. Strain, M. J. Guralnick, & H. M. Walker (Eds.), *Children's social behavior: Development, assessment, and modification* (pp. 143–179). New York: Academic Press.

Gresham, F. M., & Elliott, S. N. (1984). Assessment and classification of children's social skills: A review of methods and issues. *School Psychology Review*, *13*, 292–301.

Gross, J. J., Richards, J. M., & John, O. P. (2006). Emotion regulation in everyday life. In D. K. Snyder, J. A. Simpson, & J. N. Hughes (Eds.), *Emotion regulation in couples and families: Pathways to disfunction and health* (pp. 13–35). Washington, DC: American Psychological Association.

Han, H. S., & Thomas, M. S. (2010). No child misunderstood: Enhancing early childhood teachers' multicultural responsiveness to the social competence of diverse children. *Early Childhood Education Journal*, *37*, 469–476. https://doi.org/10.1007/s10643-009-0369-1.

Heimberg, R. G., Brozovich, F. A., & Rapee, R. M. (2010). A cognitive behavioral model of social anxiety disorder: Update and extension. In S. G. Hofmann & P. M. DiBartolo (Eds.), *Social anxiety: Clinical, developmental and social perspectives* (2nd ed., pp. 395–422). New York, NY, US: Elsevier. https://doi.org/10.1016/B978-0-12-375096-9.00015-8.

Hofmann, S. G., & Doan, S. N. (2018). *The social foundations of emotion: Developmental, cultural, and clinical dimensions*. New York, NY: American Psychological Association.

Kant, G. L., D'Zurilla, T. J., & Maydeu-Olivares, A. (1997). Social problem solving as a mediator of stress-related depression and anxiety in middle-aged and elderly community residents. *Cognitive Therapy and Research*, *21*, 73–96.

Laugeson, E. A. (2017). *PEERS for young adults: Social skills training for adult with autism spectrum disorder and other social challenges*. New York, NY, US: Routledge/Taylor & Francis Group.

Little, S. G., Swangler, J., & Akin-Little, A. (2017). Defining social skills. In J. L. Matson (Ed.), *Handbook of social behavior and skills in children* (pp. 9–17). New York, NY, US: Springer International Publishing.

MacDonald, J. D., & Gillette, Y. (1984). *Conversation engineering: A pragmatic approach to early social competence*. In *Vol. 5(03). Seminars in speech and language* (pp. 171–183): Thieme Medical Publishers, Inc.

Marroquin, B., & Nolen-Hoeksema, S. (2015). Emotion regulation and depressive symptoms: Close relationships as social context and influence. *Journal of Personality and Social Psychology*, *109*, 836–855. https://doi.org/10.1037/pspi0000034.

Masten, A. S., Burt, K. B., & Coatsworth, J. D. (2006). Competence and psychopathology in development. In D. Cicchetti & D. J. Cohen (Eds.), *Vol. 3. Developmental psychopathology* (2nd ed., pp. 696–738). New York, NY, USA: Wiley.

Matson, J. L., & Burns, C. O. (2017). History of social skills. In J. L. Matson (Ed.), *Handbook of social behavior and skills in children* (pp. 1–8). New York, NY, US: Springer International Publishing.

Matthys, W., Cuperus, J. M., & Van Engeland, H. (1999). Deficient social problem-solving in boys with ODD/CD, with ADHD, and with both disorders. *Journal of the American Academy of Child & Adolescent Psychiatry*, *38*, 311–321.

Maydeu-Olivares, A., & D'Zurilla, T. J. (1996). A factor-analytic study of the social problem-solving inventory: An integration of theory and data. *Cognitive Therapy and Research*, *20*, 115–133.

McFall, R. (1982). A review and reformulation of the concept of social skills. *Behavioral Assessment*, *4*, 1–33.

McGinnis, E. (2011a). *Skillstreaming the elementary school child: A guide for teaching prosocial skills* (3rd ed.). Champaign, IL, US: Research Press.

McGinnis, E. (2011b). *Skillstreaming the adolescent: A guide for teaching prosocial skills* (3rd ed.). Champaign, IL, US: Research Press.

Milligan, K., Astington, J. W., & Dack, L. A. (2007). Language and theory of mind: Meta-analysis of the relation between language ability and false-belief understanding. *Child Development, 78*(2), 622–646. https://doi.org/10.1111/j.1467-8624.2007.01018.x.

Milligan, K., Sibalis, A., Morgan, A., & Phillips, M. (2017). Social competence: Consideration of behavioral, cognitive, and emotional factors. In J. L. Matson (Ed.), *Handbook of social behavior and skills in children* (pp. 63–82). Cham: Springer International Publishing. https://doi.org/10.1007/978-3-319-64592-6_5.

Nangle, D. W., Grover, R. L., Holleb, L. J., Cassano, M., & Fales, J. (2010). Defining competence and identifying target skills. In D. W. Nangle, D. J. Hansen, C. A. Erdley, & P. J. Norton (Eds.), *Practitioner's guide to empirically based measures of social skills* (pp. 3–20). New York, NY: Springer. https://doi.org/10.1007/978-1-4419-0609-0_1.

Nelis, D., Kotsou, I., Quoidbach, J., Hansenne, M., Weytens, F., Dupuis, P., & Mikolajczak, M. (2011). Increasing emotional competence improved psychological and physical well-being, social relationships, and employability. *Emotion, 11*, 354–366. https://doi.org/10.1037/a0021554.

Nezu, A. M., Nezu, C. M., & Perri, M. G. (1989). *Problem-solving therapy for depression: Theory, research, and clinical guidelines*. Hoboken, NJ, US: John Wiley & Sons.

Norton, P. J., Washington, C. S., Peters, J. E., & Hayes, S. A. (2010). Diversity considerations in assessing social skills. In D. W. Nangle, D. J. Hansen, C. A. Erdley, & P. J. Norton (Eds.), *Practitioner's guide to empirically based measures of social skills*. (pp. 135–153). New York, NY: Springer. https://doi.org/10.1007/978-1-4419-0609-0_9.

Perry, N. B., Dollar, J. M., Calkins, S. D., Keane, S. P., & Shanahan, L. (2018). Childhood self-regulation as a mechanism through which early overcontrolling parenting is associated with adjustment in preadolescence. *Developmental Psychology, 54*, 1542–1554. https://doi.org/10.1037/dev0000536.

Quinn, M. M., Kavale, K. A., Mathur, S. R., Rutherford, R. B., Jr., & Forness, S. R. (1999). A meta-analysis of social skill interventions for students with emotional or behavioral disorders. *Journal of Emotional and Behavioral Disorders, 7*, 54–64.

Reid, S. C., Salmon, K., & Lovibond, P. F. (2006). Cognitive biases in childhood anxiety, depression, and aggression: Are they pervasive or specific? *Cognitive Therapy and Research, 30*(5), 531–549.

Rose-Krasnor, L. (1997). The nature of social competence: A theoretical review. *Social Development, 6*, 111–135.

Soorya, L. V., Siper, P. M., Beck, T., Soffes, S., Halpern, D., Gorenstein, M., … Wang, A. T. (2015). Randomized comparative trial of a social cognitive skills group for children with autism spectrum disorder. *Journal of the American Academy of Child & Adolescent Psychiatry, 54*(3), 208–216. https://doi.org/10.1016/j.jaac.2014.12.005.

Spence, S. H. (2003). Social skills training with children and young people: Theory, evidence and practice. *Child and Adolescent Mental Health, 8*(2), 84–96. https://doi.org/10.1111/1475-3588.00051.

Stewart, S. L., & Rubin, K. H. (1995). The social problem-solving skills of anxious-withdrawn children. *Development and Psychopathology, 7*, 323–336.

Taylor, A. B., & Asher, S. R. (1984). Children's goals and social competence: Individual differences in a game-playing context. In T. Field, J. L. Roopnarine, & M. Segal (Eds.), *Friendships in normal and handicapped children* (pp. 53–80). Norwood, NJ: Ablex.

Trevisan, D. A., Tafreshi, D., Slaney, K. L., Yager, J., & Iarocci, G. (2018). A psychometric evaluation of the multidimensional social competence scale (MSCS) for young adults. *PLoS One, 13*. https://doi.org/10.1371/journal.pone.0206800.

Trower, P. (1982). Toward a generative model of social skills: A critique and synthesis. In J. P. Curran & P. M. Monti (Eds.), *Social skills training: A practical handbook for assessment and treatment* (pp. 399–427). New York: Guilford.

Turner, S. M., Beidel, D. C., Cooley, M. R., Woody, S. R., & Messer, S. C. (1994). A multicomponent behavioral treatment for social phobia: Social effectiveness therapy. *Behaviour Research and Therapy*, *32*(4), 381–390.

von Salisch, M., & Zeman, J. L. (2018). Pathways to reciprocated friendships: A cross-lagged panel study on young adolescents' anger regulation towards friends. *Journal of Youth and Adolescence*, *47*, 673–687. https://doi.org/10.1007/s10964-017-0683-7.

Wehmeier, P. M., Schacht, A., & Barkley, R. A. (2010). Social and emotional impairment in children and adolescents with ADHD and the impact on quality of life. *Journal of Adolescent Health*, *46*(3), 209–217.

What are social skills? (2019, July 19). Retrieved from: https://www.skillsyouneed.com/ips/social-skills.html.

White, R. W. (1959). Motivation reconsidered: The concept of competence. *Psychological Review*, *66*, 297–333.

Further reading

Arcaro-McPhee, R., Doppler, E. E., & Harkins, D. A. (2002). Conflict resolution in a preschool constructivist classroom: A case study in negotiation. *Journal of Research in Childhood Education*, *17*, 19–25.

Malouff, J. M., Thorsteinsson, E. B., & Schutte, N. S. (2007). The efficacy of problem solving therapy in reducing mental and physical health problems: A meta-analysis. *Clinical Psychology Review*, *27*, 46–57.

Chapter 2

Developing social skills

Julie Newman Kingery[a], Cynthia A. Erdley[b], and Emily Scarpulla[b]
[a]*Hobart and William Smith Colleges, Geneva, NY, United States,* [b]*University of Maine, Orono, ME, United States*

Social relationships serve important functions for development across the lifespan—from preschool through adulthood, and there are key social tasks to master at each developmental stage. During the preschool years, children are developing social skills through interactions with parents and siblings, and they begin applying these skills outside the home as they are increasingly involved in peer interactions. School-age youth must learn to interact successfully with peers and adults (e.g., teachers) in more organized and rule-governed ways, and the formation of close, mutual friendships takes on greater importance. In the context of school transitions and increased electronic communications, adolescents face the challenge of interacting with a wider range of peers. At the same time, close friendships and the development of social skills needed for later romantic relationships take center stage. Throughout adulthood, social relationships continue to play an important role, both in the workplace and in everyday life. Having the necessary social skills at each of these developmental stages helps an individual to navigate these social tasks effectively, leading to high social competence. In contrast, individuals who are lacking in key social skills are less likely to master the critical social tasks associated with each stage. These individuals tend to have lower social competence, which places them at risk for a host of short- and long-term negative consequences, such as loneliness, depression, academic difficulties, externalizing problems, and difficulties with personal and professional relationships (Prinstein et al., 2018).

Identifying the correlates of the successful negotiation of social tasks at each developmental stage has led to a greater understanding of the key ingredients of social competence, which include an individual's "external" (e.g., behavioral) and "internal" (e.g., social-cognitive, emotional) skills and characteristics (Ladd, 2008). Behavioral skills associated with social competence include various prosocial behaviors (e.g., cooperation, helpfulness), which predict successful formation of friendships and peer acceptance. In contrast, deficits in prosocial behavior and/or maladaptive behavior (e.g., aggression) are related to adverse outcomes such as a lack of friends and peer rejection (for a review,

Social Skills Across the Life Span. https://doi.org/10.1016/B978-0-12-817752-5.00002-0

see Ladd, 2005). Regarding social-cognitive skills, the ways in which individuals interpret social interactions (e.g., social goals, attributions) also play a key role in their navigation of various social tasks and, therefore, predict their social adjustment (e.g., Erdley & Asher, 1999). Finally, research on emotional skills has focused on the important role that individuals' expressions of emotion, ability to understand their own and others' emotions, and ability to regulate their own emotions play in their social interactions and, consequently, various measures of social competence (e.g., Denham et al., 2003).

This chapter will examine how specific skills are related to indicators of social competence and how the relationship between skills and competence unfolds across development. Although we acknowledge that individuals with atypical development (e.g., autism spectrum disorder, intellectual disability) will display varied trajectories and unique patterns of deficits related to social skills, the scope of this chapter is limited to typical development. Specifically, we will focus on the preschool years, school-age years, adolescence, and adulthood. For each developmental period, we will first discuss the key social tasks and social contexts that characterize that stage, and then review research on the specific social skills within the behavioral, social-cognitive, and emotional domains that predict social competence during that stage.

Preschool-age children

As young as 6 months of age, infants engage in social interactions with other infants through vocalizations, smiles, gestures, and physical touch, and in their second year, toddlers begin to participate in cooperative games and experience episodes of conflict with play partners (Bukowski, Buhrmester, & Underwood, 2011). During this developmental period, children build a foundation of social skills through various interactions (e.g., observation, modeling) that occur in the context of relationships with parents and siblings. These early social interactions set the stage for the development of more sophisticated forms of play and peer engagement that emerge throughout the preschool years when children spend increasingly more time with same-aged peers. Based primarily upon proximity, reciprocal friendships during the preschool years tend to be with children of the same gender and serve the functions of companionship, intimacy, and mutual affection (Bukowski et al., 2011). Characterized by pretend play, these friendships provide opportunities for children to practice social roles and social skills such as empathy, cooperation, and conflict resolution (Bierman, Torres, & Schofield, 2010). In addition to friendships, preschoolers develop status within their classroom-based peer groups, with higher levels of peer acceptance being related to prosocial behavior and lower levels being associated with physical and relational aggression (Bukowski et al., 2011). Throughout the preschool years, children develop a variety of behavioral, social-cognitive, and emotional skills that have important implications for their future social adjustment (e.g., Goble et al., 2017).

Behavioral skills

Several key social skills in the behavioral domain are associated with social competence among preschoolers. Research has shown that preschoolers who develop effective communication skills, including good conversation abilities and accurate listening skills, are rated as more popular (e.g., friendly, outgoing) by teachers (Galejs, Dhawan, & King, 1983). Better-accepted preschoolers are also skilled at engaging in cooperative play, participating in turn taking and sharing, and entering group interactions. Furthermore, preschoolers who are skilled at initiating interactions, taking on a leadership role, and providing instrumental support to peers are rated as better liked (Ladd, Price, & Hart, 1988).

In contrast, preschoolers who show deficits in prosocial behavior and/or excesses of maladaptive behavior are less socially competent. Children who display lower levels of positive social behavior (e.g., cooperative play) and attempt peer group entry using intrusive strategies are more likely to be rejected by peers (Walker, 2004). In addition, those who exhibit more aggressive-hostile behaviors (e.g., arguing, rough play, aggression) experience higher levels of peer rejection (Rubin & Clark, 1983). Nonsocial behavior can also be a liability for children's social competence, as higher levels of reticent and withdrawn behavior (e.g., onlooking, solitary behavior during free play) are negatively associated with peer acceptance (Nelson, Rubin, & Fox, 2005).

Social-cognitive skills

Preschool children's social information processing skills also play a key role in their social competence. For example, when children are faced with ambiguous provocation situations in which some type of harm is caused, but the intent of the actor is unclear, preschoolers vary in the attributions that they make. Those children that show a tendency to make hostile intent attributions are evaluated as being more aggressive and less accepted by peers, whereas those who make benign attributions (e.g., the harm was caused by accident) are rated as more prosocial and better accepted by peers (Meece & Mize, 2010).

In addition, preschool children's social competence is related to their goals and strategies in particular social situations. For example, Kazura and Flanders (2007) found that in response to hypothetical peer conflict situations, preschoolers who endorsed friendship goals were more apt to select prosocial strategies, those who endorsed retaliation goals were more likely to pursue hostile strategies (and less likely to choose prosocial strategies), and those who endorsed avoidance goals were more apt to engage in adult-seeking strategies. Furthermore, the number of strategies that children generate as well as strategy quality (i.e., extent to which strategies are friendly, prosocial, or helpful) relates to social competence (Mize & Cox, 1990).

Emotional skills

In addition to behavioral and social-cognitive skills, social competence is closely tied to children's skills related to expressing, understanding, and regulating their emotions. According to Denham et al. (2003), emotional competence includes the following elements: emotional expressiveness (i.e., tendency to express positive versus negative affect), emotion knowledge (i.e., basic understanding of emotions), and emotion regulation (i.e., ability to modify/cope with emotional reactions). Preschoolers with more adaptive emotional skills are generally better liked by peers.

In terms of emotional expressiveness, preschoolers who express happiness are more liked by peers, whereas those with a greater proportion of angry expressions are less liked (Denham, McKinley, Couchoud, & Holt, 1990). With respect to emotion knowledge, preschoolers who can label the facial expressions of various emotions (e.g., happiness, sadness, surprise, anger) are better accepted by peers (e.g., Walden & Field, 1990) and are rated as more prosocial by adults (Mathieson & Banerjee, 2010). Moreover, preschoolers who display a greater understanding of situations related to the emotions of anger and fear are more liked by peers, and those who show difficulty differentiating expressions of happiness and sadness are less liked by peers.

Preschoolers who have difficulty regulating their emotions tend to receive lower likability ratings from peers, and these associations are stronger for boys than girls and for younger versus older preschoolers (Denham et al., 2003). Interestingly, emotion regulation may play a particularly important role when peer interactions are high in intensity (e.g., running wildly, yelling loudly). Indeed, Fabes et al. (1999) found that greater effortful control (i.e., ability to regulate behavioral, emotional, and physiological responses) among preschoolers and kindergarteners was associated with greater social competence, especially in highly intense peer interactions.

School-age children

During the elementary school years, children spend increasingly more time with peers, the features of their peer interactions change, and these relationships serve important functions for their development (Bukowski et al., 2011). In terms of qualitative changes, peer interactions become "more organized, elaborate, and rule governed" with children spending more time in large groups engaged in structured play and games with or without rules (Bierman et al., 2010, p. 125). Compared to the preschool years, rates of rough and tumble play and physical aggression decrease. However, rates of indirect or relational aggression (e.g., gossiping, ignoring, spreading rumors) and bullying increase, and children who are aggressive or socially withdrawn are at a higher risk for being victimized (Bukowski et al., 2011). Prosocial behavior (e.g., helpfulness, sharing, cooperation) continues to play a significant role in social interactions, and prosocial attitudes (e.g., kindness, empathy) take on increased importance (Bierman et al., 2010).

From middle through late childhood, children's social-cognitive abilities (e.g., perspective taking, social problem-solving) and self-regulation skills increase. Children's close friendships also change, as they become more stable, have a greater likelihood of being reciprocated, and transform in terms of various features (e.g., greater emotional reciprocity, intensity and understanding; enhanced conflict resolution). Regarding peer status, school-age children develop a greater awareness of the social standing of their classmates, and peer acceptance levels remain relatively stable across time (Bierman et al., 2010). In addition to continuing to learn social skills via direct instruction and modeling from adults such as parents and teachers, peers become increasingly important as models, teachers, and reinforcers of social skills during this developmental period. Through their social interactions, school-age children continue to develop key social skills in the behavioral, social-cognitive, and emotional domains that form a foundation for social and emotional functioning throughout their lives.

Behavioral skills

As the size of the peer group typically increases during the elementary school years, children's ability to enter ongoing interactions becomes especially important. Children who succeed in group entry behavior have been observed to attempt to understand a group's perspective before trying to join in activities or conversation. Those who make a greater number of relevant comments (i.e., directly related to the group's discussion) and accurately perceive the group's behavior are better accepted by peers (Putallaz & Gottman, 1981). In contrast, less accepted children are less cooperative and tend to direct the group's attention to themselves, which results in rejecting or ignoring responses from the group.

Prosocial behavior continues to be associated with social competence for school-age children. Across many studies with elementary school children, significant correlations between prosocial behavior (e.g., considerate of others' feelings, shares with others, helpful) and various social competence variables (e.g., popularity, quality of peer interactions, likelihood of being involved in a mutual friendship) have been reported (e.g., Andrade & Tannock, 2013).

Also as with preschool children, deficits in prosocial behavior and/or excesses in maladaptive behavior are associated with lower levels of social competence in school-aged children. Compared to their peers, rejected status children, particularly those who are aggressive, show poorer social behaviors (e.g., maladaptive response to provocation, social failure, and social success; greater proactive and reactive aggression; Volling, MacKinnon-Lewis, Rabiner, & Baradaran, 1993). Interestingly, however, there is evidence indicating that some children who engage in high levels of both prosocial and aggressive behavior (i.e., bistrategic) have higher peer status (e.g., Wurster & Xie, 2014). In terms of other behavioral difficulties, shyness and social withdrawal continue to be a liability for social competence during the school-age years, with these behaviors being negatively related to peer acceptance levels (e.g., Nelson et al., 2005).

Social-cognitive skills

Research on the social-cognitive skills of school-age youth has focused on various cognitive mediators of social behavior. Studies on children's attributions for social situations have found that compared to better-accepted peers, rejected youth are more likely to make external attributions for hypothetical social failure situations (i.e., blaming peers for negative relational outcomes; e.g., Crick & Ladd, 1993). In addition, aggressive children are more apt to make hostile attributions in response to ambiguous provocations, though this tendency decreases if the instigator is a friend (Burgess, Wojslawowicz, Rubin, Rose-Krasnor, & Booth-LaForce, 2006). Children who are victimized by peers are more likely to attribute that victimization to stable characteristics of themselves (i.e., ability and personal qualities). However, the more reciprocal friendships these children have, the less likely they are to make internal, stable attributions (Morrow, Hubbard, & Sharp, 2019). Overall, these findings suggest that participation in friendship can serve as a protective factor in terms of promoting more adaptive attributions when children encounter challenging situations with peers.

The contribution of school-aged children's social goals and strategies to their social competence has also been considered. Research by Erdley and Asher (1996) found that aggressive children were more likely to select hostile goals in response to ambiguous provocation situations, whereas behaviorally withdrawn children gave higher priority to avoidant goals, and prosocial children selected relationship-oriented goals. An investigation by Mouratidis and Sideridis (2009) revealed that children who endorse social demonstration-approach goals (i.e., aim to achieve social status and positive judgments from others) tend to have higher peer acceptance. In contrast, stronger endorsement of social demonstration-avoidance goals (i.e., focus on avoiding unfavorable judgments or rejection from peers) is associated with higher levels of loneliness. Regarding social strategies, Glick and Rose (2011) found that endorsement of avoidant/blaming strategies (in response to hypothetical situations in which a friend experienced a stressful event and the child could provide help) at the beginning of the school year was related to having fewer reciprocal friends and lower-quality friendships at the end of the school year.

Self-efficacy perceptions are also associated with various measures of social competence among school-age youth. Children who report high levels of perceived social competence (e.g., believing that it's easy to make friends, most kids like them) are more likely to be better accepted by peers (Harter, 1982). Compared to peers, aggressive children have significantly higher confidence in their ability to enact aggressive behavior and lower confidence in their ability to inhibit aggressive impulses. Interestingly, however, no differences were observed between aggressive and nonaggressive youth in perceived self-efficacy for prosocial behavior toward peers (Perry, Perry, & Rasmussen, 1986). Aggressive children also tend to expect that aggressive strategies will produce positive outcomes (e.g., tangible rewards, reduced negative treatment by others). Overall, these findings demonstrate that children's social-cognitive processes contribute to the behaviors they exhibit in their social interactions.

Emotional skills

Research examining links between emotional skills and social competence with school-age youth has focused on the domains of emotional expressiveness, emotion knowledge, and emotion regulation. Regarding emotional expressiveness, Eisenberg et al. (1995) found that children's tendency to express negative emotions predicted lower social competence (e.g., lower levels of popularity and prosocial behavior, poorer social skills) both concurrently and across a 2-year period. In terms of emotion knowledge, Custrini and Feldman (1989) reported that girls (but not boys) who were better able to express their own emotional states (i.e., encoding) and recognize expressions of emotion in others (i.e., decoding) were rated as more socially competent. Furthermore, children with better emotion understanding are more likely to be involved in a reciprocated friendship (Laghi et al., 2014).

The ability to regulate one's emotions is also a key predictor of social competence among school-age youth, both concurrently and across time (e.g., Eisenberg et al., 1995). Indeed, children with lower scores on negative emotionality and higher scores on self-regulation were rated higher on prosocial and cooperative behavior (Laible, Carlo, Murphy, Augustine, & Roesch, 2014). In one longitudinal study, Blair et al. (2015) found that greater emotion regulation skills at age five predicted more adaptive social skills at age seven, which were, in turn, related to higher-quality friendships, greater peer acceptance, and higher emotion regulation skills at age ten. Overall, these findings highlight the dynamic, interactive, and cascading effects among the emotional and social functioning variables across time (Blair et al., 2015).

Adolescence

As children move into adolescence, they interact with a wider range of peers (due to factors such as school transitions and increased use of electronic communication), there is less adult monitoring of peer interactions, and cliques (i.e., clusters of mutual friends), and crowds (i.e., loosely connected cliques with shared norms and attitudes—e.g., populars, jocks, brains) become key social structures (Bierman et al., 2010). Even more so than during childhood, adolescents increasingly turn to their peers for socialization, as they continue to acquire and refine the skills necessary for successful social interactions. One hallmark of social development during adolescence is the increased importance of friendship, along with changes in friendship features (e.g., greater intimacy, loyalty, self-disclosure; Bukowski et al., 2011). Adolescents tend to befriend peers whom they encounter often (e.g., school, neighborhood, extracurricular activities) and who are similar to themselves in terms of various characteristics (e.g., academic performance, deviant behavior, shyness; Bukowski et al., 2011). Heterosocial skills are a significant part of social competence during adolescence, as mixed-gender social interactions become more common and form a foundation for future heterosexual romantic relationships (Grover, Nangle, Serwik, & Zeff, 2007). Peer victimization increases during adolescence, along with susceptibility to peer influence (Riley, Sullivan, Hinton, & Kliewer, 2019). With increased abstract reasoning abilities, teens think about their peers' personality traits in addition to observable characteristics, and they begin to evaluate themselves in comparison to peers, which can contribute to greater social anxiety. Social withdrawal becomes less normative and is a stronger risk factor for psychological adjustment problems, especially among boys. The increasingly complex nature of peer interactions involves "active efforts at social initiation, engagement, and conversation" and requires sophisticated behavioral, social-cognitive, and emotional skills (Bierman et al., 2010, p. 129). The specific nature of these abilities and their connection to social competence will be discussed in the following sections.

Behavioral skills

As in earlier developmental stages, prosocial behavior among adolescents is associated with social competence. Teens who report higher levels of sociability (e.g., being nice to others) are better accepted by peers (Hanna, 1998). Peer ratings of prosocial behavior differ across sociometric groups, such that compared to average status peers, rejected and neglected adolescents score significantly lower and popular and controversial status teens score significantly higher (Pakaslahti, Karjalainen, & Keltikangas-Järvinen, 2002). Moreover, those who engage in prosocial behavior are more likely to be involved in a mutual best friendship, have higher-quality friendships, and experience higher friendship stability across the school year (McDonald, Wang, Menzer, Rubin, & Booth-LaForce, 2011).

Recent research also highlights the importance of examining different forms of prosocial behavior among adolescents. Proactive prosocial behavior (e.g., helping people in order to get something that the teen wants) predicts higher peer popularity (i.e., social visibility) ratings, but altruistic prosocial behavior (e.g., helping or sharing without being asked) correlates with higher peer likeability ratings (Findley-Van Nostrand & Ojanen, 2018). That is, prosocial behaviors that are self-serving versus other-oriented appear to differentially predict aspects of social competence during the adolescent years.

Interestingly, prosocial behavior appears to serve a protective function for youth exhibiting excesses in maladaptive behavior. Although high levels of aggressive behavior are typically associated with a lower likelihood of having a mutual best friend and lower friendship quality scores, if aggressive adolescents also exhibit high levels of prosocial behavior, the relationship between aggression and the friendship variables is not significant (McDonald et al., 2011).

Prosocial behavior also appears to protect adolescents, particularly boys, who exhibit elevated levels of social withdrawal from experiencing high levels of peer exclusion (Freitas, Santos, Ribeiro, Daniel, & Rubin, 2019).

As observed with younger youth, deficits in prosocial behavior and/or excesses of maladaptive behavior generally are a liability for social competence during adolescence. Relational aggression is negatively associated with peer preference, but positively associated with peer nominations of popularity (Kraft & Mayeux, 2018). With respect to social withdrawal, higher levels of social anxiety predict greater social withdrawal, which, in turn, is associated with lower levels of quality (i.e., companionship, intimacy) in adolescents' best friendships (Biggs, Vernberg, & Wu, 2012).

Notably, with increased time spent in mixed-gender peer interactions during adolescence, heterosocial competence needs to be considered. Heterosocial competence is defined as "the ability to effectively negotiate social situations that involve the other gender including acquaintanceships, friendships, romantic, and sexual relationships" (Grover et al., 2007, p. 491). Heterosocial competence involves a variety of social skills (e.g., communication, problem solving, emotional understanding) that overlap somewhat, but not completely, with the skills needed for same-gender interactions (Grover, Nangle, Serwik, Fales, & Prenoveau, 2013). Research indicates that late adolescents who have higher heterosocial skills (i.e., initiating relationships, conflict resolution, navigating sexual situations) experience fewer negative interactions in romantic relationships and other-gender friendships, and higher social support and less conflict in romantic relationships (Grover et al., 2013).

With adolescents spending increasingly more time online, a growing body of research has examined associations between behavioral patterns in teens' online communication (i.e., how they use internet-based communication technologies) and their social competence (e.g., quality of offline friendships). Overall, research supports the stimulation hypothesis (i.e., adolescents tend to use online communication tools to maintain existing friendships, and those relationships become more intimate as a result). A review by Shapiro and Margolin (2014) reported that adolescents with strong offline social skills tend to have more social connections online. In the first known study to consider how both online and offline social competence relate to peer acceptance and victimization, Resnik and Bellmore (2019) found that among a high school-aged sample, students' "social media acceptance" (i.e., "whose social media posts do you interact with the most?") was moderately positively correlated with a traditional assessment of peer acceptance but not with popularity (impact). Students' level of "social media impact" (i.e., "whose social media posts does everyone in your school pay the most attention to?") was moderately positively associated with popularity but not peer acceptance. Finally, peer victimization was negatively associated with both online and offline social skills (Resnik & Bellmore, 2019). Additional research that more adequately captures the nuances of adolescents' online social skills is needed to better understand the relationship between their online behaviors and measures of social competence.

Social-cognitive skills

Studies examining the social-cognitive skills that are linked with social competence during adolescence have focused on constructs such as social goals and attributions, social problem-solving strategies, perspective-taking abilities, and empathy. With respect to social goals, it has been found that agentic goals (i.e., focused on status, power) are negatively related to altruistic prosocial behavior (i.e., doing things for others without being asked) and reactive prosocial behavior (i.e., doing things for others because they put you in a good mood), are positively related to proactive prosocial behaviors (i.e., doing things for others to get what you want), and predict increases in relational aggression across 1 year. In contrast, communal goals (i.e., focused on closeness) are positively associated with altruistic prosocial behavior, negatively related to proactive prosocial behavior, and predict decreases in physical aggression over time (e.g., Findley-Van Nostrand & Ojanen, 2018).

Other types of social goals also predict adolescents' behavior. For example, Li and Wright (2014) found that stronger endorsement of a popularity goal (i.e., striving to be popular with peers) predicted higher levels of relational aggression and lower levels of prosocial behavior. In contrast, endorsement of a social preference goal (i.e., striving to be well liked by peers) was associated with lower levels of overt and relational aggression and more prosocial behavior. Overall, specific types of adolescents' social goals are uniquely tied to particular social behaviors.

Adolescents' attributions for various types of social situations also relate to their social competence. In a laboratory study, early adolescents were randomly assigned to an acute peer rejection versus no rejection group and subsequently participated in a game scenario that included peer judges. Compared to youth in the no-rejection group, those who experienced acute peer rejection were significantly more likely to attribute hostile intent to the peer judges and endorse aggressive responses toward them (Reijntjes et al., 2011). Other research has found that rejected status adolescents are more likely to attribute experiences of being accepted by peers to external factors, attribute experiences of peer rejection to stable factors, and endorse lower perceived control of the outcomes of social situations with peers (Toner & Munro, 1996). In contrast, better-accepted adolescents are more likely to attribute peer acceptance to internal factors and peer rejection to unstable factors, and they have higher perceived control in terms of the outcomes of social situations. Prioritizing effective social problem-solving strategies is also critical for social competence. Indeed, high-accepted adolescents are more likely than rejected peers to endorse prosocial problem-solving strategies (e.g., standing up for a classmate who is being teased; Pakaslahti et al., 2002).

Adolescents with greater empathy and more sophisticated perspective-taking abilities tend to exhibit higher levels of social competence. For example, adolescents with higher levels of empathy display greater support in their close friendships (e.g., Ciarrochi et al., 2016). Interestingly, higher levels of cognitive empathy (i.e., ability to understand when a friend is experiencing a particular emotion) among boys (but not girls) are associated with receiving a greater number of opposite-gender friendship nominations (Ciarrochi et al., 2016). These researchers speculate that the reason males do not use empathy as a criterion for selecting female friends is because they fail to recognize empathy or are indifferent to it. Theories related to a sense of safety, mate selection, and social roles/cultural context may help to explain females' tendency to befriend empathic males, but further research is needed (Ciarrochi et al., 2016).

Emotional skills

During adolescence, skills in the areas of emotional expressiveness, emotion knowledge, and emotion regulation continue to be associated with social competence. Regarding the expression of emotions, higher levels of emotional reactivity (e.g., tendency to become nervous, upset, or angry quickly) are correlated with less prosocial behavior (Carlo, Crockett, Wolff, & Beal, 2012). Notably, however, adolescents who talk about their emotions and receive supportive responses from friends are more likely to disclose emotions in subsequent conversation, a process that can improve the quality of the friendship (Legerski, Biggs, Greenhoot, & Sampilo, 2015). With respect to emotion knowledge, results of one longitudinal study revealed that adolescent girls with lower skills at identifying and describing their own emotions in eighth grade had fewer female and more male friendships in twelfth grade. Relationships among these variables were not significant for boys (Rowsell, Ciarrochi, Heaven, & Deane, 2014).

Emotion regulation skills continue to be a predictor of social competence during adolescence. For early adolescents, a specific type of emotion regulation called integrative emotion regulation (e.g., desire to understand why one feels anxious or stressed) has been found to be associated with higher levels of empathy, which, in turn, predict more prosocial behavior toward classmates (Benita, Levkovitz, & Roth, 2017). In addition, a recent study that followed seventh graders for 1 year examined the specific emotion regulation strategies of reappraisal (i.e., changing one's interpretation of a situation) and suppression (i.e., hiding one's verbal, gestural, and facial aspects of a particular emotional expression). Higher suppression was correlated with lower self-reported friendship satisfaction for boys only, both concurrently and across time (Chervonsky & Hunt, 2019).

Relationships among emotion knowledge, expression, and regulation and peer victimization have also been examined. With fifth and eighth graders, Riley and colleagues (2019) found that higher levels of emotional awareness (i.e., ability to identify one's own internal emotional experiences) were associated with more adaptive emotion regulation abilities, which, in turn, predicted lower levels of overt peer victimization (e.g., being physically harmed, being called mean names, being threatened with harm). In addition, high levels of expressive reluctance (i.e., tendency to keep negative emotions to oneself) predicted higher anger regulation abilities, which were associated with less frequent overt peer victimization. These findings illustrate how different types of emotional skills can interact to predict social competence during adolescence.

Adulthood

Adulthood is marked by distinct social skill development with the navigation of new social situations and the refinement of peer relationships over time (Bruhn & Philips, 1987). Across adulthood, there are greater complexities in social interactions that are impacted by increased cognitive abilities that affect one's ability to understand and handle subtle social cues (Holt-Lunstad & Smith, 2012). This section will provide a brief overview of social skill development during adulthood covering emerging, middle, and late adulthood. Emerging adulthood is defined as the period between 18 and 25 years of age when individuals are transitioning from adolescence to becoming independent adults (Koepke & Denissen, 2012). This period is characterized by novel social interactions, such as living away from parents and joining the workforce, that are navigated independently for the first time and set the stage for social development into middle adulthood (Chapman & Hayslip, 2006). Throughout middle adulthood, social relationships are refined to smaller, closer peer groups, and the higher quality those social relationships are, the greater overall life satisfaction (Holt-Lunstad & Smith, 2012). When transitioning into older adulthood, individuals tend to maintain a close social network and have high satisfaction with their social relationships (Luong, Charles, & Fingerman, 2011), although cognitive decline may contribute to unique difficulty with appropriate social filtering (Verhaeghen & Hertzog, 2014).

Behavioral skills

Communication skills play a critical role throughout adulthood, and in emerging adulthood these skills set a precedent for the quality of social relationships through the rest of life. Zambianchi and Bitti (2013) found that emerging adults are better able to present themselves positively while having more control over their negative emotions, which helps with more effective communication over time. The importance of effective communication skills takes on new life as emerging adults' social interactions are taking place not only in person, but also online. Mikami, Szwedo, Allen, Evans, and Hare (2010) found that online social behavior is overall congruent with in-person social behavior, and social networking websites generally serve as an extension of social contact, making it constant. This allows for more opportunity for both connection and conflict. Similar to in-person communication, extraversion and positivity relate to successful online relationships (Mikami et al., 2010). Despite being less common in middle adulthood and older adulthood, social media use is continuing to increase in these age groups. Although middle and older adults report experiencing positive social connection online, there continues to be an age gap in social competence online in regard to communication skills, such as an understanding of online culture and the implications of public information sharing (Bartsch & Dienlin, 2016).

As individuals age into late adulthood, they report higher satisfaction with social relationships (Luong et al., 2011), but they also start to lose executive control and may begin to behave in socially inappropriate ways, such as expressing unintentional prejudice (Henry, Hippel, & Baynes, 2009). Even older adults with relatively high executive control sometimes demonstrate more socially inappropriate responses to provocation than younger adults, which may be due to decreased concerns regarding social desirability (Henry et al., 2009). There is also an increase in off-target verbosity in aging populations, which is attributed to lowered cognitive inhibition (Pushkar et al., 2000). When involved in conversation, older adults often express frustration with others' verbosity, yet seem to lack awareness of their own verbosity. With these decreases in older adults' communication skills, their social partners report being less satisfied during social interactions, but interestingly, older adults report being generally satisfied with their social relationships (Pushkar et al., 2000).

Another key social skill in adulthood is conflict resolution. As emerging adults begin to navigate a variety of social situations independent from their caregivers (Manzeske & Stright, 2009), they show significant advances in conflict resolution. Laursen, Finkelstein, and Betts (2001) noted that during emerging adulthood, there is a transition from using coercive means to resolve conflict to using negotiation. Emerging adults are more able to put their self-interests aside for the benefit of their social partner and, as a result, are better able to maintain stable, higher-quality relationships (Laursen et al., 2001). However, some emerging adults struggle with adaptive conflict resolution skills, particularly those who demonstrate a hostile attribution bias that contributes to aggressive responses to conflict and leads to damaged relationships (Bailey & Ostrov, 2007).

According to Luong et al. (2011), middle and older adults are more likely to avoid conflict in relationships and, even when in conflict, they are more apt to give others the benefit of the doubt. This allows for less tension in social relationships in aging populations and more positive conflict resolution. Middle and older adults typically experience fewer negative emotions in general, which helps to prevent arguments from escalating into anger. With individuals being less reactive and overall more positive, conflicts are able to be avoided and disagreements can be more easily managed (Luong et al., 2011).

Social-cognitive skills

In addition to behavioral skills, social cognitive skills play a key role in social competence in adulthood. Social problem-solving skills that are more adaptive in maintaining positive social relationships go through further development, increasing in both quantity and quality (Laursen et al., 2001). Furthermore, emerging adults experience an increase in perspective-taking skills that enables them to better understand and appreciate others' opinions, which can help to minimize conflict and allow for more stable peer relationships (Laursen et al., 2001). Increased perspective-taking skills also contribute to emerging adults being more aware of and concerned about others' views toward them. As they become involved in new social contexts (e.g., college, the workplace), emerging adults tend to be particularly focused on positive self-presentation to promote social desirability to peers (Jackson, 2007). When using social media, emerging adults must navigate positive self-presentation from their face-to-face communication and translate that into their online presence (Mikami et al., 2010). The increased self-esteem from positive online interaction impacts online social group dynamics making for a positive social environment, whereas negative online interactions and comparing one's self-presentation with others can decrease self-esteem, demonstrating the instability of self-image and self-esteem during this period (Barker, 2009).

Moving into middle adulthood, there is a change of emphasis to smaller friendship groups rather than larger peer groups (Bruhn & Philips, 1987). With an increased stability of identity and self-esteem that comes in middle adulthood, there is more of a focus on social needs. Consequently, individuals are more likely to narrow down peer relationships to those people in their lives with whom they can form more meaningful relationships, and these relationships generally have more longevity than earlier peer relationships (Huang, 2010). Social goals during this period are more centered on creating quality social support rather than general peer acceptance (Huang, 2010).

In older adulthood, social interactions can play a key role in maintaining cognitive abilities (Kang, Boss, & Clowtis, 2016) and increasing longevity and quality of life. However, there is a bidirectional relationship between cognitive abilities and social skills (Holt-Lunstad & Smith, 2012). As cognitive skills decline, older adults tend to experience decreased social judgment and lose their social filter, which leads to decreases in social skills near the end of life (Verhaeghen & Hertzog, 2014). There is a shift in attributional style that occurs in this period as older adults tend to attribute declining social skills to their cognitive decline and see the impact on their social lives as being out of their control. There is also a decrease in cognitive flexibility that creates difficulties in social problem solving as older adults are less likely to adjust to novel ideas, which creates more conflict with peers as well as with younger adults (Verhaeghen & Hertzog, 2014). Cognitive inflexibility and cognitive decline can contribute to difficulty filtering inappropriate responses, and older adults are more likely to make comments that indicate prejudice (Henry et al., 2009). This prejudice, paired with difficulty in taking others' perspectives, may contribute to challenges in navigating conflict and, as a result, in maintaining positive social relationships (Verhaeghen & Hertzog, 2014).

Emotional skills

Social competence in adulthood is also characterized by continued emotional development. As emerging adults separate from their parents, a key task for social adjustment is the development of emotional autonomy (Koepke & Denissen, 2012). Emotion regulation skills tend to increase during this period, as does the ability to identify appropriate emotional expression, contributing to better problem-solving skills and more stable relationships (Zimmermann & Iwanski, 2014).

During middle adulthood, individuals make gains in emotional intelligence, defined as the ability to control, express, and be aware of emotions and handle interpersonal relationships appropriately. This enables individuals to employ more effective mood-management strategies in emotion regulation, such as using optimism when facing emotional stress (Chapman & Hayslip, 2006). Middle adults are also likely to express fewer emotional responses, both positive and negative, and seek less emotional support, being able to regulate independently (Zimmermann & Iwanski, 2014). As middle adults are able to successfully navigate their emotions, they also become more selective regarding with whom they choose to socialize (i.e., socioemotional selectivity theory; Carstensen, 1992). During this time, adults have closer emotional bonds with a smaller group of friends and become more emotionally close to their romantic partners. Interestingly, middle adults do not require as many social interactions to maintain emotional satisfaction as compared to younger adults (Carstensen, 1992).

Verhaeghen and Hertzog (2014) have described several characteristics of development during older adulthood. For example, this stage is marked by an increase in emotional memory, but a decrease in accurate emotional perception. Although older adults experience a general cognitive decline over time, emotional memory and social functioning do not undergo the same decline initially. Individuals enter into fewer conflicts and have more emotionally satisfying relationships while having better memory for emotionally salient events. On the other hand, there is a decline in the ability to accurately interpret emotional cues from others, which can result in misunderstandings of emotional communication and contribute to frustration in social interactions. Taken together, emotional skills in older adulthood show some strengths but also some declines that impact social competence.

Conclusion

From preschool through adulthood, as the complexity of peer interactions increases, more refined and nuanced social skills in the behavioral, social-cognitive, and emotional domains are required for social competence. Social competence during the preschool and school age years is characterized by prosocial and cooperative behavior, adaptive social-cognitive processes (e.g., prosocial strategies, relationship maintenance goals), empathy, and age-appropriate emotion regulation and understanding with relatively low levels of aggression and social withdrawal. In turn, these skills set the stage for successful social functioning during the adolescent years and beyond. In contrast, those who are lacking in one or more of these skill areas are at risk for increasingly negative social consequences. During adolescence, the social skills needed for successful dyadic friendships and romantic relationships take center stage, and adaptive communication and conflict resolution skills are needed for satisfying dyadic friendships and effective social interactions throughout adulthood. Across adulthood, small, intimate peer groups become increasingly important, with high-quality social relationships contributing to higher life satisfaction, and the cognitive declines of older adulthood posing unique challenges for social interactions. There are dynamic and interactive relationships among the different social skill domains, and the effects of adaptive social skills for social competence are cumulative across the lifespan.

References

Andrade, B. F., & Tannock, R. (2013). The direct effects of inattention and hyperactivity/impulsivity on peer problems and mediating roles of prosocial and conduct problem behaviors in a community sample of children. *Journal of Attention Disorders*, *17*(8), 670–680. https://doi.org/10.1177/1087054712437580.

Bailey, C. A., & Ostrov, J. M. (2007). Differentiating forms and functions of aggression in emerging adults: Associations with hostile attribution biases and normative beliefs. *Journal of Youth and Adolescence*, *37*(6), 713–722. https://doi.org/10.1007/s10964-007-9211-5.

Barker, V. (2009). Older adolescents' motivations for social network site use: The influence of gender, group identity, and collective self-esteem. *CyberPsychology & Behavior*, *12*(2), 209–213. https://doi.org/10.1089/cpb.2008.0228.

Bartsch, M., & Dienlin, T. (2016). Control your Facebook: An analysis of online privacy literacy. *Computers in Human Behavior*, *56*, 147–154. https://doi.org/10.1016/j.chb.2015.11.022.

Benita, M., Levkovitz, T., & Roth, G. (2017). Integrative emotion regulation predicts adolescents' prosocial behavior through the mediation of empathy. *Learning and Instruction*, *50*, 14–20. https://doi.org/10.1016/j.learninstruc.2016.11.004.

Bierman, K. L., Torres, M. M., & Schofield, H. T. (2010). Developmental factors related to the assessment of social skills. In D. W. Nangle, D. J. Hansen, C. A. Erdley, & P. J. Norton (Eds.), *Practitioner's guide to empirically based measures of social skills; Practitioner's guide to empirically based measures of social skills* (pp. 119–134). New York, NY: Springer Publishing Company. https://doi.org/10.1007/978-1-4419-0609-0_8.

Biggs, B. K., Vernberg, E. M., & Wu, Y. P. (2012). Social anxiety and adolescents' friendships: The role of social withdrawal. *The Journal of Early Adolescence*, *32*(6), 802–823. https://doi.org/10.1177/0272431611426145.

Blair, B. L., Perry, N. B., O'Brien, M., Calkins, S. D., Keane, S. P., & Shanahan, L. (2015). Identifying developmental cascades among differentiated dimensions of social competence and emotion regulation. *Developmental Psychology*, *51*(8), 1062–1073. https://doi.org/10.1037/a0039472.

Bruhn, J. G., & Philips, B. U. (1987). A developmental basis for social support. *Journal of Behavioral Medicine*, *10*(3), 213–229. https://doi.org/10.1007/bf00846536.

Bukowski, W. M., Buhrmester, D., & Underwood, M. K. (2011). Peer relations as a developmental context. In M. K. Underwood & L. H. Rosen (Eds.), *Social development: Relationships in infancy, childhood, and adolescence* (pp. 153–179). New York, NY: Guilford Press.

Burgess, K. B., Wojslawowicz, J. C., Rubin, K. H., Rose-Krasnor, L., & Booth-LaForce, C. (2006). Social information processing and coping strategies of shy/withdrawn and aggressive children: Does friendship matter? *Child Development*, *77*(2), 371–383. https://doi.org/10.1111/j.1467-8624.2006.00876.x.

Carlo, G., Crockett, L. J., Wolff, J. M., & Beal, S. J. (2012). The role of emotional reactivity, self-regulation, and puberty in adolescents' prosocial behaviors. *Social Development*, *21*(4), 667–685. https://doi.org/10.1111/j.1467-9507.2012.00660.x.

Carstensen, L. L. (1992). Social and emotional patterns in adulthood: Support for socioemotional selectivity theory. *Psychology and Aging*, *7*(3), 331–338. https://doi.org/10.1037//0882-7974.7.3.331.

Chapman, B. P., & Hayslip, B. (2006). Emotional intelligence in young and middle adulthood: Cross-sectional analysis of latent structure and means. *Psychology and Aging*, *21*(2), 411–418. https://doi.org/10.1037/0882-7974.21.2.411.

Chervonsky, E., & Hunt, C. (2019). Emotion regulation, mental health, and social wellbeing in a young adolescent sample: A concurrent and longitudinal investigation. *Emotion*, *19*(2), 270–282. https://doi.org/10.1037/emo0000432.

Ciarrochi, J., Parker, P. D., Sahdra, B. K., Kashdan, T. B., Kiuru, N., & Conigrave, J. (2016). When empathy matters: The role of sex and empathy in close friendships. *Journal of Personality*, *85*(4), 494–504. https://doi.org/10.1111/jopy.12255.

Crick, N. R., & Ladd, G. W. (1993). Children's perceptions of their peer experiences: Attributions, loneliness, social anxiety, and social avoidance. *Developmental Psychology*, *29*(2), 244–254. https://doi.org/10.1037/0012-1649.29.2.244.

Custrini, R. J., & Feldman, R. S. (1989). Children's social competence and nonverbal encoding and decoding of emotions. *Journal of Clinical Child Psychology*, *18*(4), 336–342. https://doi.org/10.1207/s15374424jccp1804_7.

Denham, S. A., Blair, K. A., DeMulder, E., Levitas, J., Sawyer, K., Auerbach-Major, S., & Queenan, P. (2003). Preschool emotional competence: Pathway to social competence. *Child Development*, *74*(1), 238–256. https://doi.org/10.1111/1467-8624.00533.

Denham, S. A., McKinley, M., Couchoud, E. A., & Holt, R. (1990). Emotional and behavioral predictors of preschool peer ratings. *Child Development*, *61*(4), 1145–1152. https://doi.org/10.2307/1130882.

Eisenberg, N., Fabes, R. A., Murphy, B., Maszk, P., Smith, M., & Karbon, M. (1995). The role of emotionality and regulation in children's social functioning: A longitudinal study. *Child Development*, *66*(5), 1360–1384. https://doi.org/10.2307/1131652.

Erdley, C. A., & Asher, S. R. (1996). Children's social goals and self-efficacy perceptions as influences on their responses to ambiguous provocation. *Child Development*, *67*(4), 1329–1344. https://doi.org/10.2307/1131703.

Erdley, C. A., & Asher, S. R. (1999). A social goals perspective on children's social competence. *Journal of Emotional and Behavioral Disorders*, *7*(3), 156–167. https://doi.org/10.1177/106342669900700304.

Fabes, R. A., Eisenberg, N., Jones, S., Smith, M., Guthrie, I., Poulin, R., … Friedman, J. (1999). Regulation, emotionality, and preschoolers' socially competent peer interactions. *Child Development*, *70*(2), 432–442. https://doi.org/10.1111/1467-8624.00031.

Findley-Van Nostrand, D., & Ojanen, T. (2018). Forms of prosocial behaviors are differentially linked to social goals and peer status in adolescents. *The Journal of Genetic Psychology: Research and Theory on Human Development*, *179*(6), 329–342. https://doi.org/10.1080/00221325.2018.1518894.

Freitas, M., Santos, A. J., Ribeiro, O., Daniel, J. R., & Rubin, K. H. (2019). Prosocial behavior and friendship quality as moderators of the association between anxious withdrawal and peer experiences in Portuguese young adolescents. *Frontiers in Psychology*, *9*, 13. https://doi.org/10.3389/fpsyg.2018.02783.

Galejs, I., Dhawan, G., & King, A. (1983). Popularity and communication skills of preschool children. *The Journal of Psychology: Interdisciplinary and Applied*, *115*, 89–95. https://doi.org/10.1080/00223980.1983.9923601.

Glick, G. C., & Rose, A. J. (2011). Prospective associations between friendship adjustment and social strategies: Friendship as a context for building social skills. *Developmental Psychology*, *47*(4), 1117–1132. https://doi.org/10.1037/a0023277.

Goble, P., Eggum-Wilkens, N., Bryce, C. I., Foster, S. A., Hanish, L. D., Martin, C. L., & Fabes, R. A. (2017). The transition from preschool to first grade: A transactional model of development. *Journal of Applied Developmental Psychology*, *49*, 55–67. https://doi.org/10.1016/j.appdev.2017.01.007.

Grover, R. L., Nangle, D. W., Serwik, A., & Zeff, K. R. (2007). Girl friend, boy friend, girlfriend, boyfriend: Broadening our understanding of heterosocial competence. *Journal of Clinical Child and Adolescent Psychology*, *36*(4), 491–502. https://doi.org/10.1080/15374410701651637.

Grover, R. L., Nangle, D. W., Serwik, A. K., Fales, J., & Prenoveau, J. M. (2013). The measure of heterosocial competence: Development and psychometric investigation. *Journal of Social and Personal Relationships*, *30*(4), 457–481. https://doi.org/10.1177/0265407512458658.

Hanna, N. A. (1998). Predictors of friendship quality and peer group acceptance at summer camp. *The Journal of Early Adolescence*, *18*(3), 291–318. https://doi.org/10.1177/0272431698018003004.

Harter, S. (1982). The Perceived Competence Scale for Children. *Child Development*, *53*(1), 87–97. https://doi.org/10.2307/1129640.

Henry, J. D., Hippel, W. V., & Baynes, K. (2009). Social inappropriateness, executive control, and aging. *Psychology and Aging*, *24*(1), 239–244. https://doi.org/10.1037/a0013423.

Holt-Lunstad, J., & Smith, T. B. (2012). Social relationships and mortality. *Social and Personality Psychology Compass*, *6*(1), 41–53. https://doi.org/10.1111/j.1751-9004.2011.00406.x.

Huang, C. (2010). Mean-level change in self-esteem from childhood through adulthood: Meta-analysis of longitudinal studies. *Review of General Psychology*, *14*(3), 251–260. https://doi.org/10.1037/a0020543.

Jackson, T. (2007). Protective self-presentation, sources of socialization, and loneliness among Australian adolescents and young adults. *Personality and Individual Differences*, *43*(6), 1552–1562. https://doi.org/10.1016/j.paid.2007.04.012.

Kang, D.-H., Boss, L., & Clowtis, L. (2016). Social support and cognition. *Western Journal of Nursing Research*, *38*(12), 1639–1659. https://doi.org/10.1177/0193945916655796.

Kazura, K., & Flanders, R. (2007). Preschool children's social understanding: A pilot study of goals and strategies during conflict situations. *Psychological Reports*, *101*(2), 547–554. https://doi.org/10.2466/PR0.101.6.547-554.

Koepke, S., & Denissen, J. J. (2012). Dynamics of identity development and separation–individuation in parent–child relationships during adolescence and emerging adulthood—A conceptual integration. *Developmental Review*, *32*(1), 67–88. https://doi.org/10.1016/j.dr.2012.01.001.

Kraft, C., & Mayeux, L. (2018). Associations among friendship jealousy, peer status, and relational aggression in early adolescence. *The Journal of Early Adolescence*, *38*(3), 385–407. https://doi.org/10.1177/0272431616670992.

Ladd, G. W. (2005). *Children's peer relationships and social competence: A century of progress*. New Haven, CT: Yale University Press.

Ladd, G. W. (2008). Social competence and peer relations: Significance for young children and their service-providers. *Early Childhood Services*, *2*, 129–148. https://doi.org/10.4324/9780203841198.ch3.

Ladd, G. W., Price, J. M., & Hart, C. H. (1988). Predicting preschoolers' peer status from their playground behaviors. *Child Development*, *59*(4), 986–992. https://doi.org/10.2307/1130265.

Laghi, F., Baiocco, R., Di Norcia, A., Cannoni, E., Baumgartner, E., & Bombi, A. S. (2014). Emotion understanding, pictorial representations of friendship and reciprocity in school-aged children. *Cognition and Emotion*, *28*(7), 1338–1346. https://doi.org/10.1080/02699931.2014.881779.

Laible, D., Carlo, G., Murphy, T., Augustine, M., & Roesch, S. (2014). Predicting children's prosocial and co-operative behavior from their temperamental profiles: A person-centered approach. *Social Development*, *23*(4), 734–752. https://doi.org/10.1111/sode.12072.

Laursen, B., Finkelstein, B. D., & Betts, N. T. (2001). A developmental meta-analysis of peer conflict resolution. *Developmental Review*, *21*(4), 423–449. https://doi.org/10.1006/drev.2000.0531.

Legerski, J., Biggs, B. K., Greenhoot, A. F., & Sampilo, M. L. (2015). Emotion talk and friend responses among early adolescent same-sex friend dyads. *Social Development*, *24*(1), 20–38. https://doi.org/10.1111/sode.12079.

Li, Y., & Wright, M. F. (2014). Adolescents' social status goals: Relationships to social status insecurity, aggression, and prosocial behavior. *Journal of Youth and Adolescence*, *43*(1), 146–160. https://doi.org/10.1007/s10964-013-9939-z.

Luong, G., Charles, S. T., & Fingerman, K. L. (2011). Better with age: Social relationships across adulthood. *Journal of Social and Personal Relationships*, *28*(1), 9–23. https://doi.org/10.1177/0265407510391362.

Manzeske, D. P., & Stright, A. D. (2009). Parenting styles and emotion regulation: The role of behavioral and psychological control during young adulthood. *Journal of Adult Development*, *16*(4), 223–229. https://doi.org/10.1007/s10804-009-9068-9.

Mathieson, K., & Banerjee, R. (2010). Pre-school peer play: The beginnings of social competence. *Educational and Child Psychology*, *27*(1), 9–20.

McDonald, K. L., Wang, J., Menzer, M. M., Rubin, K. H., & Booth-LaForce, C. (2011). Prosocial behavior moderates the effects of aggression on young adolescents' friendships. *International Journal of Developmental Science*, *5*(1-2), 127–137. Retrieved from https://ezproxy.hws.edu/login?url=https://search-proquest-com.ezproxy.hws.edu/docview/1030208202?accountid=27680.

Meece, D., & Mize, J. (2010). Multiple aspects of preschool children's social cognition: Relations with peer acceptance and peer interaction style. *Early Child Development and Care*, *180*(5), 585–604. https://doi.org/10.1080/03004430802181452.

Mikami, A. Y., Szwedo, D. E., Allen, J. P., Evans, M. A., & Hare, A. L. (2010). Adolescent peer relationships and behavior problems predict young adults' communication on social networking websites. *Developmental Psychology*, *46*(1), 46–56. https://doi.org/10.1037/a0017420.

Mize, J., & Cox, R. A. (1990). Social knowledge and social competence: Number and quality of strategies as predictors of peer behavior. *The Journal of Genetic Psychology: Research and Theory on Human Development*, *151*(1), 117–127. https://doi.org/10.1080/00221325.1990.9914648.

Morrow, M. T., Hubbard, J. A., & Sharp, M. K. (2019). Preadolescents' internal attributions for negative peer experiences: Links to child and classroom peer victimization and friendship. *Journal of Abnormal Child Psychology*, *47*(3), 393–404. https://doi.org/10.1007/s10802-018-0460-4.

Mouratidis, A. A., & Sideridis, G. D. (2009). On social achievement goals: Their relations with peer acceptance, classroom belongingness, and perceptions of loneliness. *Journal of Experimental Education*, *77*(3), 285–307. https://doi.org/10.3200/JEXE.77.3.285-308.

Nelson, L. J., Rubin, K. H., & Fox, N. A. (2005). Social withdrawal, observed peer acceptance, and the development of self-perceptions in children ages 4 to 7 years. *Early Childhood Research Quarterly*, *20*(2), 185–200. https://doi.org/10.1016/j.ecresq.2005.04.007.

Pakaslahti, L., Karjalainen, A., & Keltikangas-Järvinen, L. (2002). Relationships between adolescent prosocial problem-solving strategies, prosocial behaviour, and social acceptance. *International Journal of Behavioral Development*, *26*(2), 137–144. https://doi.org/10.1080/01650250042000681.

Perry, D. G., Perry, L. C., & Rasmussen, P. (1986). Cognitive social learning mediators of aggression. *Child Development*, *57*(3), 700–711. https://doi.org/10.2307/1130347.

Prinstein, M. J., Rancourt, D., Adelman, C. B., Ahlich, E., Smith, J., & Guerry, J. D. (2018). Peer status and psychopathology. In W. M. Bukowski, B. Laursen, & K. H. Rubin (Eds.), *Handbook of peer interactions, relationships, and groups* (2nd ed., pp. 617–636). New York: Guilford.

Pushkar, D., Basevitz, P., Arbuckle, T., Nohara-Leclair, M., Lapidus, S., & Peled, M. (2000). Social behavior and off-target verbosity in elderly people. *Psychology and Aging*, *15*(2), 361–374. https://doi.org/10.1037//0882-7974.15.2.361.

Putallaz, M., & Gottman, J. M. (1981). An interactional model of children's entry into peer groups. *Child Development*, *52*(3), 986–994. https://doi.org/10.2307/1129103.

Reijntjes, A., Thomaes, S., Kamphuis, J. H., Bushman, B. J., de Castro, B. O., & Telch, M. J. (2011). Explaining the paradoxical rejection-aggression link: The mediating effects of hostile intent attributions, anger, and decreases in state self-esteem on peer rejection-induced aggression in youth. *Personality and Social Psychology Bulletin*, *37*(7), 955–963. https://doi.org/10.1177/0146167211410247.

Resnik, F., & Bellmore, A. (2019). Connecting online and offline social skills to adolescents' peer victimization and psychological adjustment. *Journal of Youth and Adolescence*, *48*(2), 386–398. https://doi.org/10.1007/s10964-018-0953-z.

Riley, T. N., Sullivan, T. N., Hinton, T. S., & Kliewer, W. (2019). Longitudinal relations between emotional awareness and expression, emotion regulation, and peer victimization among urban adolescents. *Journal of Adolescence*, *72*, 42–51. https://doi.org/10.1016/j.adolescence.2019.02.005.

Rowsell, H. C., Ciarrochi, J., Heaven, P. C. L., & Deane, F. P. (2014). The role of emotion identification skill in the formation of male and female friendships: A longitudinal study. *Journal of Adolescence*, *37*(2), 103–111. https://doi.org/10.1016/j.adolescence.2013.11.005.

Rubin, K. H., & Clark, M. L. (1983). Preschool teacher's ratings of behavioral problems: Observational, sociometric, and social-cognitive correlates. *Journal of Abnormal Child Psychology*, *11*(2), 273. Retrieved from https://ezproxy.hws.edu/login?url=https://search-proquest-com.ezproxy.hws.edu/docview/1300101425?accountid=27680.

Shapiro, L. A. S., & Margolin, G. (2014). Growing up wired: Social networking sites and adolescent psychosocial development. *Clinical Child and Family Psychology Review*, *17*(1), 1–18. https://doi.org/10.1007/s10567-013-0135-1.

Toner, M. A., & Munro, D. (1996). Peer-social attributions and self-efficacy of peer-rejected preadolescents. *Merrill-Palmer Quarterly*, *42*(3), 339–357.

Verhaeghen, P., & Hertzog, C. (2014). *The Oxford handbook of emotion, social cognition, and problem solving in adulthood*. New York: Oxford University Press.

Volling, B. L., MacKinnon-Lewis, C., Rabiner, D., & Baradaran, L. P. (1993). Children's social competence and sociometric status: Further exploration of aggression, social withdrawal, and peer rejection. *Development and Psychopathology*, *5*(3), 459–483. https://doi.org/10.1017/S0954579400004521.

Walden, T. A., & Field, T. M. (1990). Preschool children's social competence and production and discrimination of affective expressions. *British Journal of Developmental Psychology*, *8*(1), 65–76. https://doi.org/10.1111/j.2044-835X.1990.tb00822.x.

Walker, S. (2004). Teacher reports of social behavior and peer acceptance in early childhood: Sex and social status differences. *Child Study Journal*, *34*(1), 13–28.

Wurster, T., & Xie, H. (2014). Aggressive and prosocial behaviors: The social success of bistrategic preadolescents. *International Journal of Behavioral Development*, *38*(4), 367–377. https://doi.org/10.1177/0165025414531463.

Zambianchi, M., & Bitti, P. E. R. (2013). The role of proactive coping strategies, time perspective, perceived efficacy on affect regulation, divergent thinking and family communication in promoting social well-being in emerging adulthood. *Social Indicators Research*, *116*(2), 493–507. https://doi.org/10.1007/s11205-013-0307-x.

Zimmermann, P., & Iwanski, A. (2014). Emotion regulation from early adolescence to emerging adulthood and middle adulthood: Age differences, gender differences, and emotion-specific developmental variations. *International Journal of Behavioral Development*, *38*, 182–194. https://doi.org/10.1177/0165025413515405.

Chapter 3

Linking social skills and adjustment

Kimberly E. Kamper-DeMarco[a], Jessica Shankman[b], Eliot Fearey[b], Hannah R. Lawrence[b], and Rebecca A. Schwartz-Mette[b]
[a]*State University of New York Buffalo State College, Buffalo, NY, United States,* [b]*University of Maine, Orono, ME, United States*

Linking social skills and emotional adjustment

An individual's ability to successfully navigate social situations plays a significant role in promoting adjustment across development, predicting better trajectories and psychological well-being over time. Successful navigation of social situations often entails a wide range of cognitive, behavioral, and emotional abilities (Crick & Dodge, 1994; Lemerise & Arsenio, 2000). For example, adaptive social responding requires accurate processing of social information (cognitive), conversing and interacting appropriately (behavioral), and effectively regulating emotions (emotional). As such, it is clear that social skills involve a broad range of components that form the foundation for positive relationships, which contribute to psychological adjustment across the lifespan.

A number of theories highlight the association between social skills and well-being, focusing on how cognition, behavior, and emotion play unique roles in adjustment over time. We first briefly review major theoretical lenses linking social skills to positive psychological adjustment to help clarify the processes through which social skills and social skills development are linked to well-being and adjustment. However, social skill development is an ever-evolving process across the lifespan. An understanding of associations between social skills and positive adjustment across each developmental stage is necessary in order to appreciate the applicability of these theories. Lastly, it is well established that social skills are often impacted in individuals with emotional deficits and that these social skills difficulties are often associated with poorer outcomes (Bellini, Peters, Benner, & Hopf, 2007; Phillips, 1978). We review how social skills deficits are associated with different types of psychopathology.

Social Skills Across the Life Span. https://doi.org/10.1016/B978-0-12-817752-5.00003-2

Theoretical lenses

Theories that address the association between social skills and adjustment generally assert that social interactions provide individuals with a context in which the social skills necessary to form close bonds and successfully navigate interpersonal conflict develop. Quality relationships, then, facilitate positive emotional adjustment. This section details theories that address the links between social skills and emotional adjustment across the lifespan.

Social bonding perspective

The social bonding perspective (Salvas et al., 2011) asserts that developing close social relationships engenders feelings of emotional security and connectedness to others, which promotes adaptive functioning. This theoretical lens incorporates psychoanalytic and Neo-Freudian theories, attachment and personality theories, and social constructivist theories, which underscore that social skills lay the foundation for close social relationships and subsequent psychological well-being.

Each of these incorporated theories proposes specific links between social interactions and adjustment. Specifically, psychoanalytic theory proposes that as social skills develop through interactions with parents and peers, youth become more autonomous. This maturation enables the psychological and emotional preparedness required to handle situations independently (Blos, 1967). Neo-Freudian perspectives extend this thinking and posit that the skills needed to form social relationships are key to psychological well-being, not just in childhood, but across the lifespan (Erikson, 1963).

From an attachment perspective, children are thought to form mental schemas or representations based on their interactions with others, which then shape their behavior in social situations and their subsequent well-being (Bowlby, 1969). Additionally, it is thought that those children who demonstrate positive social skills develop positive schemas and thus view themselves and the world as positive and secure, whereas those who lack or otherwise struggle with social skills are likely to experience poorer adjustment (Ainsworth & Bowlby, 1991). Social constructivists further suggest that social interactions provide children with a context in which to experience conflict. Through the successful navigation of conflict (i.e., conflict resolution), children develop perspective-taking skills to better understand the needs of others (Rubin, Bukowski, & Parker, 2006).

Interpersonal theories of psychopathology

In line with a social bonding perspective, Sullivan's interpersonal theory of psychiatry (1953) underscores the relative importance of various types of interpersonal relationships across development, with a particular focus on poor adjustment outcomes that result from maladaptive functioning at each stage.

The first important social relationships occur in infancy between children and their caregivers, with positive functioning in these relationships linked with positive emotional adjustment. In childhood, relationships with caregivers remain of central importance, but a shift occurs in which youth are increasingly interested in relationships with peers. Acceptance from and strong connections with the peer group further facilitate positive emotional adjustment. In adolescence, dyadic friendships are a primary focus, and the intimacy that develops between close friends is thought to directly contribute to positive emotional functioning. In adulthood, the context of focus shifts to romantic relationships, with the emotional and physical intimacy derived from these partnerships contributing to emotional adjustment.

Sullivan posited that poor emotional adjustment, namely, psychopathology, results from missed social opportunities to master particular developmental tasks that typically develop in the context of different relationships across the lifespan. For example, adolescents who do not successfully form close dyadic friendships may not hone social skills that develop intimacy (e.g., reciprocal self-disclosure). These missed opportunities and underdeveloped skills then contribute to emotional adjustment consequences. Although Sullivan's theory was among the first to directly link specific relationships (and the social skills developed therein) to emotional adjustment, the theory is broad and does not speak to how interpersonal functioning specifically contributes to different types of psychopathology. Later theories, such as Coyne's interpersonal theory of depression (1976), build on the foundation of Sullivan's theory and speak directly to the process by which social skills impact depressive symptomology, and vice versa.

Coyne's theory (1976) posits that depressive symptoms and poor interpersonal functioning constitute a vicious, transactional cycle from which it is difficult to disengage. Depressed individuals are thought to lack adaptive ways of seeking and receiving desired social support. This skill deficit facilitates problematic social behaviors (e.g., excessive reassurance seeking) that are aversive and erode relationships. The resultant lack of social support from these deteriorated relationships then predicts increased depression over time. Coyne's theory has been enhanced and extended in recent decades (Joiner, 2007; Joiner & Metalsky, 1995; Rudolph, 2009) and remains a focus of empirical study. Importantly, interpersonal theories have not yet been as thoroughly developed and tested for other disorders, although it is clear that interpersonal dysfunction exists across many types of psychopathology (e.g., Girard et al., 2017).

Social learning theory

According to social learning theories, relationships provide a behavioral guide for navigating the world. Individuals learn how to successfully interact using direct (e.g., reward/punishment responses to new behavior) and indirect (e.g., observation) experiences. Initially proposed by Bandura (1977), social learning theory highlights the importance of learning through trial and error. When entering into unknown situations, individuals employ different techniques and discern which responses are rewarded and punished (Bandura & Walters, 1963). As direct experience does not account for all learned behavior, Bandura (1977) further highlighted the importance of observational learning, noting that individuals' behavior is also shaped by watching whether others' behavior is rewarded or punished. As such, social learning theory emphasizes the impact of behavioral social skills on adjustment via learned behavior. Individuals who quickly learn what behavior is rewarded or punished in different situations, and adjust their own behavior accordingly, will, in turn, be better adjusted. Bandura (1977) also suggested a cognitive component to social learning whereby the observer must attend to and retain information or behavior presented. In this, he noted that with development, individuals become capable of understanding which observed behaviors will lead to positive or negative outcomes, as well as whether they have the ability, or self-efficacy, to use those behaviors successfully (Bandura & Schunk, 1981). This attention and feelings of being able to achieve the observed goal then lead to replication. Social learning theory implies that individuals are more likely to focus attention on others who are particularly interesting or display admired qualities.

Social information processing

More recently, researchers have further emphasized the role of cognition, namely, social information processing (SIP), in social skill development and adjustment. The SIP framework highlights the nuanced role of cognition in social skill development and adjustment (Crick & Dodge, 1994). Specifically, the SIP model addresses how individuals encode, interpret, understand, and respond in social situations, positing that appraisals and social interpretations contribute to self-perception and subsequent psychological adjustment.

Modifying Dodge's initial SIP model (1991), Crick and Dodge (1994) proposed an interactional model in which individuals evaluate and learn from their social experiences. Specifically, individuals enter social situations with a database of predetermined (e.g., biological, experiential) capabilities, memories, and knowledge. As individuals process both internal (e.g., emotions) and external (e.g., environmental) cues, they integrate this database with their own personal experiences. Using all of this information, individuals clarify a social goal. They then generate possible responses based on past experiences and cues from the current social situation(s). From these options, individuals choose a response that they feel they are most capable of enacting and that is likely to have the most beneficial outcome. The chosen response is enacted, and the response they receive from others then influences future social responding. Social experiences are subsequently integrated into future social responses.

According to the SIP model, there are often situations in which social information processing goes awry. For example, children who are aggressive are more likely to have errors throughout the social information processing progression. During the initial steps in the model (i.e., encoding and interpretation), children who have previous experiences with aggression (i.e., aggressive experiences are part of their database) may be more likely to interpret benign situations as being hostile (Godleski & Ostrov, 2010; Martinelli, Ackermann, Bernhard, Freitag, & Schwenck, 2018). These children subsequently decide to respond to such situations with aggression, due to a belief that aggression will result in a desired outcome (e.g., a toy, higher status among peers, less future victimization; Crick & Dodge, 1994). This cycle tends to be reinforced, with aggressive children (particularly those engaging in reactive aggression) struggling to learn to appropriately identify nonaggressive situations and respond accordingly, leading to increased risk of multiple forms of psychopathology.

Although the SIP perspective is primarily applied to the study of the development of poor social functioning, the model also provides a framework and associated evidence for understanding the development of positive social skills. For example, when children are able to appropriately encode and interpret interactions and social behaviors, they are better able to identify and select from a range of more adaptive responses. Children who are able to engage in more adaptive SIP steps have been shown to demonstrate a host of positive outcomes, including social and emotional adjustment (Dodge & Price, 1994), as well as cognitive adjustment (i.e., school readiness and success; Ziv, 2013).

These theories offer nuanced differences in perspective, but each emphasizes the importance of social skills developed in the context of interpersonal relationships. These skills then foster adaptive social interactions to build positive social relationships, which then promote positive emotional adjustment. As previously noted, the developmental nature of social skills growth and associated developmental outcomes are vital to fully understanding the complexity of these theoretical perspectives. Next, we discuss in more detail how adaptive social skills contribute to positive emotional adjustment across the lifespan.

Social skills and emotional adjustment across development

Although the specific impact of social skills on emotional adjustment differs as a function of typical abilities and tasks at each developmental stage, associations between social skills and a variety of emotional adjustment outcomes are strong throughout development. For example, adaptive social skills have been linked with greater self-esteem (Riggio, Throckmorton, & Depaola, 1990), self-efficacy (Segrin & Taylor, 2007), self-control (Taylor, Liang, Tracy, Williams, & Seigle, 2002), happiness (Argyle & Lu, 1990; Demir, Jaafar, Bilyk, & Mohd Ariff, 2012), life satisfaction (Kelly, Fincham, & Beach, 2003; Riggio, Watring, & Throckmorton, 1993), engagement (Ladd & Price, 1987), and coping (Mota & Matos, 2013). This section focuses on general links between social skills and emotional adjustment outcomes during major developmental stages.

Infancy and toddlerhood

Social skills first develop in infancy as children increase observation of and reaction to others (Baillargeon et al., 2015). Infants show the most interest in caregivers, but they may also engage in simple gestures and interactions directed at other infants (Hay, Caplan, & Nash, 2006). As they grow, infants develop abilities thought to underlie basic social skills (e.g., joint attention) that are linked to a range of positive adjustment outcomes (e.g., adaptive emotion regulation; Beauchamp & Anderson, 2010).

In toddlerhood (12–18 months of age), interactions among peers, including play and conflict, are readily observed (Parker, Rubin, Erath, Wojslawowicz, & Buskirk, 2006). The shift toward more multifaceted social interactions with individuals other than primary caregivers demonstrates the increased skill demanded of this developmental stage. Toddlers increasingly engage in parallel and imitative play (Howes, 1996) and learn appropriate responses to peers (Bandura, 1977; Crick & Dodge, 1994). During this period, toddlers also begin to display prosocial behavior (e.g., helping, sharing, inclusion behavior), demonstrate turn-taking ability, and start to establish friendships (Hay, Payne, & Chadwick, 2004; Parker et al., 2006). Research demonstrates that infants and toddlers who display more complex social skills are better adjusted across childhood (Howes, 1996).

Childhood

Early childhood (preschool years) is characterized by increased specificity and preference in peer selection, suggesting more intricate social abilities. Specifically, children learn more elaborate ways in which to play with their peers, shifting to interactive play and the formation of stable, lasting friendships. Children are even able to rate peers on social competence and likeability (Kamper-DeMarco & Ostrov, 2019), evidencing a greater focus on social preferences and the development of perspective-taking abilities (Rubin et al., 2006). The positive impacts of children's adaptive social skill development have significant empirical support (Hay et al., 2004; Ladd, Kochenderfer, & Coleman, 1996; Maguire & Dunn, 1997).

A considerably larger body of research documents the negative impacts of poor social skills in childhood. Preschoolers with poor social skills (e.g., shyness, solitary play) are more likely to experience poorer psychological adjustment (Coplan, Gavinski-Molina, Lagacé-Séguin, & Wichmann, 2001; Graham & Coplan, 2012). Further, young children who are rejected by peers (i.e., an indicator of poor social skills) are at greater risk for higher levels of peer victimization and subsequent anxiety and depression (Kamper-DeMarco & Ostrov, 2017).

The majority of research on social skills and emotional adjustment focuses on middle childhood (elementary school years), given the central focus of peer acceptance at this time (Hay et al., 2004; Rubin et al., 2006). Children during this developmental period spend significantly more time with peers, and friendships become more stable and complex (Fabes, Martin, & Hanish, 2009; Gifford-Smith & Brownell, 2003). However, as with early childhood, disruption or impairment of social skills during middle childhood can contribute to negative affect over time, particularly when associated with poorer peer relations (Bukowski, Laursen, & Hoza, 2010). In fact, Visconti and Troop-Gordon (2010) found that when youth struggle with behavioral and emotional regulation, they are more likely to experience subsequent loneliness, anxiety, and externalizing behavior.

Adolescence

During adolescence, close dyadic friendships take center stage, as adolescents spend more time with friends than with others (e.g., parents), and the influence of peers is at its strongest (Lodder, Scholte, Goossens, & Verhagen, 2017; Parker et al., 2006). At the same time, adolescents are forming their own identities. It follows that the skills developed and maintained in this peer context are critical to adolescents' emotional adjustment. Indeed, when individuals display appropriate social skills (e.g., prosociality), they are more likely to have stable friendships (Bowker, Rubin, Burgess, Booth-LaForce, & Rose-Krasnor, 2006). Moreover, the social skills required to support high-quality friendships (e.g., supportive communication) often contribute to more prosocial behavior and less jealousy, which can be protective against internalizing symptoms (e.g., Parker, Walker, Low, & Gamm, 2005). Having no friends or having problematic friendships is consistently linked to negative adjustment (e.g., internalizing and externalizing problems; Rubin et al., 2006). Adolescents who display dysregulated or aggressive behavior are more likely to struggle with peer relations and subsequently experience adjustment difficulties (Petraitis, Flay, & Miller, 1995).

Likewise, social skills are fundamental for navigating romantic relationships, which normatively emerge during adolescence (Engels, Finkenauer, Meeus, & Dekovic, 2001). Such relationships can contribute to positive adjustment by fostering a sense of self-worth and self-concept (Connolly & McIsaac, 2009). However, adolescents who engage in very early romantic experiences face particular challenges and stress that can give rise to problematic emotional adjustment, including substance use, deviant behavior, depression, anxiety, and disordered eating (Collibee & Furman, 2015; Davila, 2008; Starr et al., 2012). This may occur in part because early adolescents lack the sophisticated social skills to manage these complex peer relationships.

Adulthood

By adulthood, romantic relationships typically are the most salient with regard to their impact on individuals' adjustment and well-being (Kelly et al., 2003), and much research indicates that social skills likely drive this association (Argyle & Lu, 1990; Riggio et al., 1993). As in previous developmental stages, social skills are linked with emotional adjustment across adulthood (Demir et al., 2012; Uchino, 2006). For instance, research has demonstrated that when adults feel regulated and in control, they are more likely to have positive relations with their family and friends, leading to positive adjustment and sense of purpose (Chrouser Ahrens & Ryff, 2006). Additionally, adults' adaptive social information processing skills are related to greater well-being (Lilgendahl & McAdams, 2011).

In late adulthood, individuals tend to strengthen important social relationships and pare down peripheral connections (English & Carstensen, 2014). As older adults face shifting goals and potential cognitive declines, cognitive and behavioral social skills (e.g., communication, perspective taking) are often less emphasized, while emotional aspects of social skills (e.g., emotion regulation) increase (Carstensen & Mikels, 2005). This shift in social skills to those most vital during older adulthood, along with fewer but stronger social relationships, tends to support high life satisfaction and well-being during the end stages of life (Luong, Charles, & Fingerman, 2010).

Although social skill development across the lifespan has clear links to positive outcomes, the range of social skills varies across each individual. Along with a solid body of evidence that adaptive social skills generally contribute to positive emotional adjustment, researchers have investigated specific social skills deficits linked with particular forms of psychopathology. The following section provides an overview of social skills deficits associated with specific classes of disorder, noting where additional empirical study is needed.

Social skills deficits and psychopathology

When social skills acquisition lags behind developmental norms or social skills are deficient, risk for psychopathology increases. Poor social skills are associated with a wide array of psychological disorders across the lifespan and are believed to contribute to psychopathology via limited social interaction and/or poor quality relationships (Bellini et al., 2007). The *Diagnostic and Statistical Manual of Mental Disorders* (DSM-V; APA, 2013) includes information on the social difficulties inherent in multiple syndromes. The following sections discuss specific social skill deficits associated with various forms of psychopathology.

Neurodevelopmental disorders

Neurodevelopmental disorders include autism spectrum disorder (ASD), attention deficit hyperactivity disorder (ADHD), intellectual disability (ID), and learning disabilities (LD). Such disorders are grouped together due to their typical origins in early childhood and links with developmental deficits and impairment, including those that are social. Significant social skill deficits are noted across all neurodevelopmental disorders with recent research proposing biological differences that are both structural (e.g., differences in the cerebellum; Stoodley, 2016) and functional (e.g., differences in how individuals experience tactile stimulation; Cascio, 2010) and that may underlie the associated deficits.

Given the cascading effect of social skills deficits in early childhood on subsequent social development (Burt, Obradović, Long, & Masten, 2008), these social skills deficits are of significant concern.

Social skills difficulties are a core feature of ASD and a well-established deficit in individuals with ADHD (Bagwell, Molina, Pelham, & Hoza, 2001). Normative social behaviors such as eye gaze, imitation, and joint attention may be limited or lacking among individuals with ASD (Davis & Carter, 2014), whereas lack of awareness, poor perspective-taking ability, and regulation problems contribute to poor peer relations in individuals with ADHD (e.g., Friedman et al., 2003). As such, these social skill deficits likely drive the association between neurodevelopmental disorders and poor outcomes. In fact, previous research suggests that individuals with ASD and ADHD are both at increased risk for social isolation and rejection (Howlin, Goode, Hutton, & Rutter, 2004; Hoza, 2007), educational and/or vocational underachievement (Arnold, Hodgkins, Kahle, Madhoo, & Kewley, 2015; Eaves & Ho, 2008), and depression and anxiety (Kim, Szatmari, Bryson, Streiner, & Wilson, 2000; Kok, Groen, Fuemaier, & Tucha, 2016; Landau & Moore, 1991).

Links between other neurodevelopmental disorders (e.g., ID, learning disabilities) and social skill deficits are less understood, but still supported by empirical findings. Substantial research has shown that, although social skills deficits are not always apparent to observers (e.g., Hughes et al., 1999; Kavale & Forness, 1996), individuals with these disabilities are less likely to initiate interactions with and respond to peers than typically developing individuals (Sukhodolsky & Butter, 2007). This reduced social interaction could thus contribute to the development of subsequent psychopathology (Mishna, 2003).

From a SIP perspective, individuals with neurodevelopmental disorders may struggle to accurately identify others' intentions, either due to lack of awareness or understanding of social situations. These individuals may subsequently have difficulty adequately generating appropriate responses to social situations, leading to either social reticence (e.g., in those with ID; Hughes et al., 1999) or inappropriate regulatory skills (e.g., in those with ADHD; Ros & Graziano, 2017). These SIP errors may help to explain links between neurodevelopmental disorders and subsequent forms of psychopathology.

Of note, neurodevelopmental disorders are commonly classified along a spectrum of severity, ranging from mild to more severe. As such, the severity of neurodevelopmental disorders is crucial to take into account in understanding both the range of social deficits that may be present and the impact on related emotional adjustment outcomes. For example, individuals with more severe syndromes may have limited self-awareness, which may be protective in terms of the impact of social rejection on internalizing symptoms.

Externalizing disorders

Externalizing psychopathology includes disorders in which there is overt, external, problematic behavior. The development of these disorders (e.g., disruptive behavior disorder, conduct disorder, substance-use disorders) likely represents a reciprocal relationship with social skill deficits. In fact, the SIP model was initially proposed to explain aggressive behavior (Crick & Dodge, 1994; Dodge, 1991), and studies have proliferated on the SIP of children exhibiting externalizing behavior. These children demonstrate deficits in appropriately attending to social cues, which leads them to attribute hostile intentions in ambiguous situations (Burke, Loeber, & Birmaher, 2004).

Like neurodevelopmental disorders, externalizing disorders are often associated with a limited ability to generate adequate responses in social interactions, leading to a reliance on aggressive and maladaptive responses (e.g., substance use). Limited social skills via poor attributions and inadequate response generation can render these individuals likely to be rejected by mainstream peers and to associate instead with deviant peers, leading to rule breaking and/or aggressive behavior (Burke et al., 2004). Social skill deficits that result in poor peer relationships early in development significantly contribute to later conduct problems, again emphasizing the importance of adequate social skills for positive development (Miller-Johnson, Coie, Maumary-Gremaud, & Bierman, 2002).

Relatedly, social learning theory has been used to understand the development of deviant behavior (e.g., substance use; Petraitis et al., 1995). In particular, Petraitis et al. (1995) note that individuals are more likely to engage in substance use and other risky behavior when they have poor observational models of social behavior (e.g., adults or peers who use substances and encourage substance use) and difficulty resisting peer pressure, a developmentally important social skill. Researchers have also highlighted the role of self-control in the development of substance-use disorders (e.g., Homer et al., 2008; Meldrum, Trucco, Cope, Zucker, & Heitzeg, 2018). Sussman, McCuller, and Dent (2003) found that social skills deficits, such as behavioral undercontrol, significantly contribute to the development of problems, including delinquency and substance use (Sussman et al., 2003).

Internalizing disorders

Internalizing disorders (i.e., anxiety and depression) are often thought to occur in individuals who exhibit overcontrol of their behavior (Kovacs & Devlin, 1998). Although diagnostic criteria for internalizing disorders do not articulate explicit social skills deficits, research suggests that these deficits are often present. In fact, some theories outline direct associations between social skill deficits and internalizing disorders (e.g., Rudolph, 2009). For example, interpersonal theories of depression focus on the difficulties that individuals with internalizing behaviors have in adequately seeking and receiving support from others (e.g., Coyne, 1976; Joiner, 2007).

Links to SIP difficulties in individuals with internalizing disorders also are apparent. For example, individuals with anxiety and depressive disorders often make erroneous attributions of others' behavior (Bell, Luebbe, Swenson, & Allwood, 2009; Hofmann, 2007) as a result of over attending to negative (e.g., potentially threatening) aspects of a social situation. Individuals who experience internalizing problems are more likely to make negative, internal attributions in which they are highly critical of themselves in social situations (Bell et al., 2009; Rubin et al., 2006). This may lead to generation of fewer responses from which to choose regarding how react or respond to particular social situations. Each of these SIP deficits may help to elucidate the associations among internalizing disorders, social skill deficits, and poor adjustment.

Self-destructive behaviors, such as nonsuicidal self-injury (NSSI) and suicidality, are frequently associated with mood disorders and interpersonal problems. These behaviors are often preceded by social distress (Schwartz-Mette & Lawrence, 2019). Importantly, research has sought to understand the social skill deficits that might contribute to these extreme behaviors for the purposes of prevention and treatment. Studies consistently document that interpersonal distress is a primary trigger for NSSI (Taylor et al., 2018) and that deficits in multiple domains of social functioning (e.g., emotion dysregulation, social problem solving, social avoidance, and impulsivity) significantly contribute to increased suicide risk (Becker-Weidman, Jacobs, Reinecke, Silva, & March, 2010).

Eating disorders

Eating disorders (ED) are characterized by overregulation (e.g., anorexia nervosa) or underregulation (e.g., bulimia nervosa, binge-eating disorder) of eating behavior. There are clear links between ED and social skill deficits that impact overall adjustment. For example, in a systematic review, Arcelus and colleagues (Arcelus, Haslam, Farrow, & Meyer, 2013) found that individuals with ED felt socially ineffective, were less able to assert themselves successfully in social situations, and experienced high levels of social anxiety. The authors purport a number of etiological pathways that clarify links between social difficulties and ED: (1) challenges with solving interpersonal problems, (2) difficulties with emotional expression, and (3) fear of conflict and negative interactions (Arcelus et al., 2013). From a SIP perspective, these difficulties in response generation and selection appear to play a significant role in the proliferation of negative adjustment outcomes (e.g., low self-esteem) associated with ED. Difficulty in emotion identification and generation, along with SIP and regulatory challenges, appear to be significant contributors to the poor emotional adjustment experienced by those with ED.

Schizophrenia spectrum disorders

Schizophrenia spectrum disorders (SSD) are related to deficits in social cognition, leading researchers to examine whether social skill deficits are present prior to onset, or whether social skills decline after individuals present with

SSD. Individuals with SSD perform significantly worse than healthy controls on broad measures of social skills, and research has found that these social deficits may be present prior to experiencing onset of SSD (Mueser, Bellack, Morrison, & Wixted, 1990; Pinkham, Penn, Perkins, Graham, & Siegel, 2007). Social skill deficits also appear to be more strongly related to negative symptoms (e.g., blunted affect, anhedonia) as compared to positive symptoms (e.g., hallucination, delusions; Bellack, Morrison, Wixted, & Mueser, 1990). Given the cognitive, behavioral, and emotional components of negative symptoms, this finding appears to further support the notion that deficits in social skills contribute to limited peer relations and subsequent adjustment problems.

Personality disorders

Individuals with personality disorders (PD) are often described as inflexible and having longstanding problematic behavior that interferes with social relationships (APA, 2013; Oltmanns, Melley, & Turkheimer, 2002). Although this inherently suggests deficits in social skills, few empirical studies have examined social skills in relation to specific PDs. Thus, we have included a brief review of social deficits across more commonly researched PDs.

Antisocial personality disorder (ASPD) is often described as an extreme version of externalizing disorder, and social deficits linked with externalizing disorders likely are comparable to those in ASPD (Holmes, Slaughter, & Kashani, 2001). Individuals with ASPD may have further difficulties recognizing facial affect, limiting empathy and perspective-taking (Marsh & Blair, 2008). On the other hand, borderline personality disorder (BPD) is characterized by instability of emotion, cognition, and behavior. DSM-5 criteria explicitly identify social skills as a fundamental deficit (APA, 2013). Difficulty solving social problems and generating social responses likely contribute to maladjustment in BPD (Bray, Barrowclough, & Lobban, 2007). Relatedly, individuals with BPD often misinterpret facial expressions, are easily hurt, and act impulsively, which can contribute to rejection (Dyck et al., 2009). Narcissistic personality disorder (NPD) is a disorder characterized by self-importance and lack of empathy. It is associated with difficulty understanding the emotional experience of others (Baskin-Sommers, Krusemark, & Ronningstam, 2014) and self-reported deficits in perspective-taking skills (Ritter et al., 2011). Thus, like many of the aforementioned diagnostic groups, individuals with PDs likely struggle to adequately identify the needs and social cues of others. This lack of social awareness or general misinterpretation of social events may explain social skill deficits among those with PDs.

Neurocognitive disorders of older age

Neurocognitive disorders are primarily identified as a function of cognitive deficits that appear in the context of aging. Impairment in social skills is common and often reflects initial behavior changes at onset of neurocognitive decline.

These deficits include problems in perspective-taking, poor empathy, difficulty attending to and encoding social cues, and abnormal social behavior (Henry, von Hippel, Molenberghs, Lee, & Sachdev, 2016). Across disorders, a primary cause of social skills deficits is change in brain functioning. Both structural and functional changes in the brain (e.g., decreased brain mass, neurochemical decreases) have been associated with social skill decline (Desmarais, Lanctôt, Masellis, Black, & Herrmann, 2018). Importantly, these declining social skills may reflect biomarkers in a number of neurocognitive disorders and may represent important benchmarks in the assessment and treatment of these disorders (Bora, Velakoulis, & Walterfang, 2016).

Conclusions

As evidenced in this review, social interactions are the basis in which social skill development occurs. Individuals' ability to skillfully interact with their family, peers, and acquaintances provides a context in which social skills develop and subsequently impact the quality of interpersonal relationships, which, in turn, are essential to positive emotional adjustment. However, understanding the role of social skill development (or lack thereof) across development is fundamental to adequately identifying where individuals may struggle or excel. Because these skills differ significantly over the lifespan, developmental theory has sought to provide the basis for understanding social skill development. The SIP model, a leading and well-cited theory, approaches social skill development and deficits from a cognitive framework. It assesses social skills as a learned skill through the way that we take in, think about, and react to our social environment. Social bonding theories underscore the importance of social interaction and social skill development in aiding future adjustment, noting that these social situations provide us the bases for security and autonomy. Interpersonal theories, like social bonding theories, articulate the importance of social skills on adjustment through understanding when poor outcomes are associated with social skill deficits. As can be seen, these lagging or deficient social skills can contribute to, and be an outgrowth of, poor adjustment outcomes including psychopathology. Lastly, social learning theories contribute to our understanding of the impacts of the environment and how through observation, modeling, and subsequent cognitive awareness of how others engage socially, individuals learn how different social responses contribute to both positive and negative outcomes. Poor social skills are associated with a wide array of psychological disorders across the lifespan. Research further establishing and clarifying these associations is a critical area of empirical inquiry with potentially wide ranging clinical implications.

References

Ainsworth, M. D. S., & Bowlby, J. (1991). An ethological approach to personality development. *American Psychologist, 46*(4), 333–341. https://doi.org/10.1037/0003-066X.46.4.333.

APA. (2013). *Diagnostic and statistical manual of mental disorders* (5th ed.). American Psychiatric Association.

Arcelus, J., Haslam, M., Farrow, C., & Meyer, C. (2013). The role of interpersonal functioning in the maintenance of eating: A systematic review and testable model. *Clinical Psychology Review, 33*(1), 156–167. https://doi.org/10.1016/j.cpr.2012.10.009.

Argyle, M., & Lu, L. (1990). Happiness and social skills. *Personality and Individual Differences, 11*(12), 1255–1261. https://doi.org/10.1016/0191-8869(90)90152-H.

Arnold, L. E., Hodgkins, P., Kahle, J., Madhoo, M., & Kewley, G. (2015). Long-term outcomes of ADHD: Academic achievement and performance. *Journal of Attention Disorders*, https://doi.org/10.1177/1087054714566076.

Bagwell, C. L., Molina, B. S., Pelham, W. E., & Hoza, B. (2001). Attention-deficit hyperactivity disorder and problems in peer relations: Predictions from childhood to adolescence. *Journal of the American Academy of Child & Adolescent Psychiatry, 40*(11), 1285–1292. https://doi.org/10.1097/00004583-200111000-00008.

Baillargeon, R., Scott, R. M., He, Z., Sloane, S., Setoh, P., Jin, J., … Bian, L. (2015). Psychological and sociomoral reasoning in infancy. In M. Mikulineer & P. R. Shaver (Eds.), *Attitudes and social cognition*: Vol. 1. APA handbook of personality and social psychology. (pp. 79–150). Washington, DC: American Psychological Association. https://doi.org/10.21426/B615110376.

Bandura, A. (1977). *Social learning theory*. Oxford, England: Prentice-Hall.

Bandura, A., & Schunk, D. H. (1981). Cultivating competence, self-efficacy, and intrinsic interest through proximal self-motivation. *Journal of Personality and Social Psychology, 41*(3), 586–598. https://doi.org/10.1037/0022-3514.41.3.586.

Bandura, A., & Walters, R. H. (1963). *Social learning and personality development*. New York, NY: Holt Rinehart and Winston.

Baskin-Sommers, A., Krusemark, E., & Ronningstam, E. (2014). Empathy in narcissistic personality disorder: From clinical and empirical perspectives. *Personality Disorders: Theory, Research, and Treatment, 5*(3), 323–333. https://doi.org/10.1037/per0000061.

Beauchamp, M. H., & Anderson, V. (2010). SOCIAL: An integrative framework for the development of social skills. *Psychological Bulletin, 136*(1), 39–64. https://doi.org/10.1037/a0017768.

Becker-Weidman, E. G., Jacobs, R. H., Reinecke, M. A., Silva, S. G., & March, J. S. (2010). Social problem-solving among adolescents treated for depression. *Behaviour Research and Therapy, 48*(1), 11–18. https://doi.org/10.1016/j.brat.2009.08.006.

Bell, D. J., Luebbe, A. M., Swenson, L. P., & Allwood, M. A. (2009). The children's evaluation of everyday social encounters questionnaire: Comprehensive assessment of children's social information processing and its relation to internalizing problems. *Journal of Clinical Child and Adolescent Psychology, 38*(5), 705–720. https://doi.org/10.1080/15374410903103585.

Bellack, A. S., Morrison, R. L., Wixted, J. T., & Mueser, K. T. (1990). An analysis of social competence in schizophrenia. *British Journal of Psychiatry, 156*(6), 809–818. https://doi.org/10.1192/bjp.156.6.809.

Bellini, S., Peters, J. K., Benner, L., & Hopf, A. (2007). A meta-analysis of school-based social skills interventions for children with autism spectrum disorders. *Remedial and Special Education, 28*(3), 153–162. https://doi.org/10.1177/07419325070280030401.

Blos, P. (1967). The second individuation process of adolescence. *The Psychoanalytic Study of the Child, 22*, 162–186.

Bora, E., Velakoulis, D., & Walterfang, M. (2016). Social cognition in Huntington's disease: A meta-analysis. *Behavioural Brain Research, 297*, 131–140. https://doi.org/10.1016/j.bbr.2015.10.001.

Bowker, J. C. W., Rubin, K. H., Burgess, K. B., Booth-LaForce, C., & Rose-Krasnor, L. (2006). Behavioral characteristics associated with stable and fluid best friendship patterns in middle childhood. *Merrill-Palmer Quarterly, 52*(4), 671–693. https://doi.org/10.1353/mpq.2006.0000.

Bowlby, J. (1969). *Attachment and loss, Vol. 1: Attachment*. New York, NY: Basic Books.

Bray, S., Barrowclough, C., & Lobban, F. (2007). The social problem-solving abilities of people with borderline personality disorder. *Behaviour Research and Therapy*, *45*(6), 1409–1417. https://doi.org/10.1016/j.brat.2006.06.011.

Bukowski, W. M., Laursen, B., & Hoza, B. (2010). The snowball effect: Friendship moderates escalations in depressed affect among avoidant and excluded children. *Development and Psychopathology*, *22*(4), 749–757. https://doi.org/10.1017/S095457941000043X.

Burke, J. D., Loeber, R., & Birmaher, B. (2004). Oppositional defiant disorder and conduct disorder: A review of the past 10 years, part II. *Journal of the American Academy of Child & Adolescent Psychiatry*, *41*(11), 1275–1293. https://doi.org/10.1097/00004583-200211000-00009.

Burt, K. B., Obradović, J., Long, J. D., & Masten, A. S. (2008). The interplay of social competence and psychopathology over 20 years: Testing transactional and cascade models. *Child Development*, *72*(2), 359–374. https://doi.org/10.1111/j.1467-8624.2007.01130.x.

Carstensen, L. L., & Mikels, J. A. (2005). At the intersection of emotion and cognition: Aging and the positivity effect. *Current Directions in Psychological Science*, *14*(3), 117–121. https://doi.org/10.1111/j.0963-7214.2005.00348.x.

Cascio, C. J. (2010). Somatosensory processing in neurodevelopmental disorders. *Journal of Neurodevelopmental Disorders*, *2*(2), 62–69. https://doi.org/10.1007/s11689-010-9046-3.

Chrouser Ahrens, C. J., & Ryff, C. D. (2006). Multiple roles and well-being: Sociodemographic and psychological moderators. *Sex Roles*, *55*, 801–815. https://doi.org/10.1007/s11199-006-9134-8.

Collibee, C., & Furman, W. (2015). Quality counts: Developmental shifts in associations between romantic relationship qualities and psychosocial adjustment. *Child Development*, *86*(5), 1639–1652. https://doi.org/10.1111/cdev.12403.

Connolly, J., & McIsaac, C. (2009). Adolescents' explanations for romantic dissolutions: A developmental perspective. *Journal of Adolescence*, *32*(5), 1209–1223. https://doi.org/10.1016/j.adolescence.2009.01.006.

Coplan, R. J., Gavinski-Molina, M. H., Lagacé-Séguin, D. G., & Wichmann, C. (2001). When girls versus boys play alone: Nonsocial play and adjustment in kindergarten. *Developmental Psychology*, *37*(4), 464–474. https://doi.org/10.1037/0012-1649.37.4.464.

Coyne, J. C. (1976). Depression and the response of others. *Journal of Abnormal Psychology*, *85*, 186–193. https://doi.org/10.1037/0021-843X.85.2.186.

Crick, N. R., & Dodge, K. A. (1994). A review and reformulation of social-information processing mechanisms in children's social adjustment. *Psychological Bulletin*, *115*(1), 74–101. https://doi.org/10.1037/0033-2909.115.1.74.

Davila, J. (2008). Depressive symptoms and adolescent romance: Theory, research, and implications. *Child Development Perspectives*, *2*(1), 26–31. https://doi.org/10.1111/j.1750-8606.2008.00037.x.

Davis, N. O., & Carter, A. S. (2014). Social development in autism. In F. R. Volkmar, S. J. Rogers, R. Paul, & K. A. Pelphrey (Eds.), *Handbook of autism and pervasive developmental disorders: Diagnosis, development, and brain mechanisms* (pp. 212–229). Hoboken, NJ: John Wiley & Sons Inc. https://doi.org/10.1002/9781118911389.hautc09.

Demir, M., Jaafar, J., Bilyk, N., & Mohd Ariff, M. R. (2012). Social skills, friendship and happiness: A cross-cultural investigation. *Journal of Social Psychology*, *152*(3), 379–385. https://doi.org/10.1080/00224545.2011.591451.

Desmarais, P., Lanctôt, K. L., Masellis, M., Black, S. E., & Herrmann, N. (2018). Social inappropriateness in neurodegenerative disorders. *International Psychogeriatrics*, *30*(2), 197–207. https://doi.org/10.1017/S1041610217001260.

Dodge, K. A. (1991). Emotion and social information processing. In J. Garber & K. A. Dodge (Eds.), *Cambridge studies in social and emotional development. The development of emotion regulation and dysregulation* (pp. 159–181). New York, NY: Cambridge University Press.

Dodge, K. A., & Price, J. M. (1994). On the relation between social information processing and socially competent behavior in early school-aged children. *Child Development*, *65*(5), 1385–1397. https://doi.org/10.2307/1131505.

Dyck, M., Habel, U., Slodczyk, J., Schlummer, J., Backes, V., Schneider, F., & Reske, M. (2009). Negative bias in fast emotion discrimination in borderline personality disorder. *Psychological Medicine*, *39*(5), 855–864. https://doi.org/10.1017/S0033291708004273.

Eaves, L. C., & Ho, H. H. (2008). Young adult outcome of autism spectrum disorders. *Journal of Autism and Developmental Disorders*, *38*(4), 739–747. https://doi.org/10.1007/s10803-007-0441-x.

Engels, R.C.M.E., Finkenauer, C., Meeus, W., & Dekovic, M. (2001). Parental attachment and adolescents' emotional adjustment: The associations with social skills and relational competence. *Journal of Counseling Psychology*, *48*(4), 428–439. https://doi.org/10.1037/0022-0167.48.4.428.

English, T., & Carstensen, L. L. (2014). Selective narrowing of social networks across adulthood is associated with improved emotional experience in daily life. *International Journal of Behavioral Development*, *38*(2), 195–202. https://doi.org/10.1177/0165025413515404.

Erikson, E. H. (1963). *Childhood and society*. New York, NY: Norton.

Fabes, R. A., Martin, C. L., & Hanish, L. D. (2009). Children's behaviors and interactions with peers. In K. H. Rubin, W. M. Bukowski, & B. Laursen (Eds.), *Handbook of peer interactions, relationships, and groups: Social, emotional, and personality development in context* (pp. 45–62). New York, NY: Guilford Press.

Friedman, S. R., Rapport, L. J., Lumley, M., Tzelepis, A., Vanvoorhis, A., Stettner, L., & Kakaati, L. (2003). Aspects of social and emotional competence in adult attention deficit/hyperactivity disorder. *Neuropsychology*, *17*(1), 50–58. https://doi.org/10.1013/0894-4105.17.1.50.

Gifford-Smith, M. E., & Brownell, C. A. (2003). Childhood peer relationships: Social acceptance, friendships, and peer networks. *Journal of School Psychology*, *41*(4), 235–284. https://doi.org/10.1016/S0022-4405(03)00048-7.

Girard, J. M., Wright, A. G. C., Beeney, J. E., Lazarus, S. A., Scott, L. N., Stepp, S. D., & Pilkonis, P. A. (2017). Interpersonal problems across levels of the psychopathology hierarchy. *Comprehensive Psychiatry*, *79*, 53–69. https://doi.org/10.1016/j.comppsych.2017.06.014.

Godleski, S. A., & Ostrov, J. M. (2010). Relational aggression and hostile attribution biases: Testing multiple statistical methods and models. *Journal of Abnormal Child Psychology*, *38*(4), 447–458. https://doi.org/10.1007/s10802-010-9391-4.

Graham, A., & Coplan, R. J. (2012). Shyness, sibling relationships, and young children's socioemotional adjustment at preschool. *Journal of Research in Childhood Education*, *26*(4), 435–449. https://doi.org/10.1080/02568543.2012.711802.

Hay, D. F., Caplan, M., & Nash, A. (2006). The beginnings of peer relations. In K. H. Rubin, W. M. Bukowski, & B. Laursen (Eds.), *Handbook of child psychology* (pp. 121–142). New York, NY: Guilford Publications.

Hay, D. F., Payne, A., & Chadwick, A. (2004). Peer relations in childhood. *Journal of Child Psychology and Psychiatry*, *45*(1), 84–108. https://doi.org/10.1046/j.0021-9630.2003.00308.x.

Henry, J. D., von Hippel, W., Molenberghs, P., Lee, T., & Sachdev, P. S. (2016). Clinical assessment of social cognitive function in neurological disorders. *Nature Reviews Neurology*, *12*(1), 28–39. https://doi.org/10.1038/nrneurol.2015.229.

Hofmann, S. G. (2007). Cognitive factors that maintain social anxiety disorder: A comprehensive model and its treatment implications. *Cognitive Behaviour Therapy*, *36*(4), 193–209. https://doi.org/10.1080/16506070701421313.

Holmes, S. E., Slaughter, J. R., & Kashani, J. (2001). Risk factors in childhood that lead to the development of conduct disorder and antisocial personality disorder. *Child Psychiatry and Human Development*, *31*(3), 183–193. https://doi.org/10.1023/A:1026425304480.

Homer, B. D., Solomon, T. M., Moeller, R. W., Mascia, A., DeRaleau, L., & Halkitis, P. N. (2008). Methamphetamine abuse and impairment of social functioning: A review of the underlying neurophysiological causes and behavioral implications. *Psychological Bulletin, 134*(2), 301–310. https://doi.org/10.1037/0033-2909.134.2.301.

Howes, C. (1996). The earliest friendships. In W. M. Bukowski, A. F. Newcomb, & W. W. Hartup (Eds.), *The company they keep: Friendship in childhood and adolescence* (pp. 66–86). New York, NY: Cambridge University Press.

Howlin, P., Goode, S., Hutton, J., & Rutter, M. (2004). Adult outcome for children with autism. *Journal of Child Psychology and Psychiatry, 45*(2), 212–229. https://doi.org/10.1111/j.1469-7610.2004.00215.x.

Hoza, B. (2007). Peer functioning in children with ADHD. *Journal of Pediatric Psychology, 32*(6), 655–663. https://doi.org/10.1016/j.ambp.2006.04.011.

Hughes, C., Rodi, M. S., Lorden, S. W., Pitkin, S. E., Derer, K. R., Hwang, B., & Cai, X. (1999). Social interactions of high school students with mental retardation and their general education peers. *American Journal on Mental Retardation, 104*(6), 533–544.

Joiner, T. E. (2007). *Why people die by suicide*. Cambridge, MA: Harvard University Press.

Joiner, T. E., & Metalsky, G. I. (1995). A prospective test of an integrative interpersonal theory of depression: A naturalistic study of college roommates. *Journal of Personality and Social Psychology*, https://doi.org/10.1037/0022-3514.69.4.778.

Kamper-DeMarco, K. E., & Ostrov, J. M. (2017). Prospective associations between peer victimization and social-psychological adjustment problems in early childhood. *Aggressive Behavior, 43*(5), 471–482. https://doi.org/10.1002/ab.21705.

Kamper-DeMarco, K. E., & Ostrov, J. M. (2019). The influence of friendships on aggressive behavior in early childhood: Examining the interdependence of aggression. *Child Psychiatry and Human Development, 50*(3), 520–531. https://doi.org/10.1007/s10578-018-0857-x.

Kavale, K. A., & Forness, S. R. (1996). Social skill deficits and learning disabilities: A meta-analysis. *Journal of Learning Disabilities, 29*(3), 226–237. https://doi.org/10.1177/002221949602900301.

Kelly, A. B., Fincham, F. D., & Beach, S. R. H. (2003). Communication skills in couples: A review and discussion of emerging perspectives. In J. O. Greene & B. R. Burleson (Eds.), *Handbook of communication and social interaction skills* (pp. 723–751). Mahway, NJ: Lawrence Erlbaum Associates, Inc.

Kim, J. A., Szatmari, P., Bryson, S. E., Streiner, D. L., & Wilson, F. J. (2000). The prevalence of anxiety and mood problems among children with autism and Asperger syndrome. *Autism, 4*(2), 117–132. https://doi.org/10.1177/1362361300004002002.

Kok, F. M., Groen, Y., Fuemaier, A. B., & Tucha, O. (2016). Problematic peer functioning in girls with ADHD: A systematic literature review. *PLoS One, 11*(11), https://doi.org/10.1371/journal.pone.0165119.

Kovacs, M., & Devlin, B. (1998). Internalizing disorders in childhood. *Journal of Child Psychology and Psychiatry and Allied Disciplines, 39*(1), 47–63. https://doi.org/10.1017/S0021963097001765.

Ladd, G. W., Kochenderfer, B. J., & Coleman, C. C. (1996). Friendship quality as a predictor of young children's early school adjustment. *Child Development, 67*(3), 1103–1118. https://doi.org/10.2307/1131882.

Ladd, G. W., & Price, J. M. (1987). Predicting children's social and school adjustment following the transition from preschool to kindergarten. *Child Development*, 1168–1189. https://doi.org/10.2307/1130613.

Landau, S., & Moore, L. (1991). Social skill deficits in children with attention-deficit hyperactivity disorder. *School Psychology Review, 20*(2), 235–251.

Lemerise, E. A., & Arsenio, W. F. (2000). An integrated model of emotion processes and cognition in social information processing. *Child Development, 71*(1), 107–118. https://doi.org/10.1111/1467-8624.00124.

Lilgendahl, J. P., & McAdams, D. P. (2011). Constructing sotires of self-growth: How individual differences in patterns of autobiographical reasoning relate to well-being in midlife. *Journal of Personality*, *79*(2), 391–428. https://doi.org/10.1111/j.1467-6494.2010.00688.x.

Lodder, G. M. A., Scholte, R. H. J., Goossens, L., & Verhagen, M. (2017). Loneliness in early adolescence: Friendship quantity, friendship quality, and dyadic processes. *Journal of Clinical Child and Adolescent Psychology*, *46*(5), 709–720. https://doi.org/10.1080/15374416.2015.1070352.

Luong, G., Charles, S. T., & Fingerman, K. L. (2010). Better with age: Social relationships across adulthood. *Journal of Social and Personal Relationships*, *28*(1), 9–23. https://doi.org/10.1177/0265407510391362.

Maguire, M. C., & Dunn, J. (1997). Friendships in early childhood, and social understanding. *International Journal of Behavioral Development*, *21*(4), 669–686. https://doi.org/10.1080/016502597384613.

Marsh, A. A., & Blair, R. J. R. (2008). Deficits in facial affect recognition among antisocial populations: A meta-analysis. *Neuroscience and Biobehavioral Reviews*, *32*(3), 454–465. https://doi.org/10.1016/j.neubiorev.2007.08.003.

Martinelli, A., Ackermann, K., Bernhard, A., Freitag, C. M., & Schwenck, C. (2018). Hostile attribution bias and aggression in children and adolescents: A systematic literature review on the influence of aggression subtype and gender. *Aggression and Violent Behavior*, *39*, 25–32. https://doi.org/10.1016/j.avb.2018.01.005.

Meldrum, R. C., Trucco, E. M., Cope, L. M., Zucker, R. A., & Heitzeg, M. M. (2018). Brain activity, low self-control, and delinquency: An fMRI study of at-risk adolescents. *Journal of Criminal Justice*, *56*, 107–117. https://doi.org/10.1016/j.jcrimjus.2017.07.007.

Miller-Johnson, S., Coie, J. D., Maumary-Gremaud, A., & Bierman, K. L. (2002). Peer rejection and aggression and early starter models of conduct disorder. *Journal of Abnormal Child Psychology*, *30*(3), 217–230. https://doi.org/10.1023/A:1015198612049.

Mishna, F. (2003). Learning disabilities and bullying: Double jeopardy. *Journal of Learning Disability*, *36*(4), 336–347. https://doi.org/10.1177/00222194030360040501.

Mota, C. P., & Matos, P. M. (2013). Peer attachment, coping, and self-esteem in institutionalized adolescents: The mediating role of social skills. *European Journal of Psychology of Education*, *28*, 87–100. https://doi.org/10.1007/s10212-012-0103-z.

Mueser, K. T., Bellack, A. S., Morrison, R. L., & Wixted, J. T. (1990). Social competence in schizophrenia: Premorbid adjustment, social skill, and domains of functioning. *Journal of Psychiatric Research*, *24*(1), 51–63. https://doi.org/10.1016/0022-3956(90)90024-K.

Oltmanns, T. F., Melley, A. H., & Turkheimer, E. (2002). Impaired social functioning and symptoms of personality disorders assessed by peer and self-report in a nonclinical population. *Journal of Personality Disorders*, *16*(5), 437–452. https://doi.org/10.1521/pedi.16.5.437.22123.

Parker, J. G., Rubin, K. H., Erath, S. A., Wojslawowicz, J. C., & Buskirk, A. A. (2006). Peer relationships, child development, and adjustment: A developmental psychopathology perspective. In D. Cicchetti & D. J. Cohen (Eds.), *Developmental psychopathology, Vol. 1: Theory and method* (2nd ed., pp. 419–493). Hoboken, NJ: John Wiley & Sons Inc. https://doi.org/10.1002/9780470939383.ch12.

Parker, J. G., Walker, A. R., Low, C. M., & Gamm, B. K. (2005). Friendship jealousy in young adolescents: Individual differences and links to sex, self-esteem, aggression, and social adjustment. *Developmental Psychology*, *41*(1), 235–250. https://doi.org/10.1037/0012-1649.41.1.235.

Petraitis, J., Flay, B. R., & Miller, T. Q. (1995). Reviewing theories of adolescent substance use: Organizing pieces in the puzzle. *Psychological Bulletin*, *117*(1), 67–86. https://doi.org/10.1037/0033-2909.117.1.67.

Phillips, E. L. (1978). *The social skills basis of psychopathology, personality, and temperament: Alternatives to abnormal psychology and psychiatry*. New York: G. & Stratton.

Pinkham, A. E., Penn, D. L., Perkins, D. O., Graham, K. A., & Siegel, M. (2007). Emotion perception and social skill over the course of psychosis: A comparison of individuals "at-risk" for psychosis and individuals with early and chronic schizophrenia spectrum illness. *Cognitive Neuropsychiatry*, *12*(3), 198–212. https://doi.org/10.1080/13546800600985557.

Riggio, R. E., Throckmorton, B., & Depaola, S. (1990). Social skills and self-esteem. *Personality and Individual Differences*, *11*, 799–804. https://doi.org/10.1016/0191-8869(90)90188-W.

Riggio, R. E., Watring, K. P., & Throckmorton, B. (1993). Social skills, social support, and psychosocial adjustment. *Personality and Individual Differences*, *15*, 275–280. https://doi.org/10.1016/0191-8869(93)90217-Q.

Ritter, K., Dziobek, I., Preißler, S., Rüter, A., Vater, A., Fydrich, T., … Roepke, S. (2011). Lack of empathy in patients with narcissistic personality disorder. *Psychiatry Research*, *187*(1), 241–247. https://doi.org/10.1016/j.psychres.2010.09.013.

Ros, R., & Graziano, P. A. (2017). Social functioning in children with or at risk for attention deficit/hyperactivity disorder: A meta-analytic review. *Journal of Clinical Child & Adolescent Psychology*, *47*(2), 213–235. https://doi.org/10.1080/15374416.2016.1266644.

Rubin, K. H., Bukowski, W. M., & Parker, J. G. (2006). Peer interactions, relationships, and groups. In N. Eisenberg, W. Damon, & R. M. Lerner (Eds.), *Handbook of child psychology: Social, emotional, and personality development* (pp. 571–645). Hoboken, NJ: John Wiley & Sons Inc.

Rudolph, K. D. (2009). The interpersonal context of adolescent depression. In S. Nolen-Hoeksema & L. M. Hilt (Eds.), *Handbook of depression in adolescents* (pp. 377–418). New York, NY: Routledge/Taylor & Francis Group.

Salvas, M. C., Vitaro, F., Brendgen, M., Lacourse, É., Boivin, M., & Tremblay, R. E. (2011). Interplay between friends' aggression and friendship quality in the development of child aggression during the early school years. *Social Development*, *20*(4), 645–663. https://doi.org/10.1111/j.1467-9507.2010.00592.x.

Schwartz-Mette, R. A., & Lawrence, H. R. (2019). Peer socialization of non-suicidal self-injury in adolescents' close friendships. *Journal of Abnormal Child Psychology*, https://doi.org/10.1007/s10802-019-00569-8.

Segrin, C., & Taylor, M. (2007). Positive interpersonal relationships mediate the association between social skills and psychological well-being. *Personality and Individual Differences*, *43*(4), 637–646. https://doi.org/10.1016/j.paid.2007.01.017.

Starr, L. R., Davila, J., Stroud, C. B., Clara Li, P. C., Yoneda, A., Hershenberg, R., & Ramsay Miller, M. (2012). Love hurts (in more ways than one): Specificity of psychological symptoms as predictors and consequences of romantic activity among early adolescent girls. *Journal of Clinical Psychology*, *68*(4), 403–420. https://doi.org/10.1002/jclp.20862.

Stoodley, C. J. (2016). The cerebellum and neurodevelopmental disorders. *Cerebellum*, *15*(1), 34–37. https://doi.org/10.1007/s12311-015-0715-3.

Sukhodolsky, D. G., & Butter, E. M. (2007). Social skills training for children with intellectual disabilities. In J. W. Jacobson, J. A. Mulick, & J. Rojahn (Eds.), *Handbook of intellectual disabilities* (pp. 601–618). Boston, MA: Springer.

Sullivan, H. S. (1953). *The interpersonal theory of psychiatry*. New York, NY: W. W. Norton & Co.

Sussman, S., McCuller, W. J., & Dent, C. W. (2003). The associations of social self-control, personality disorders, and demographics with drug use among high-risk youth. *Addictive Behaviors*, *28*(6), 1159–1166. https://doi.org/10.1016/S0306-4603(02)00222-8.

Taylor, P. J., Jomar, K., Dhingra, K., Forrester, R., Shahmalak, U., & Dickson, J. M. (2018). A meta-analysis of the prevalence of different functions of non-suicidal self-injury. *Journal of Affective Disorders*, *227*, 759–769. https://doi.org/10.1016/j.jad.2017.11.073.

Taylor, C. A., Liang, B., Tracy, A. J., Williams, L. M., & Seigle, P. (2002). Gender differences in middle school adjustment, physical fighting, and social skills: Evaluation of a social competency program. *Journal of Primary Prevention*, *23*(2), 259–272. https://doi.org/10.1023/A:1019976617776.

Uchino, B. N. (2006). Social support and health: A review of physiological processes potentially underlying links to disease outcomes. *Journal of Behavioral Medicine*, *29*(4), 377–387. https://doi.org/10.1007/s10865-006-9056-5.

Visconti, K. J., & Troop-Gordon, W. (2010). Prospective relations between children's responses to peer victimization and their socioemotional adjustment. *Journal of Applied Developmental Psychology*, *31*(4), 261–272. https://doi.org/10.1016/j.appdev.2010.05.003.

Ziv, Y. (2013). Social information processing patterns, social skills, and school readiness in preschool children. *Journal of Experimental Child Psychology*, *114*(2), 306–320. https://doi.org/10.1016/j.jecp.2012.08.009.

Part II

Assessment and intervention

Chapter 4

Assessing youth

Cynthia A. Erdley and Melissa S. Jankowski
University of Maine, Orono, ME, United States

A long history of research on the peer relations of children and adolescents has firmly established that those youth with social skills deficits are more likely to have poorer peer relationship experiences, including peer rejection, lack of friendships/low-quality friendships, and peer victimization (Ladd, 2005). In addition, social skills deficits can negatively impact child-adult interactions, as well as daily living skills. These negative interpersonal experiences increase youths' risk for short- and long-term adjustment problems, such as loneliness, depressive symptoms, suicidality, academic difficulties, delinquency, substance use, and sexual risk behavior (Prinstein et al., 2018). Thus, it is critical to assess youths' social skills to identify deficits or excesses in specific social behaviors that may contribute to negative peer interactions. This information can be highly valuable in determining what skills to target when planning intervention and for evaluating the effectiveness of intervention.

When considering youths' social functioning, Gresham (2016) distinguishes among social skills, social tasks, and social competence. Social skills are defined as a specific class of behaviors enacted by an individual to complete a social task successfully. Examples of social tasks include making a friend, entering a peer group, or handling conflict. Social competence is viewed as an evaluative construct, given that competence is based on others' judgments that a person has performed a social task adequately. Thus, social skills are the building blocks that can contribute to successful task performance and judgments of social competence by others.

In this chapter, we first consider the various categories of informants (i.e., parents, teachers, trained observers, peers, self) who might provide evaluations of youths' social skills, as well as the advantages and disadvantages associated with each informant type and the value of gaining insights from multiple informants. We then discuss the variety of methods currently used by researchers and clinicians to assess the social skills of children and adolescents. These include interviews, rating scales, naturalistic observation, structured observation, and the use of virtual social environments. Examples of these methods are described, and the strengths and drawbacks of these techniques are highlighted.

Social Skills Across the Life Span. https://doi.org/10.1016/B978-0-12-817752-5.00004-4

Finally, we review the ways in which the social skills of youth from special populations, including those with autism spectrum disorders, intellectual disabilities, externalizing problems, and internalizing problems, are assessed.

The use of various informants to assess youths' social skills

Researchers and clinicians often rely on multiple information sources when obtaining assessments of youths' social skills. These include parents, teachers, trained observers, peers, and the children themselves. Use of each type of informant has advantages and disadvantages, and frequently it is recommended that evaluations be collected from multiple informants to capitalize on their unique perspective and gain a more complete picture of children's social functioning across different contexts.

Parents

Because parents have a long history of observing their children at home and in other social contexts, they are frequently asked to provide evaluations of their children's social skills (Gresham et al., 2018). An advantage of using parents as informants is that they have had extensive experience observing their children across time in a large range of social situations. However, parents often have less opportunity to observe their children interacting with peers, especially in the school context, and particularly as their children reach adolescence and increasingly engage in peer interactions outside the purview of adults. Another drawback of using parents as informants is that they evaluate behavior from an adult perspective, imposing their own values when assessing their children's social skills. In addition, parents often do not have much experience with other children, and consequently they may not have access to information about what types and frequencies of behavior are normative (Bierman, 2004). Finally, because of their emotional attachment to their children, parents may evaluate their child's behavior in a more positive manner (e.g., downplay their child's physical aggression).

Teachers

Teachers are also a key source for providing evaluations of children's social skills. Unlike parents, teachers tend to have extensive opportunities to observe children interacting with peers in the school context. In addition, given their experience with numerous children within a particular age range, teachers have more knowledge about what types of behavior are normative (Murray, Ruble, Willis, & Molloy, 2009). Nevertheless, teachers' observations and perceptions of a child are typically based on just a few months of observing children's peer interactions, primarily within instructional settings, and teachers often are only indirectly involved in children's peer interactions (Gresham et al., 2018; Kwon, Kim, & Sheridan, 2012). Importantly, the validity of teachers' evaluations of children's social skills may vary as a function of child age. Although teachers of preschool and elementary school students may spend a significant part of the school day with their students, teachers of middle- and high-school students may have fairly limited contact with specific students, seeing them for only a few hours each week. Therefore, teachers of adolescents may have a relatively small set of observations on which to base their behavioral assessments. Furthermore, like parents, teachers evaluate youths' behaviors from an adult perspective, which may impact their judgments. Finally, teachers may have certain biases that could influence their evaluations (e.g., having specific expectations about a child's social skills based on knowing the child's older sibling).

Trained observers

Trained observers are another useful source for assessing children's social skills. One advantage of using observers as informants is that they are more apt to be objective, given that they do not have a personal relationship with the children. Observers can be trained to be proficient in coding the behaviors of interest, and interrater reliability can be established and monitored. However, there are various drawbacks to the use of observers. Certainly it can take a significant amount of time to train the observers, carry out the observations, and code the data. There are also concerns that the children who are being observed might be reactive to the observer, possibly showing behavioral excesses or becoming more behaviorally withdrawn, thus compromising the validity of the observations (Merrell, 2001). Therefore, observers should spend time establishing rapport with the children prior to the actual observation session. Alternatively, observations may be conducted unobtrusively (e.g., through a one-way mirror or using hidden cameras). Observations may be limited in that they provide only a snapshot of the child's behaviors within a short timeframe. Moreover, behaviors of key interest (e.g., group entry strategies, dealing with peer conflict) may not occur within the observation period, and more subtle behaviors (e.g., emotional expressions, relational aggression) may happen outside the purview of the observer (Erdley, Nangle, Burns, Holleb, & Kaye, 2010).

Peers

In addition to using adults as evaluators of children's social skills, peers can be an important source of information. A major advantage of obtaining input from peers is that they tend to have experiences with children in a wide variety of social situations and contexts, including settings that adults may have limited access to (e.g., table in the back corner of the lunchroom, secluded spots on the playground, online interactions). Furthermore, peers are generally more attuned to the value and effectiveness of social skills that are key for attaining social success in the peer group. Indeed, one study found that peer ratings of third- to fifth-grade students' social skills were stronger predictors of children's outcomes (e.g., acceptance, peer popularity) than were teacher ratings (Kwon et al., 2012). Also of note, because peer ratings are obtained from multiple people, the risk that individual bias may impact the results is lessened, and the reliability of the assessments is enhanced (Bierman, 2004).

Nevertheless, reputational biases may influence peers' evaluations of a particular child's social skills (Hymel, Wagner, & Butler, 1990). For example, a child with a reputation as a bully who has recently shown significant improvements in his behavior may continue to be evaluated by peers as engaging in high levels of aggressive behavior and low levels of prosocial behavior. Another potential disadvantage associated with peer evaluators is that they may be less aware of certain types of behavior, particularly more subtle behaviors. Consistent with this idea, Younger, Schwartzman, and Ledingham (1986) found that children were not able to report reliably on socially withdrawn behaviors until they were about 8 years old. Finally, there are numerous practical challenges involved in collecting social skills assessments from peers. Researchers must obtain parental consent, and parents may be reluctant to allow their children to evaluate (and be evaluated by) their peers (Mayeux, Underwood, & Risser, 2007). In addition, given that peer ratings are commonly completed in the school context, school administrators and teachers must agree to allow data collection to occur during class time.

Self-reports

Although evaluations of youths' social skills are frequently obtained from other people, children can also be valuable sources of information regarding their social functioning. Of course, youth have full access to the wide range of social contexts in which they have been involved and may have the best insights into the thoughts and emotions that underlie their behavioral choices (Junttila, Voeten, Kaukiainen, & Vaurus, 2006). However, when reporting about the self, youth may be subject to social desirability biases such that they inflate reports of positive social skills and minimize reports of negative behaviors (Junttila et al., 2006). Merrell (2001) has cautioned that it is unclear whether youth with significant social behavior problems can provide accurate reports regarding their social skills. Regardless of the child's level of social competence, clinicians and researchers must ensure that the assessment procedure is developmentally appropriate, with items and response formats that are understandable to the respondent.

Multiple informants

It has long been recommended that when assessing the social skills of children and adolescents, responses from multiple types of informants should be obtained (Renk & Phares, 2004). As described earlier, different informants have varying experiences with children across many contexts, and combining several evaluations can provide a more complete picture of the child's social functioning with different social interaction partners and in various settings. Nevertheless, there continues to be strong interest regarding discrepancies in informants' evaluations.

Most research examining such discrepancies has focused on responses to behavior rating scale measures. For example, Gresham, Elliott, Cook, Vance, and Kettler (2010) examined cross-informant correlations across the various social skills and problem behavior domains of the Social Skills Improvement System Rating Scales (SSIS-RS; Gresham & Elliott, 2008). They found that for total social skills ratings, correlations were relatively low, but statistically significant: teacher-parent ($r=.30$), parent-student ($r=.21$), and teacher-student ($r=.21$). Of note, one drawback in making these comparisons is that the item content was not consistent across the forms. In fact, the SSIS-RS teacher and parent forms have 80% of the items in common, whereas the teacher and student forms have only 67% overlap in items. Lack of consistency in item content is likely to account for some of the lower agreement among raters.

More recently, Gresham et al. (2018) investigated agreement among informant pairs of teachers, parents, and students in response to the Social Skills Improvement System-Social-Emotional Learning Edition (SSIS SEL) rating forms (Gresham & Elliott, 2017), which are revisions of the SSIS-RS (Gresham & Elliott, 2008). To complete these forms, teachers and parents indicate the frequency with which students demonstrate a particular social-emotional skill on a scale of 1 (*never*) to 4 (*almost always*). Students respond to the same items, but indicate on a scale of 1 (*not true*) to 4 (*very true*) whether they engage in the skill. Gresham et al. (2018) found that interrater correlations were significant, with teacher-parent informants having higher correlations ($r=.34$) than teacher-student ($r=.27$) or parent-student ($r=.29$) informants. Moreover, the correlations between the ratings provided by pairs of similar informants (e.g., two teachers) were significantly higher than those between dissimilar informants (e.g., a teacher and a parent). The cross-informant correlations were higher in the Gresham et al. (2018) study than in the Gresham et al. (2010) study, likely in part because the items on the teacher, parent, and student forms of the SSIS-SEL were the same. However, the fact that the item-ranking anchors were different on the student form than on the parent and teacher versions of the form was a limitation.

Notably, findings from the Gresham et al. (2018) study were consistent with results obtained in a meta-analysis of 74 studies of cross-informant ratings of children's and adolescents' social skills conducted by Renk and Phares (2004). Specifically, parents and teachers demonstrated higher agreement with one another than either group did with students. This finding may reflect the fact that parents and teachers share a similar perspective as adult outside observers who do not have access to the full range of child social interactions, whereas students have greater insights regarding their social behaviors. Interestingly, the Renk and Phares (2004) meta-analysis also revealed that among various cross-informant pairs, the strongest correlations of ratings were between teachers and children's peers. This relatively higher level of agreement might be related to the fact that both teachers and peers base their assessments primarily on observations of children's social behavior in the same context, namely, the school.

Overall, studies of cross-informant ratings indicate that there is much more agreement than disagreement among raters (Gresham et al., 2018). Although cross-informant discrepancies may be attributed to source effects (e.g., informants' biased perspectives, lack of awareness, unreliable reporting), it seems likely that informant discrepancies more strongly reflect context effects rather than source effects. That is, differences in informants' evaluations may represent real differences in children's behavior across the particular social situations in which the informant has observed them (Gresham et al., 2018). For example, parents may report that a child is relatively skilled at initiating interactions, but teachers may rate the child as low on this skill. This discrepancy may reflect the fact that the child may have little difficulty initiating interactions with family members in the familiar setting of the home, but may struggle with this skill when faced with a large peer group at school.

Gresham et al. (2018) note that informant discrepancies can have an impact on the identification and treatment of social-behavioral difficulties. Therefore, it is critical to seek feedback from multiple informants to obtain a more comprehensive evaluation of the child's social skills. In addition, Gresham et al. (2018) recommend that ratings from multiple informants be supplemented with other data, including direct observations and interviews, which can be useful in explaining the reasons for discrepancies in informants' reports and better understanding the particular social contexts that are challenging for the child.

Methods used for assessing social skills

Numerous methods are used by researchers and clinicians to assess the social skills of children and adolescents. These include interviews, rating scales, naturalistic observation, structured observation, and the use of virtual social environments. In the following section, examples of these different methodological approaches are described, and the strengths and drawbacks of these techniques are discussed.

Interviews

One technique for obtaining information about youths' social skills is through interviews of the child, the parent, and/or a teacher who is very familiar with the child's behavior. As Merrell (2001) notes, this is quite an adaptable assessment technique, as interviews can range from highly structured to less structured formats. An advantage of using interviews is that they can provide important information about the particular environmental conditions and social situations in which the child exhibits certain social behaviors. Insights can also be gained regarding the antecedent and consequent conditions associated with the target behavior (Merrell, 2001).

Interviews of youth themselves can provide valuable insights regarding their thought processes as they encounter particular types of social situations. Importantly, the interviewer should make sure that the procedure (e.g., response format, length of interview) and language used are developmentally appropriate. Younger children tend to be more vulnerable to suggestibility, so the interviewer must be careful about how questions are presented and should avoid the use of leading questions that might bias children's responses. Given advances in their perspective-taking abilities, adolescents tend to be more self-conscious and more concerned about the social desirability of their responses. Thus, it is especially important to try to build rapport so that the respondent feels more comfortable in sharing candid responses (Erdley et al., 2010).

The Enactive Social Knowledge Interview (Mize & Ladd, 1988) is used to assess how preschool-aged children might respond to six hypothetical challenging social situations (e.g., being excluded from play). To make the process more engaging, children convey their response by using a puppet to act out what strategies they would use. In the Home Interview with Child (Valente, 1994), children (kindergarten through third grade) are presented with a series of eight drawings that depict two types of social situations: ambiguous minor harm (e.g., being hit by a ball) and unsuccessful peer group entry (e.g., being ignored by children in a group). The interviewer reads a brief description of each situation, and children are asked to make attributions regarding the peers' intent and to report how they would respond to the situation. Similarly, in the Social Cognitive Assessment Profile—Revised (Hughes, Meehan, & Cavell, 2004), an interviewer presents elementary school-aged children with vignettes involving overtly or relationally aggressive provocation. The interviewer instructs children to imagine being involved in each vignette, and then asks children questions regarding their attributions, social goals, behavioral strategies, and outcome expectations. In the Interpersonal Negotiation Strategies Interview (Schultz, Yeates, & Selman, 1988), a youth (ages 8–17 years) is presented with a series of four hypothetical dyadic interpersonal dilemmas. The interviewer then asks a set of standard questions after each dilemma (e.g., "What do you think is the best way to solve the problem?") to assess youths' social skills knowledge.

The Vineland Adaptive Behavior Scales—Third Edition (Vineland-3; Sparrow, Cicchetti, & Saulnier, 2016) includes a widely used interview that assesses behavior in three major domains: communication, daily living skills, and socialization. There are also two optional domains, motor skills and maladaptive behavior, that can be included if these are areas of concern. The Interview Form is completed by a professional who interviews an adult informant (e.g., parent, teacher) that is familiar with the individual's everyday functioning. The interviewer asks general, open-ended questions designed to begin discussion of the content area, and item-specific problems can be used to help in scoring individual items. Normative scores are available for across the lifespan, from birth through age 90+, and psychometric properties (e.g., inter-interviewer reliability, internal consistency, test-retest reliability) are strong (Burger-Caplan, Saulnier, & Sparrow, 2018).

Rating scales

Behavior rating scales, which typically obtain informant estimates of the frequency with which a youth enacts specific behaviors, are the most frequently used measures for assessing social skills (Gresham, 2016). Gresham et al. (2018) assert that rating scales should be considered indirect measures of behavior, given that they typically do not assess behaviors at the time and place of occurrence that they have happened. Instead, informants are asked to reflect retrospectively on the youth's behaviors when completing their ratings. There are a variety of advantages associated with the use of behavior rating scales, including: (a) data are quantifiable and can be analyzed regarding their reliability and validity, (b) a broad range of behaviors, including prosocial skills and problem behaviors, can be evaluated, (c) multiple informants can be used, representing a variety of perspectives (e.g., parents, teachers, youth), and (d) normative data can be employed to determine how an individual's ratings compare with representative samples of others (Gresham et al., 2018; Gresham & Elliott, 2008). In addition, completion of rating scales takes relatively little time and training, and informants can base their ratings on their observations of the youth's behavior over time and across a variety of social situations. Some of the disadvantages of rating scales are that responses can be biased by the informant's perception of the behavior being rated (as opposed to its actual occurrence), and they are relatively insensitive to short-term changes in behavior, given that ratings tend to represent summaries of behavior over time (Gresham, 2016). Numerous rating scale measures are available (see Crowe, Beauchamp, Catoppa, & Anderson, 2011; Humphrey et al., 2011 for reviews), and several of the most widely used measures are described in the following paragraphs.

The Social Skills Improvement System Rating Scales (SSIS-RS; Gresham & Elliott, 2008), which is a revised version of the Social Skills Rating System (SSRS; Gresham & Elliott, 1990), have been used extensively around the world (Gresham, 2016). Forms are available for teachers, parents, and youth, and all forms contain common items across seven social skills subdomains, including Communication, Cooperation, Engagement, Assertion, Responsibility, Empathy, and Self-Control. Items are rated based on the frequency with which they occur (0=*never*, 1=*seldom*, 2=*often*, 3=*almost always*), as well as how important they are (0=*not important*, 1=*important*, 2=*critical*). The Problem Behavior scale includes five subdomains: Externalizing, Internalizing, Bullying, Hyperactivity/Inattention, and Autism Spectrum, and these are rated on the 4-point frequency scale. The measure has strong psychometric properties, including high internal consistency, test-retest reliability, and validity. The SSIS-RS has been standardized based on a nationally representative sample of youth (ages 3–18 years) and differentiates between the standardization sample and various special populations (e.g., attention-deficit/hyperactivity disorder (ADHD), emotional disturbance, intellectual disability; Gresham & Elliott, 2008).

The Matson Evaluation of Social Skills with Youngsters-II (MESSY-II; Matson, 2010) is a rating scale measure that assesses both appropriate and inappropriate social behaviors in youth (ages 2–16 years). Items are evaluated using a 5-point scale ranging from 1 (*not at all*) to 5 (*very much*). Internal consistency has been found to be good for different age groups (2–5 years, 6–9 years, 10–16 years), though notably the internal consistency is highest for the 10- to 16-year-old group, suggesting that older children display more consistency in their social skills (Matson, 2010). Convergent and divergent validity are good to strong, though the validity is lower for the 2- to 5-year-old group, perhaps due to greater variability in their behavior. The MESSY-II consists of three factors: Adaptive/Appropriate, Hostile, and Inappropriately Assertive/Over-Confident (Matson, Neal, Worley, Kozlowski, & Fodstad, 2012). Matson, Kozlowski, Neal, Worley, and Fodstad (2011) established cutoffs as a function of age cohort for each of the three factors of the MESSY-II. A strength of the MESSY-II is that it allows for a more nuanced interpretation of deficits or excesses in social skills tailored for the child's age.

A broader scale with utility for assessing social skills is the Achenbach System of Empirically Based Assessment (ASEBA; Achenbach & Rescorla, 2001). This is a series of questionnaires used by clinicians and researchers to assess both adaptive and maladaptive behaviors and overall functioning, including social functioning (e.g., social participation, aggression, withdrawn/depressed behavior), in children and adolescents. The system includes the Child Behavior Checklist (CBCL), which is completed by caregivers regarding their child's behavior and social connections. The CBCL is among the most widely used parent-report measures of youth emotional and behavioral problems in both clinical and research settings. The Youth Self Report Form (YSR) is completed by youth regarding their own experiences. Finally, the Teacher Report Form (TRF) is completed by the youth's teacher(s). There are two age versions for the CBCL and TRF: preschool (1½ to 5 years) and school-age (6–18 years), and the YSR is designed for youth ages 11–18 years. The total number of items varies, and there is not a one-to-one correspondence between each individual item across the different report forms. Items are scored 0 (*not true*) to 2 (*very true or often true*). Test-retest reliability, interrater reliability, and validity have all been demonstrated in the ASEBA scales. Additionally, these scales have been translated into over 100 languages, and there are a variety of multicultural applications, including a Multicultural Family Assessment Module (MFAM). This supplement allows the clinician or researcher to compare data from the other Achenbach system measures (e.g., CBCL, TRF, YSR) to cultural norms.

The report generated by the supplement documents how the youth's behavior compares to the cultural norms of his or her society, as well as other cultures.

Additional broad rating scale measures used extensively by researchers and practitioners are part of the Behavioral Assessment System for Children (BASC-3; Reynolds & Kamphaus, 2015). The BASC-3 components provide a comprehensive system of assessing behavioral and emotional functioning in children and adolescents/young adults between the ages of 2 and 25 years. The BASC-3 includes Teacher Rating Scales (TRS) and Parent Rating Scales (PRS), each of which has three levels: preschool (2–5 years), child (6–11 years), and adolescent (12–21 years). Items are scored on a 0 (*never*) to 3 (*almost always*) scale. Among the composite scores generated, the BASC-3 yields a score for Adaptive Skills (e.g., social skills, leadership, functional communication). Other behaviors that may impact social functioning are also assessed (e.g., aggression, withdrawal). The TRS, PRS, and SRP all have high levels of internal consistency, test-retest reliability, and validity. Moreover, norms have been developed based on large, demographically representative samples.

Observations in the natural environment

Although interviews and rating scales can provide useful descriptions of the social skills of children and adolescents, responses can be biased by the evaluator's perception of the youth's behavior. Observing youths' behavior in natural social settings is considered to be the most ecologically valid method of assessing social skills (Gresham, 2016). Naturalistic behavior observation involves having trained, objective observers recording behaviors at the time of occurrence in natural settings (Merrell, 2001). Observations should be carried out in settings where youth are typically interacting with others, and traditionally the school context has been the most frequently used. It is preferable to observe during less structured times (e.g., lunchtime, recess) when youth have more freedom to interact. Various approaches to observation may be adopted, including event sampling (i.e., number of times a specific behavior occurs during the observation period is noted) and time sampling (i.e., observational period is divided into intervals and particular behaviors that are enacted within each interval are recorded).

Observations of the child in his or her natural environment can help the clinician to understand the antecedents and consequences that may maintain adaptive and/or problematic social behaviors. For example, a clinician might observe the child at school to determine the types of events that tend to precipitate the behavior of interest (e.g., aggression, withdrawal). These observations can serve to inform case conceptualization and guide treatment. However, numerous challenges are associated with clinical observation of the child in his or her natural environment, including potential barriers to gaining access to the setting, the time needed to conduct the observations, and the potential for the child or peers to be reactive to being observed. Additionally, there are various cultural considerations, which, if not taken into account, could lead to inaccurate conclusions regarding social skills. For example, many Asian cultures socialize youth to avoid direct confrontation, whereas Arabic cultures often encourage staring at people that one finds interesting (Damico & Damico, 1993). Cultural norms must be factored in when evaluating the quality of culturally diverse youths' behaviors in social interactions.

Structured observations

Although naturalistic observations generally yield findings with high ecological validity, oftentimes it may be difficult to observe social behaviors of key interest because they occur at low frequency or out of the range of the observer. To address these challenges, structured or analogue observation can be used, in which circumstances are created that will increase the opportunity to observe the behavior of interest in a more controlled setting. Such work has often been conducted within a research setting. For example, to examine children's peer group entry strategies, Putallaz (1983) had two experimental confederates who were of the same gender and of about the same age as the participant play a game. The participant was then sent into the room, and the child's behaviors when attempting to join the ongoing interaction were observed. In a study that focused on children's responses to ambiguous provocation, Hudley and Graham (1993) set up a game involving two participants who had a chance to win a prize. However, the conditions of the game were such that the children's ability to win was thwarted. Of interest was how the participants would interpret and respond to the provocation, given that it appeared that the other peer had caused the loss.

Structured observations can be especially useful when assessing adolescents' peer interactions, given that the majority of adolescents' everyday social interactions occur in more private, less easily observable settings. The Contextual Assessment of Social Skills (CASS; Ratto, Turner-Brown, Rupp, Mesibov, & Penn, 2011) is a role-play assessment of conversational skills for adolescents and young adults that can be used with typically developing individuals, as well as those with high-functioning autism spectrum disorder (ASD). In the CASS, participants engage in two 3-min role play conversations with two different confederates (unfamiliar peers) who are of the opposite gender. In the first interaction, the confederate shows social interest and engagement. In the second interaction, the confederate displays boredom and disengagement. The conversations are recorded, and participants' verbal and nonverbal behaviors are coded in 10 categories (e.g., asking questions, topic changes, overall involvement, overall quality of rapport). Asking questions and topic changes are coded as behavioral counts, whereas the other categories are scored by two trained raters on a scale of 1 (*low*) to 7 (*high*). Ratto et al. (2011) found that the internal consistency of the CASS was quite high, and interrater reliability was adequate.

Although primarily used in the research context, structured observations also can be used clinically. However, the clinician must be aware of confidentiality concerns and informed consent requirements. Given these challenges, particularly regarding bringing confederates into the clinical setting, it may be easier for the clinician to set up structured interactions outside of the clinic in ways that uphold the client's confidentiality. For example, a client who has social anxiety might be asked to initiate a conversation with a stranger in a public setting while the clinician observes.

Virtual environments

Given the many challenges related to conducting naturalistic or structured behavioral observations, some researchers have capitalized on advances in technology to create virtual environments in which youths' social skills can be assessed. Virtual environments allow users to interact with computer-based characters in various social contexts and at any time. One such virtual environment is that of computer games, which can provide an engaging method for both assessment and learning of social skills. Moreover, computer games have several advantages over traditional assessment methods, including minimal training requirements and the elimination of subjective bias from coding. Further, they allow for accurate data collection that can be used to quickly build databases of social comparison data.

One recently developed computer game is Zoo U (zoougame; Derosier, Craig, & Sanchez, 2012). Zoo U is a computer game platform that implements a performance-based assessment of social skills. Children are presented with virtual situations that are analogous to those commonly experienced in school settings. In addition to a teacher and student, the scene contains zoo animals to provide an opportunity for fun engagement and opportunities for novel problem-solving tasks (e.g., working with other students to feed and care for the animals). Children must interact with the characters in Zoo U to complete six virtual social situations (communication, cooperation, empathy, emotion regulation, impulse control, and social initiation). Evidence indicates that children who demonstrate high social competence on the Zoo U platform are significantly more likely to exhibit positive adjustment in the school setting (e.g., Derosier & Thomas, 2018).

Additionally, virtual environment computer games have been developed and tested to assess social skills in several special populations. One such example is a chat room task created by Mikami, Huang-Pollock, Pfiffner, McBurnett, and Hangai (2007) used to assess social skills in youth with ADHD. Children with ADHD tend to display an array of behaviors that may negatively impact their social skills. Specifically, those with ADHD-combined type (ADHD-C) tend to exhibit an aggressive and disruptive behavioral style that may contribute to subsequent rejection by peers. Conversely, those with ADHD-inattentive type (ADHD-I) may appear passive and withdrawn, which may interfere with the formation of peer relationships.

To address difficulties in assessing these differences, Mikami et al. (2007) constructed a "chat room" task to compare the social behavior of children with ADHD-C and ADHD-I. Children in the study were instructed to interact in a chat room with a computer program that simulated interactions with four peers. They were informed in advance that the "peers" were part of a computer program and were free to respond in their own way. Children with ADHD-C made more off-topic and hostile responses, and those with ADHD-I provided fewer responses and showed poor memory for the conversation. Importantly, parent and teacher ratings and in vivo observations of social skills were found to correlate with this chat room task. This suggests that this novel assessment paradigm can be used by clinicians and researchers who are interested in observational measures of social skills that may be more objective and less subject to bias than other measures. Further, the design of this chat room task is such that it can be administered to a single child whenever is most convenient.

Finally, a virtual environment social skills assessment called Pegasys-VR (Wong-Sarver, Beidel, & Spitalnik, 2014) has been developed specifically for children with Social Anxiety Disorder (SAD). Pegasys-VR includes age-appropriate avatars with differing gender, race, and roles (i.e., teacher, principal, classmate, or bully) that users interact with in various settings (i.e., hallways, classrooms). Le and Beidel (2017) found that the Pegasys-VR was more feasible to implement than traditional role-playing tasks in that it took less personnel time, cost less, and demonstrated moderate concurrent validity with self-reported ratings of anxiety. Overall, the use of virtual environments to assess social skills appears to be an efficient, reliable, and engaging method that has immense potential.

Although evaluations of the use of these virtual environments have been restricted to research settings, there is reason to believe that they hold promise for practicing clinicians as well. For example, Le and Beidel (2017) found that virtual environments require significantly less personnel time and costs when compared to traditional role-playing tasks that may be used when assessing social competence. Specifically, Le and Beidel (2017) reported that a clinician could conduct four virtual environment assessments for the cost of one traditional role playing assessment. Over time, this savings would offset the initial cost of purchasing the virtual environment software. Given this, virtual environments have the potential to offer nonintrusive, economical methodology to directly observe a youth's social skills in a clinical setting.

Assessing social skills in special populations

Deficits in social skills typically are hallmarks of various developmental and psychological disorders, such as autism spectrum disorders, intellectual disabilities, and externalizing and internalizing problems. Thus, it is critical to have social skills assessment tools that are reliable and valid to use with these special populations, as well as sensitive to the unique social challenges that these youth might experience. In the following section, issues that need to be considered when assessing social skills in youth from various special populations are described.

Autism spectrum disorder

Deficits in social skills are a defining feature of autism spectrum disorders (ASD). In addition, those with ASD exhibit impairments in communication and tend to demonstrate stereotyped patterns of behavior, interests, and activities (American Psychiatric Association, 2013). Given that social skills deficits are a key characteristic of ASD, there is a great need for assessment tools that can be used to identify specific skill deficits to guide intervention efforts as well as to evaluate the effectiveness of intervention. Although the social skills of youth with ASD have often been assessed using measures that were initially developed and normed with typically developing populations, measures also have been created to evaluate social skills specifically in youth with ASD.

Examples of measures that were developed initially to assess typically developing children but have commonly been used to evaluate children with ASD are the Social Skills Rating Scale (SSRS; Gresham & Elliott, 1990) and the Preschool and Kindergarten Behavior Scale (PKBS-2; Merrell, 1994). Importantly, there is evidence that both measures are internally consistent and highly reliable in assessing the social skills of young children with ASD (Wang, Sandall, Davis, & Thomas, 2011). Likewise, the Matson Evaluation of Social Skills with Youngsters-II (MESSY-II; Matson, 2010), originally normed based on typically developing populations, has been shown to be sensitive to social skill differences in typically developing children versus those with ASD (e.g., Matson et al., 2011), who tend to show deficits in appropriate social skills, but not excesses in inappropriate social skills.

A rating scale designed specifically for use with those with ASD is the Social Responsiveness Scale, Second Edition (SRS-2; Constantino & Gruber, 2012). The School-Age Form is appropriate for youth aged 4–18 years and assesses characteristic features of ASD involving interpersonal behavior, communication, and stereotypic and restricted behaviors and interests. Informants (typically parents and teachers) rate the frequency of behaviors on a scale of 1 (*not true*) to 4 (*almost always true*). Use of a continuous scale is consistent with the conceptualization of ASD symptoms and impairments on a continuum of severity (American Psychiatric Association, 2013). The five treatment subscales (Social Awareness, Social Cognition, Social Communication, Social Motivation, and Restricted Interests and Repetitive Behavior) can be useful for targeting intervention needs and assessing treatment effects (Donnelly et al., 2018).

The TRIAD Social Skills Assessment (TSSA; Stone, Ruble, Coonrod, Hepburn, & Pennington, 2003) is a criterion-based, multi-informant measure that is used to describe the social behavior of those with ASD. The questionnaire assesses four areas of social functioning: (a) ability to understand emotions and perspectives of others, (b) ability to initiate interactions, (c) ability to maintain interactions, and (d) ability to respond to others. Ratings are made on a 1 (*not very well*) to 4 (*very well*) scale. Research by Murray et al. (2009) found that parents and teachers demonstrated moderate agreement in their overall social skills rating scores. However, there was low agreement regarding ratings of specific social skills, which may reflect the varying social contexts in which parents versus teachers observe children.

A variety of observational measures are also available for assessing the social skills of youth with ASD. A widely employed observational measure is the Autism Diagnostic Observation Schedule, Second Edition (ADOS-2; Lord et al., 2012). The ADOS-2 is a semistructured observational measure that can be used with those from age 12 months through adulthood. Five versions are available, and choice of the appropriate version is based on the individual's expressive language level and chronological age. The individual with ASD engages in a series of interactive activities with a trained examiner, and then behaviors are coded and scored following an algorithm. Observations focus on communication, social interaction, play, and restricted and repetitive behaviors.

The Social Skills Observation Measure (SOM) is a direct observational method for social skills that was developed for use with children with ASD in naturalistic situations in school (Dekker, Nauta, Mulder, Sytema, & de Bildt, 2016). The SOM has been implemented with youth between the ages of 9 and 13 years and involves two separate 15-min observation periods. One observation occurs in a naturalistic, unstructured situation in the class (e.g., free play time), and the other takes place in a naturalistic, unstructured situation on the playground. Each 1-min interval includes 40 s of observation, followed by 20 s of coding. Coding focuses on specific behavior (e.g., solitary unoccupied, cooperative interaction, reactive aggression), quality of behavior (i.e., assertive, subassertive, aggressive/dominant), and number of children interacted with. These observations and the coding are carried out by observers who are blind to the child's status, allowing for an objective assessment of social behavior. Dekker et al. (2016) report that the SOM has high interrater reliability, but convergent validity is low, suggesting that this measure provides additional information on the frequency and quality of social behavior of children with ASD beyond that obtained from other measures (e.g., the ADOS-2). A major strength of this measure is its focus on the peer interactions of children with ASD in two naturalistic situations, enabling observation of a broader spectrum of behaviors.

An observational research method used with adolescents is the Contextual Assessment of Social Skills (CASS; Ratto et al., 2011) that was previously described in the "Structured observations" section. Ratto et al. (2011) evaluated the CASS with participants (ages 16–22 years) who had high-functioning autism spectrum disorder (HFASD) or were typically developing. Results indicated that compared to the typically developing participants, those with HFASD were less likely to perceive changes in social context (interested vs bored partner) and were less apt to change their conversational behaviors. Ratto et al. (2011) found support for convergent and discriminant validity of the CASS, given that the total change score of the CASS was associated with verbal IQ and theory of mind. In addition, the total change score significantly predicted the presence of ASD, supporting the predictive validity of this measure. Thus, it appears that the CASS is an ecologically valid measure of social skills that can be effective for assessing the interactions of adolescents with HFASD.

Intellectual disability

Social skills challenges are common in youth with intellectual disabilities (ID; Greenspan, 1999). These youth often face social demands that are difficult to navigate (e.g., receiving special education). Further, most studies suggest that these youth have fewer peer interactions and longstanding friendships (e.g., Webster & Carter, 2007). Limited involvement in general education settings and extracurricular activities further exacerbates relationship challenges. In addition, youth with intellectual disabilities tend to have difficulty understanding the social contexts of situations, understanding jokes, and taking the perspective of others (i.e., de Bildt et al., 2005).

Often, the Vineland Adaptive Behavior Scales, Third Edition (Vineland-3; Sparrow et al., 2016), are used to assess social skills in youth with ID. As described in the "Interviews" section, one aspect of the Vineland-3 is an interview form that is completed by a professional who interviews the parent or teacher. Behavior is assessed across various domains, and in particular, the communication (i.e., receptive, expressive, and written) and socialization (i.e., interpersonal relationships, play and leisure time, and coping skills) domains can provide valuable insights into the social skills of youth with ID. In addition to the widely used interview form, the Vineland-3 includes a Parent/Caregiver Form that asks about home and family-life behavior using a questionnaire format completed by a parent or caregiver, as well as a Teacher Form, which collects a teacher's experiences with adaptive behavior in school, preschool, or in a structured daycare setting. The Vineland-3 has demonstrated strong reliability and validity for assessing youth with ID (Sparrow et al., 2016). Additionally, the SSIS-RS (Gresham & Elliott, 2008) and MESSY-II (Matson, 2010), described in the "Rating scales" section, are used with many special populations, including those with ID.

Externalizing disorders

Children with ADHD often encounter problems in social interactions with peers and are at risk for peer rejection and social isolation (e.g., Mash & Barkley, 2003). These social problems include frequent shifts in conversation, difficulty listening, initiating conversations at inappropriate times, and engaging in off-task behavior. Given the centrality of peer relationships in youth, assessing and addressing these issues are important.

As described in the "Rating scales" section, the Social Skills Improvement System Rating Scales (SSIS-RS; Gresham & Elliott, 2008) have been used with a number of special populations, including youth with ADHD. Van der Oord et al. (2005) found support for three of the four factor structures of the SSRS in an ADHD sample (e.g., cooperation, self-control, assertion). However, they also observed low agreements across informants, specifically for the ADHD sample. According to Gresham and Elliott (1990), however, the agreement between raters in ADHD populations is not expected to be high, due to the situational specificity of social behavior. Given the evidence that social skills in children with ADHD are likely to differ across social scenarios, it is especially important to combine information from as many sources as possible. In addition, as described in the "Virtual environments" section, a novel way to address informant/situation discrepancy issues in assessing social skills in ADHD may be through the use of computer-administered assessment paradigms (e.g., chat room task; Mikami et al., 2007).

Internalizing disorders

Socially anxious and socially phobic youth have been found to have deficits in social skills, and youths' self-reports of anxiety tend to increase as parental ratings of social skills decrease (e.g., Ginsburg, La Greca, & Silverman, 1998). Further, youth diagnosed with social phobia are noted to participate in fewer social interactions and initiate interactions less frequently (Spence, Donovan, & Brechman-Toussaint, 1999). Despite evidence supporting these deficits, studies examining objective ratings of behavior in this population have not obtained consistent results. For example, Segrin and Kinney (1995) and Strahan and Conger (1998) found no differences in observer ratings for socially anxious and nonsocially anxious youth, whereas a more recent study (Inderbitzen-Nolan, Anderson, & Johnson, 2007) found that objective raters (confederates and audience members during behavioral role plays) rated socially anxious youth as being less socially skilled than their nonanxious counterparts. Despite these inconsistencies in objective ratings of social skills in anxious youth, subjective ratings in this population are found to be consistent. Evidence indicates that socially anxious youth rate themselves as performing poorer than their peers, and these lower ratings align with those of outside observers (Inderbitzen-Nolan et al., 2007). As described in the "Virtual environments" section, Wong-Sarver et al. (2014) have created the Pegasys-VR for use specifically with individuals with Social Anxiety Disorder. This task has been found to be more feasible to implement than traditional role playing tasks, costs less, and has concurrent validity with self-reported ratings of anxiety.

Concluding comments

Assessing the social skills of youth is an important task, given extensive evidence that youth with social skills deficits and/or behavioral excesses are at risk for low peer acceptance and victimization, which in turn are related to greater vulnerability to socioemotional adjustment problems both concurrently and in the long-term (Prinstein et al., 2018). Identifying behaviors that need to be targeted for intervention is critical for designing programs that can effectively build youth's social skills. Furthermore, the use of social skills assessments is important in determining whether such interventions have resulted in improvements in youth's social skills. Many different informants, such as parents, teachers, trained observers, peers, and youth themselves, may be called upon to provide evaluations of youth's social skills. Each informant has unique information and perspectives regarding the target child, and it is strongly recommended that multiple informants be used to obtain a more complete profile of the child's social skills across a range of contexts (Renk & Phares, 2004). A wide variety of techniques for assessing the social skills of youth is available, including interviews, rating scales, naturalistic and structured observations, and use of virtual environments. Each approach has particular strengths and drawbacks, and it is recommended that multiple techniques be used to provide a more comprehensive understanding of a child's social functioning (Merrell, 2001). Given that difficulties with social skills are commonly seen in those from special populations (e.g., ASD, ID, externalizing and internalizing disorders), it is critical that social skills assessments be sensitive to the unique characteristics of these groups. Moreover, as clinicians will increasingly be working with diverse youth, who themselves are interacting with more diverse youth, it must be recognized that the meaning and value of specific social behaviors can vary depending on the youth's culture. Thus, diversity issues must be taken into account when interpreting the results of social skills assessments.

References

Achenbach, T. M., & Rescorla, L. A. (2001). *Manual for the ASEBA school-age forms and profiles*. Burlington, VT: University of Vermont Research Center for Children, Youth, & Families.

American Psychiatric Association. (2013). *Diagnostic and statistical manual of mental disorders* (5th ed.). Arlington, VA: American Psychiatric Publishing.

Bierman, K. L. (2004). *Peer rejection: Developmental processes and intervention strategies*. New York, NY: Guilford Press.

Burger-Caplan, R., Saulnier, C. A., & Sparrow, S. S. (2018). Vineland Adaptive Behavior Scales. In J. Kreutzer, et al. (Eds.), *Encyclopedia of clinical neuropsychology* (pp. 1–5): Springer International Publishing. https://doi.org/10.1007/978-3-319-56782-2_1602-4.

Constantino, J. N., & Gruber, C. P. (2012). *Social Responsiveness Scale, Second Edition (SRS-2)*. Torrance, CA: Western Psychological Services.

Crowe, L. M., Beauchamp, M. H., Catoppa, C., & Anderson, V. (2011). Social function assessment tools for children and adolescents: A systematic review from 1988 to 2010. *Clinical Psychology Review*, *31*, 767–785. https://doi.org/10.1016/j.cpr.2011.03.00.

Damico, J. S., & Damico, S. K. (1993). Language and social skills from a diversity perspective: Considerations for the speech-language pathologist. *Language, Speech, and Hearing Services in Schools, 24*(4), 236–243. https://doi.org/10.1044/0161-1461.2404.236.

de Bildt, A., Serra, M., Luteijn, E., Kraijer, D., Sytema, S., & Minderaa, R. (2005). Social skills in children with intellectual disabilities with and without autism. *Journal of Intellectual Disability Research, 49*(5), 317–328. https://doi.org/10.1111/j.1365-2788.2005.00655.x.

Dekker, V., Nauta, M. H., Mulder, E. J., Sytema, S., & de Bildt, A. (2016). A fresh pair of eyes: A blind observation method for evaluating social skills of children with ASD in a naturalistic peer situation in school. *Journal of Autism and Developmental Disorders, 46*, 2890–2904. https://doi.org/10.1007/s10803-016-2829-y.

Derosier, M. E., Craig, A. B., & Sanchez, R. P. (2012). Zoo U: A stealth approach to social skills assessment in schools. *Advances in Human-Computer Interaction, 2012*, 1–7. https://doi.org/10.1155/2012/654791.

Derosier, M. E., & Thomas, J. M. (2018). Establishing the criterion validity of Zoo U's game-based social emotional skills assessment for school-based outcomes. *Journal of Applied Developmental Psychology, 55*, 52–61. https://doi.org/10.1016/j.appdev.2017.03.001.

Donnelly, J. P., Lopata, C., Jordan, A. K., Thomeer, M. L., Rodgers, J. D., McDonald, C. A., & Nelson, A. T. (2018). Informant discrepancies in the assessment of ASD symptoms of high-functioning children with ASD using the SRS-2. *Measurement and Evaluation in Counseling and Development, 51*, 60–70. https://doi.org/10.1080/07481756.2017.1395706.

Erdley, C. A., Nangle, D. W., Burns, A. M., Holleb, L. J., & Kaye, A. J. (2010). Assessing children and adolescents. In D. W. Nangle, D. J. Hansen, C. A. Erdley, & P. J. Norton (Eds.), *Practitioner's guide to empirically based measures of social skills* (pp. 69–85). New York: Springer.

Ginsburg, G. S., La Greca, A. M., & Silverman, W. K. (1998). Social anxiety in children with anxiety disorders: Relation with social and emotional functioning. *Journal of Abnormal Child Psychology, 26*, 175–185. https://doi.org/10.1023/A:1022668101048.

Greenspan, S. (1999). A contextualist perspective on adaptive behavior. In R. L. Schalock (Ed.), *Adaptive behavior and its measurement: Implications for the field of mental retardation* (pp. 61–80). Washington, DC: American Association on Mental Retardation.

Gresham, F. M. (2016). Social skills assessment and intervention for children and youth. *Cambridge Journal of Education, 46*, 319–332. https://doi.org/10.1080/0305764X.2016.1195788.

Gresham, F. M., & Elliott, S. N. (1990). *The social skills rating system*. Circle Pines, MN: American Guidance Service.

Gresham, F. M., & Elliott, S. N. (2008). *Social Skills Improvement System Rating Scales*. Minneapolis, MN: Pearson Assessments.

Gresham, F. M., & Elliott, S. N. (2017). *Social Skills Improvement System Social Emotional Learning Edition Rating Forms*. Minneapolis, MN: Pearson Assessments.

Gresham, F. M., Elliott, S. N., Cook, C. R., Vance, M. J., & Kettler, R. (2010). Cross-informant agreement for ratings for social skill and problem behavior ratings: An investigation of the Social Skills Improvement System—Rating scales. *Psychological Assessment, 22*, 157–166. https://doi.org/10.1037/a0018124.

Gresham, F. M., Elliott, S. N., Metallo, S., Byrd, S., Wilson, E., & Cassidy, K. (2018). Cross-informant agreement of children's social-emotional skills: An investigation of ratings by teachers, parents, and students from a nationally representative sample. *Psychology in the Schools, 55*, 208–223. https://doi.org/10.1002/pits.22101.

Hudley, C., & Graham, S. (1993). An attributional intervention to reduce peer-directed aggression among African American boys. *Child Development, 64*, 124–138. https://doi.org/10.1111/j.1467-8624.1993.tb02899.x.

Hughes, J. N., Meehan, B., & Cavell, T. A. (2004). Development and validation of a gender-balanced measure of aggression-relevant social cognition. *Journal of Clinical Child & Adolescent Psychology*, *33*, 292–302. https://doi.org/10.1207/s15374424jccp3302_11.

Humphrey, N., Kalambouka, A., Wigelsworth, M., Lendrum, A., Deighton, J., & Wolpert, M. (2011). Measures of social and emotional skills for children and young people: A systematic review. *Educational and Psychological Measurement*, *71*, 617–637. https://doi.org/10.1177/0013164410382896.

Hymel, S., Wagner, E., & Butler, L. J. (1990). Reputational biases: View from the peer group. In S. R. Asher & J. D. Coie (Eds.), *Peer rejection in childhood* (pp. 156–186). Cambridge, England: Cambridge University Press.

Inderbitzen-Nolan, H. M., Anderson, E. R., & Johnson, H. S. (2007). Subjective versus objective behavioral ratings following two analogue tasks: A comparison of socially phobic and non-anxious adolescents. *Journal of Anxiety Disorders*, *21*(1), 76–90. https://doi.org/10.1016/j.janxdis.2006.03.013.

Junttila, N., Voeten, M., Kaukiainen, A., & Vaurus, M. (2006). Multisource assessment of children's social competence. *Educational and Psychological Measurement*, *66*, 874–895. https://doi.org/10.1177/0013164405285546.

Kwon, K., Kim, E. M., & Sheridan, S. M. (2012). A contextual approach to social skills assessment in the peer group: Who is the best to judge? *School Psychology Quarterly*, *27*, 121–133. https://doi.org/10.1037/a0028696.

Ladd, G. W. (2005). *Children's peer relations and social competence: A century of progress*. New Haven, CT: Yale University Press.

Le, T., & Beidel, D. C. (2017). Psychometric properties of a social skills assessment using a virtual environment. *Journal of Psychopathology and Behavioral Assessment*, *39*(2), 230–240. https://doi.org/10.1007/s10862-017-9589-7.

Lord, C., Rutter, M., DiLavore, P. C., Risi, S., Gotham, K., & Bishop, S. (2012). *Autism Diagnostic Observation Schedule, second edition (ADOS-2) manual (Part I): Modules 1–4*. Torrance, CA: Western Psychological Services.

Mash, E. J., & Barkley, R. A. (2003). *Child psychopathology* (2nd ed.). New York: Guilford Press.

Matson, J. L. (2010). *The Matson Evaluation of Social Skills with Youngsters-II (MESSY-II)*. Baton Rouge, LA: Disability Consultants, LLC.

Matson, J. L., Kozlowski, A. M., Neal, D., Worley, J. A., & Fodstad, J. (2011). Cutoffs for the Matson Evaluation of Social Skills with Youngsters-II (MESSY-II) for typically developing children and for children diagnosed with autism spectrum disorders. *Research in Autism Spectrum Disorders*, *5*, 798–802. https://doi.org/10.1016/j.rasd.2010.09.008.

Matson, J. L., Neal, D., Worley, J. A., Kozlowski, A. M., & Fodstad, J. C. (2012). Factor structure of the Matson Evaluation of Social Skills with Youngsters-II (MESSY-II). *Research in Developmental Disabilities*, *33*, 2067–2071. https://doi.org/10.1016/j.ridd.2010.09.026.

Mayeux, L., Underwood, M. K., & Risser, S. D. (2007). Perspectives on the ethics of sociometric research with children. *Merrill-Palmer Quarterly*, *53*, 53–78. https://doi.org/10.1353/mpq.2007.0002.

Merrell, K. W. (1994). *The Preschool and Kindergarten Behavior Scales*. Austin, TX: PRO-ED.

Merrell, K. W. (2001). Assessment of children's social skills: Recent developments, best practices, and new directions. *Exceptionality*, *9*, 3–18. https://doi.org/10.1207/S15327035EX091&2_2.

Mikami, A. Y., Huang-Pollock, C. L., Pfiffner, L. J., McBurnett, K., & Hangai, D. (2007). Social skills differences among attention-deficit/hyperactivity disorder types in a chat room assessment task. *Journal of Abnormal Child Psychology, 35*(4), 509–521. https://doi.org/10.1007/s10802-007-9108-5.

Mize, J., & Ladd, G. W. (1988). Predicting preschoolers' peer behavior and status from their interpersonal strategies: A comparison of verbal and enactive responses to hypothetical social dilemmas. *Developmental Psychology, 24*, 782–788. https://doi.org/10.1037/0012-1649.24.6.782.

Murray, D. S., Ruble, L. A., Willis, H., & Molloy, C. A. (2009). Parent and teacher report of social skills in children with autism spectrum disorders. *Language, Speech, and Hearing Services in Schools, 40*, 109–115. https://doi.org/10.1044/0161-1461(2008/07-0089).

Prinstein, M. J., Rancourt, D., Adelman, C. B., Ahlich, E., Smith, J., & Guerry, J. D. (2018). Peer status and psychopathology. In W. M. Bukowski, B. Laursen, & K. H. Rubin (Eds.), *Handbook of peer interactions, relationships, and groups* (2nd ed., pp. 617–636). New York: Guilford.

Putallaz, M. (1983). Predicting children's sociometric status from their behavior. *Child Development, 54*, 1417–1426. https://doi.org/10.1111/j.1467-8624.1983.tb00057.x.

Ratto, A. B., Turner-Brown, L., Rupp, B. M., Mesibov, G. B., & Penn, D. L. (2011). Development of the Contextual Assessment of Social Skills (CASS): A role play measure of social skill for individuals with high-functioning autism. *Journal of Autism and Developmental Disorders, 41*, 1277–1286. https://doi.org/10.1007/s10803-010-1147-z.

Renk, K., & Phares, V. (2004). Cross-informant ratings of social competence in children and adolescents. *Clinical Psychology Review, 24*, 239–254. https://doi.org/10.1016/j.cpr.2004.01.004.

Reynolds, C. R., & Kamphaus, R. W. (2015). *Behavior Assessment System for Children manual* (3rd ed.). Bloomington, MN: Pearson.

Schultz, L. S., Yeates, K. O., & Selman, R. L. (1988). *The Interpersonal Negotiations Strategies Interview: A scoring manual.* Boston: The Group for the Study of Interpersonal Development.

Segrin, C. G., & Kinney, T. (1995). Social skills deficits among the socially anxious: Rejection from others and loneliness. *Motivation and Emotion, 19*(1), 1–24.

Sparrow, S. S., Cicchetti, D. V., & Saulnier, C. A. (2016). *Vineland Adaptive Behavior Scales manual* (3rd ed.). Bloomington, MN: NCS Pearson, Inc.

Spence, S. H., Donovan, C., & Brechman-Toussaint, M. (1999). Social skills, social outcomes, and cognitive features of childhood social phobia. *Journal of Abnormal Psychology, 108*, 211–221. https://doi.org/10.1037/0021-843X.108.2.211.

Stone, W., Ruble, L., Coonrod, E., Hepburn, S., & Pennington, M. (2003). *TRIAD Social Skills Assessment manual.* Nashville, TN: Treatment and Research Institute for Autism Spectrum Disorders.

Strahan, E., & Conger, A. J. (1998). Social anxiety and its effects on performance and perception. *Journal of Anxiety Disorders, 12*(4), 293–305. https://doi.org/10.1016/S0887-6185(98)00016-4.

Valente, E. (1994). *Home Interview with Child.* Technical Report. Nashville, TN: Vanderbilt University.

Van der Oord, S., Van der Meulen, E. M., Prins, P. J. M., Oosterlaan, J., Buitelaar, J. K., & Emmelkamp, P. M. G. (2005). A psychometric evaluation of the Social Skills Rating System in children with attention deficit hyperactivity disorder. *Behaviour Research and Therapy, 43*(6), 733–746. https://doi.org/10.1016/j.brat.2004.06.004.

Wang, H. T., Sandall, S. R., Davis, C. A., & Thomas, C. J. (2011). Social skills assessment in young children with autism: A comparison evaluation of the SSRS and PKBS. *Journal of Autism and Developmental Disorders, 41*, 1487–1495. https://doi.org/10.1007/s10803-010-1175-8.

Webster, A. A., & Carter, M. (2007). Social relationships and friendships of children with developmental disabilities: A systematic review. *Journal of Intellectual and Developmental Disability, 32*, 200–213. https://doi.org/10.1080/13668250701549443.

Wong-Sarver, N., Beidel, D. C., & Spitalnik, J. (2014). The feasibility and acceptability of virtual environments in the treatment of childhood social anxiety disorder. *Journal of Clinical Child & Adolescent Psychology*, *43*, 63–73. https://doi.org/10.1080/15374416.2013.843461.

Younger, A. J., Schwartzman, A. E., & Ledingham, J. E. (1986). Age-related differences in children's perceptions of social deviance: Change in behavior or in perspective? *Developmental Psychology*, *22*, 531–542.

Chapter 5

Assessing adults

Sarah Fischer[a], Peter J. Norton[b], William Spaulding[a], and James A. Courtney[b]
[a]*University of Nebraska-Lincoln, Lincoln, NE, United States,* [b]*Monash University, Melbourne, VIC, Australia*

Social skill deficits that begin in childhood may persist into adulthood, or new social skill problems may arise in adults due to trauma, mental illness, injury, or other reasons. Issues and considerations in the assessment of social skills in adult populations are, in many ways, similar to those observed in assessing social skills in children or adolescents but can be complicated by greater difficulty in obtaining observations of naturalistic behavior and social performance. For reasons that will be described later in this chapter, most social skill assessment strategies for adults have traditionally relied on self-report or observation in analogue or role-played interactions. The strengths and limitations of each of these approaches will be discussed in detail.

The valid assessment of social skills in adults is complicated by a range of individual and group factors. These include, but are certainly not limited to, varying levels of functioning and associated social skills performance norms in adults being assessed, variations in expectations of social behavior in differing social roles, and cultural differences in expected or appropriate social behaviors. As such, assessment of social skills must be evaluated across potentially multiple performance contexts.

Due to the complicated nature of measuring social skills across settings and contexts, it is often necessary to consider varied types of assessment methods. Prior to any skill evaluation, the key to making decisions regarding the type of assessment to use is often a well-formed question. Is the priority to determine social functioning or, perhaps, to measure specific social skills? Is the individual being assessed the primary source of information, or is there the potential for collateral information from other sources? Clarifying the question at hand will provide the framework for making decisions about which method to use to assess social skills in each case.

Social Skills Across the Life Span. https://doi.org/10.1016/B978-0-12-817752-5.00005-6

General assessment methods

The methods for evaluating social skills are varied. Each method has its own unique strengths and weaknesses that are important to consider when making decisions as to which assessment method is most appropriate. Assessment tools for social skills in adults generally exist as self-report questionnaires or as systems for observing social behaviors in person. Use of a clinical interview has also been suggested as a further strategy (e.g., Meier & Hope, 1998). There are strengths and limitations inherent to each of these assessment approaches. A multimethod approach that consists of a combination of these approaches can provide a holistic overview of social skill and performance functioning, as no single assessment or method can account for all aspects of social functioning.

Self-report measures of social skills

Self-report questionnaires are the most widely used tools for assessing social skills in adults (Norton, Grills-Taquechel, & Raouf, 2010). Of particular benefit, these instruments typically can be completed quite quickly outside of an assessment session, thereby minimizing time and cost, and can be administered repeatedly to assess client progress during interventions (Nelson, 1981). Self-report measures do not directly sample behaviors or skill performance and may therefore be subject to bias due to poor insight or social desirability. Regardless, this approach is often the simplest and most quantifiable, and outcomes can be assessed against existing norms when available. Additionally, although individual measures can be limited in scope (e.g., specifically assessing assertiveness), the range of available measures affords the practitioner the ability to quickly and reliably assess clients' perceptions of their social functioning (see Nangle, Hansen, Erdley, & Norton, 2010). Available self-report assessment tools typically also offer strong psychometric evidence of reliability and validity. However, it must be noted that many of these tools were developed in the 1970s or 1980s and therefore might not align with contemporary social or situational norms, including use of mobile or internet technology. Further, these measures may reflect standards of behavior that are not appropriate for individuals of a range of diverse backgrounds (Kim, Yan, & Kulkarni, 2017; Morgan, Hsiao, Dobbins, Brown, & Lyons, 2015; Norton, Washington, Peters, & Hayes, 2010).

Global social skills

When wanting the "big picture" of social functioning, or when it is prudent to complete broad testing in order to determine an individual's strengths and weaknesses in social functioning, measures that assess global social skills may be very valuable. Several self-report instruments have been developed to assess general global social skills. These include the Interpersonal Competence Questionnaire (ICQ; Buhrmester, Furman, Wittenberg, & Reis, 1988),

Inventory of Interpersonal Problems (IIP; Horowitz, Rosenberg, Baer, Ureño, & Villaseñor, 1988), and the Social Skills Inventory (SSI; Riggio, 1986).

The 40-item Interpersonal Competence Questionnaire (ICQ; Buhrmester et al., 1988) assesses social functioning across five domains: Initiating Relationships, Disclosing Personal Information, Providing Emotional Support, Negative Assertion, and Conflict Management. Items are rated on a five-point scale, and scales are obtained by taking the average of the eight items per scale. The measure has predominantly been evaluated using undergraduate university student samples (Buhrmester et al., 1988), although one study has successfully employed the ICQ with elderly individuals with schizophrenia (Semple et al., 1999). It has been translated into multiple languages, each resulting in psychometric properties similar to the original scale, including internal consistency and a factor structure across studies (Giromini et al., 2016; Górska, 2011).

The Inventory of Interpersonal Problems (IIP) contains 127 items across two sections, the first of which is prefaced "It is hard for me to…" (78 items) and the second prefaced with "These are things I do too much…" (49 items; Horowitz et al., 1988). Items are scored on a five-point (0 = *not at all*; 4 = *extremely*) scale. Factor analysis suggests six domains are assessed (Assertiveness, Controllingness, Intimacy, Responsibility, Sociability, and Submissiveness), and a total score can be calculated. The IIP has been shown to demonstrate strong construct validity (Gurtman, 1996) and has been adapted into a 64-item version and a 32-item version. It can also be used as a pre- and posttreatment outcome measure that is sensitive to change (McFarquhar, Luyten, & Fonagy, 2018; Ruiz et al., 2004).

The Social Skills Inventory (SSI; Riggio, 1986) is a 90-item measure of general social skills across six domains: Emotional Expressivity, Emotional Sensitivity, Emotional Control, Social Expressivity, Social Sensitivity, and Social Control. Previous versions of the SSI also contained an additional 15-item Social Manipulation scale. All items are rated on a five-point (1 = *not at all like me*, 5 = *exactly like me*) scale. It was designed with the goal of understanding and measuring individual differences in social skills. It has strong test-retest reliability and acceptable to good internal consistency. The SSI has been adapted many times for specific populations and languages, including French, German, Italian, and Swedish.

Assertiveness

Arguably the most frequently sampled social skill domain among self-report measures has been assertiveness, although interest in assertiveness appears to have waned. This may be due to the publication of the DSM-III (APA, 1980) wherein the diagnosis of social phobia (now social anxiety disorder) subsumed many difficulties associated with assertive behavior. As such, many measures of social anxiety directly assess problems with assertiveness among difficulties in other social performance situations, or assess underlying fears of evaluation.

Measuring and addressing assertiveness is also a key component in several other circumstances and diagnoses. Survivors of childhood trauma often struggle to engage in an assertive interpersonal style (Cloitre, Cohen, & Koenen, 2011) due to abuse and poor modeling. Individuals diagnosed with borderline personality disorder also experience difficulty in being assertive, often instead falling into nonassertive or aggressive interpersonal strategies (Liebke et al., 2017). Unfortunately, there are few measures of assertiveness that have been recently validated. When looking to measure assertiveness in a clinical setting, it may be most useful to complete a clinical interview, asking relevant questions based on the client's situation and the evidence-based treatment literature.

Published and psychometrically evaluated measures that specifically assess assertiveness include the Rathus Assertiveness Schedule (RAS; Rathus, 1973) and the Scale for Interpersonal Behaviour (SIB; Arrindell, de Groot, & Walburg, 1984; Arrindell & van der Ende, 1985). Although each of these tools differs slightly, all generally tap into the ability or willingness of the respondent to (a) refuse unreasonable requests and (b) ask others to change their behavior.

The 30-item Rathus Assertiveness Schedule (RAS) is a widely used measure that assesses the extent to which various assertive (e.g., "When I am asked to do something, I insist upon knowing why.") and nonassertive (e.g., "I often have a hard time saying 'No.'") statements are descriptive of the respondent. Items are rated on a +3 (*very characteristic of me, extremely descriptive*) to −3 (*very uncharacteristic of me, extremely nondescriptive*) scale with no zero point. Nonassertive items are reverse-scored. The RAS has been shown to have high test-rest reliability (Rathus, 1973).

The Scale for Interpersonal Behaviour (SIB; Arrindell et al., 1984; Arrindell & van der Ende, 1985) contains 50 items describing assertive behaviors, with 46 contributing to 4 subscales: Negative Assertion, Personal Limitations, Initiative Assertiveness, and Positive Assertion. A total Assertiveness score is obtained by summing all items. Two 5-point scales are used for each item, with the first being a self-rating of distress caused by that assertive behavior, and the second assessing the likelihood of engaging in that assertive behavior. SIB scores are not affected by gender or age (Arrindell, Sanderman, & Ranchor, 1990). This measure has been validated in both inpatient (Arrindell et al., 2005) and outpatient (Arrindell & van der Ende, 1985) populations and has strong internal consistency and convergent validity.

Observational assessment of social skills

Although self-report tools are most commonly used in assessing social skills, behavioral observations are generally seen as the gold standard (Norton, Grills-Taquechel, et al., 2010; Norton, Washington, et al., 2010) as they allow for the analysis of actual, real-world social skill performance as opposed to an individual's self-reported perceptions of their social skills. While naturalistic behavioral observation is perhaps the most valuable and information-rich type of social skill assessment method, it typically is not feasible outside of institutional settings. This is due to issues of access, privacy, and consent, in that observing client behavior in various scenarios (e.g., at work, interacting with friends) would encounter a host of privacy, feasibility, and reactivity issues. For example, attempts to observe and assess the social functioning of an adult in the workplace would be limited by possible barriers to being in the workplace, privacy concerns for the individual being observed, and possible consent issues regarding others in the workplace with whom they are interacting.

Behavioral observation approaches are designed to be either structured or unstructured. Structured behavioral observations retain much of the quantifiability and norm-based referencing advantages of self-report measures, but the structured behavioral simulations may not reflect individually or culturally relevant situations. Unstructured behavioral observations allow for the most individually tailored assessment of personally and culturally relevant social performance situations, but often reflect simple molar-level assessor judgments of skill performance.

Due to the difficulties inherent in naturalistic behavioral observation, most behavior observations are done in analogue or role play, although debate exists with regard to the extent that behavior displayed in analogue settings is representative of naturalistic behavior. In nonclinical samples, for example, Segrin (1998) surreptitiously recorded participants' social behavior in a waiting room while they believed that they were waiting for a third participant to arrive (participants were later debriefed regarding the waiting room recordings and given the option to have their videos destroyed). Ratings of their social behavior were compared to those of two samples that each completed a different analogue interaction in which they had been given instructions and were informed that they were being observed. On indices of talk duration, speaking turns, gaze duration, and gaze frequency, participants in the waiting room condition showed lower social interaction than did participants in either of the other two analogue conditions. Interestingly, the interaction indices were correlated in the expected directions with a self-report measure of conversation skills only for participants in the waiting room condition, suggesting that analogue interactions may provide an overestimate of social skills when participants are aware that they are being observed.

Similarly, Gorecki, Dickson, Anderson, and Jones (1981) and Frisch and Higgins (1986) reported higher levels of assertive behavior in role-played interactions than in interactions that participants believed to be actually occurring, although St. Lawrence, Kirksey, and Moore (1983) reported no differences in assertiveness between role play and in vivo interactions among a sample of female undergraduate students selected for high or low self-reported assertiveness. In institutional settings, Monti, Corriveau, and Curran (1982) reported low correspondence between staff ratings of social skills made from observations of patient behavior in a day-hospital psychiatric setting, and ratings made during a role-played assessment test, while Curran (1982) found reasonably high correspondence between performance on a role-played assessment and naturalistic observations of psychiatric inpatients. As such, clinicians should be cognizant that there is equivocal evidence that assessments of role-played or analogue social behavior may provide an exaggerated picture of a client's typical functioning.

Role play instructions and prompts

Another issue that must be considered relates to the instructions given for the role play, as demand characteristics can impact skills performance (Meier & Hope, 1998; Norton & Hope, 2001). Nelson, Hayes, Felton, and Jarrett (1985) have demonstrated significant differences in skill performance quality when both skilled and unskilled participants are given general instructions such as "act as you normally do" versus high demand instructions such as "act as you believe a highly skilled person would do." As such, the combination of "act as you normally would" instructions may serve to assess current skill performance, whereas high demand instructions may be useful in determining either an individual's awareness of what constitutes skilled social behavior or their possible current upper limits of skill performance (Segrin, 1998).

Beyond initial instructions, the use of single or multiple prompts during the analogue assessment must also be considered. The Simulated Social Interaction Test (Curran, 1982), for example, provides a brief narrator description of a social interaction (e.g., "You have had an argument with a close friend. She says to you…" after which a confederate states "I don't want to talk about it. I'm leaving."). The participant's response to this prompt is video recorded and rated by judges. The rationale for this format, described by Curran (1982), was to be able to sample multiple different social interactions rather than a fewer number of longer duration, reduce participant and judge burden, and maintain methodological rigor as ongoing prompts could not be standardized across all possible responses to the first prompt.

Despite these advantages, it has been suggested that deficits in social skill performance may require multiple back-and-forth exchanges before they become evident (Bellack, 1983). Kirchner, Kennedy, and Draguns (1979) reported that in a study of incarcerated offenders and nonoffending community members, aggressive responses to negative social prompts in a multiprompt role play did not differ between offenders and nonoffenders after the first two prompts, but began to emerge thereafter. Unfortunately, Kirchner et al. (1979) did not report whether similar patterns existed for nonaggressive assertive responses. Galassi and Galassi (1976) did note that single-prompt methodologies yielded significantly longer participant responses than did multiple-prompt approaches.

Molar vs molecular level of analysis

The level at which ratings of social skills are made also warrants consideration, particularly in the context of the specific assessment questions. Molecular ratings are assessments of multiple specific behaviors or observations, such as eye contact, rate of speech, or use of gestures, and can be rated in terms of their occurrence, frequency, intensity, and/or duration. As ineffective or unskilled behavior can occur at both ends of the spectrum of many social behaviors, such as minimal or no verbal response and pressured speech, or lack of eye-contact versus intense staring, molecular ratings allow for a fine-grained analysis of specific skill performance difficulties that can be targeted for intervention. However, molecular ratings typically require high levels of training and would necessitate the use of audio/video recording in order to assess multiple target molecular behaviors. Additionally, molecular ratings may be more susceptible to mischaracterizing individual-level or culture-specific behaviors, like degree of eye contact or use of nonverbal gestures that can differ across people of different ethnic and cultural backgrounds (Norton, Grills-Taquechel, et al., 2010; Norton, Washington, et al., 2010). Finally, some (e.g., Conger & Conger, 1986) have questioned the extent to which molecular assessments fully capture the gestalt of social performance.

Molar ratings, on the other hand, are a single rating of global skill performance or a specific skill domain such as assertiveness. Molar ratings are most common in analogue assessment methodologies (see later), due to their simplicity and ability to gauge overall skill performance, although they lack the ability to identify specific factors contributing to skilled or unskilled performances. Indeed, studies (e.g., Conger & Farrell, 1981) and reviews (e.g., Bellack, 1983; Norton, Grills-Taquechel, et al., 2010; Norton, Washington, et al., 2010) have identified that eye contact and verbal content are the predominant contributors to molar ratings, and that deficits in other molecular behaviors may therefore be underidentified through molar ratings. Optimally, a combination of molar- and molecular-level assessments could be employed sequentially, as needed. Molar assessments could be made initially to identify the extent to which poor performance is apparent, followed by molecular-level analyses of specific behaviors or characteristics to help identify contributors.

Standardized vs individualized role play formats

A final consideration in selecting or designing an analogue observational assessment for social skills focuses on the extent to which the role-played social scenarios are standardized or individualized to the person being assessed. Individualized scenarios hold clear appeal in that they would have direct relevance to the individual's current environment and can better reflect a diverse range of individual factors than can predetermined or standardized scenarios. Individualized scenarios, however, make it difficult, if not impossible, to benchmark ratings with established norms in order to assess the extent to which performance or behaviors compares with others. Standardized role plays, in contrast, often provide norms or benchmarks against which individual scores can be compared. Published standardized assessments also typically adopt scoring systems that have established psychometric strengths, as well as established scenarios that cover a range of common interactions and elicit specific social skills.

However, even highly generic social scenarios (e.g., asking someone out on a date) may contravene or not capture individual differences (e.g., religious or cultural proscriptions regarding dating). As with instructional demands and molar/molecular levels of analyses, a combination of standardized and individualized scenarios may be optimal.

One assessment tool, the Ideographic Role Play Test (IRP; Kern, 1991a, 1991b), attempts to bridge the structured versus individualized gap by asking participants to describe examples of six types of assertion scenarios (e.g., being requested to do something undesirable) from their recent personal experience. Each situation is role-played with a trained partner and is scored on a six-point scale from total assertiveness to total submission or aggression. Although Kern (1991a) reported excellent reliability and concurrent validity using the IRP, no norms were presented and no copies of the manual (Kern, 1991b) can be located through academic or global databases.

Published behavioral observational assessments of social skills

Several published and evaluated behavioral observation assessments have been reported in the literature and are described now. Only systems designed for clinical use—that is, not specifically designed for use solely in a research study—and for which published norms are available have been included. Due to their clinical nature, these assessments likely focus on deficits and may not be appropriate for individuals in nonclinical populations. It should be noted that the most recently developed of these systems are approximately three decades old, and the extent to which the scenarios reflect contemporary social interactions is unclear. Several other assessments, including the Social Skill Behavioral Assessment System (Caballo & Buela, 1988), Social Interaction Test (Trower, Bryant, & Argyle, 1978), and Behavioral Role Playing Assertion Test (McFall & Lillesand, 1971), were either developed for a specific research assessment or do not currently have available norms.

Standardized behavioral observation

Multiple standardized observation assessments of social skills in adults have been developed, including the Assessment of Interpersonal Problem-Solving Skills (AIPSS; Donahoe et al., 1990), Behavioral Assertiveness Test—Revised (BAT-R; Eisler, Hersen, Miller, & Blanchard, 1975), and the Simulated Social Interaction Test (SSIT; Curran, 1982).

The Assessment of Interpersonal Problem-Solving Skills (AIPSS; Donahoe et al., 1990) is an assessment consisting of 13 videotaped scenes depicting various social interactions. In 10 of the scenes, interpersonal problems are depicted between the actors. For each scene, the individual being assessed is asked to identify with one of the actors, detect if there was an interpersonal problem, propose how they would respond as one of the actors, and then role play the proposed solution. A relatively complex scoring system is used for assessing identification of a problem, describing the problem, processing a solution to the problem, verbal content of the role-played re-enactment, performance of the role-played re-enactment, and overall role play effectiveness. Norms for nonclinical individuals and adult male patients with schizophrenia are available (Donahoe et al., 1990; Grant, Addington, Addington, & Konnert, 2001). No norms are available for other skill-impaired populations. Donahoe et al. (1990) reported good psychometric estimates.

The 32-situation Behavioral Assertiveness Test-Revised (BAT-R) consists of a range of written single-prompt standardized social scenarios that are narrated to the participant. Participants are asked to imagine themselves in each situation and, when prompted, respond as they normally would. Scenarios cover a range of situations requiring positive or negative assertion, and vary by the gender and familiarity level of the imagined other. Participant responses are video recorded and scored by trained independent judges on a molar index of overall assertiveness, molecular ratings of nonverbal behaviors, and specific negative and positive assertion behaviors are identified. Norms for high and low assertive male psychiatric patients are available (Eisler et al., 1975), and strong psychometric estimates have been reported for psychiatric inpatients, individuals in treatment for alcohol use, and college students across a number of studies (e.g., Bellack, Hersen, & Turner, 1979; Pachman, Foy, Massey, & Eisler, 1978). No contemporary norms or psychometric evaluations have been reported.

The Simulated Social Interaction Test (SSIT; Curran, 1982) comprises 12 single-prompt role-played scenarios, 4 of which are for practice and 8 are scored. Each scenario is narrated, and a single prompt is delivered by a role-play partner, the gender of whom varies across scenarios. Scenarios cover a range of social situations, including heterosexual interaction, interpersonal loss, receiving criticism or rejection, and receiving compliments. Both participants themselves and trained judges rate each response on two 11-point molar scales assessing social effectiveness and social anxiety, respectively. Norms for nonclinical adults and male psychiatric inpatients are available (Curran, Wessberg, Monti, Corriveau, & Coyne, 1980), and strong psychometric estimates have been reported across multiple studies (Curran, 1982; Curran et al., 1980), although no contemporary psychometric data have been published.

Interview-based assessment of social skills

Only one semistructured clinical interview for assessing social skills has been presented in the literature (untitled interview; Meier & Hope, 1998); however, it has not been subjected to any evaluations of reliability or validity. The clinical interview questions begin with obtaining a social functioning history to identify possible recurrent themes or problems. The nature, number, and closeness of friendships in childhood, adolescence, and adulthood are explored, as are the number, frequency, and success of intimate or romantic relationships.

The second section involves questions regarding the types of social situations and relationships in which the individual feels he or she has difficulties, including work or school, home, public places, recreational settings, and dating or sexual relationships. Within each identified area of difficulty, the interviewer explores how the individual interacts with a range of same- and opposite-gender individuals, such as friends, coworkers, bosses, children, or professionals, in those situations. Further, in each area described as difficult, individuals are asked to recount the most recent time that they were in that situation, including antecedents, goals, or motivations for the situation, perceptions of their verbal and nonverbal performance, and the outcomes of the situation, as well as an exploration of their views of what they may have done differently to achieve a more successful or positive outcome. Finally, interviewees are asked to rank-order the identified situations according to their perceived difficulty as a basis for treatment planning (Meier & Hope, 1998). The goals that are created based on the information gathered during the interview will then be consistently revisited and updated. No scoring instructions are provided by the authors.

Assessing social skills in skill-impaired populations

In certain populations, including individuals with autism spectrum disorder (ASD), intellectual disability (ID), and schizophrenia, impairments or deficits in social functioning are typical. ASD, by definition, is characterized by "persistent deficits in social communication and social interaction across multiple contexts" (APA, 2013, p. 61), whereas ID and schizophrenia both frequently present with social skill deficits. Although ASD and ID are typically diagnosed in childhood, accurate assessment of social functioning in adulthood remains critical for both intervention planning and determining level of support that may be necessary for optimal care and independent living (Lecavalier & Butter, 2010). This is especially true given that researchers are becoming more interested in individual differences and determining how to use a person's strengths to compensate for deficits (e.g., Livingston, Colvert, Bolton, Social Relationships Study Team, & Happé, 2019).

Although each of these diagnoses carries unique differences in the types of deficits and the presumed impairments leading to the deficits (see Fakhoury, 2015; Lecavalier & Butter, 2010), an emerging common theme is that skill assessment tools developed for nondisordered or typically developing adults may not be appropriate or sufficiently sensitive to adequately assess social functioning in these populations (Gerhardt & Mayville, 2010). As such, social skill and functioning assessments for individuals with each of these diagnoses have been developed.

Autism spectrum disorder and intellectual disability

The Adaptive Behavior Assessment System-3rd Edition (ABAS-3; Harrison & Oakland, 2015) is a rating scale, which, in the Adult form, is designed to assess adaptive behaviors in adults aged 16–89 years. The ABAS-3 is designed to assess adaptive behavior across a range of populations, including individuals with ASD and ID. The ABAS-3 has an extensive psychometric and normative base. The Adult form can be administered as a self-report measure. Separate Parent and Teacher forms may be used with adults up to the age of 21. Conceptual, Social, and Practical domain composite scores are derived, along with 11 adaptive skill areas (depending on the specific form and age group).

The Vineland Adaptive Behavior Scales—3rd Edition (VABS-3; Sparrow, Cicchetti, & Saulnier, 2016) are arguably the most widely used measures of adaptive behavior (Burger-Caplan, Saulnier, & Sparrow, 2018). The VABS-3 assesses three domains of adaptive behaviors: communication, daily living, and socialization, with an additional optional motor skills assessment. The VABS is available in interview, parent/caregiver rating scale, and teacher rating scale forms, with the former two being applicable for adults up to 90 years of age. The teacher rating scales are applicable up to age 21. Although developed for the assessment of adaptive behavior in individuals with ID, the VABS-3 has been used clinically and in research with individuals with other developmental disorders including ASD (see Gerhardt & Mayville, 2010). The VABS-3 has extensive standardization and psychometric data (Burger-Caplan et al., 2018).

Other commonly used rating scales of social skills in adults with ID include the Matson Evaluation of Social Skills for Individuals with Severe Mental Retardation (MESSIER; Matson, 1995; Matson & Boisjoli, 2008) for adults with severe ID, and the Social Performance Survey Schedule—Revised (SPSS-R; Matson, Helsel, Bellack, & Senatore, 1983) for adults with mild-to-moderate ID and traumatic brain injury (Long, McDonald, Tate, Togher, & Bornhofen, 2008).

Schizophrenia

Individuals diagnosed with a schizophrenia spectrum disorder often experience unique social cognition deficits and circumstances that may result in lost opportunities to develop social skills (e.g., long-term hospitalization). Select measures are uniquely appropriate to measure these deficits. The Social Functioning Scale (SFS; Birchwood, Smith, Cochrane, Wetton, & Copestake, 1990) is a 71- to 79-item questionnaire that was specifically developed to assess occupational and social functioning of individuals with diagnosed serious mental illnesses. Some evidence suggests that the SFS may show ceiling effects on several domains when assessing nonclinical samples (Schneider, Reininghaus, van Nierop, Janssens, Myin-Germeys, & GROUP Investigators, 2017). It assesses functioning in domains necessary for independent living, including employment, independent-competence, independent-performance, interpersonal behaviors, prosocial activities, recreation, and social engagement/withdrawal. Both self-report and informant-report versions have been evaluated and show a high degree of concordance (Dickerson, Ringel, & Parente, 1997). Multiple studies support the psychometric characteristics of the SFS (e.g., Dickerson, Parente, & Ringel, 2000), and separate norms based on nonclinical controls and both first-episode and multiepisode individuals with a diagnosis of schizophrenia.

One analogue assessment protocol has been specifically developed for use with individuals experiencing schizophrenia and other serious mental illness that may result in social functioning deficits, the Maryland Assessment of Social Competence (MASC; Bellack & Thomas-Lohrman, 2003). Four scenarios are enacted: initiating a conversation with a casual acquaintance, a discussion with a healthcare worker, a conversation where the respondent must assert his/her rights, and a conversation requiring compromise, each of which can be adapted to specific client contexts. The MASC is delivered in a multiple prompt/response format, with the nonassessed role-play actor given the option of multiple ongoing prompts or responses based on the client's responses. Ratings are made from a video recording of the interactions, and verbal skills, nonverbal skills, and overall social effectiveness ratings are made on five-point scales. Two studies (Bellack & Thomas-Lohrman, 2003; Bellack et al., 2004) report good psychometrics characteristics of the MASC among individuals with serious mental illness.

Finally, the Time-Sample Behavioral Checklist and Staff-Resident Interaction Chronograph (TSBC/SRIC; Paul, 1987, 1988) is an extensive observational coding system for use on inpatient units that requires extensive training. The systems assess 69 specific behaviors across 7 domains (TSBC) and 94 codes for patient/staff interactions. Together, the TSCB/SRIC has been reported to predict successful discharge and postdischarge community function with an extremely high degree of accuracy (Paul, 2000), but the number of observers and the amount of required training and coding limit the feasibility of employing the TSBC/SRIC in many settings.

Measures of social cognition

Of special interest in the last decade is the proliferation of research related to the concept of social cognition, which primarily consists of the ability to recognize and understand the emotions and intentions of others, and forms the foundation on which other social skills can build. One study found that social cognitive ability (measured at pre- and posttraining), along with demographic characteristics, was a strong predictor of functional social skills (Sasson, Morrison, Kelsven, & Pinkham, 2019). Most measures of social cognition are designed for the laboratory, although many can be used in a clinical setting as well when appropriate.

The Social Cognition Psychometric Evaluation Study (SCOPE; Pinkham et al., 2013; Pinkham, Harvey, & Penn, 2017) is a large-scale study that aims to identify psychometrically strong measures of social cognition, and through expert panels has identified four primary domains of social cognition into the following categories: emotion processing, social perception, theory of mind, and attribution style/bias (Pinkham et al., 2013). SCOPE, along with other reviews (Morrison et al., 2019), have identified key measures for evaluation and improvement.

Clinically relevant emotion processing measures, such as the Bell Lysaker Emotion Recognition Task (BLERT; Bryson, Bell, & Lysaker, 1997) and the Penn Emotion Recognition Task (ER-40; Kohler et al., 2003), utilize computer static and dynamic images to assess the ability to identify emotional expression in human faces. The BLERT was originally designed to assess emotion recognition in individuals diagnosed with schizophrenia, but has since been used with adults with ASD and normative community samples. It is composed of dynamic images of emotional expressions. The BLERT has demonstrated good reliability, validity, and stability. The ER-40 also targets emotion recognition in faces, but it uses static images to do so. Like the BLERT, the ER-40 was originally used with individuals diagnosed with schizophrenia but has also been used in other populations, such as those with ASD.

Key measures of social perception include the Relationships Across Domains task (RAD; Sergi et al., 2009) and the Benton facial recognition task (Benton et al., 1994). The RAD is designed for measuring relationship perception in healthy individuals and individuals diagnosed with schizophrenia. It consists of questions regarding 25 vignettes; participants are asked to identify how the subjects of the vignettes are connected. The RAD demonstrates good internal consistency in outpatient participants with schizophrenia and healthy controls. The Benton facial recognition task is a well-established and widely used measure that has long been used to assess impairments in facial recognition in participants with brain legions. It has also recently been tested in normative samples (Rossion & Michel, 2018), tested with individuals diagnosed with congenital prosopagnosia (Palermo et al., 2017), and adapted for individuals with traumatic brain injuries (Rigon, Voss, Turkstra, Mutlu, & Duff, 2018).

Theory of Mind, the concept that one knows that others have distinct mental states (e.g., beliefs, emotions), is a deficit seen in several populations, most notably in individuals diagnosed with ASD. Common measures of interest for Theory of Mind include the awareness of social inference task (TASIT; McDonald, Flanagan, Rollins, & Kinch, 2003; McDonald et al., 2006), the hinting task (Corcoran & Frith, 2003), the reading the mind in the eyes task (RMET; Baron-Cohen, Wheelwright, Hill, Raste, & Plumb, 2001), and the cartoon theory of mind intentions subscale (CToM Intentions; Brüne, 2003).

The TASIT measure is a three-part Theory of Mind/social perception task that assesses emotion recognition and the ability to recognize and differentiate comments that are meant to be taken literally or nonliterally. It has primarily been used in normative samples and in individuals with a traumatic brain injury (McDonald, 2012; McDonald et al., 2006). The hinting task is perhaps one of the most well-known and often-used measures of Theory of Mind, and is primarily used with individuals with psychosis (Lindgren et al., 2018; Mallawaarachchi, Cotton, Anderson, Killackey, & Allott, 2019) and schizophrenia (Bora, Yucel, & Pantelis, 2009). The hinting task may be the easiest to use in a clinical setting.

The RMET is another very commonly used measure with good test-retest validity (Fernández-Abascal, Cabello, Fernández-Berrocal, & Baron-Cohen, 2013) that has been widely employed across populations, including healthy controls, individuals with ASD (Baron-Cohen et al., 2001), individuals that demonstrate psychopathy (Richell et al., 2003), and individuals with borderline personality disorder (Fertuck et al., 2009). Some recent research suggests that the RMET is not sensitive enough for normative samples (Black, 2019) and is vulnerable to the confound of gender (Kynast & Schroeter, 2018).

Attribution style is the way in which individuals attribute the causes of events in their lives to themselves, others, and the environment/luck. One commonly used measure of attribution style is the ambiguous intentions and hostility questionnaire (AIHQ; Combs, Penn, Wicher, & Waldheter, 2007), which specifically targets the social cognitive basis for paranoia. The intended population is anyone that tends to experience paranoia and increased hostility, especially when paired with psychosis proneness. It has been found to have adequate internal consistency and test-retest reliability and was able to distinguish controls from individuals diagnosed with schizophrenia (Buck et al., 2017) and individuals with persecutory delusions or ideas (Combs et al., 2009).

Other factors to consider

When assessing social skills in adults, there are several factors that are crucial to consider, including culture (see Norton, Grills-Taquechel, et al., 2010; Norton, Washington, et al., 2010), environmental factors, gender and gender roles, and the wide adoption of the internet and mobile technologies. The importance of culture cannot be overstated. Consider, for example, an individual from a more socially reserved collectivistic culture who has recently moved to the United States. The social expectations of behavior and social performance would likely differ between this individual interacting with extended family and her social behavior with her coworkers or new friends. If we were to assess her social skills using only measures designed for white, male, English-speaking individuals, we would not be able to ascertain the full extent of her social skills.

Culture and context can impact social priorities, habits, and skills. For example, Chinese mothers and European mothers have been found to endorse different values in regard to their children's social skills and habits (Cheah & Rubin, 2003). This can also include language; assessments that are translated should be independently validated to ensure that the psychometric properties are sound, and the experiments avoid bias that comes with using measurements that do not appropriately measure constructs in that culture (He & van de Vijver, 2012). Nonverbal social behavior differs across cultures as well (Poyatos, 1988). Specific molecular social behaviors, such as eye contact, rate of speech, and gestural intensity, can also differ considerably across various cultural groups (Norton, Washington, et al., 2010).

Other environmental factors are also important to consider. For instance, trauma, especially childhood trauma, can impact social development in fundamental ways (Cloitre et al., 2011). Gender and gender roles must be accounted for as well. Socioeconomic status has also been shown to impact facets of social development, such as evidence suggesting that social emotional scores fluctuate with the combined effects of SES and ethnicity (Kuo, Casillas, Walton, Way, & Moore, 2020). Other diversity factors, such as special group status, age or generation, acculturation, LGBTQ group membership, and so forth, may also be worth considering when choosing an assessment, as well as when choosing an assessment, and are important to recognize as they may relate to potential biases during observational measurement (Norton, Grills-Taquechel, et al., 2010; Norton, Washington, et al., 2010).

Moving forward, it is anticipated that mobile data collection will become increasingly popular. While arguably in its infancy, mobile self-report assessment can provide more detailed and accurate information than typical self-report mechanisms. Mobile assessment tools can also often supply immediate feedback, connect to the researcher or treatment team, and capture real-time changes in social ability, offering valuable information regarding how the environment impacts social ability (Granholm, Ben-Zeev, Link, Bradshaw, & Holden, 2011; Moore et al., 2015). Generally speaking, the use of technology is becoming more prevalent in the world of social skill assessment and training. Virtual reality has been especially promising, allowing for in vivo observations and practice without having to actually be in vivo. Recent projects include social cognition training for children (Didehbani, Allen, Kandalaft, Krawczyk, & Chapman, 2016; Moon & Ke, 2019) and young adults (Yang et al., 2017) with ASD, individuals diagnosed with schizophrenia (Rus-Calafell, Gutiérrez-Maldonado, & Ribas-Sabaté, 2014), and even training programs designed for managers and sales representatives (Taupiac, Rodriguez, Strauss, & Beney, 2019). Current trends seem to be focused on training and treatment. However, programs that use VR to assess social skills is a growing field.

Conclusions and summary

This chapter has reviewed the assessment of social skills in adult populations and highlighted the issues involved in obtaining observations of naturalistic behavior and social performance. When compared to assessing similar domains in children, adult assessment is complicated by a number of specific factors that underpin a preference to rely on self-report or analogue observational-based methodologies. While potentially appealing, these approaches are likewise complicated, resulting in the need to evaluate skills across multiple performance domains. Although numerous assessment instruments have been developed to assist in this context, limitations can be identified in most, leading to the conclusion that a combination of approaches is required to provide a more holistic and meaningful assessment outcome.

Another important consideration relates to the age of available assessment tools and published norms. Indeed, much of the literature in this field was published in the last century with some notable exceptions. This challenges the clinician to select or exclude specific instruments on the basis of contemporary application. Factors related to sociocultural progressions in the global community should continue to be at the forefront as new social skill measures are created and old ones are adapted and used. At this time, available measures might not accurately assess current social values, standards, and expected behaviors. In contrast, a more progressive approach to assessing social skills in special needs groups is reflected through the development of some more contemporary measures; namely, the ABAS-3 (Harrison & Oakland, 2015) and the VBAS-3 (Sparrow et al., 2016), both described in the preceding section. Unfortunately, there is relatively less development in the context of assessing social skills in individuals with schizophrenia or for inpatient settings (e.g., the NOSIE-30 was published in 1965), despite changes in psychiatric management and movements in the social conceptualization of these conditions.

In sum, there are a number of assessment tools available to the clinician to assist in the assessment of social skills in adult populations, including those with special needs. This chapter presents some of the challenges inherent in the selection of strategy and approach and limitations relevant to the assessment context and applicability of measures. Social skills are varied and complex, and the clinician must have a question in mind when choosing an assessment, whether that involves establishing a client's broad level of social functioning or evaluating specific facets of social functioning. It is vital that the central role of the clinician is observed in the assessment process such that formal measures are carefully selected on an informed basis to assist and not replace careful diagnosis and intervention.

References

American Psychiatric Association. (1980). *Diagnostic and statistical manual of mental disorders* (3rd ed.). Washington, DC: American Psychiatric Association.

American Psychiatric Association. (2013). *Diagnostic and statistical manual of mental disorders* (5th ed.). Arlington, VA: Author.

Arrindell, W. A., Akkerman, A., van der Ende, J., Schreurs, P. J., Brugman, A., Stewart, R. E., … Sanderman, R. (2005). Normative studies with the Scale for Interpersonal Behaviour (SIB): III. Psychiatric inpatients. *Personality and Individual Differences*, *38*, 941–952. https://doi.org/10.1016/j.paid.2004.06.019.

Arrindell, W. A., de Groot, P. M., & Walburg, J. A. *De Schaal voor Interpersoonlijk Gedrag (SIG). Handleiding deel 1* [The Scale for Interpersonal Behaviour (SIB). Test manual, part I]. (1984). Lisse, The Netherlands: Swets & Zeitlinger.

Arrindell, W. A., Sanderman, R., & Ranchor, A. (1990). The Scale for Interpersonal Behaviour and the Wolpe-Lazarus Assertiveness Scale: A correlational comparison in a non-clinical sample. *Personality and Individual Differences*, *11*, 509–513. https://doi.org/10.1016/0191-8869(90)90064-X.

Arrindell, W. A., & van der Ende, J. (1985). Cross-sample invariance of the structure of self-reported distress and difficulty in assertiveness: Experiences with the Scale for Interpersonal Behaviour. *Advances in Behaviour Research and Therapy*, *7*, 205–243. https://doi.org/10.1016/0146-6402(85)90013-X.

Baron-Cohen, S., Wheelwright, S., Hill, J., Raste, Y., & Plumb, I. (2001). The "Reading the Mind in the Eyes" test revised version: A study with normal adults, and adults with Asperger syndrome or high-functioning autism. *The Journal of Child Psychology and Psychiatry and Allied Disciplines*, *42*, 241–251. https://doi.org/10.1111/1469-7610.00715.

Bellack, A. S. (1983). Recurrent problems in the behavioral assessment of social skill. *Behaviour Research and Therapy*, *21*, 29–41. https://doi.org/10.1016/0005-7967(83)90123-7.

Bellack, A. S., Hersen, M., & Turner, S. M. (1979). The relationship of role playing and knowledge of appropriate behavior to assertion in the natural environment. *Journal of Consulting and Clinical Psychology*, *47*, 670–678. https://doi.org/10.1037/0022-006X.47.4.670.

Bellack, A. S., Schooler, N. R., Marder, S. R., Kane, J. M., Brown, C. H., & Yang, Y. (2004). Do clozapine and risperidone affect social competence and problem solving? *American Journal of Psychiatry*, *161*, 364–367. https://doi.org/10.1176/appi.ajp.161.2.364.

Bellack, A. S., & Thomas-Lohrman, S. (2003). *Maryland Assessment of Social Competence*. Baltimore, MD: Unpublished assessment manual.

Benton, A. L., Abigail, B., Sivan, A. B., Hamsher, K. D., Varney, N. R., & Spreen, O. (1994). *Contributions to neuropsychological assessment: A clinical manual*. USA: Oxford University Press. https://doi.org/10.1037/021683.

Birchwood, M., Smith, J., Cochrane, R., Wetton, S., & Copestake, S. (1990). The Social Functioning Scale: The development and validation of a new scale of social adjustment for use in family intervention programs with schizophrenic patients. *British Journal of Psychiatry*, *157*, 853–859. https://doi.org/10.1192/bjp.157.6.853.

Black, J. E. (2019). An IRT analysis of the Reading the Mind in the Eyes test. *Journal of Personality Assessment*, *101*, 425–433. https://doi.org/10.1080/00223891.2018.1447946.

Bora, E., Yucel, M., & Pantelis, C. (2009). Theory of mind impairment in schizophrenia: Meta-analysis. *Schizophrenia Research*, *109*, 1–9. https://doi.org/10.1016/j.schres.2008.12.020.

Brüne, M. (2003). Theory of mind and the role of IQ in chronic disorganized schizophrenia. *Schizophrenia Research*, *60*, 57–64. https://doi.org/10.1016/S0920-9964(02)00162-7.

Bryson, G., Bell, M., & Lysaker, P. (1997). Affect recognition in schizophrenia: A function of global impairment or a specific cognitive deficit. *Psychiatry Research*, *71*, 105–113. https://doi.org/10.1016/S0165-1781(97)00050-4.

Buck, B., Iwanski, C., Healey, K. M., Green, M. F., Horan, W. P., Kern, R. S., … Penn, D. L. (2017). Improving measurement of attributional style in schizophrenia: A psychometric evaluation of the Ambiguous Intentions Hostility Questionnaire (AIHQ). *Journal of Psychiatric Research*, *89*, 48–54. https://doi.org/10.1016/j.jpsychires.2017.01.004.

Buhrmester, D., Furman, W., Wittenberg, M. T., & Reis, H. T. (1988). Five domains of interpersonal competence in peer relationships. *Journal of Personality and Social Psychology*, *55*, 991–1008. https://doi.org/10.1037//0022-3514.55.6.991.

Burger-Caplan, R., Saulnier, C. A., & Sparrow, S. S. (2018). Vineland adaptive behavior scales. In J. Kreutzer, J. DeLuca, & B. Caplan (Eds.), *Encyclopedia of clinical neuropsychology* (2nd ed.). New York: Springer. https://doi.org/10.1007/springrreference_184293.

Caballo, V. E., & Buela, G. (1988). Molar/molecular assessment in an analogue situation: Relationships among several measures and validation of a behavioral assessment instrument. *Perceptual and Motor Skills*, *67*, 591–602. https://doi.org/10.2466/pms.1988.67.2.591.

Cheah, C., & Rubin, K. H. (2003). European American and Mainland Chinese mothers' socialization beliefs regarding preschoolers' social skills. *Parenting*, *3*(1), 1–21. https://doi.org/10.1207/S15327922PAR0301_01.

Cloitre, M., Cohen, L. R., & Koenen, K. C. (2011). *Treating survivors of childhood abuse: Psychotherapy for the interrupted life*. New York: The Guilford Press. https://doi.org/10.1037/e517322011-039.

Combs, D. R., Penn, D. L., Michael, C. O., Basso, M. R., Wiedeman, R., Siebenmorgan, M., … Chapman, D. (2009). Perceptions of hostility by persons with and without persecutory delusions. *Cognitive Neuropsychiatry*, *14*, 30–52. https://doi.org/10.1080/13546800902732970.

Combs, D. R., Penn, D. L., Wicher, M., & Waldheter, E. (2007). The Ambiguous Intentions Hostility Questionnaire (AIHQ): A new measure for evaluating hostile social-cognitive biases in paranoia. *Cognitive Neuropsychiatry*, *12*, 128–143. https://doi.org/10.1080/13546800600787854.

Conger, J. C., & Conger, A. J. (1986). Assessment of social skills. In A. R. Ciminero, K. S. Calhoun, & H. E. Adams (Eds.), *Handbook of behavioral assessment* (2nd ed., pp. 526–560). New York: John Wiley & Sons. https://doi.org/10.3928/0279-3695-19870801-18.

Conger, J. C., & Farrell, A. D. (1981). Behavioral components of heterosocial skills. *Behavior Therapy*, *12*, 41–55. https://doi.org/10.1016/S0005-7894(81)80105-0.

Corcoran, R., & Frith, C. D. (2003). Autobiographical memory and theory of mind: Evidence of a relationship in schizophrenia. *Psychological Medicine*, *33*(5), 897–905. https://doi.org/10.1017/s0033291703007529.

Curran, J. P. (1982). A procedure for the assessment of social skills: The simulated social interaction test. In J. P. Curran & P. M. Monti (Eds.), *Social skills training: A practical handbook for assessment and treatment* (pp. 348–373). New York: The Guilford Press. https://doi.org/10.1017/S0141347300011137.

Curran, J. P., Wessberg, H. W., Monti, P. M., Corriveau, D. P., & Coyne, N. A. (1980). *Patients versus controls on a social skills/anxiety role-play test*. In *Paper presented at the 88th annual convention of the American Psychological Convention, Montreal, Quebec, Canada*.

Dickerson, F. B., Parente, F., & Ringel, N. (2000). The relationship among three measures of social functioning in outpatients with schizophrenia. *Journal of Clinical Psychology*, *56*, 1509–1519. https://doi.org/10.1002/1097-4679(200012)56:12<1509::AID-3>3.0.CO;2-J.

Dickerson, F. B., Ringel, N. B., & Parente, F. (1997). Ratings of social functioning in outpatients with schizophrenia: Patient self-report versus caregiver assessment. *Evaluation and Program Planning*, *20*, 415–420. https://doi.org/10.1016/S0149-7189(97)00020-7.

Didehbani, N., Allen, T., Kandalaft, M., Krawczyk, D., & Chapman, S. (2016). Virtual reality social cognition training for children with high functioning autism. *Computers in Human Behavior*, *62*, 703–711. https://doi.org/10.1016/j.chb.2016.04.033.

Donahoe, C. P., Carter, M. J., Bloem, W. D., Hirsch, G. L., Laasi, N., & Wallace, C. J. (1990). Assessment of interpersonal problem-solving skills. *Psychiatry*, *53*, 329–339. https://doi.org/10.1080/00332747.1990.11024517.

Eisler, R. M., Hersen, M., Miller, P. M., & Blanchard, E. B. (1975). Situational determinants of assertive behaviors. *Journal of Consulting and Clinical Psychology*, *43*, 330–340. https://doi.org/10.1016/B978-0-08-023719-0.50045-0.

Fakhoury, M. (2015). Autistic spectrum disorders: A review of clinical features, theories and diagnosis. *International Journal of Developmental Neuroscience*, *43*, 70–77. https://doi.org/10.1016/j.ijdevneu.2015.04.003.

Fernández-Abascal, E. G., Cabello, R., Fernández-Berrocal, P., & Baron-Cohen, S. (2013). Test-retest reliability of the 'Reading the Mind in the Eyes' test: A one-year follow-up study. *Molecular Autism*, *4*, 33. https://doi.org/10.1186/2040-2392-4-33.

Fertuck, E. A., Jekal, A., Song, I., Wyman, B., Morris, M. C., Wilson, S. T., … Stanley, B. (2009). Enhanced 'Reading the Mind in the Eyes' in borderline personality disorder compared to healthy controls. *Psychological Medicine*, *39*, 1979–1988. https://doi.org/10.1017/S003329170900600X.

Frisch, M. B., & Higgins, R. L. (1986). Instructional demand effects and the correspondence among role-play, self-report, and naturalistic measures of social skill. *Behavioral Assessment*, *8*, 221–236.

Galassi, M. D., & Galassi, J. P. (1976). The effects of role playing variations on the assessment of assertive behavior. *Behavior Therapy*, *7*, 343–347. https://doi.org/10.1016/S0005-7894(76)80061-5.

Gerhardt, P. F., & Mayville, E. (2010). Assessment of social skills and social competence in learners with autism spectrum disorders. In D. W. Nangle, D. J. Hansen, C. A. Erdley, & P. J. Norton (Eds.), *Practitioner's guide to empirically based measures of social skills* (pp. 193–206). New York: Springer. https://doi.org/10.1007/978-1-4419-0609-0_13.

Giromini, L., de Campora, G., Brusadelli, E., D'Onofrio, E., Zennaro, A., Zavattini, G. C., & Lang, M. (2016). Validity and reliability of the Interpersonal Competence Questionnaire: Empirical evidence from an Italian study. *Journal of Psychopathology and Behavioral Assessment*, *38*, 113–123. https://doi.org/10.1007/s10862-015-9499-5.

Gorecki, P. R., Dickson, A. L., Anderson, H. N., & Jones, G. E. (1981). Relationship between contrived in vivo and role-play assertive behavior. *Journal of Clinical Psychology*, *37*, 104–107. https://doi.org/10.1002/1097-4679(198101)37:1<104::aid-jclp2270370119>3.0.co;2-1.

Górska, M. (2011). Psychometric properties of the Polish version of the Interpersonal Competence Questionnaire (ICQ-R). *European Journal of Psychological Assessment*, *27*, 186–192. https://doi.org/10.1027/1015-5759/a000066.

Granholm, E., Ben-Zeev, D., Link, P. C., Bradshaw, K. R., & Holden, J. L. (2011). Mobile Assessment and Treatment for Schizophrenia (MATS): A pilot trial of an interactive text-messaging intervention for medication adherence, socialization, and auditory hallucinations. *Schizophrenia Bulletin*, *38*, 414–425. https://doi.org/10.1093/schbul/sbr155.

Grant, C., Addington, J., Addington, D., & Konnert, C. (2001). Social functioning in first- and multi-episode schizophrenia. *Canadian Journal of Psychiatry*, *46*, 746–749. https://doi.org/10.1177/070674370104600808.

Gurtman, M. B. (1996). Interpersonal problems and the psychotherapy context: The construct validity of the inventory of interpersonal problems. *Psychological Assessment*, *8*, 241. https://doi.org/10.1037/1040-3590.8.3.241.

Harrison, P. L., & Oakland, T. (2015). *ABAS-3: Adaptive Behavior Assessment System* (3rd ed.). Torrance, CA: Western Psychological Services.

He, J., & van de Vijver, F. (2012). Bias and equivalence in cross-cultural research. *Online Readings in Psychology and Culture*, *2*(2), 8. https://doi.org/10.9707/2307-0919.1111.

Horowitz, L. M., Rosenberg, S. E., Baer, B. A., Ureño, G., & Villaseñor, V. S. (1988). Inventory of interpersonal problems: Psychometric properties and clinical applications. *Journal of Consulting and Clinical Psychology*, *56*, 885–892. https://doi.org/10.1037//0022-006x.56.6.885.

Kern, J. M. (1991a). An evaluation of a novel role-play methodology: The standardized idiographic approach. *Behavior Therapy*, *22*, 13–29. https://doi.org/10.1016/S0005-7894(05)80240-0.

Kern, J. M. (1991b). *Manual for the idiographic role-play test of assertion* [Unpublished test manual]. Las Vegas: University of Nevada.

Kim, S., Yan, M. C., & Kulkarni, S. S. (2017). Social-skill interventions for culturally and linguistically diverse students with disabilities: A comprehensive review. *Exceptionality Education International*, *27*, 85–98. Retrieved from https://ir.lib.uwo.ca/eei/vol27/iss1/5.

Kirchner, E. P., Kennedy, R. E., & Draguns, J. G. (1979). Assertion and aggression in adult offenders. *Behavior Therapy*, *10*, 452–471. https://doi.org/10.1016/S0005-7894(79)80050-7.

Kohler, C. G., Turner, T. H., Bilker, W. B., Brensinger, C. M., Siegel, S. J., Kanes, S. J., & Gur, R. C. (2003). Facial emotion recognition in schizophrenia: Intensity effects and error pattern. *American Journal of Psychiatry*, *160*, 1768–1774. https://doi.org/10.1176/appi.ajp.160.10.1768.

Kuo, Y. L., Casillas, A., Walton, K. E., Way, J. D., & Moore, J. L. (2020). The intersectionality of race/ethnicity and socioeconomic status on social and emotional skills. *Journal of Research in Personality*, *84*, 103905. https://doi.org/10.1016/j.jrp.2019.103905.

Kynast, J., & Schroeter, M. L. (2018). Sex, age, and emotional valence: Revealing possible biases in the 'Reading the Mind in the Eyes' Task. *Frontiers in Psychology*, *9*, 570. https://doi.org/10.3389/fpsyg.2018.00570.

Lecavalier, L., & Butter, E. M. (2010). Assessment of social skills and intellectual disability. In D. W. Nangle, D. J. Hansen, C. A. Erdley, & P. J. Norton (Eds.), *Practitioner's guide to empirically based measures of social skills* (pp. 179–192). New York: Springer. https://doi.org/10.1007/978-1-4419-0609-0_12.

Liebke, L., Bungert, M., Thome, J., Hauschild, S., Gescher, D. M., Schmahl, C., & Lis, S. (2017). Loneliness, social networks, and social functioning in borderline personality disorder. *Personality Disorders: Theory, Research, and Treatment*, *8*, 349. https://doi.org/10.1037/per0000208.

Lindgren, M., Torniainen-Holm, M., Heiskanen, I., Voutilainen, G., Pulkkinen, U., Mehtälä, T., … Therman, S. (2018). Theory of mind in a first-episode psychosis population using the hinting task. *Psychiatry Research*, *263*, 185–192. https://doi.org/10.1016/j.psychres.2018.03.014.

Livingston, L. A., Colvert, E., Social Relationships Study Team, Bolton, P., & Happé, F. (2019). Good social skills despite poor theory of mind: Exploring compensation in autism spectrum disorder. *Journal of Child Psychology and Psychiatry*, *60*, 102–110. https://doi.org/10.1111/jcpp.12886.

Long, E., McDonald, S., Tate, R., Togher, L., & Bornhofen, C. (2008). Assessing social skills in people with very severe traumatic brain injury: Validity of the Social Performance Survey Schedule (SPSS). *Brain Impairment*, *9*, 274–281. https://doi.org/10.1375/brim.9.3.274.

Mallawaarachchi, S. R., Cotton, S. M., Anderson, J., Killackey, E., & Allott, K. A. (2019). Exploring the use of the Hinting Task in first-episode psychosis. *Cognitive Neuropsychiatry*, *24*, 65–79. https://doi.org/10.1080/13546805.2019.1568864.

Matson, J. L. (1995). *The Matson Evaluation of Social Skills for Individuals with Severe Retardation (MESSIER)*. Baton Rouge, LA: Scientific Publishers, Inc.

Matson, J. L., & Boisjoli, J. A. (2008). Cutoff scores for the Matson Evaluation of Social Skills for Individuals with Severe Retardation (MESSIER) for adults with intellectual disability. *Behavior Modification*, *32*, 109–120. https://doi.org/10.1177/0145445507307466.

Matson, J. L., Helsel, W. J., Bellack, A. S., & Senatore, V. (1983). Development of a rating scale to assess social skills deficits in mentally retarded adults. *Applied Research in Mental Retardation*, *4*, 399–407. https://doi.org/10.1016/0270-3092(83)90038-3.

McDonald, S. (2012). New frontiers in neuropsychological assessment: Assessing social perception using a standardised instrument, The Awareness of Social Inference Test. *Australian Psychologist*, *47*, 39–48. https://doi.org/10.1111/j.1742-9544.2011.00054.x.

McDonald, S., Bornhofen, C., Shum, D., Long, E., Saunders, C., & Neulinger, K. (2006). Reliability and validity of The Awareness of Social Inference Test (TASIT): A clinical test of social perception. *Disability and Rehabilitation*, *28*, 1529–1542. https://doi.org/10.1080/09638280600646185.

McDonald, S., Flanagan, S., Rollins, J., & Kinch, J. (2003). TASIT: A new clinical tool for assessing social perception after traumatic brain injury. *Journal of Head Trauma Rehabilitation*, *18*, 219–238. https://doi.org/10.1097/00001199-200305000-00001.

McFall, R. M., & Lillesand, D. B. (1971). Behavioral rehearsal with modeling and coaching in assertion training. *Journal of Abnormal Psychology*, *77*, 313–323. https://doi.org/10.1037/h0031010.

McFarquhar, T., Luyten, P., & Fonagy, P. (2018). Changes in interpersonal problems in the psychotherapeutic treatment of depression as measured by the Inventory of Interpersonal Problems: A systematic review and meta-analysis. *Journal of Affective Disorders*, *226*, 108–123. https://doi.org/10.1016/j.jad.2017.09.036.

Meier, V. J., & Hope, D. A. (1998). Assessment of social skills. In A. S. Bellack & M. Hersen (Eds.), *Behavioral assessment: A practical handbook* (4th ed.). Needham Heights, MA: Allyn & Bacon.

Monti, P. M., Corriveau, D. P., & Curran, J. P. (1982). Assessment of social skills in the day hospital: Does the clinician see something other than the researcher sees? *International Journal of Partial Hospitalization*, *1*, 245–250.

Moon, J., & Ke, F. (2019). Exploring the treatment integrity of virtual reality-based social skills training for children with high-functioning autism. *Interactive Learning Environments*, 1–15. https://doi.org/10.1080/10494820.2019.1613665.

Moore, R. C., Fazeli, P. L., Patterson, T. L., Depp, C. A., Moore, D. J., Granholm, E., … Mausbach, B. T. (2015). UPSA-M: Feasibility and initial validity of a mobile application of the UCSD Performance-Based Skills Assessment. *Schizophrenia Research*, *164*, 187–192. https://doi.org/10.1016/j.schres.2015.02.014.

Morgan, J. J., Hsiao, Y. J., Dobbins, N., Brown, N. B., & Lyons, C. (2015). An observation tool for monitoring social skill implementation in contextually relevant environments. *Intervention in School and Clinic*, *51*, 3–11. https://doi.org/10.1177/1053451215577474.

Morrison, K. E., Pinkham, A. E., Kelsven, S., Ludwig, K., Penn, D. L., & Sasson, N. J. (2019). Psychometric evaluation of social cognitive measures for adults with autism. *Autism Research*, *12*, 766–778. https://doi.org/10.1002/aur.2084.

Nangle, D. W., Hansen, D. J., Erdley, C. A., & Norton, P. J. (Eds.), (2010). *Practitioner's guide to empirically based measures of social skills*. New York: Springer.

Nelson, R. O. (1981). Realistic dependent measures for clinical use. *Journal of Consulting and Clinical Psychology*, *49*, 168–182. https://doi.org/10.1037//0022-006x.49.2.168.

Nelson, R. O., Hayes, S. C., Felton, J. L., & Jarrett, R. B. (1985). A comparison of data produced by different behavioral assessment techniques with implications for models of social skills inadequacy. *Behaviour Research and Therapy*, *23*, 1–11. https://doi.org/10.1016/0005-7967(85)90137-8.

Norton, P. J., Grills-Taquechel, A. E., & Raouf, M. (2010). Assessing adults. In D. W. Nangle, D. J. Hansen, C. A. Erdley, & P. J. Norton (Eds.), *Practitioner's guide to empirically based measures of social skills*. (pp. 87–98). New York: Springer. https://doi.org/10.1007/978-1-4419-0609-0.

Norton, P. J., & Hope, D. A. (2001). Analogue observational methods in the assessment of social functioning in adults. *Psychological Assessment*, *13*, 59–72. https://doi.org/10.1037//1040-3590.13.1.59.

Norton, P. J., Washington, C., Peters, J. E., & Hayes, S. A. (2010). Diversity considerations. In I. D. W. Nangle, D. J. Hansen, C. A. Erdley, & P. J. Norton (Eds.), *Practitioner's guide to empirically based measures of social skills*. (pp. 135–154). New York: Springer. https://doi.org/10.1007/978-1-4419-0609-0.

Pachman, J. S., Foy, D. W., Massey, F., & Eisler, R. M. (1978). A factor analysis of assertive behaviors. *Journal of Consulting and Clinical Psychology*, *46*, 347. https://doi.org/10.1037/0022-006X.46.2.347.

Palermo, R., Rossion, B., Rhodes, G., Laguesse, R., Tez, T., Hall, B., … Al-Janabi, S. (2017). Do people have insight into their face recognition abilities? *The Quarterly Journal of Experimental Psychology*, *70*(2), 218–233. https://doi.org/10.1080/17470218.2016.1161058.

Paul, G. L. (Ed.), (1987). *Observational assessment instrumentation for service and research: The Time-Sample Behavior Checklist: Assessment in residential treatment settings: Part 2*. Champaign, IL: Research Press.

Paul, G. L. (Ed.), (1988). *Observational assessment instrumentation for service and research: The Staff-Resident Interaction Chronograph: Assessment in residential treatment settings: Part 3*. Champaign, IL: Research Press.

Paul, G. L. (2000). Evidence-based practices in inpatient and residential facilities. *The Clinical Psychologist*, *53*, 3–11.

Pinkham, A. E., Harvey, P. D., & Penn, D. L. (2017). Social cognition psychometric evaluation: Results of the final validation study. *Schizophrenia Bulletin*, *44*, 737–748. https://doi.org/10.1093/schbul/sbx117.

Pinkham, A. E., Penn, D. L., Green, M. F., Buck, B., Healey, K., & Harvey, P. D. (2013). The social cognition psychometric evaluation study: Results of the expert survey and RAND panel. *Schizophrenia Bulletin*, *40*, 813–823. https://doi.org/10.1093/schbul/sbt081.

Poyatos, F. (1988). New research perspectives in cross-cultural psychology through nonverbal communication studies. In F. Poyatos (Ed.), *Cross-cultural perspectives in nonverbal communication* (pp. 35–69). Toronto: C. J. Hogrefe. https://doi.org/10.2307/3172816.

Rathus, S. A. (1973). A 30-item schedule for assessing assertive behavior. *Behavior Therapy*, *4*, 398–406. https://doi.org/10.1016/S0005-7894(73)80120-0.

Richell, R. A., Mitchell, D. G., Newman, C., Leonard, A., Baron-Cohen, S., & Blair, R. J. R. (2003). Theory of mind and psychopathy: Can psychopathic individuals read the 'language of the eyes'? *Neuropsychologia*, *41*, 523–526. https://doi.org/10.1016/s0028-3932(02)00175-6.

Riggio, R. (1986). Assessment of basic social skills. *Journal of Personality and Social Psychology*, *51*, 649–660. https://doi.org/10.1037/0022-3514.51.3.649.

Rigon, A., Voss, M. W., Turkstra, L. S., Mutlu, B., & Duff, M. C. (2018). Different aspects of facial affect recognition impairment following traumatic brain injury: The role of perceptual and interpretative abilities. *Journal of Clinical and Experimental Neuropsychology*, *40*, 805–819. https://doi.org/10.1080/13803395.2018.1437120.

Rossion, B., & Michel, C. (2018). Normative accuracy and response time data for the computerized Benton Facial Recognition Test (BFRT-c). *Behavior Research Methods*, *50*, 2442–2460. https://doi.org/10.3758/s13428-018-1023-x.

Ruiz, M. A., Pincus, A. L., Borkovec, T. D., Echemendia, R. J., Castonguay, L. G., & Ragusea, S. A. (2004). Validity of the Inventory of Interpersonal Problems for predicting treatment outcome: An investigation with the Pennsylvania Practice Research Network. *Journal of Personality Assessment*, *83*, 213–222. https://doi.org/10.1207/s15327752jpa8303_05.

Rus-Calafell, M., Gutiérrez-Maldonado, J., & Ribas-Sabaté, J. (2014). A virtual reality-integrated program for improving social skills in patients with schizophrenia: A pilot study. *Journal of Behavior Therapy and Experimental Psychiatry*, *45*, 81–89. https://doi.org/10.1016/j.jbtep.2013.09.002.

Sasson, N. J., Morrison, K. E., Kelsven, S., & Pinkham, A. E. (2019). Social cognition as a predictor of functional and social skills in autistic adults without intellectual disability. *Autism Research*, https://doi.org/10.1002/aur.2195. [Epub ahead of print].

Schneider, M., Reininghaus, U., van Neirop, M., Janssens, M., Myin-Germeys, I., & GROUP Investigators. (2017). Does the Social Functioning Scale reflect real-life social functioning? An experience sampling study in patients with a non-affective psychotic disorder and healthy control individuals. *Psychological Medicine*, *47*, 2777–2786. https://doi.org/10.1017/S0033291717001295.

Segrin, C. (1998). The impact of assessment procedures on the relationship between paper and pencil and behavioral indicators of social skill. *Journal of Nonverbal Behavior*, *22*, 229–251. https://doi.org/10.1023/A:1022944505955.

Semple, S. J., Patterson, T. L., Shaw, W. S., Grant, I., Moscona, S., & Jeste, D. V. (1999). Self-perceived interpersonal competence in older schizophrenia patients: The role of patient characteristics and psychosocial factors. *Acta Psychiatrica Scandinavica*, *100*, 126–135. https://doi.org/10.1111/j.1600-0447.1999.tb10833.x.

Sergi, M. J., Fiske, A. P., Horan, W. P., Kern, R. S., Kee, K. S., Subotnik, K. L., … Green, M. F. (2009). Development of a measure of relationship perception in schizophrenia. *Psychiatry Research*, *166*, 54–62. https://doi.org/10.1016/j.psychres.2008.03.010.

Sparrow, S. S., Cicchetti, D. V., & Saulnier, C. A. (2016). *Vineland Adaptive Behavior Scales* (3rd ed. (Vineland-3)). Bloomington: NCS Pearson.https://doi.org/10.1007/springerreference_184293.

St. Lawrence, J. S., Kirksey, W. A., & Moore, T. (1983). External validity of role play assessment of assertive behavior. *Journal of Behavioral Assessment*, *5*, 25–34. https://doi.org/10.1007/BF01343636.

Taupiac, J. D., Rodriguez, N., Strauss, O., & Beney, P. (2019). *Social skills training tool in Virtual Reality, intended for managers and sales representatives*. In *IEEE-VR: Conference on Virtual Reality and 3D user interfaces*. https://doi.org/10.1109/vr.2019.8798317.

Trower, P., Bryant, B., & Argyle, M. (1978). *Social skills and mental health*. Pittsburgh: University of Pittsburgh Press. https://doi.org/10.1016/0005-7967(78)90019-0.

Yang, Y. D., Allen, T., Abdullahi, S. M., Pelphrey, K. A., Volkmar, F. R., & Chapman, S. B. (2017). Brain responses to biological motion predict treatment outcome in young adults with autism receiving Virtual Reality Social Cognition Training: Preliminary findings. *Behaviour Research and Therapy*, *93*, 55–66. https://doi.org/10.1016/j.brat.2017.03.014.

Further reading

Dickerson, F., Boronow, J. J., Ringel, N., & Parente, F. (1999). Social functioning and neurocognitive deficits in outpatients with schizophrenia: A 2 year follow-up. *Schizophrenia Research*, *37*, 13–20. https://doi.org/10.1016/s0920-9964(98)00134-0.

Floyd, R., Shands, E. I., Alfonso, V. C., Phillips, J. F., Autry, B. K., Mosteller, J. A., … Irby, S. (2015). A systematic review and psychometric evaluation of adaptive behavior scales and recommendations for practice. *Journal of Applied School Psychology*, *31*, 83–113. https://doi.org/10.1080/15377903.2014.979384.

Heimberg, R. G., Chiauzzi, E. J., Becker, R. E., & Madrazo-Peterson, R. (1983). Cognitive mediation of assertive behavior: An analysis of the self-statement patterns of college students, psychiatric patients, and normal adults. *Cognitive Therapy and Research*, *7*, 455–463. https://doi.org/10.1007/BF01187173.

Herson, M., Bellack, A. S., Turner, S. M., Williams, M. T., Harper, K., & Watts, J. G. (1979). Psychometric properties of the Wolpe-Lazarus Assertiveness Scale. *Behaviour Research and Therapy*, *17*, 63–69. https://doi.org/10.1016/0005-7967(79)90051-2.

Honigfeld, G., Gillis, R. D., & Klett, C. J. (1965). Nurses' observation scale for inpatient evaluation: A new scale for measuring improvement in chronic schizophrenia. *Journal of Clinical Psychology*, *21*, 65–71. https://doi.org/10.1002/1097-4679(196501)21:1<65::aid-jclp2270210122>3.0.co;2-i.

Kanning, U. P. (2006). Development and validation of a German-language version of the Interpersonal Competence Questionnaire (ICQ). *European Journal of Psychological Assessment*, *22*, 43–51. https://doi.org/10.1027/1015-5759.22.1.43.

Kogan, E. S., Hersen, M., & Kabacoff, R. I. (1995). Psychometric properties of the Wolpe-Lazarus Assertiveness Scale with community-dwelling older adults. *Journal of Psychopathology and Behavioral Assessment*, *17*, 97–109. https://doi.org/10.1007/BF02214730.

Lyall, D., Hawley, C., & Scott, K. (2004). Nurses' Observation Scale for Inpatient Evaluation: Reliability update. *Journal of Advanced Nursing*, *46*, 390–394. https://doi.org/10.1111/j.1365-2648.2004.03006.x.

Meyer, L. H., Reichle, J., McQuarter, R., Cole, D. A., Vandercook, T., Evans, I., … Kishi, G. (1985). *Assessment of Social Competence (ASC): A scale of social competence functions (revised).* Syracuse, NY: Syracuse University. https://doi.org/10.13140/RG.2.1.3004.5528.

Penn, D. L., Spaulding, W., Reed, D., & Sullivan, M. (1996). The relationship of social cognition to ward behavior in chronic schizophrenia. *Schizophrenia Research*, *20*, 327–335. https://doi.org/10.1016/0920-9964(96)00010-2.

Schwartz, R. M., & Gottman, J. M. (1976). Toward a task analysis of assertive behavior. *Journal of Consulting and Clinical Psychology*, *44*, 910–920. https://doi.org/10.1037/0022-006X.44.6.910.

Wolpe, J., & Lazarus, A. A. (1966). *Behavior therapy techniques: A guide to the treatment of neuroses.* Elmsford, NY: Pergamon. https://doi.org/10.1001/archpsyc.1967.01730200121020.

Chapter 6

Intervening with youth

Laura A. Andrews[a], Rachel L. Grover[b], Michelle L. Buffie[a], and Douglas W. Nangle[a]
[a]*University of Maine, Orono, ME, United States,* [b]*Loyola University Maryland, Baltimore, MD, United States*

Social skills training (SST) interventions are designed to assist youth who have difficulty navigating social interactions with peers due to deficits in social skills. SST interventions, based in social learning and behavioral theories, aim to systematically increase knowledge and appropriate use of social skills. Social skills are essential for well-being, and many developmental milestones of childhood and adolescence depend on adaptive social relationships (Hartup, 1989). In contrast, social skill deficits are associated with a broad range of social and emotional problems or disorders in childhood and adolescence (Gresham, 2017). SST can be used as a standalone intervention or as a component of an integrated treatment package to build or bolster skills and improve socioemotional functioning. Programs are delivered in both individual and group formats in a variety of settings (e.g., clinic, school-based, summer camp) using behavioral, social-cognitive, educational, and/or peer-mediated methods. The design and delivery of SST is dependent upon the type of social skills deficit requiring intervention. A key distinction for clinicians to make is between skill-acquisition and performance deficits. Some youth lack particular social skills, whereas others cannot effectively use them due to anxiety or other impairments. In such cases, SST may need to be replaced or augmented with another intervention.

This chapter begins with a review of the core SST target skills and the training components used to teach the skills, followed by a discussion of several variations and implementation considerations. A broad review of the evidence base is provided focusing on meta-analytic literature, and then attention is directed to more specific populations with examples of effective SST programs.

Core intervention skills

The first step in any SST intervention is a comprehensive assessment of skills deficits (both acquisition and performance), as well as problematic social situations. Using the results, the intervention should be tailored to match the

Social Skills Across the Life Span. https://doi.org/10.1016/B978-0-12-817752-5.00006-8

particular needs of the youth. SST interventions are often flexible, modular approaches, comprising several individual social skills that can be taught as needed. Some interventions focus on foundational microskills (e.g., eye contact), whereas others are designed to facilitate competency in more complex sets of skills (e.g., conversation, assertiveness, social problem solving) or particular situations (e.g., date initiation, responding to bullying). SST typically proceeds in a systematic fashion using several core behavioral components to teach skills (see next section). The core intervention skills for SST can be grouped into those that focus on behavioral social interaction skills (e.g., communication skills, conflict resolution) and those that address social-cognitive and emotional skills (e.g., attributions and perspective taking, emotion regulation). No matter the focus, interventions should also include consideration of matching the necessary social skills to the relevant context (e.g., developmental, cultural) and situations (e.g., friendship, school situations).

Behavioral social interaction skills interventions concentrate on a range of issues from basic conversational skills to higher-order skill sets, such as assertiveness and conflict resolution. Basic conversational skills are the building blocks of all social interactions and are vital facilitators of play, academic achievement, and further socialization (Kelly, 1982). As such, these skills are often emphasized in SST, including eye contact; body posture; vocal volume, tone, and pace; facial expressions; head movements; and listening (Spence, 2003). These basic skills can be seen as foundational to more complex communication skills, including initiating and maintaining conversations, taking turns, selecting appropriate topics, engaging in self-disclosure, and ending conversations. However, it should be noted that microskills deficits are probably not the sole cause of ineffective social behavior. Social behavior is likely multiply determined and may depend on several factors, including foundational skills, motivations, solution selection, and emotion regulation (Cavell, 1990).

At times, SST programs focus on specific clusters of skills related to a similar theme or social problem area. For example, negotiation and conflict resolution skills programs focus on teaching the social skills needed to manage conflict situations. Such programs often include psychoeducation about conflict, as well as communication, anger management, perspective taking, and mediation skills (Coleman & Prywes, 2014). Negotiation and conflict resolution skill training is implemented in a variety of settings, including schools (through peer mediation programs), and yields positive results (e.g., Ibarrola-Garcia, Iriarte, & Aznarez-Sanado, 2017). Often categorized under the umbrella of conflict resolution programs, effective antibullying programs work to reduce bullying and increase prosocial behaviors by creating a positive school climate through policies and teacher training as well as fostering social and emotional skills in students (e.g., empathy, assertiveness, friendship, and conversational skills; Algozzine, Daunic, & Smith, 2010; Frey et al., 2005).

Some interventions also include groups of skills related to assertiveness and romantic relationships. Assertiveness training focuses specifically on the social skills necessary to accurately and respectfully make and refuse requests and to communicate opinions, feelings, and boundaries (Duckworth & Mercer, 2006). Specific to youth, assertiveness training has been used to increase sexual assertiveness in adolescent girls (Rowe, Jouriles, & McDonald, 2015) and is included in broader social skills interventions, including the Skillstreaming program for children (McGinnis, 2011a) and adolescents (McGinnis, 2011b). For teens, important social skill competencies might also include "date-initiation" skills, as well as the skills needed to maintain dating relationships. Although this class of skills overlaps with general social skills (e.g., initiating and maintaining conversations), the romantic relationship context demands an additional set of skills, including initiating physical intimacy, communicating desired level of commitment, and managing a break-up (Grover, Nangle, Serwik, Fales, & Prenoveau, 2013).

Other social skills interventions focus on the social-cognitive and emotional skills components of social competence. Social-cognitive skills are those that connect thinking strategies to social interactions. For example, social problem-solving refers to the process of identifying and solving social problems (Bell & D'Zurilla, 2009). Social perspective taking, another common social-cognitive skill, is the ability to consider another's perspective in a social situation and to use this knowledge to inform actions (Tamnes et al., 2018). Also, recognizing that emotions can help or hinder the performance of effective social skills, other programs include emotion regulation skill components. The Tools4U social skills intervention for juvenile delinquent youth (van der Stouwe, Asscher, Hoeve, van der Laan, & Stams, 2016) is an exemplar of this integration of skills. Tools4U takes a cognitive-behavioral approach and focuses on the skills that youth need to manage difficult situations (e.g., peer pressure). The program provides social problem solving skills to increase prosocial responses and social perspective taking skills to increase empathy and decrease assumptions of hostile intent. At the same time, Tools4U addresses cognitive distortions to reduce the incidence of rigid or dichotomous thinking.

Core training components

Target skills vary across interventions, but there is a fair degree of consistency in intervention procedures. Rooted in the behavioral tradition, SST interventions typically incorporate several core training components to facilitate skill acquisition. These behavioral components include psychoeducation and direct instruction, modeling, behavioral rehearsal, feedback, reinforcement, and reduction of inhibiting and competing behaviors. In addition, social-cognitive components (e.g., perspective-taking, modification of attributions) are often used to complement the behavioral approaches. Despite the presentation of these components as separate entities, it is important to note that they are often used together in intervention programs. For example, an intervention may present social-problem solving as a social-cognitive component, and use psychoeducation, modeling, and feedback to help teach social-problem solving.

Psychoeducation and direct instruction

Once target skills are identified, these skills can be addressed in intervention occurring in one-on-one therapy, group therapy, or within the school context. Typically, the new skill is broken down into small steps, explained, and discussed (Segrin & Givertz, 2003). In addition, the rationale for why the skill is important is shared with the child. Take the social skill of "starting a conversation" as an example. Direct instruction would involve listing a few important steps (e.g., identify someone who is not currently in a conversation, make a comment about something neutral like the weather or a noncontroversial current event, and ask an open-ended question). The psychoeducation component serves to explain each of the skill steps (e.g., "If you want to start a conversation with someone, it is helpful to find someone not already in a conversation, because that person is available. Otherwise, you might interrupt another conversation and be perceived as rude"). As each step of the skill is introduced, the rationale is explained so that the learner can understand both the component skill, as well as its importance. In addition, the therapist and child discuss the skill and situational factors that might affect the skill performance. For instance, the therapist and child might discuss several hypothetical and real-life situations where it might be appropriate to start a conversation.

Modeling

Once the skill steps and rationale are discussed, the target skill is typically modeled. Modeling allows the participant to observe appropriate production of the skill, as well as positive outcomes related to skill use. Modeling can occur in vivo or via video. In vivo modeling involves an adult or peer acting out the target skill while the child observes. Both adult models and peer models are effective (Shukla-Mehta, Miller, & Callahan, 2010), although Bandura (1977) highlights the importance of having a relatable model, preferably one that is similar to the child, to facilitate learning. Video modeling allows the clinician to focus the attention of the child on the relevant behaviors and encourage the child to replicate and practice the behaviors. Video modeling, compared to in vivo, has the technological advantage of being able to pause, rewind, and replay aspects of the social interaction or skill. In fact, in a small sample study of children with Autism spectrum disorders, Charlop-Christy, Le, and Freeman (2000) found faster skill acquisition and higher levels of generalization when using video as compared to in vivo modeling. The authors suggest that the video format may be more motivating and engaging for these youth and that it may also have an advantage of limiting visual and auditory distractions. However, in a direct comparison of the two approaches with preschoolers with autism, Wilson (2013) found mixed results, suggesting that some youth may respond better to in vivo, whereas others may respond better to video modeling. As such, Wilson (2013) recommends considering the learning style of the child in selecting the mode of modeling intervention.

Behavioral rehearsal

After watching a model enact the skill, it is important to rehearse the skill. Just like learning any new skill, practice should take place as soon and as frequently as possible. Practice often first occurs as a role play in session where the participant can repeat different steps as needed, until the skill is learned. Skill steps may also be verbally or imaginally rehearsed. For complex skills, or skills that are particularly difficult for the child, it may be more helpful to enact a series of graduated rehearsals, with each practice incorporating an additional step of the social skill. Finally, it is important to practice outside of session, and rehearsal (verbal, imaginal, and/or in vivo) can be assigned as homework. For example, a child with social anxiety might first role play with her clinician to practice inviting a friend to a social event. Then the child might imagine asking an actual friend, taking time to imagine different outcomes and responses. Finally, the child would be encouraged to practice the skills with peers. Practicing a new skill both in and out of the therapeutic setting helps ensure the generalization of that skill across a variety of situations. In addition, this rehearsal likely increases the potential maintenance of the skill through operant conditioning as the individual is apt to be rewarded for their attempts. Behavioral rehearsal is one of the key strategies identified to promote generalization of new behaviors (Stokes & Osnes, 1989) and is routinely included in SST interventions.

Feedback and reinforcement

Constructive feedback is essential during the initial acquisition and refinement of social skills. Feedback is provided by the therapist during role plays and other practice. In group SST interventions, this initial feedback may also be given by peers in the social skills group. Inclusion of peers in this process may facilitate learning by providing natural reinforcements for the demonstrated social skills (Stokes & Osnes, 1989). For example, the PEERS (Program for the Education and Enrichment of Relational Skills) curriculum, a manualized social skills intervention for adolescents with autism spectrum disorder (ASD), also has a peer-mediated version that includes trained typically developing teen mentors who give positive reinforcement for initiations of social skills (Matthews et al., 2018). The PEERS with Peers program showed a slight advantage in the areas of social skills knowledge and social functioning as compared with the traditional curriculum (Matthews et al., 2018). Parents, teachers, and partners can also be trained to be social skills coaches and to give feedback outside of the sessions (Spence, 2003).

Behaviors that are positively reinforced are more likely to reoccur, so it is important for praise to be a central part of initial feedback. Instructors, coaches, and peers need to stress the positive aspects of the learner's performance, as well as give constructive feedback on the areas in need of refinement (e.g., "Nice job looking Sarah in the eye as you asked your question. Next time speak just a bit louder so she can hear you"). Youth who are anxious, or otherwise not intrinsically motivated to engage in the social skill, may need other external reinforcements (e.g., small prizes as motivators) to facilitate skill practice. Hopefully, over time, the natural and positive effects of social skill performance will be enough to maintain the skill.

Reduction of inhibiting and competing behaviors

Depending on the needs of the youth, SST might also address inhibiting and competing behaviors (Spence, 2003). Inhibiting and competing behaviors are those that serve to impede the adoption of adaptive social skills (Gresham, 2016). For example, a young child might hit another child to get a toy instead of using appropriate play joining skills and may be inadvertently rewarded for this behavior by the acquisition of the toy. In this case, SST directs attention to those social situations and teaches the child a positive replacement behavior (e.g., asking to share the desired toy; Maag, 2005). For a positive replacement behavior to be effective, it must be functionally equivalent and garner as much, or more, positive reinforcement than the original behavior (Gresham, 2017). Once identified, the replacement behavior is taught, modeled, and practiced as described earlier, often in combination with other interventions, such as time out or contingency management to reduce aggression. Anxiety can also be conceptualized as an inhibiting force resulting in performance deficits. For example, an adolescent may have some of the requisite skills to make friends, but be unable to enact the behaviors needed due to anxiety. As such, anxiety management may be effectively paired with social skills interventions. One program, Social Effectiveness Therapy for Children and Adolescents (SET-C), with both social anxiety management and social skills components, yielded significant improvements in both areas compared to a control (Beidel, Turner, Young, & Paulson, 2005).

Social-cognitive components

The behavioral components described earlier are often paired with social-cognitive components to teach social monitoring, to enhance social-cognitive skills like social problem-solving or perspective-taking, or to change counterproductive attributions or thoughts. A large part of SST involves teaching the learner to be aware of peer reactions to their own behavior and to use those reactions as important constructive feedback. As such, SST interventions often include a metacognitive component to teach effective social monitoring. For example, social problem-solving interventions like Tools for Getting Along (Daunic et al., 2012) routinely teach the importance of monitoring the outcomes of social behavior to inform future social decision making. Social problem-solving interventions might emphasize changing the child's problem orientation to be one of approach rather than avoidance or improving specific problem-solving skills, such as increasing the amount of possible generated solutions or learning how to better evaluate the effectiveness of a possible solution (D'Zurilla & Nezu, 2010).

Social perspective-taking components might involve practice in identifying the feelings and thoughts of others. For example, one intervention that showed promising results involves parents reading narratives that tell the same story from different characters' perspectives to their children with autism (Tsunemi, Tamura, Ogawa, Isomura, & Masataka, 2014). SST programs may also include cognitive restructuring components like collecting evidence or challenging assumptions about social situations or other's intent (e.g., "What made you think that Alonzo bumped you on purpose? Could another explanation be more likely?"). Skills training components used to facilitate emotion regulation may include practice recognizing the emotions of self and others, emotion labeling, as well as self-monitoring and understanding of emotional triggers (Einfeld et al., 2018). For example, a review of social skills treatments for youth with attention deficit/hyperactivity disorder (ADHD) revealed that interventions typically included training in macroskills, such as social problem solving, emotion regulation, and perspective taking (Willis, Siceloff, Morse, Neger, & Flory, 2019).

Social skills training variations

SST can be delivered in multiple formats across a variety of populations with differing degrees of intensity and duration. When designing or implementing training programs, the characteristics of the child should be considered to maximize outcomes and address specific needs. The benefits and potential disadvantages of delivering training in group or individual formats should also be compared, and the options for various settings, as well as the utility of including parents, peers, and teachers to increase social validity and generalization of skills across contexts should be considered.

Individual and group formats

One-on-one and group-based training formats have relative advantages and potential disadvantages. Group-based approaches involve an inherent social context in the intervention setting. Therefore, groups allow participants to interact with peers in a safe environment, engage in structured or unstructured practice of newly acquired skills, observe appropriate skill modeling from peers, and receive feedback from both the facilitator and group members (Hansen, Nangle, & Meyer, 1998). The group setting may also afford more variability in social contexts (e.g., dyadic vs group interactions), responses during practiced social interactions, and diversity in peer characteristics (e.g., age, types of social deficits, personality) compared to a one-on-one treatment setting. These factors may serve to enhance the social validity of SST and increase generalization to more diverse situations outside of treatment. Group interventions are most effective when participants have a similar type and severity of skill deficit to focus on the same skills and progress at an even rate (Kelly, 1982). However, many settings may not permit this degree of matching. It is also possible that challenges may arise from a high degree of peer similarity, such as risk for negative peer influence and deviancy training among youth with antisocial behavior (Arnold & Hughes, 1999).

Compared to group formats, one-on-one training allows the intervention to be individually tailored according to the type and severity of deficits and other important characteristics of the child. Closer monitoring of individual progress during delivery also enables therapists to adjust training according to specific needs (e.g., pace, generalization). Additional time and attention can be allocated to social skills that the child has difficulty mastering. In individual formats, the child also has the opportunity to practice and master skills before interacting with peers. This may be particularly beneficial for some youth, such as children with social anxiety, who may otherwise be hesitant to participate in SST. Individual training also affords benefits to children and families with flexibility in scheduling. Notably, in terms of effectiveness, it appears that the positive effects of training steadily increase as the size of the treatment group decreases to an individual, one-on-one format (Schneider, 1992). In fact, some findings suggest that individual treatment is significantly more effective compared to larger classmate groups in school settings for socially isolated children (Erwin, 1994). However, meta-analyses have also found that that the size of the intervention group is not a significant predictor of outcomes (Schneider, 1992).

School-based interventions

Social skills programs are commonly implemented in the educational setting for students with identified skills deficits or through classroom-wide prevention and intervention efforts. For example, the majority of the conflict resolution skill programs are housed in schools and are considered universal interventions delivered to all students (Algozzine et al., 2010). School settings allow for broad-scale impact, and, in some cases, facilitate peer integration. For example, classroom-based social skills interventions for ADHD may impact peer status, as well as the social skill of the target child (Willis et al., 2019). One example of a universal intervention is the Social-Skills Improvement System—Classwide Intervention (Elliott & Gresham, 2007). This manualized assessment and intervention system is designed to increase prosocial behavior and decrease problem behavior at the classroom level for preschool through high school-aged youth. Across 10 units, students learn receptive skills (e.g., listening to others, following steps and rules) and interactive skills (e.g., communication, cooperation, reading and managing emotions), as well as education-based skills about selective input (e.g., paying attention to work) and productivity (e.g., asking a question) with scripted lessons, video vignettes, and exercises presented in student booklets.

Meta-analytic findings suggest that universal intervention programs show modest changes in social behavior for most students, with the greatest benefits found for preschool or kindergarten children and high school-aged youth (January, Casey, & Paulson, 2011). Interventions implemented with more active instructional methods and extended programming (mean number of hours = 25) tend to be most effective (January et al., 2011). For example, the Fast Track program and PATHS curriculum (Promoting Alternative Thinking Strategies) uses varied teaching methods during two or more brief sessions per week across several months (Greenberg, Kusche, Cook, & Quamma, 1995). Interestingly, recent research has investigated the cost effectiveness of such programs, and findings suggest that there may be an optimal age for delivery (e.g., second grade compared to first grade; Hunter, DiPerna, Hart, & Crowley, 2018). Other school-based interventions are intended for specific populations of students, such as youth with ASD. Evidence for school-based interventions for youth with ASD are more mixed, showing minimal to large effects overall. Most evidence points to the greater success of inclusion-based classroom delivery compared to "pullout interventions" in an independent setting, which provides youth with ASD the opportunity to regularly interact with typically developing peers to maximize outcomes (Bellini, Peters, Benner, & Hopf, 2007; Camargo et al., 2016).

Peer-mediated components

Peers can also be put to effective use in peer-mediated programs. In peer-mediated programs, peers help to deliver the intervention. In the PEERS with Peers program, Matthews et al. (2018) included trained typically developing adolescent peers in their social skills intervention for teens with ASD. These peer mediators attended the social skills groups, modeled new skills, and gave positive reinforcement for target behaviors exhibited by youth with ASD. In addition, the peer mediators engaged in a phone call with a youth with ASD each week to encourage homework compliance and give more positive reinforcement. Typically, conflict resolution interventions contain a peer mediation component. In this case, peer mediators are students, trained in conflict resolution skills, who model and practice the skills with their fellow students in response to specific conflicts (Algozzine et al., 2010). Other programs integrate untrained peers, such as in SET-C (Beidel, Turner, & Morris, 2004). During specialized generalization sessions, socially anxious youth interact with socially skilled peers in naturalistic settings to observe appropriate modeling of target behaviors and expand existing peer networks.

Additional considerations

Intensity and duration

The intensity and duration of SST can also vary greatly depending on the type of treatment program and child needs. Though most interventions are implemented in time-limited and/or location-specific sessions, ongoing full-day programs in school settings or summer camps provide much greater intensity. The duration of SST may vary by session length, number, and frequency to adequately meet the child's needs. Many SST programs are delivered in weekly or biweekly sessions across approximately 12–16 weeks (e.g., Beidel et al., 2004; Laugeson & Frankel, 2010). Other programs extend for several months, such as the PATHS curriculum, which can be delivered across the length of an academic year, or across multiple years, such as the entire Fast Track Program (Greenberg et al., 1995). More time-limited, yet intensive, programs are also available in the form of summer programs lasting 5–8 weeks (e.g., Pelham & Hoza, 1996). Some interventions offer booster sessions after the program is completed for additional skills practice to encourage maintenance of gains over time. In terms of research evidence, little is known about the adequate dose of SST required for children and adolescents to experience meaningful changes. A meta-analysis by Schneider and Byrne (1985), including SST interventions for youth who are typically developing, socially isolated, learning disabled, behaviorally disordered, or developmentally delayed, did not find an association between length and outcome, suggesting that short-term programs may be adequate.

Social validity

To ensure socially meaningful and generalizable outcomes, interventions should be designed to enhance the social validity of SST. Social validity concerns the degree to which interventions and targeted skills reflect the natural social environment, are accepted and valued by participants, and are likely to produce positive outcomes and reinforcement in the social environment (Spence, 2003). Effort should be taken to select social skills for intervention based on participant involvement and empirical evidence for their social validity. Training may also be enhanced through integration in the naturalistic setting for better generalization. For example, SET-C includes peer generalization sessions to provide youth with opportunities to engage with socially skilled peers in other settings (e.g., pizza parlors, recreation centers; Beidel et al., 2004). In addition to peer involvement, teacher (e.g., DeRosier, 2004) and parent (e.g., Mikami, Lerner, Griggs, McGrath, & Calhoun, 2010) participation may increase generalization by creating opportunities for modeling, practice, and reinforcement of appropriate use of skills in natural settings in everyday life.

Diversity

Social interactions are embedded in context and are culturally based. With the increasing diversity of youth, it is crucial that aspects of diversity and individual differences are considered in SST (Cartledge & Loe, 2001). Unfortunately, however, the SST literature parallels the youth psychotherapy literature in that little is known about the relative impact of SST with youth of diverse identities. Some professionals argue that evidence-based interventions are effective across cultural groups based on shared universal principles related to therapeutic change. However, others believe that interventions are less effective for individuals with diverse identities because programs have not been developed or evaluated for the specific population and may overlook important cultural considerations in treatment (Huey & Polo, 2017).

As such, we are left with recommendations for tailoring SST according to youth identity and culture. Cultural influences span across domains of social expressiveness (e.g., behavioral, emotional, verbal, and nonverbal), as well as social and family orientations (e.g., collective, cooperative communities) and spiritual and religious traditions (Rivera & Adkinson, 1997). At times, youth from culturally and linguistically diverse backgrounds may be improperly identified as having social skills deficits when social context and cultural differences are overlooked (Cartledge & Loe, 2001). For example, expectations for appropriate use of eye contact differ between cultures, making it more likely for a child who engages in limited eye contact as an act of deference to be improperly identified as having a nonverbal skill deficit. Therefore, individual and cultural aspects of diversity must be recognized when assessing and selecting social skills for intervention.

SST can be delivered in a culturally sensitive manner with adaptations guided by a child-specific cultural assessment and additional resources about cultural diversity (e.g., Cartledge & Milburn, 1996). Interventions may be adapted to consider the child's preferences for language, treatment context, and therapist characteristics as well as for target behaviors. Some bilingual or multilingual children may prefer to participate in SST training with the language that they anticipate using in social settings most often, while others may be most comfortable with a bilingual facilitator. Contextual preferences can include those relating to the intervention setting (e.g., classroom), intervention group size (e.g., one-on-one vs group training), or specific training methods (e.g., inclusion of family members). For example, culturally based beliefs or behaviors may make it less likely for some youth or families to participate in SST in a medical or clinic-based setting compared to a familiar location, such as a school or community center. SST interventions may also consider the match between the child and facilitator's ethnicity and culture and incorporate training for facilitators to increase multicultural competence.

Importantly, culturally informed SST may incorporate cultural values and beliefs into training with culturally relevant target behaviors and with culturally based metaphors or ideas (Cartledge & Loe, 2001). For example, SST may emphasize collective cooperation or demonstrate effective responding with preferred cultural behaviors. Culturally informed SST not only must teach skills for the immediate peer group but also should support skill building for settings within the child's cultural group. Interventions focused on social skills related to romantic relationships must also consider the cultural context, as different cultures have a variety of social norms concerning appropriate dating behavior (Grover et al., 2013).

One example of a culturally informed SST program is The Positive Adolescents Choices Training (PACT) program designed for African American youth (Hammond, Warfield, & Yung, 2015). PACT aims to reduce the risk of perpetration or victimization by violence and is typically implemented as a group intervention in the school setting with students identified as having social skill deficits, behavioral or aggression problems, and a history of involvement in violence. Comprising three main components, violence-risk education, anger management, and prosocial skills training, PACT teaches skills using videos featuring African American peer role models demonstrating appropriate communication and negotiation skills with culturally relevant conflict situations for minority youth. The small group format also facilitates social support among peers of the same race and can provide opportunities to discuss and process social challenges related to diversity, such as racial labels.

Developmental differences

Research about developmental factors, such as age, suggests that SST is more effective during the preschool (3–4 years old) or adolescent (14–19 years old) periods than at other ages (Schneider & Byrne, 1985). This pattern is particularly pronounced when SST is delivered through adult instruction with modeling or coaching. Age-related differences may be associated with developmental changes in the motivation or ability to receive instruction from adults about social behaviors. It is possible that children are less open to information from adults about social relationships compared to adolescents who may have greater motivation to learn skills after developing uncertainty or concern about their social abilities or status (Schneider & Byrne, 1985). Increases in self-awareness and metacognition, or awareness of thinking processes, may also improve efficacy in the adolescent years. Additionally, younger children may not be as responsive to interventions that are more cognitive and conceptual in nature. These approaches may be best suited for adolescents, whereas younger children may be likely to benefit from interventions emphasizing behavioral or more basic socioemotional components. Despite these differences, numerous intervention programs are available for each developmental stage and age range.

Review of evidence base

Research on the efficacy and effectiveness of SST for children and adolescents spans decades and extends across a variety of populations, settings, and intervention components. Overall, the evidence suggests that SST is moderately effective for different groups of children and adolescents, including young children with developmental delays and older adolescents with aggressive behavior. In general, SST interventions are associated with positive results and yield small-to-large effect sizes for short-term outcomes (Beelmann, Pfingsten, & Lösel, 1994; Erwin, 1994; Schneider, 1992; Schneider & Byrne, 1985). Though there is evidence that SST is generally effective for improving skills and other socioemotional outcomes in the short term, whether benefits persist for longer periods remains uncertain. Limited available outcome data suggest that gains may be largely maintained for up to 1 year (Schneider, 1992), but other findings show less promising long-term outcomes (Beelmann et al., 1994). It should be noted that the question of whether SST works can be particularly difficult to answer due to the variety of interventions, target populations, and participant age ranges. Following content are examples of applications of SST in specific populations with available information about empirical support for each group.

Evidence-based interventions by problem area/program type

A multitude of SST programs have been developed in recent years, covering a range of diagnoses, ages, formats, and settings. Examples of effective programs for different problem areas are described, including programs for youth with autism spectrum disorders, developmental delays and intellectual disabilities, social anxiety disorder, depression, attention-deficit/hyperactivity disorder, and conduct problems. These evidence-based programs are supported by multiple empirical investigations and have manuals and/or materials available to assist with effective implementation.

Autism spectrum disorder

Collectively, randomized controlled trials and single-subject design studies provide evidence to support the efficacy of SST for youth with ASD in both group programs and inclusive education settings. In the domain of social competence, meta-analytic findings suggest that group interventions demonstrate moderate effects for youth with ASD (Gates, Kang, & Lerner, 2017). Though large effect sizes are often found in studies using self-reported assessments, these changes are fully explained by youth gaining knowledge about social skills rather than implementing/enacting these skills (Gates et al., 2017). In practice, it may be important to encourage the selection and implementation of appropriate behaviors in multiple contexts to support more robust gains and generalization outside the clinic. Other meta-analytic findings indicate moderate-to-large effect sizes for group interventions provided to youth with high-functioning ASD (Wolstencroft et al., 2018). These interventions demonstrate improvements in social communication and reductions of restricted interests and repetitive behaviors, two of the main components of ASD.

Interventions for youth with ASD between the ages of 2–6 years most commonly use the methods and principles of applied behavior analysis (ABA). Interventions using ABA typically include repeated trials of verbal or behavioral prompting (e.g., "Give her a block") and reinforcement (e.g., "Good smiling!" "That's the way to play"), imitation and modeling paradigms, and self-monitoring (Reichow & Volkmar, 2010). To encourage and reinforce social interaction and responding, interventions often focus on the monitoring of others' and the use of one's own verbal and nonverbal communication (e.g., eye contact, facial expressions, body movements). ABA methods can be flexibly applied through delivery by clinicians, parents, or peers in clinic, home, or school settings as an independent intervention or in combination with other approaches.

One widespread application of ABA for the treatment of ASD is the application of the Lovaas model (Lovaas & Smith, 1989). The Lovaas model and early intensive behavioral interventions (EIBIs) more generally have been demonstrated to be effective in treating youth with ASD across several meta-analyses and independent investigations (Reichow, 2012). The EIBI paradigm involves 40h per week of one-on-one therapy delivered by trained clinicians, often in the child's home, for 2 or more years (Reichow & Volkmar, 2010). The Lovaas model utilizes primarily discrete trial training and operant conditioning techniques to teach cognitive, social, and self-care skills, as well as to foster language development.

Interventions for older youth with high-functioning ASD are often implemented in group formats. One such group intervention for children is the Secret Agent Society Small Group Program (SAS; formerly called the Junior Detective Training Program), designed for youth aged 8–12 years (Einfeld et al., 2018). The SAS program has demonstrated sustained improvements in emotion regulation, social competence, and social problem solving as a school-based intervention (Einfeld et al., 2018). The SAS program has a fun multimedia espionage-themed curriculum and includes activities (e.g., a board game and secret agent "gadgets"), discussion, role plays, and "home missions" completed on a computer game. Participants are taught skills across 9 weekly sessions to recognize emotions in themselves and others, express feelings in appropriate ways, communicate and play, build and maintain friendships, solve social problems, and detect and manage bullying. Another evidence-based social skills program is the PEERS Program designed for adolescents (i.e., ages 12–17 years; Laugeson & Frankel, 2010). The PEERS Program was found to be effective in increasing youths' social skill knowledge and overall social functioning (Laugeson & Frankel, 2010). This 14-week group intervention provides youth skills to successfully initiate and maintain friendships, with topics spanning from use of appropriate conversation skills, entering and exiting conversations, and choosing appropriate friends to more varied instruction in areas of humor, changing a bad reputation, and handling rejection, teasing and bullying.

Developmental delays and intellectual disabilities

Children with intellectual disabilities and developmental disorders often exhibit impairments in social functioning. Research has found mixed evidence for SST interventions with this population, with effect sizes ranging from small to large in different meta-analyses (Beelmann et al., 1994; Schneider & Byrne, 1985). Interventions using behavioral methods (e.g., social or material reinforcement) may be associated with larger effect sizes compared to other approaches, such as modeling or coaching (Schneider & Byrne, 1985). The U.S. Department of Education's What Works Clearinghouse (WWC) has also reviewed SST as an intervention for children with disabilities in early childhood education, citing a small evidence base for improvements to the domain of social-emotional development and behavior, and no discernible effects for cognition (U.S. Department of Education, Institute of Education Sciences, What Works Clearinghouse, 2013).

One manualized evidence-based social skills program for youth (i.e., ages 13–17 years) with developmental delays is the Superheroes Social Skills Program (Jenson et al., 2011). The Superheroes Social Skills Program was found to be effective in improving targeted social skills and increasing generalization of skills across settings (O'Handley, Ford, Radley, Helbig, & Wimberly, 2016). The program teaches 17 core skills, including engaging in conversations, responding to questions and requests, recognizing emotions in oneself and others, expressing wants and needs, participating and turn taking, perspective taking, problem solving, and recognizing, reporting, and responding to bullying. Social skills are introduced by superhero characters in animations, modeled by peers through video scenarios, and reviewed in social narratives with comics. Participants practice skills in session with role plays and games using multimedia materials, and in generalized settings at home and school.

Attention deficit/hyperactivity disorder

SST is a component of broader interventions that are effective for ADHD, but SST has little support as a standalone treatment for this population. In its summary, Division 53 of the American Psychological Association (Society of Clinical Child and Adolescent Psychology) gave SST a low effectiveness rating for ADHD, indicating that SST interventions have been evaluated in well-designed studies and have not demonstrated positive results (Effective Child Therapy, 2019; Evans, Owens, & Bunford, 2014). In contrast to traditional, clinic-based SST, however, behavioral interventions that include contingency management for social functioning in recreational settings are considered a well-established treatment for ADHD (Evans et al., 2014). One such intervention is the Summer Treatment Program (STP) for youth aged 5–16 years (Pelham & Hoza, 1996). The STP has been demonstrated to be effective in reducing the frequency of negative behaviors related to ADHD, improving social skills, and enhancing peer relationships (Hantson et al., 2012). Trained group leaders implement behavioral interventions and teach relevant skills. Youth are then able to practice and apply the acquired skills in the context of cooperative team games. Other SST components of effective interventions for ADHD often include parent training, parent-administered skill teaching, and parent generalization components. One example is the Parental Friendship Coaching program (PFC; Mikami et al., 2010), which was found to be effective in increasing social skills and friendship quality in youth aged 6–10 years (Mikami et al., 2010). PFC consists of eight parent group sessions with psychoeducation, modeling, role plays, and homework focused on the individual child's needs.

Social anxiety disorder

For youth anxiety more generally, the Society of Clinical Child and Adolescent Psychology rated SST as an experimental intervention, suggesting a need for more research in this area (Higa-McMillan, Francis, Rith-Najarian, & Chorpita, 2016). Only one available study (i.e., DeRosier, 2004) using the Social Skills Group Intervention (S.S. GRIN) program showed a small positive effect for improving peer relations and reducing social anxiety symptoms. S.S. GRIN is a school-based intervention designed for elementary school children aged 8–11 years who lack appropriate social skills (e.g., impulse control problems) and experience peer relationship difficulties such as peer rejection and bullying. S.S. GRIN is delivered across 8 weeks using didactic instruction, role plays, modeling, and interactive activities. The program teaches basic social skills (e.g., verbal and nonverbal communication, initiation), reinforces prosocial attitudes and behavior (e.g., cooperation, compromise, and negotiation), and builds adaptive coping strategies for social problems such as teasing through strategies of positive reinforcement, corrective feedback, and cognitive reframing.

SST is also a component of several broader cognitive-behavioral intervention packages shown to be effective in treating youth with social anxiety disorder (SAD). One intervention based in cognitive behavioral therapy (CBT) is the Brave Program for Social Anxiety designed for youth aged 7–17 years (Spence, Donovan, & Brechman-Toussaint, 2000). Both in person and online versions of this program have been demonstrated to be effective in increasing social skills and reducing symptoms of anxiety (e.g., Spence et al., 2000). This 12-week program focuses on SST, cognitions associated with SAD, and exposure to social situations. Another intervention delivered as an integrated treatment for socially anxious youth (i.e., ages 7–17 years) is Social Effectiveness Therapy for Children and Adolescents (SET-C; Beidel et al., 2004). SET-C has been demonstrated to be effective in increasing social skills and reducing symptoms of social anxiety, with gains being maintained for multiple years (Beidel et al., 2005). SET-C consists of 24 sessions delivered across 12 weeks with components of psychoeducation for children and parents, peer generalization, and exposure (administered individually). This intervention was adapted for implementation in the school setting for students aged 11–18 years and is known as the Skills for Academic and Social Success (SASS) program (Fisher, Masia-Warner, & Klein, 2004). Spanning 12 weeks, SASS is a comprehensive system that includes weekly group skills training, weekend social events and in-class exposures, focused individual sessions, and psychoeducation sessions for parents and teachers.

Depression

Broadly, meta-analytic findings suggest that SST has moderate effects for children with internalizing and externalizing problems in areas such as social interaction and self-concept, but limited evidence is available for the independent effect of SST on depression (Schneider, 1992; Schneider & Byrne, 1985). SST is a component of several intervention packages shown to be effective in treating youth with depression using CBT or interpersonal psychotherapy (IPT). Typically, SST for depression involves psychoeducation, modeling, behavioral rehearsal, and exposure (Sburlati, Lyneham, Schniering, & Rapee, 2014). A widely used CBT intervention that includes a social skills component is the Coping with Depression Course for Adolescents (CWD-A; Clarke, Lewinsohn, & Hops, 1990). Intended for youth aged 13–18 years, CWD-A is delivered in a group format across 12–16 sessions, with psychoeducation, structured social activities, and social skill building with corresponding homework. Social skills targets might include verbal and nonverbal communication, practicing introductions, or starting and maintaining conversations. In addition to CBT interventions, IPT has demonstrated efficacy in treating youth with depression both as a preventative program with Interpersonal Psychotherapy-Adolescent Skills Training (IPT-AST; Young, Mufson, & Davies, 2006) and as an intervention with Interpersonal Psychotherapy-A (IPT-A; Mufson et al., 1994) for youth aged 12–18. These treatments emphasize building communication skills and interpersonal problem-solving abilities through didactic training, role plays, and behavioral rehearsal.

Conduct problems and aggression

SST interventions and prevention programs for antisocial and aggressive youth show small-to-moderate effects overall with improvements in social skills, externalizing behaviors, social adjustment, and self-esteem, as well as modest improvements in antisocial behavior (Ang & Hughes, 2002; Losel & Beelmann, 2003). One evidence-based comprehensive program incorporating SST is the Fast Track Program and corresponding PATHS curriculum for preschool and elementary-age youth (Greenberg et al., 1995). The Fast Track program and PATHS curriculum have been demonstrated to effectively reduce the occurrence of conduct problems and to increase social skills in youth (Conduct Problems Prevention Research Group, 2011). The PATHS curriculum typically consists of two 20- to 30-min sessions per week, though it can be flexibly applied, with the complete program spanning an academic year. The lessons and activities aim to increase social competence, positive peer relations, interpersonal problem-solving skills, and emotional understanding and regulation, as well as decrease internalizing and externalizing problems.

Another noteworthy intervention is the Incredible Years training series for youth aged 3–8 years, which can be implemented as a treatment for children with conduct problems or ADHD, as well as a prevention program in schools or clinics (Webster-Stratton, 2001). The Incredible Years series, comprising parent, teacher, and child training modules, has been demonstrated to be effective in reducing disruptive behavior and increasing social skills (Webster-Stratton, 2001). The parent training component encourages the development of a strong parent-child relationship through child-directed play and effective parenting practices (e.g., management of misbehavior, rule and limit setting, and use of praise and incentives). Teacher training focuses on classroom management strategies and promotes prosocial behavior and school readiness. The core social skills and problem-solving curriculum for children teaches emotion management skills (e.g., talking about feelings, identifying and understanding others' feelings), social skills (e.g., how to make friends, enter groups, and play with others), problem-solving skills (e.g., solving problems step by step), and classroom behavior skills (e.g., listening, following rules) through video modeling, discussion groups, and individualized feedback.

Another effective intervention for conduct problems is the Superheroes Social Skills program adapted slightly for aggressive and disruptive behavior (Jenson et al., 2011). The Superheroes Social Skills program has been shown to effectively decrease the occurrence of disruptive and aggressive behavior among children aged 7–12 years with high incidence disabilities (e.g., learning disabilities, emotional and behavioral disorders, mild intellectual disabilities, speech and language impairment, and other health impairments; O'Handley, Radley, & Cavell, 2016). Training occurs across 10 sessions to introduce skills such as instructional control and turn taking with video modeling, behavioral rehearsal, self-monitoring, and reinforcement strategies. As mentioned earlier, the Superheroes Social Skills program can also be used for individuals with developmental delays and intellectual disabilities.

Conclusions and future directions

SST is an important intervention for children and adolescents who have difficulty navigating peer interactions due to acquisition- or performance-based social skills deficits. Rooted in social learning and behavioral theories, SST includes target skills ranging from foundational conversational skills (e.g., eye contact) to more complex communication skills (e.g., initiating conversations, conflict resolution) and social-cognitive and emotional skills (e.g., perspective taking, emotion regulation). Skills are taught through psychoeducation and direct instruction, modeling, behavioral rehearsal, feedback, and reinforcement and are supported by social-cognitive training components. SST can be delivered in individual or groups formats across clinical or educational settings for a variety of youth populations. Training should be individualized according to child characteristics and cultural preferences to meet specific needs and maximize intervention outcomes.

Across different populations and implementation approaches, SST appears to be effective in improving social skills and other domains of social and behavioral functioning with small-to-moderate effects. Although some suggest that these effects are indicative of clinically meaningful and noticeable differences, others interpret the small effects of SST more critically (Schneider, 1992). Youth with social skills deficits are likely to experience multiple social and emotional challenges, which may need to be addressed with various intervention approaches. For this reason, it has been suggested that SST may be inadequate as a sole intervention (e.g., Spence, 2003), but may provide important contributions as part of a comprehensive treatment package (Gresham, Cook, Crews, & Kern, 2004).

More research is needed to understand how effects from SST can be maximized for different populations of children and adolescents, particularly relating to factors of diversity. Future research should focus on previously overlooked groups, such as children with depression or psychosis, as well as examine outcomes for youth with diverse cultural identities to inform potential adaptations for these populations. Other important future research considerations include increasing the correspondence between behaviors taught and measured, differentiating between social skill knowledge and performance, and assessing the generalizability of skills to other contexts. Intervention studies may also aim to improve the social validity of SST components (e.g., socially significant goals) and outcome measures to those that are likely to predict socially important outcomes (e.g., peer status; Gresham et al., 2004). Lastly, though ample evidence suggests that SST is effective in the short term, little is known about the maintenance of gains over time. A crucial area of future inquiry is the evaluation of long-term outcomes and maintenance of skills with consideration for different intervention strategies and degrees of intensity and duration.

References

Algozzine, D., Daunic, A. P., & Smith, S. W. (2010). Conflict resolution, peer mediation, and bullying prevention. In R. Algozzine, A. P. Daunic, & S. W. Smith (Eds.), *Preventing problem behaviors: Schoolwide programs and classroom practices* (5th ed., pp. 113–132). Thousand Oaks, CA: Corwin.

Ang, R., & Hughes, J. (2002). Differential benefits of skills training with antisocial youth based on group composition: A meta-analytic investigation. *School Psychology Review*, *31*(2), 164–185.

Arnold, M. E., & Hughes, J. N. (1999). First do no harm: Adverse effects of grouping deviant youth for skills training. *Journal of School Psychology*, *37*(1), 99–115. https://doi.org/10.1016/S0022-4405(98)00027-2.

Bandura, A. (1977). *Social learning theory*. Englewood Cliffs, NJ: Prentice-Hall.

Beelmann, A., Pfingsten, U., & Lösel, F. (1994). Effects of training social competence in children: A meta-analysis of recent evaluation studies. *Journal of Clinical Child Psychology*, *23*(3), 260–271. https://doi.org/10.1207/s15374424jccp2303_4.

Beidel, D. C., Turner, S. M., & Morris, T. L. (2004). *Social effectiveness therapy for children and adolescents (SET-C)*. Toronto: Multi-Health Systems, Inc. Ontario.

Beidel, D. C., Turner, S. M., Young, B., & Paulson, A. (2005). Social effectiveness therapy for children: Three-year follow-up. *Journal of Consulting and Clinical Psychology*, *73*(4), 721–725. https://doi.org/10.1037/0022-006x.73.4.721.

Bell, A. C., & D'Zurilla, T. J. (2009). Problem-solving therapy for depression: A meta-analysis. *Clinical Psychology Review*, *29*(4), 348–353. https://doi.org/10.1016/j.cpr.2009.02.003.

Bellini, S., Peters, J. K., Benner, L., & Hopf, A. (2007). A meta-analysis of school-based social skills interventions for children with autism spectrum disorders. *Remedial and Special Education*, *28*(3), 153–162. https://doi.org/10.1177/07419325070280030401.

Camargo, S. P. H., Rispoli, M., Ganz, J., Hong, E. R., Davis, H., & Mason, R. (2016). Behaviorally based interventions for teaching social interaction skills to children with ASD in inclusive settings: A meta-analysis. *Journal of Behavioral Education, 25*(2), 223–248. https://doi.org/10.1007/s10864-015-9240-1.

Cartledge, G., & Loe, S. (2001). Cultural diversity and social skill instruction. *Exceptionality, 9*(1), 33–46. https://doi.org/10.1207/s15327035ex091&2_4.

Cartledge, G., & Milburn, J. F. (1996). *Cultural diversity and social skills instruction: Understanding ethnic and gender differences*. Champaign, IL: Research Press.

Cavell, T. (1990). Social adjustment, social performance, and social skills: A tri-component model of social competence. *Journal of Clinical Child & Adolescent Psychology, 19*(2), 111–122. https://doi.org/10.1207/s15374424jccp1902_2.

Charlop-Christy, M. H., Le, L., & Freeman, K. A. (2000). A comparison of video modeling with in vivo modeling for teaching children with autism. *Journal of Autism and Developmental Disorders, 30*(6), 537–552. https://doi.org/10.1023/A:1005635326276.

Clarke, G. N., Lewinsohn, P. M., & Hops, H. (1990). *Instructor's manual for the adolescent coping with depression course*. Portland, OR: Kaiser Permanente Center for Health Research.

Coleman, S. W., & Prywes, Y. (2014). Teaching conflict resolution in a workshop. In P. T. Coleman, M. Deutsch, & E. C. Marcus (Eds.), *The handbook of conflict resolution: Theory and practice* (3rd ed., pp. 849–876). San Francisco, CA: Josey Bass.

Conduct Problems Prevention Research Group. (2011). The effects of the Fast Track preventive intervention on the development of conduct disorder across childhood. *Child Development, 82*, 331–345. https://doi.org/10.1111/j.1467-8624.2010.01558.x.

D'Zurilla, T. J., & Nezu, A. M. (2010). Problem-solving therapy. In K. S. Dobson (Ed.), *Handbook of cognitive-behavioral therapies* (3rd ed., pp. 197–225). New York, NY: Guilford Press.

Daunic, A. P., Smith, S. W., Garvan, C. W., Barber, B. R., Becker, M. K., Peters, C. D., … Naranjo, A. H. (2012). Reducing developmental risk for emotional/behavioral problems: A randomized controlled trial examining the Tools for Getting Along curriculum. *Journal of School Psychology, 50*, 149–166. https://doi.org/10.1016/j.jsp.2011.09.003.

DeRosier, M. E. (2004). Building relationships and combating bullying: Effectiveness of a school-based social skills group intervention. *Journal of Clinical Child and Adolescent Psychology, 33*(1), 196–201. https://doi.org/10.1207/s15374424jccp3301_18.

Duckworth, M. P., & Mercer, V. (2006). Assertiveness training. In J. E. Fisher & W. T. O'Donohue (Eds.), *Practitioner's guide to evidence-based psychotherapy* (pp. 80–92). Boston, MA: Springer.

Effective Child Therapy. (2019). Retrieved from https://effectivechildtherapy.org/.

Einfeld, S. L., Beaumont, R., Clark, T., Clarke, K. S., Costley, D., Gray, K. M., … Howlin, P. (2018). School-based social skills training for young people with autism spectrum disorders. *Journal of Intellectual & Developmental Disability, 43*(1), 29–39. https://doi.org/10.3109/13668250.2017.1326587.

Elliott, S. N., & Gresham, F. M. (2007). *Social skills improvement system: Classwide intervention program*. Minneapolis, MN: Pearson Assessments.

Erwin, P. G. (1994). Effectiveness of social skills training with children: A meta-analytic study. *Counselling Psychology Quarterly, 7*(3), 305–310. https://doi.org/10.1080/09515079408254154.

Evans, S. W., Owens, J. S., & Bunford, N. (2014). Evidence-based psychosocial treatments for children and adolescents with attention-deficit/hyperactivity disorder. *Journal of Clinical Child & Adolescent Psychology, 43*(4), 527–551. https://doi.org/10.1080/15374416.2013.850700.

Fisher, P. H., Masia-Warner, C., & Klein, R. G. (2004). Skills for social and academic success: A school-based intervention for social anxiety disorder in adolescents. *Clinical Child and Family Psychology Review, 7*(4), 241–249. https://doi.org/10.1007/s10567-004-6088-7.

Frey, K. S., Hirschstein, M. K., Snell, J. L., Edstrom, L. V., MacKenzie, E. P., & Broderick, C. J. (2005). Reducing playground bullying and supporting beliefs: An experimental trial of the steps to respect program. *Developmental Psychology*, *41*(3), 479–491. http://dx.doi.org.proxy-ln.researchport.umd.edu/10.1037/0012-1649.41.3.479.

Gates, J. A., Kang, E., & Lerner, M. D. (2017). Efficacy of group social skills interventions for youth with autism spectrum disorder: A systematic review and meta-analysis. *Clinical Psychology Review*, *52*, 164–181. https://doi.org/10.1016/j.cpr.2017.01.006.

Greenberg, M. T., Kusche, C. A., Cook, E. T., & Quamma, J. P. (1995). Promoting emotional competence in school-aged children: The effects of the PATHS curriculum. *Development and Psychopathology*, *7*, 117–136. https://doi.org/10.1017/s0954579400006374.

Gresham, F. M. (2016). Social skills assessment and intervention for children and youth. *Cambridge Journal of Education*, *46*(3), 319–332. https://doi.org/10.1080/0305764x.2016.1195788.

Gresham, F. M. (2017). Evidence-based interventions for social skill deficits in children and adolescents. In L. A. Theodore (Ed.), *Handbook of evidence-based interventions for children and adolescents* (pp. 365–376). New York, NY: Springer Publishing Company.

Gresham, F. M., Cook, C. R., Crews, S. D., & Kern, L. (2004). Social skills training for children and youth with emotional and behavioral disorders: Validity considerations and future directions. *Behavioral Disorders*, *30*(1), 32–46. https://doi.org/10.1177/019874290403000101.

Grover, R. L., Nangle, D. W., Serwik, A., Fales, J., & Prenoveau, J. (2013). The measure of heterosocial competence: Development and psychometric investigation. *Journal of Social and Personal Relationships*, *30*, 457–481. https://doi.org/10.1177/0265407512458658.

Hammond, W. R., Warfield, J. R., & Yung, B. R. (2015). *Positive adolescent choices training (PACT): A model for violence prevention groups with African American youth* (2nd ed.). Champaign, IL: Research Press.

Hansen, D. J., Nangle, D. W., & Meyer, K. A. (1998). Enhancing the effectiveness of social skills interventions with adolescents. *Education and Treatment of Children*, *21*, 489–513.

Hantson, J., Wang, P. P., Grizenko-Vida, M., Ter-Stepanian, M., Harvey, W., Joober, R., & Grizenko, N. (2012). Effectiveness of a therapeutic summer camp for children with ADHD: Phase I clinical intervention trial. *Journal of Attention Disorders*, *16*, 610–617. https://doi.org/10.1177/1087054711416800.

Hartup, W. W. (1989). Social relationships and their developmental significance. *American Psychologist*, *44*, 120–126. https://doi.org/10.1037//0003-066x.44.2.120.

Higa-McMillan, C. K., Francis, S. E., Rith-Najarian, L., & Chorpita, B. F. (2016). Evidence base update: 50 years of research on treatment for child and adolescent anxiety. *Journal of Clinical Child & Adolescent Psychology*, *45*(2), 91–113. https://doi.org/10.1080/15374416.2015.1046177.

Huey, S. J., Jr., & Polo, A. J. (2017). Evidence-based psychotherapies with ethnic minority children and adolescents. In J. R. Weisz & A. E. Kazdin (Eds.), *Evidence-based psychotherapies for children and adolescents* (3rd ed., pp. 361–378). New York, NY: The Guilford Press.

Hunter, L. J., DiPerna, J. C., Hart, S. C., & Crowley, M. (2018). At what cost? Examining the cost effectiveness of a universal social–emotional learning program. *School Psychology Quarterly*, *33*(1), 147–154. https://doi.org/10.1037/spq0000232.

Ibarrola-Garcia, S., Iriarte, C., & Aznarez-Sanado, M. (2017). Self-awareness emotional learning during mediation procedures in the school context. *Electronic Journal of Research in Educational Psychology*, *15*, 75–105. https://doi.org/10.14204/ejrep.41.15175.

January, A. M., Casey, R. J., & Paulson, D. (2011). A meta-analysis of classroom-wide interventions to build social skills: Do they work? *School Psychology Review*, *40*(2), 242–257.

Jenson, W. R., Bowen, J., Clark, E., Block, H., Gabriensen, T., Hood, J., & Springer, B. (2011). *Superheroes social skills*. Eugene, OR: Pacific Northwest.

Kelly, J. A. (1982). *Social-skills training: A practical guide for interventions*. New York: Springer.

Laugeson, E. A., & Frankel, F. (2010). *Social skills for teenagers with developmental and autism spectrum disorders: The PEERS treatment manual*. New York: Routledge.

Losel, F., & Beelmann, A. (2003). Effects of child skills training in preventing antisocial behavior: A systematic review of randomized evaluations. *The Annals of the American Academy of Political and Social Science*, *587*(1), 84–109. https://doi.org/10.1177/0002716202250793.

Lovaas, O. I., & Smith, T. (1989). A comprehensive behavioral theory of autistic children: Paradigm for research and treatment. *Journal of Behavior Therapy and Experimental Psychiatry*, *20*, 17–29. https://doi.org/10.1016/0005-7916(89)90004-9.

Maag, J. W. (2005). Social skills training for youth with emotional and behavioral disorders and learning disabilities: Problems, conclusions, and suggestions. *Exceptionality*, *13*(3), 155–172. https://doi.org/10.1207/s15327035ex1303_2.

Matthews, N. L., Orr, B. C., Warriner, K., DeCarlo, M., Sorensen, M., Laflin, J., & Smith, C. J. (2018). Exploring the effectiveness of a peer-mediated model of the PEERS curriculum: A pilot randomized control trial. *Journal of Autism and Developmental Disorders*, *48*(7), 2458–2475. https://doi.org/10.1007/s10803-018-3504-2.

McGinnis, E. (2011a). *Skillstreaming the elementary school child: A guide for teaching prosocial skills* (3rd ed.). Champaign, IL: Research Press.

McGinnis, E. (2011b). *Skillstreaming the adolescent: A guide for teaching prosocial skills* (3rd ed.). Champaign, IL: Research Press.

Mikami, A. Y., Lerner, M. D., Griggs, M. S., McGrath, A., & Calhoun, C. D. (2010). Parental influence on children with attention-deficit/hyperactivity disorder: II. Results of a pilot intervention training parents as friendship coaches for children. *Journal of Abnormal Child Psychology*, *38*, 737–749. https://doi.org/10.1007/s10802-010-9403-4.

Mufson, L., Moreau, D., Weissman, M. M., Wickramaratne, P., Martin, J., & Samoilov, A. (1994). Modification of interpersonal psychotherapy with depressed adolescents (IPT-A): Phase I and II studies. *Journal of the American Academy of Child & Adolescent Psychiatry*, *33*, 695–705. https://doi.org/10.1097/00004583-199406000-00011.

O'Handley, R. D., Ford, W. B., Radley, K. C., Helbig, K. A., & Wimberly, J. K. (2016). Social skills training for adolescents with intellectual disabilities: A school-based evaluation. *Behavior Modification*, *40*, 541–567. https://doi.org/10.1177/0145445516629938.

O'Handley, R. D., Radley, K. C., & Cavell, H. J. (2016). Utilization of superheroes social skills to reduce disruptive and aggressive behavior. *Preventing School Failure: Alternative Education for Children and Youth*, *60*, 124–132. https://doi.org/10.1080/1045988x.2015.1038775.

Pelham, W. E., & Hoza, B. (1996). Intensive treatment: A summer treatment program for children with ADHD. In E. D. Hibbs & P. S. Jensen (Eds.), *Psychosocial treatments for child and adolescent disorders: Empirically based strategies for clinical practice* (pp. 311–340). Washington, DC: American Psychological Association.

Reichow, B. (2012). Overview of meta-analyses on early intensive behavioral intervention for young children with autism spectrum disorders. *Journal of Autism and Developmental Disorders*, *42*, 512–520. https://doi.org/10.1007/s10803-011-1218-9.

Reichow, B., & Volkmar, F. R. (2010). Social skills interventions for individuals with autism: Evaluation for evidence-based practices within a best evidence synthesis framework. *Journal of Autism and Developmental Disorders*, *40*(2), 149–166. https://doi.org/10.1007/s10803-009-0842-0.

Rivera, B. D., & Adkinson, D. R. (1997). Culturally sensitive interventions: Social skills training with children and parents from culturally and linguistically diverse backgrounds. *Intervention in School and Clinic*, *33*(2), 75–80. https://doi.org/10.1177/105345129703300201.

Rowe, L. S., Jouriles, E. N., & McDonald, R. (2015). Reducing sexual victimization in adolescent girls: A randomized controlled pilot trial of my voice, my choice. *Behavior Therapy*, *46*, 315–327. https://doi.org/10.1016/j.beth.2014.11.003.

Sburlati, E. S., Lyneham, H. J., Schniering, C. A., & Rapee, R. M. (Eds.), (2014). *Evidence-based CBT for anxiety and depression in children and adolescents: A competencies based approach*. Malden, MA: John Wiley & Sons.

Schneider, B. H. (1992). Didactic methods for enhancing children's peer relations: A quantitative review. *Clinical Psychology Review*, *12*(3), 363–382.

Schneider, B. H., & Byrne, B. M. (1985). Children's social skills training: A meta-analysis. In B. H. Schneider, K. R. Rubin, & J. E. Ledingham (Eds.), *Children's peer relations: Issues in assessment and intervention*. New York: Springer-Verlag.

Segrin, C., & Givertz, M. (2003). Methods of social skills training and development. In J. O. Greene & B. R. Burleson (Eds.), *Handbook of communication and social interaction skills* (pp. 135–176). Mahwah, NJ: Erlbaum.

Shukla-Mehta, S., Miller, T., & Callahan, K. J. (2010). Evaluating the effectiveness of video instruction on social and communication skills training for children with autism spectrum disorders: A review of the literature. *Focus on Autism and Other Developmental Disabilities*, *25*(1), 23–36. https://doi.org/10.1177/1088357609352901.

Spence, S. H. (2003). Social skills training with children and young people: Theory, evidence and practice. *Child and Adolescent Mental Health*, *8*(2), 84–96. https://doi.org/10.1111/1475-3588.00051.

Spence, S. H., Donovan, C., & Brechman-Toussaint, M. (2000). The treatment of childhood social phobia: The effectiveness of a social skills training-based, cognitive-behavioural intervention, with and without parental involvement. *Journal of Child Psychology and Psychiatry*, *41*, 713–726. https://doi.org/10.1111/1469-7610.00659.

Stokes, T. F., & Osnes, P. G. (1989). An operant pursuit of generalization. *Behavior Therapy*, *20*(3), 337–355. https://doi.org/10.1016/s0005-7894(89)80054-1.

Tamnes, C. K., Overbye, K., Ferschmann, L., Fjell, A. M., Walhovd, K. B., Blakemore, S. J., & Dumontheil, I. (2018). Social perspective taking is associated with self-reported prosocial behavior and regional cortical thickness across adolescence. *Developmental Psychology*, *54*(9), 1745–1757. https://doi.org/10.31234/osf.io/xp2gk.

Tsunemi, K., Tamura, A., Ogawa, S., Isomura, T., & Masataka, N. (2014). Intensive exposure to narrative in story books as a possibly effective treatment of social perspective-taking in schoolchildren with autism. *Frontiers in Psychology*, *5*, 2. https://doi.org/10.3389/fpsyg.2014.00002.

U.S. Department of Education, Institute of Education Sciences, What Works Clearinghouse. (2013). *Early childhood education interventions for children with disabilities intervention report: Social skills training*. Retrieved from http://whatworks.ed.gov.

van der Stouwe, T., Asscher, J. J., Hoeve, M., van der Laan, P. H., & Stams, G. J. M. (2016). Social skills training for juvenile delinquents: Post treatment changes. *Journal of Experimental Criminology*, *12*, 515–536. https://doi.org/10.1007/s11292-016-9262-2.

Webster-Stratton, C. (2001). The incredible years: Parents, teachers, and children training series. *Residential Treatment for Children & Youth*, *18*, 31–45. https://doi.org/10.1300/j007v18n03_04.

Willis, D., Siceloff, E. R., Morse, M., Neger, E., & Flory, K. (2019). Stand-alone social skills training for youth with ADHD: A systematic review. *Clinical Child and Family Psychology Review*, 1–19. https://doi.org/10.1007/s10567-019-00291-3.

Wilson, K. P. (2013). Teaching social-communication skills to preschoolers with autism: Efficacy of video versus in vivo modeling in the classroom. *Journal of Autism and Developmental Disorders*, *43*(8), 1819–1831. https://doi.org/10.1007/s10803-012-1731-5.

Wolstencroft, J., Robinson, L., Srinivasan, R., Kerry, E., Mandy, W., & Skuse, D. (2018). A systematic review of group social skills interventions, and meta-analysis of outcomes, for children with high functioning ASD. *Journal of Autism and Developmental Disorders*, *48*(7), 2293–2307. https://doi.org/10.1007/s10803-018-3485-1.

Young, J. F., Mufson, L., & Davies, M. (2006). Efficacy of interpersonal psychotherapy-adolescent skills training: An indicated preventive intervention for depression. *Journal of Child Psychology and Psychiatry*, *47*, 1254–1262. https://doi.org/10.1111/j.1469-7610.2006.01667.x.

Chapter 7

Intervening with adults

Samantha J. Gregus[a], Elissa R. Failes[a], Elizabeth Ramirez[a], Raegan Harrington[b], Phoebe Welcome[b], and Rebecca A. Schwartz-Mette[b]
[a]*Wichita State University, Wichita, KS, United States,* [b]*University of Maine, Orono, ME, United States*

Social relationships are centrally important to adults' health and well-being. Friendships decrease loneliness, boost happiness, and provide social support (e.g., Arnett, 2013; Demir, 2010), and strong communication with a romantic partner can facilitate validation, deepen connections, and increase relationship satisfaction (Bodenmann, Bradbury, & Pihet, 2009). Social skills are foundational to social interactions, and social skills deficits are linked with harmful physiological effects (e.g., Snyder, Castellani, & Whisman, 2006), psychological problems (e.g., Horn, Xu, Beam, Turkheimer, & Emery, 2013), educational attrition (e.g., Foley Nicpon et al., 2006), poor job outcomes (e.g., Huffcutt, Conway, Roth, & Stone, 2001), and cognitive decline (e.g., Zunzunegui, Alvarado, Del Ser, & Otero, 2003).

Fortunately, interventions are available to improve outcomes for individuals with social skills deficits. Social skills training (SST) aims to increase socially desirable behavior and reduce inappropriate behavior. This chapter provides an overview of SST programs for adults (including core components, intervention targets, and general efficacy) and offers a sampling of exemplar SST programs for many presenting concerns.

Overview of SST programs for adults

SST is grounded in social learning theory, which posits that people learn by observing and imitating others. First proposed by Bandura (1969), the theory states that behavior is best explained in terms of continuous, reciprocal interactions between the individual and his or her environment. Effective social skills are conceptualized as the ability to create a favorable social climate whereby others respond according to an individual's expectations and desires (Eisler & Frederiksen, 1980). In contrast, social skills deficits refer to an inability to produce appropriate social behavior needed to function effectively. Deficits in social skills may result from learning environments failing to provide appropriate

Social Skills Across the Life Span. https://doi.org/10.1016/B978-0-12-817752-5.00007-X

social models and/or punishing appropriate social behavior, a lack of social intelligence, or the result of underlying psychological and/or neurological disorders [e.g., autism spectrum disorders (ASD), schizophrenia], which prevent individuals from interacting effectively with others. Resulting social interactions can be experienced as unsatisfying, distressing, and disruptive, which can exacerbate deficits and increase avoidance strategies. Social isolation further prevents refinement of existing skills, inciting a negatively reinforced, cyclical process. SST relies on the social learning premise that, if provided the right context and reinforcement, individuals can generalize social skills learned and practiced in an artificial setting to real-world contexts, resulting in functional improvement.

Core components

SST programs include core components aimed at helping individuals acquire and implement effective social skills. Adult SST begins with identifying goals via collaborative discussions and/or baseline assessment (e.g., Kurtz, Boelter, Jarmolowicz, Chin, & Hagopian, 2011; Pratt, Mueser, Wolfe, Santos, & Bartels, 2017; Westerhof-Evers, Visser-Keizer, Fasotti, & Spikman, 2019). Complex skills (e.g., maintaining conversation) are then operationally defined and broken down into smaller behaviors (e.g., eye contact, responding).

Core techniques begin with psychoeducation. The trainer teaches the client in what circumstances, why, and how to use the skill. Next, the trainer models the skill to demonstrate effective use. Demonstrations can be completed in person, by video, and/or in role plays with the client. Next, the trainer provides opportunities for the client to practice the skill. Rehearsal may involve repetition, role plays with the trainer or other group members, and practices in simulated environments where the skill is to be used. During these role plays, the trainer provides feedback on how well the client used the skill and on his or her use of nonverbal behaviors (e.g., voice tone, body posture, language). The trainer will then offer specific recommendations to refine the skill. Trainers will shape more complex skills by combining smaller skills and providing reinforcement for approximations toward the desired end goal.

The process is repeated until individuals master and generalize the skills to new contexts. Once goals are achieved, problem solving is used to navigate barriers to implementation and generalization of new skills. Trainers also emphasize the long-term value of continued use of new skills, even when short-term negative consequences may appear (e.g., unexpected reactions from others). In some cases, the trainer may involve family and friends in treatment to enhance outcomes.

Implementation and service delivery variations

SST programs vary with regard to setting, trainers, program duration, methods utilized, and whether SST functions as a standalone intervention or single component in a larger program. These choice points offer clinicians flexibility.

Consistent with evidence-based practice, considerations of the clients' values and preferences should be embedded throughout treatment to collaboratively determine appropriate targets and procedures.

Setting

SST can be delivered to individuals or groups of clients with similar deficits. Groups usually range from 6 to 10 members (Harrison-Felix et al., 2018; Herbert et al., 2005). Individualized formats offer greater focus on the client's goals, whereas group formats benefit from increased opportunities for skill practice, observation, and feedback. Culture may play a role in which format is most acceptable to clients, as structured group settings might help with destigmatization, whereas individual therapy helps to protect confidentiality (Hays, 2009).

Most SST sessions occur face to face in outpatient or community settings, although some have been implemented successfully in inpatient and residential treatment settings (e.g., Laugeson, Gantman, Kapp, Orenski, & Ellingsen, 2015) and via a telephone or computer (Axelrod, Perepletchikova, Holtzman, & Sinha, 2011; Schlegel, Vicaria, Isaacowitz, & Hall, 2017). In-person SST provides opportunities for real-world skills practice and may increase attention to idiosyncratic nuances such as nonverbal communication patterns. However, programs offered through other means (e.g., telephone) reduce barriers for clients who might otherwise lack access. For example, in a program combining motivational interviewing and communication skills training for adults with HIV, telephone coaching helped increase access for geographically isolated individuals and alleviate confidentiality concerns (Lovejoy & Heckman, 2014).

Trainers

Some SST programs use licensed psychologists, psychologist trainees, or master's level therapists (Axelrod et al., 2011; Doyle et al., 2013), and others employ trained undergraduate students, case managers, or other staff (Pratt et al., 2017; Tiger, Hanley, & Bruzek, 2008). Trainer education level is often determined by the complexity of the skills being taught and the severity of the population's presenting concerns. Group programs often use two trainers to model intervention strategies and keep the group on track.

Duration

Sessions are typically scheduled on a weekly basis for a specified number of weeks (Laugeson et al., 2015; Westerhof-Evers et al., 2017). Focused programs that target one or two problem areas (e.g., assertiveness, couple distress) might last only one session (Markman, Stanley, & Blumberg, 2001). Other, more comprehensive programs targeting severe symptom presentations [e.g., ASD, traumatic brain injury (TBI)] can last several months to more than a year (Laugeson et al., 2015; Pratt et al., 2017). While larger effect sizes may be observed in long-term interventions, brief interventions tend to reduce attrition, be more affordable, and promote self-management of symptoms (Robinson & Reiter, 2016). For example, problem-solving therapy (PST) has been adapted for use in integrated primary care settings and has been found to be effective in as few as three or four sessions (Mynors-Wallis, Gath, Day, & Baker, 2000; Nguyen, Chen, & Denburg, 2018).

Involvement of others

As noted, training programs may involve family members or caregivers. Programs such as Program for the Education and Enrichment of Relational Skills (PEERS) for Young Adults (Laugeson, 2017) and functional communication training (FCT) (Tiger et al., 2008) teach family members how to promote clients' skill acquisition and generalization (Bellack, Mueser, Gingerich, & Agresta, 2013). Programs might also include significant others to improve their relationship with the client (e.g., Westerhof-Evers et al., 2019). Family involvement may be especially important to members of ethnically and racially diverse backgrounds who might value a collective approach to treatment (Hays, 2009).

Methods utilized

Traditional, in vivo skills practice is by far the most common intervention method with the strongest research base to support its effectiveness (e.g., Bell & D'Zurilla, 2009; Jeste & Maglione, 2013). Clients practice skills directly with the trainer(s), other group members, or in simulated/real-world environments (e.g., "field trips") that allow practice of newly acquired skills and enhance generalization effects. Notably, technology-assisted modeling procedures are also gaining traction. In video modeling, for example, clients watch a model on video engage in a target behavior and are asked to imitate the behavior. The video can be shown in its entirety or in smaller segments with the client completing small approximations of the target behavior in between clips (Mason, Rutar Shuman, & Cook, 2013).

Research findings are mixed or emerging with regard to the effectiveness of video and computer methods. Some data support the use of video modeling for teaching academic, social, and daily living skills (Mason et al., 2013), but insufficient research evidence supports video modeling with individuals with ASD (Anderson et al., 2017) and social anxiety disorder (Smits, Powers, Buxkamper, & Telch, 2006). Computer training programs have been used to increase emotion recognition skills, but effects appear to be limited to young and middle-aged adults (Schlegel et al., 2017). Virtual reality is another emerging area and has been tested among individuals with schizophrenia to improve conversational and communication skills (Park et al., 2011; Rus-Calafell, Gutiérrez-Maldonado, & Ribas-Sabaté, 2014) and among individuals with ASD to improve social cognition and job skills (Kandalaft, Didehbani, Krawczyk, Allen, & Chapman, 2013; Smith et al., 2014). Reviews of these emerging areas are promising, but small samples and noncontrolled designs limit the degree to which findings are conclusive or generalizable.

"Standalone" intervention or program component

Some SST programs were developed as standalone interventions; however, it is common for SST to be embedded within a larger treatment package. In these cases, one or two sessions might focus on enhancing social skills in a targeted fashion while remaining sessions focus on increasing motivation to change, changing cognitions, or building other coping skills (e.g., Reilly & Shopshire, 2002). Standalone interventions benefit from an intensive focus on social skills, whereas combined treatments can help alleviate social impairments often exacerbated by co-occurring psychological disorders.

Primary targets

Adult SST programs generally involve one or more of four primary targets: communication skills, social cognitive skills, relationship building skills, and vocational skills/independent living skills. Programs targeting multiple domains are typically organized into modules with individual sessions focused on one or two areas. Although many programs are manualized, they can be flexibly tailored to client needs. Furthermore, specific skills can be tailored to individual cultural preferences.

Communication skills include microlevel skills, complex skills, assertiveness skills, and conflict management skills. Microlevel skills involve vocal cues, affect, gestures, eye contact, and gait proximity (Almerie et al., 2015) and are beneficial to those whose social skills deficits are more generalized (e.g., ASD; Spain & Blainey, 2015). Complex communication skills include initiating and maintaining conversation, empathetic listening, and turn taking (Nangle, Hansen, Erdley, & Norton, 2010) and are commonly included in treatments for couple distress, social anxiety, TBI, and ASD (Finch, Copley, Cornwell, & Kelly, 2016; Heimberg & Barlow, 1991; NICE, 2016). Assertiveness skills encompass learning to apologize, express (dis)approval, refuse, request change, compromise and negotiate, and defend oneself (Smith, 1985) and are typically included in programs for depression, anxiety, and substance abuse (Cuijpers, Van Straten, Andersson, & Van Oppen, 2008; Reilly & Shopshire, 2002). Conflict management skills consist of how to communicate during and resolve conflict and are often involved in couple or family therapy and personality disorder treatment (Jakubowski, Milne, Brunner, & Miller, 2004).

Social cognitive skills include perspective taking, emotion regulation, and social problem solving (Van Manen, Prins, & Emmelkamp, 2001), and training in this area bolsters critical thinking and evaluation of alternative perspectives. Emotion regulation skills training involves teaching appropriate identification, understanding, and expression of emotion. Social problem solving consists of learning how to define a problem, generate solutions, make decisions, implement solutions, and assess effectiveness (Bell & D'Zurilla, 2009). Social cognitive skills are commonly taught in the treatment of mood and anxiety disorders, schizophrenia, ASD, and TBI (Schlegel et al., 2017; Spain & Blainey, 2015; Westerhof-Evers et al., 2017, 2019).

Relationship-building skills include developing and sustaining friendships and romantic relationships (Jakubowski et al., 2004; Owen, Manthos, & Quirk, 2013) and are largely derived from the communication and social cognitive skills domain (Jakubowski et al., 2004; Owen et al., 2013). Skills include how to meet new people, accept and give compliments, get to know someone, respond to requests, initiate dates, be intimate, and have safe sex. Relationship skills are often taught among individuals with personality disorders, TBI, schizophrenia, and ASD.

Although not all skills in the vocational and independent living domain are "social" in nature, many include foundational components of communication, social cognition, and/or relationship building. For example, vocational programs help clients practice interview skills, engage in salary negotiation, ask for help, communicate with coworkers, and accept feedback (Anderson et al., 2017; Hedley et al., 2017). Independent living skills target use of public transportation, money management, community safety, medical care, and relationships with roommates or residential staff. Such programs are common among adults with ASD, intellectual disability (ID), TBI, and cognitive decline, as these individuals often require additional services and assistance to support their functioning and wellbeing (e.g., Fadyl & McPherson, 2009).

General efficacy of social skills training programs

SST programs have been developed for adults with a wide range of problems. Although the adult SST literature is significantly smaller than the youth SST literature, developing and evaluating SST for adults is a growing priority. Studies evaluating the efficacy of adult SST programs vary across program, population, and setting. Hundreds of programs have been evaluated as standalone interventions, and many reflect single-case designs for specific clients. Others are embedded as a component of larger therapy packages. Fewer programs have been manualized and tested for specific populations, like PEERS for Young Adults (Laugeson, 2017), HOPES-I (Pratt et al., 2017), and T-ScEmo (Westerhof-Evers et al., 2017, 2019).

Published reviews evaluating SST have generally found moderate effects for improved social functioning and reduced impairment in individuals with schizophrenia, bipolar, and depression (e.g., Bartels et al., 2014; Bellack et al., 2013; Pratt et al., 2017). Some psychiatric problems have a larger body of research and a stronger evidence base than others (e.g., severe mental illness, schizophrenia; Pratt et al., 2017; Roberts et al., 2014), but fewer studies have tested adult SST for disorders commonly diagnosed in youth, such as ASD or ID. Further, although social validity (i.e., degree to which SST is acceptable to clients or caregivers) is not consistently assessed, analysis of available data typically indicates support (e.g., Anderson et al., 2017; Chezan, Drasgow, & Martin, 2014). The strength of conclusions can be affected by the sample size, degree of methodological rigor, and variations in measurement outcomes.

SST interventions by problem area

SST programs target a range of psychological issues and disorders. In the following section, we provide an overview of interventions for selected problem areas. We also identify one or two model programs with supportive research outcomes in each area.

Neurodevelopmental disorders

Autism spectrum disorders

Adults with ASD face social isolation, problems in daily living, lower educational attainment, unemployment, and health problems (e.g., Hendricks, 2010; Howlin, Goode, Hutton, & Rutter, 2004), as well as challenges in making friends, forming romantic relationships, and living independently (e.g., Müller, Schuler, & Yates, 2008). Services for adults with ASD tend to be more limited than services for children with ASD, and the literature examining SST programs for adults is also much smaller in comparison.

Despite limited research, the National Institute for Health Care Excellence recommends SST for people with ASD (NICE, 2016). Most programs target communication, social functioning, emotion recognition and regulation, and problem-solving (Spain & Blainey, 2015), and others include vocational and living skills (e.g., Anderson et al., 2017; Hedley et al., 2017). Most interventions are group-based, include 6–10 participants and two or more facilitators, and run for at least 8 weeks. Techniques used include didactics, modeling, role play, rehearsal of skills, feedback, evaluating videos, and social events (Spain & Blainey, 2015). Systematic reviews suggest SST improves social cognition, empathy, self-rated social skills, social support, and loneliness, with less support for improving mental health and quality of life (Lorenc et al., 2018; Spain & Blainey, 2015). Behavioral skills training in vocational programs also improves job-related outcomes (Anderson et al., 2017; Hedley et al., 2017). Although many studies lack social validity data, treatment outcomes were rated "acceptable" in some studies, based on observations and self/caregiver reports (Anderson et al., 2017; Howlin & Yates, 1999).

PEERS for Young Adults (Laugeson, 2017) aims to improve social skills in adults with ASD. PEERS was originally developed and evaluated for use with adolescents with ASD. However, as adults with ASD also struggle with social impairment, PEERS was evaluated with adults in two randomized controlled trials (Gantman, Kapp, Orenski, & Laugeson, 2012; Laugeson et al., 2015) and is considered to be the first evidence-based group treatment for adult ASD. PEERS involves 16 weekly, 90-min group sessions for adults and caregivers, who attend concurrent groups each week. PEERS provides concrete guidance for developing and maintaining relationships and managing peer conflict and rejection. Groups use didactics, skills demonstrations, role plays, coaching, feedback, and homework. Improvements were reported in social skills, responsiveness, engagement, knowledge, and empathy (Gantman et al., 2012; Laugeson et al., 2015), with many gains maintained after 16 weeks.

Intellectual disability

ID originates in childhood, can be comorbid with communication, learning, and psychiatric problems, and often is linked to social skills deficits (Chadsey-Rusch, Rusch, & O'Reilly, 1991). Most studies of SST for adult ID involve very small samples, target different social behaviors, and/or test different intervention strategies (e.g., didactic teaching, reinforcement, shaping, modeling, role playing, feedback, social stories; Gül, 2016; O'Reilly et al., 2004). Given these methodological challenges and variations, sufficient evaluation of each form of SST for ID in adults has not yet amassed.

One SST program accumulating support is FCT for adults with ID. FCT aims to replace maladaptive behaviors with adaptive communication. Problem behaviors are conceptualized via functional analysis. Appropriate communicative responses are chosen, and shaping procedures (e.g., differential reinforcement; Kurtz et al., 2011) aim to develop and solidify new behaviors. FCT has convincing outcomes among adults (Chowdhury & Benson, 2011) and is considered probably efficacious for treating adults with ID (Kurtz et al., 2011). Staff members involved with FCT also report participant benefit and that the intervention is relatively easy to implement (Chezan et al., 2014).

Severe mental illness

Schizophrenia

Individuals with schizophrenia experience deficits in social cognition and problem solving, problems integrating prior experiences into appropriate future use, communication difficulties, social anhedonia, and isolation (Bellack, 2004; Bellack et al., 2013; Penn, Corrigan, Bentall, Racenstein, & Newman, 1997), placing them at risk for emergency room visits, hospitalization, and early nursing home placement (Bartels & Pratt, 2009; Miller & Rosenheck, 2006). SST programs target individuals' social cognitive, communication, and daily living skills, such as managing finances, using public transportation, and medication compliance (Jeste & Maglione, 2013). Duration ranges from 1 month to a year of weekly sessions. SST can be delivered in individual, group, or virtual settings and utilizes modeling, role play, and feedback (Bellack et al., 2013). While antipsychotic medications are used to control positive symptoms (e.g., hallucinations, delusions) of schizophrenia, SST addresses the negative symptoms (e.g., blunted affect, lack of speech, reduced social drive) and enhances rehabilitation (Almerie et al., 2015; Kurtz & Mueser, 2008).

Systematic reviews indicate that SST generally enhances social functioning, reduces relapse risk, and improves the quality of life for those with schizophrenia (Almerie et al., 2015). In a meta-analysis of randomized controlled trials,

SST resulted in large effect sizes for knowledge of training material; moderate effect sizes for performance of social and daily living skills, community functioning, and negative symptom improvement; and small effect sizes for reducing relapse (Kurtz & Mueser, 2008). Targeting social cognition appears to enhance theory of mind and affect recognition (Grant, Lawrence, Preti, Wykes, & Cella, 2017). Data further suggest that gains generalize and are maintained for 3 years (Bartels et al., 2014; Bellack et al., 2013).

Social Cognition and Interaction Training (SCIT; Roberts & Penn, 2009) for adults with schizophrenia aims to improve social deficits. SCIT is implemented in 18–24 weekly, 1-h group sessions (Combs et al., 2007). Therapists use psychoeducation, skills practice, rehearsal, and homework assignments to address skills deficits. Participants identify a partner with whom to practice skills outside session, and trainers follow up with partners to increase compliance. Modules target social cognitive skills, including emotion perception, attributional biases, and theory of mind (Roberts & Penn, 2009). Initial studies supported the feasibility of SCIT in inpatient and outpatient settings and its promise in improving social cognition (Combs et al., 2007; Roberts & Penn, 2009). In a randomized controlled trial, Roberts et al. (2014) found small-to-medium effect sizes for reductions in hostile attributions, decreased negative symptoms, and improvements in social functioning. Client feedback also indicated the intervention was useful and helpful, despite some reported difficulty understanding content.

Another empirically supported SST intervention for older adults with schizophrenia is Helping Older People Experience Success (HOPES). HOPES has been evaluated in group (Pratt, Bartels, Mueser, & Forester, 2008) and individual formats (i.e., HOPES-I; Pratt et al., 2017) and consists of weekly sessions facilitated by trained case managers, interns, and master's-level therapists. HOPES teaches skills in five domains (leisure time, effective communication, establishing friendships, independent living, and health self-management) through goal setting, role play, facilitating in vivo practice of skills in community settings, and individualized feedback. The individual and group treatments last 9–12 and 24 months, respectively. A randomized control trial of the group model supported gains in independent living skills, community and social functioning, and health care (Mueser et al., 2010). HOPES has also been associated with long-term reductions in negative symptoms of schizophrenia (Bartels et al., 2014).

Bipolar disorder

Bipolar disorder is linked with significant social and vocational impairment (Depp et al., 2010). Although specific SST programs for adults with bipolar disorders are underdeveloped, elements of SST do appear and have been evaluated in the context of family-based psychoeducational therapies. As the family unit plays an important role in bipolar illness (Fiorillo et al., 2015), family therapy for bipolar disorder addresses maladaptive interaction cycles via communication and problem-solving skills training. Sessions last 60–90 min for 1–2 years, with studies observing reduced rates of relapse and hospitalization, increased time to relapse, decreased mood symptoms, and reduced health risks and burden for caregivers (see Miziou et al., 2015). A recent trial further noted improvements for patients' functioning and social outcomes, as well as reduced family burden (Fiorillo et al., 2015).

Personality disorders

Borderline personality disorder

Individuals with BPD struggle with regulating cognition, emotion, and behavior, which negatively impacts social functioning (Axelrod et al., 2011). Social deficits in BPD include hostile attributional bias, rejection fears, and interpersonal hostility (Lis & Bohus, 2013). The current, gold-standard treatment for BPD is dialectical behavioral therapy (DBT), a comprehensive treatment that aims to reduce self-destructive behaviors and enhance adaptive regulation (Linehan, 2015). Social skills are targeted via core SST techniques (e.g., didactics, modeling, role play, rehearsal, feedback). Two domains directly aim to improve social cognition and interpersonal functioning: emotion regulation (identifying emotions, decreasing difficult emotions, managing emotional intensity) and interpersonal effectiveness (assertiveness, creating, and maintaining relationships). Weekly 90-min skills groups are held in addition to weekly individual sessions and telephone coaching for up to 20 weeks. Facilitators are master's- or doctoral-level clinicians trained extensively in DBT.

DBT is an empirically supported treatment for adults with BPD (Axelrod et al., 2011; Linehan et al., 2006). A systematic review found DBT was efficacious in reducing self-harm and suicidality (Panos, Jackson, Hasan, & Panos, 2014), and randomized controlled trials examining secondary outcomes support the efficacy of DBT for improving social adjustment (e.g., Pistorello, Fruzzetti, MacLane, Gallop, & Iverson, 2012). Dewe and Krawitz (2007) conducted a component analysis to evaluate perceptions of DBT among BPD patients and found that patients viewed emotion regulation skills and interpersonal effectiveness as especially useful.

Antisocial personality disorder

Individuals with antisocial personality disorder (ASPD) experience social difficulties, including violating social norms, aggression, impulsiveness, deceitfulness and manipulation, and poor problem solving (APA, 2013). Research is limited in regards to effective treatment approaches; however, CBT, including problem solving and interpersonal skills training, has been examined with mixed results. In particular, studies have shown CBT to reduce reoffending, have no result, or to incite iatrogenic effects (e.g., clients learned skills to better manipulate others; see Hare & Hart, 1993).

Enhanced thinking skills (ETS), a variant of CBT, is gaining support. ETS teaches impulse control, flexible thinking, general and moral reasoning, and interpersonal problem-solving skills in 20 2-h group sessions over a period of 5 weeks. ETS has been shown to be successful among male prisoners with ASPD in reducing recidivism rates and improving functioning related to avoidance, aggressiveness, impulsivity, resentment, and paranoia (Doyle et al., 2013), as well as improved social problem-solving skills (McDougall, Perry, Clarbour, Bowles, & Worthy, 2009).

Major depressive disorder

Depressed individuals often struggle in interpersonal relationships due to a tendency to smile less, express negative vocal cues, maintain less eye contact, converse about negative content, and experience social discomfort (Segrin, 2000). Although standalone SST programs for depression exist (Bellack, Hersen, & Himmelhoch, 1981), SST is most often included as a component of larger treatment packages (e.g., CBT) with one or two sessions devoted to assertiveness, communication, and problem-solving skills training.

One exemplar SST intervention for depression is PST. PST has been evaluated as a standalone intervention, but also is used in conjunction with CBT for depression (Cuijpers et al., 2008). PST views social problem solving as integral to the association between stress and well-being and encourages a positive problem orientation and rational problem-solving style. PST typically lasts 12 sessions, though some forms can be quite short (e.g., four sessions) or longer term (Mynors-Wallis et al., 2000; Nguyen et al., 2018). On its own, PST appears as effective at reducing depression as medication and other psychotherapies and is significantly more effective than supportive therapy or no treatment (Bell & D'Zurilla, 2009; Kirkham, Choi, & Seitz, 2015). In seven meta-analyses by Cuijpers et al. (2008), PST was equally efficacious as CBT, behavioral activation, and psychodynamic therapy and was more efficacious than supportive therapies. PST appears most effective when it includes training in all four major problem-solving skills: problem definition, generation of alternatives, decision making, and solution implementation and verification (Bell & D'Zurilla, 2009). Additionally, dropout was lower in PST compared to other treatments, and data document patient satisfaction with PST (Mynors-Wallis, Davies, Gray, Barbour, & Gath, 1997; Mynors-Wallis, Gath, Lloyd-Thomas, & Tomlinson, 1995), providing some evidence for social validity.

Social anxiety disorder

Individuals with SAD may have underlying social skills deficits such as ineffective communication skills (Hopko, McNeil, Zvolensky, & Eifert, 2001; Schneider & Turk, 2014; c.f. Rapee & Lim, 1992; Thompson, Van Zalk, Marshall, Sargeant, & Stubbs, 2019), which may be improved with SST (Heimberg & Barlow, 1991). Alternately, fears of social rejection in SAD can deter effective social interactions, leading to performance deficits in the absence of skills deficits (Beidel, Rao, Scharfstein, Wong, & Alfano, 2010; Heimberg & Becker, 2002). Many treatments for SAD include an SST component, but the unique contribution of SST is rarely assessed (Barkowski et al., 2016). A meta-analysis by Acarturk, Cuijpers, van Straten, and de Graaf (2009) suggests there is scant evidence for using SST in isolation and little indication that SST increases overall effect sizes within treatment packages (Acarturk et al., 2009).

One effective treatment, including an SST component, is Herbert and colleagues' modified version of cognitive behavioral group therapy (CBGT; 2005). The original version (Heimberg & Becker, 2002) is an extensively researched treatment for SAD (Chambless & Ollendick, 2001). Herbert et al. (2005) evaluated whether adding an SST component to the original CBGT enhanced its efficacy. The modified treatment includes identification of social skills deficits, psychoeducation, modeling, in-session rehearsal, feedback, and out-of-session homework integrated within the larger treatment package that includes cognitive restructuring and exposure. Groups include four to six clients who meet on a weekly basis for 12 2-h sessions. Posttreatment evaluation revealed moderate-to-large effect sizes reflecting significant improvement for those who received the SST component compared to those who did not.

Traumatic brain injuries

Individuals with TBI may experience deficits in social cognition and communication, which can lead to relationship and occupational problems that persist over time (e.g., Hoofien, Gilboa, Vakil, & Donovick, 2001; Kersel, Marsh, Havill, & Sleigh, 2001). In Finch et al.'s (2016) review, manualized SST for TBI resulted in improved social communication and quality of life but not social participation or engagement. The strongest effects emerged for group therapy involving goal identification, group-based activities, homework, and feedback.

One exemplar program is group interactive structured treatment for social competence (GIST; e.g., Dahlberg et al., 2007; Harrison-Felix et al., 2018). Groups include six to eight participants and two facilitators, a speech language pathologist, and a therapist. Groups meet for 13 weeks in community or residential settings, and each session typically lasts 90 min. Topics include goal setting, communication skills, assertiveness skills, problem-solving skills, social boundaries, and conflict resolution. The program incorporates weekly homework and in vivo practice. Skills are rehearsed in the group with therapists and group members providing feedback. In a randomized control trial, Dahlberg et al. (2007) found evidence for improved social communication, global life satisfaction, and attainment of communication goals that were maintained after 3 and 6 months. Harrison-Felix et al. (2018) observed improved social competence goals resulting from GIST presented in both interactive and didactic formats.

A notable emergent program is the treatment for social cognition and emotion regulation (T-ScEmo; Westerhof-Evers et al., 2017, 2019) that targets emotion perception, perspective taking, theory of mind, awareness and inhibition of inappropriate social behavior, and use of socially appropriate behavior. T-ScEmo involves 16–20 individual, 1-h sessions in a medical setting once or twice a week. Neuropsychologists are recommended as facilitators, given the complexity of TBI deficits. Significant others also participate to learn coaching strategies and improve relationships. Westerhof-Evers et al. (2017) compared T-ScEmo to a computerized program for improving general cognition. Participants in both conditions showed gains in social participation, empathetic behavior, attainment of treatment goals, and quality of relationships, but effects favored T-ScEmo. Further, T-ScEmo significantly improved affect recognition, theory of mind, and quality of life, with effects lasting five months. Low dropout was observed, and treatment satisfaction was reported by clients and caregivers.

Couple problems

SST programs for couple distress aim to reduce negative communication patterns and improve problem solving. According to two meta-analyses, SST programs for married or dating couples are very efficacious (Hawkins, Blanchard, Baldwin, & Fawcett, 2008; Hawkins & Fackrell, 2010) for improving conflict management, problem solving, and communication. Partners also report less intense relationship problems and a reduction in negative interactions (e.g., aggression, violence) within the relationship (Owen et al., 2013).

An effective SST program for couples is the Prevention and Relationship Education Program (PREP), created to improve communication and conflict management, deepen commitment, and increase connections (Markman et al., 2001). PREP is taught in a group format and includes lectures, discussions, activities, workbooks, and homework. Videotaped examples of couple interactions are used for modeling and discussion. PREP is 12-h long, taught over a weekend or over multiple weeks. Supportive outcomes include social skill development, increased positive interactions and satisfaction, and decreased negative interactions and distress (Markman, Renick, Floyd, Stanley, & Clements, 1993; Stanley, Allen, Markman, Rhoades, & Prentice, 2010), with effects lasting up to 5 years (Stanley, Markman, St. Peters, & Leber, 1995).

Conclusions and future directions

Although by no means exhaustive, our review presents evidence that SST is effective for some problem areas (e.g., schizophrenia, ASD, couple problems) and promising for others (e.g., bipolar, ID). Still more research is needed to understand the efficacy, effectiveness, and social validity of SST. Component analyses also are needed to understand the incremental contribution of SST to larger treatment packages, particularly in light of movements to reduce lengthy manualized treatments to core components and adapt them to primary care settings (Robinson & Reiter, 2016). In addition, future research requires utilization of methodologically rigorous designs with control groups, testing moderators of treatment effects, and exploring efficacy for underrepresented populations. Finally, although adult SST programs are not as readily available as those for children (especially for disorders commonly diagnosed in childhood; e.g., neurodevelopmental disorders), many adults require ongoing support for social impairments. Future studies should also examine the cost effectiveness of interventions in order to influence policy makers and ensure resources are available to adults across the lifespan.

References

Acarturk, C., Cuijpers, P., van Straten, A., & de Graaf, R. (2009). Psychological treatment of social anxiety disorder: A meta-analysis. *Psychological Medicine*, *39*, 241–254. https://doi.org/10.1017/S0033291708003590.

Almerie, M. Q., Okba Al Marhi, M., Jawoosh, M., Alsabbagh, M., Matar, H. E., Maayan, N., & Bergman, H. (2015). Social skills programmes for schizophrenia. *Cochrane Database of Systematic Reviews*, *6*, https://doi.org/10.1002/14651858.CD009006.

American Psychiatric Association (APA). (2013). *Diagnostic and statistical manual of mental disorders* (5th ed.). Arlington, VA: American Psychiatric Association.

Anderson, A., Moore, D. W., Rausa, V. C., Finkelstein, S., Pearl, S., & Stevenson, M., (2017). A systematic review of interventions for adults with autism spectrum disorder to promote employment. *Review Journal of Autism and Developmental Disorders*, *4*, 26–38. https://doi.org/10.1007/s40489-016-0094-9.

Arnett, J. J. (2013). The evidence for generation we and against generation me. *Emerging Adulthood*, *1*, 5–10. https://doi.org/10.1177/2167696812466842.

Axelrod, S. R., Perepletchikova, F., Holtzman, K., & Sinha, R. (2011). Emotion regulation and substance use frequency in women with substance dependence and borderline personality disorder receiving dialectical behavior therapy. *The American Journal of Drug and Alcohol Abuse*, *37*, 37–42. https://doi.org/10.3109/00952990.2010.535582.

Bandura, A. (1969). Social-learning theory of identificatory processes. In D. Goslin (Ed.), *Handbook of socialization theory and research* (pp. 213–262). Chicago, IL: Rand McNally & Company.

Barkowski, S., Schwartze, D., Strauss, B., Burlingame, G. M., Barth, J., & Rosendahl, J. (2016). Efficacy of group psychotherapy for social anxiety disorder: A meta-analysis of randomized-controlled trials. *Journal of Anxiety Disorders*, *39*, 44–64. https://doi.org/10.1016/j.janxdis.2016.02.005.

Bartels, S. J., & Pratt, S. I. (2009). Psychosocial rehabilitation and quality of life for older adults with serious mental illness: Recent findings and future research directions. *Current Opinion in Psychiatry*, *22*, 381–385. https://doi.org/10.1097/YCO.0b013e32832c9234.

Bartels, S. J., Pratt, S. I., Mueser, K. T., Forester, B. P., Wolfe, R., Cather, C., … Feldman, J. (2014). Long-term outcomes of a randomized trial of integrated skills training and preventive healthcare for older adults with serious mental illness. *The American Journal of Geriatric Psychiatry*, *22*, 1251–1261. https://doi.org/10.1016/j.jagp.2013.04.013.

Beidel, D. C., Rao, P. A., Scharfstein, L., Wong, N., & Alfano, C. A. (2010). Social skills and social phobia: An investigation of DSM-IV subtypes. *Behaviour Research and Therapy*, *48*, 992–1001. https://doi.org/10.1016/j.brat.2010.06.005.

Bell, A. C., & D'Zurilla, T. J. (2009). Problem-solving therapy for depression: A meta-analysis. *Clinical Psychology Review*, *29*, 348–353. https://doi.org/10.1016/j.cpr.2009.02.003.

Bellack, A. S. (2004). Skills training for people with severe mental illness. *Psychiatric Rehabilitation Journal, 27*, 375–391. https://doi.org/10.2975/27.2004.375.391.

Bellack, A. S., Hersen, M., & Himmelhoch, J. (1981). Social skills training compared with pharmacotherapy and psychotherapy in the treatment of unipolar depression. *The American Journal of Psychiatry*, https://doi.org/10.1176/ajp.138.12.1562.

Bellack, A. S., Mueser, K. T., Gingerich, S., & Agresta, J. (2013). *Social skills training for schizophrenia: A step-by-step guide*. New York, NY: Guilford Publications.

Bodenmann, G., Bradbury, T. N., & Pihet, S. (2009). Relative contributions of treatment-related changes in communication skills and dyadic coping skills to the longitudinal course of marriage in the framework of marital distress prevention. *Journal of Divorce & Remarriage, 50*, 1–21. https://doi.org/10.1080/10502550802365391.

Chadsey-Rusch, J., Rusch, F. R., & O'Reilly, M. F. (1991). Transition from school to integrated communities. *RASE: Remedial & Special Education, 12*, 23–33. https://doi.org/10.1177/074193259101200605.

Chambless, D. L., & Ollendick, T. H. (2001). Empirically supported psychological interventions: Controversies and evidence. *Annual Review of Psychology, 52*, 685–716. https://doi.org/10.1146/annurev.psych.52.1.685.

Chezan, L. C., Drasgow, E., & Martin, C. A. (2014). Discrete-trial functional analysis and functional communication training with three adults with intellectual disabilities and problem behavior. *Journal of Behavioral Education, 23*, 221–246. https://doi.org/10.1007/s10864-013-9192-2.

Chowdhury, M., & Benson, B. A. (2011). Use of differential reinforcement to reduce behavior problems in adults with intellectual disabilities: A methodological review. *Research in Developmental Disabilities, 32*, 383–394. https://doi.org/10.1016/j.ridd.2010.11.015.

Combs, D. R., Adams, S. D., Penn, D. L., Roberts, D., Tiegreen, J., & Stem, P. (2007). Social cognition and interaction training (SCIT) for inpatients with schizophrenia spectrum disorders: Preliminary findings. *Schizophrenia Research, 91*, 112–116. https://doi.org/10.1016/j.schres.2006.12.010.

Cuijpers, P., Van Straten, A., Andersson, G., & Van Oppen, P. (2008). Psychotherapy for depression in adults: A meta-analysis of comparative outcome studies. *Journal of Consulting and Clinical Psychology, 76*, 909. https://doi.org/10.1037/a0013075.

Dahlberg, C. A., Cusick, C. P., Hawley, L. A., Newman, J. K., Morey, C. E., Harrison-Felix, C. L., & Whiteneck, G. G. (2007). Treatment efficacy of social communication skills training after traumatic brain injury: A randomized treatment and deferred treatment controlled trial. *Archives of Physical Medicine and Rehabilitation, 88*, 1561–1573. https://doi.org/10.1016/j.apmr.2007.07.033.

Demir, M. (2010). Close relationships and happiness among emerging adults. *Journal of Happiness Studies: An Interdisciplinary Forum on Subjective Well-Being, 11*, 293–313. https://doi.org/10.1007/s10902-009-9141-x.

Depp, C. A., Mausbach, B. T., Harvey, P. D., Bowie, C. R., Wolyniec, P. S., Thornquist, M. H., … Patterson, T. L. (2010). Social competence and observer-rated social functioning in bipolar disorder. *Bipolar Disorder, 12*, 843–850. https://doi.org/10.1111/j.1399-5618.2010.00880.x.

Dewe, C., & Krawitz, R. (2007). Component analysis of dialectical behavior therapy skills training. *Australasian Psychiatry, 15*, 222–225. https://doi.org/10.1080/10398560701320345.

Doyle, M., Khanna, T., Lennox, C., Shaw, J., Hayes, A., Taylor, J., … Dolan, M. (2013). The effectiveness of an enhanced thinking skills programme in offenders with antisocial personality traits. *The Journal of Forensic Psychiatry & Psychology, 24*, 1–15. https://doi.org/10.1080/14789949.2012.752519.

Eisler, R. M., & Frederiksen, L. W. (1980). On the nature of social skills. In R. M. Eisler & L. W. Frederiksen (Eds.), *Perfecting social skills: A guide to interpersonal behavior development* (pp. 3–21). https://doi.org/10.1007/978-1-4613-3186-5_1.

Fadyl, J. K., & McPherson, K. M. (2009). Approaches to vocational rehabilitation after traumatic brain injury: A review of the evidence. *The Journal of Head Trauma Rehabilitation*, *24*, 195–212. https://doi.org/10.1097/HTR.0b013e3181a0d458.

Finch, E., Copley, A., Cornwell, P., & Kelly, C. (2016). Systematic review of behavioral interventions targeting social communication difficulties after traumatic brain injury. *Archives of Physical Medicine and Rehabilitation*, *97*, 1352–1365. https://doi.org/10.1016/j.apmr.2015.11.005.

Fiorillo, A., Del Vecchio, V., Luciano, M., Sampogna, G., De Rosa, C., Malangone, C., … Maj, M. (2015). Efficacy of psychoeducational family intervention for bipolar I disorder: A controlled, multicentric, real-world study. *Journal of Affective Disorders*, *172*, 291–299. https://doi.org/10.1016/j.jad.2014.10.021.

Foley Nicpon, M., Huser, L., Hull Banks, E., Sollenberger, S., Befort, C., & Kurpius, S. E. (2006). The relationship of loneliness and social support with college freshmen's academic performance and persistence. *Journal of College Student Retention*, *8*, 345–358. https://doi.org/10.2190/A465-356M-7652-783R.

Gantman, A., Kapp, S. K., Orenski, K., & Laugeson, E. A. (2012). Social skills training for young adults with high-functioning autism spectrum disorders: A randomized controlled pilot study. *Journal of Autism and Developmental Disorders*, *42*, 1094–1103. https://doi.org/10.1007/s10803-011-1350-6.

Grant, N., Lawrence, M., Preti, A., Wykes, T., & Cella, M. (2017). Social cognition interventions for people with schizophrenia: A systematic review focusing on methodological quality and intervention modality. *Clinical Psychology Review*, *56*, 55–64. https://doi.org/10.1016/j.cpr.2017.06.001.

Gül, S. O. (2016). The combined use of video modeling and social stories in teaching social skills for individuals with intellectual disability. *Kuram ve Uygulamada Eğitim Bilimleri/Educational Sciences: Theory & Practice*, *16*, 83–107. https://doi.org/10.12738/estp.2016.1.0046.

Hare, R. D., & Hart, S. D. (1993). Psychopathy, mental disorder, and crime. In S. Hodgins (Ed.), *Mental disorder and crime* (pp. 104–115). Thousand Oaks, CA: Sage.

Harrison-Felix, C., Newman, J. K., Hawley, L., Morey, C., Ketchum, J. M., Walker, W. C., … Howe, L. (2018). Social competence treatment after traumatic brain injury: A multicenter, randomized controlled trail of interactive group treatment versus noninteractive treatment. *Archives of Physical Medicine and Rehabilitation*, *99*, 2131–2142. https://doi.org/10.1016/j.apmr.2018.05.030.

Hawkins, A. J., Blanchard, V. L., Baldwin, S. A., & Fawcett, E. B. (2008). Does marriage and relationship education work? A meta-analytic study. *Journal of Consulting and Clinical Psychology*, *76*, 723. https://doi.org/10.1037/a0012584.

Hawkins, A. J., & Fackrell, T. A. (2010). Does relationship and marriage education for lower-income couples work? A meta-analytic study of emerging research. *Journal of Couple & Relationship Therapy*, *9*, 181–191. https://doi.org/10.1080/15332691003694927.

Hays, P. A. (2009). Integrating evidence-based practice, cognitive-behavior therapy, and multicultural therapy: Ten steps for culturally competent practice. *Professional Psychology: Research and Practice*, *40*, 354. https://doi.org/10.1037/a0016250.

Hedley, D., Uljarevic, M., Cameron, L., Halder, S., Richdale, A., & Dissanayake, C. (2017). Employment programmes and interventions targeting adults with autism spectrum disorder: A systematic review of the literature. *Autism*, *21*, 929–941. https://doi.org/10.1177/1362361316661855.

Heimberg, R. G., & Barlow, D. H. (1991). New developments in cognitive-behavioral therapy for social phobia. *The Journal of Clinical Psychiatry*, *52*(Suppl), 21–30.

Heimberg, R. G., & Becker, R. E. (2002). *Cognitive-behavioral group therapy for social phobia: Basic mechanisms and clinical strategies*. New York: Guilford Press.

Hendricks, D. (2010). Employment and adults with autism spectrum disorders: Challenges and strategies for success. *Journal of Vocational Rehabilitation*, *32*, 125–134. https://doi.org/10.3233/JVR-2010-0502.

Herbert, J. D., Gaudiano, B. A., Rheingold, A. A., Myers, V. H., Dalrymple, K., & Nolan, E. M. (2005). Social skills training augments the effectiveness of cognitive behavioral group therapy for social anxiety disorder. *Behavior Therapy*, *36*, 125–138. https://doi.org/10.1016/S0005-7894(05)80061-9.

Hoofien, D., Gilboa, A., Vakil, E., & Donovick, P. J. (2001). Traumatic brain injury (TBI) 10–20 years later: A comprehensive outcome study of psychiatric symptomatology, cognitive abilities and psychosocial functioning. *Brain Injury*, *15*, 189–209. https://doi.org/10.1080/02699050130005659.

Hopko, D. R., McNeil, D. W., Zvolensky, M. J., & Eifert, G. H. (2001). The relation between anxiety and skill in performance-based anxiety disorders: A behavioral formulation of social phobia. *Behavior Therapy*, *32*, 185–207. https://doi.org/10.1016/S0005-7894(01)80052-6.

Horn, E. E., Xu, Y., Beam, C. R., Turkheimer, E., & Emery, R. E. (2013). Accounting for the physical and mental health benefits of entry into marriage: A genetically informed study of selection and causation. *Journal of Family Psychology*, *27*, 30–41. https://doi.org/10.1037/a0029803.

Howlin, P., Goode, S., Hutton, J., & Rutter, M. (2004). Adult outcome for children with autism. *Journal of Child Psychology and Psychiatry*, *45*, 212–229. https://doi.org/10.1111/j.1469-7610.2004.00215.x.

Howlin, P., & Yates, P. (1999). The potential effectiveness of social skills groups for adults with autism. *Autism*, *3*, 299–307. https://doi.org/10.1177/1362361399003003007.

Huffcutt, A. I., Conway, J. M., Roth, P. L., & Stone, N. J. (2001). Identification and meta-analytic assessment of psychological constructs measured in employment interviews. *Journal of Applied Psychology*, *86*, 897–913. https://doi.org/10.1037/0021-9010.86.5.897.

Jakubowski, S. F., Milne, E. P., Brunner, H., & Miller, R. B. (2004). A review of empirically supported marital enrichment programs. *Family Relations*, *53*, 528–536. https://doi.org/10.1111/j.0197-6664.2004.00062.x.

Jeste, D. V., & Maglione, J. E. (2013). Treating older adults with schizophrenia: Challenges and opportunities. *Schizophrenia Bulletin*, *39*, 966–968. https://doi.org/10.1093/schbul/sbt043.

Kandalaft, M. R., Didehbani, N., Krawczyk, D. C., Allen, T. T., & Chapman, S. B. (2013). Virtual reality social cognition training for young adults with high-functioning autism. *Journal of Autism and Developmental Disorders*, *43*, 34–44. https://doi.org/10.1007/s10803-012-1544-6.

Kersel, D. A., Marsh, N. V., Havill, J. H., & Sleigh, J. W. (2001). Psychosocial functioning during the year following severe traumatic brain injury. *Brain Injury*, *15*, 683–696. https://doi.org/10.1080/02699050010013662.

Kirkham, J. G., Choi, N., & Seitz, D. P. (2015). Meta-analysis of problem solving therapy for the treatment of depression in older adults. *The American Journal of Geriatric Psychiatry*, *23*, S129–S130. https://doi.org/10.1016/j.jagp.2014.12.131.

Kurtz, M. M., & Mueser, K. T. (2008). A meta-analysis of controlled research on social skills training for schizophrenia. *Journal of Consulting and Clinical Psychology*, *76*, 491–504. https://doi.org/10.1037/0022-006X.76.3.491.

Kurtz, P. F., Boelter, E. W., Jarmolowicz, D. P., Chin, M. D., & Hagopian, L. P. (2011). An analysis of functional communication training as an empirically supported treatment for problem behavior displayed by individuals with intellectual disabilities. *Research in Developmental Disabilities*, *32*, 2935–2942. https://doi.org/10.1016/j.ridd.2011.05.009.

Laugeson, E. A. (2017). *PEERS for young adults: Social skills training for adults with autism spectrum disorder and other social challenges* (1st ed.). New York, NY: Routledge.

Laugeson, E. A., Gantman, A., Kapp, S. K., Orenski, K., & Ellingsen, R. (2015). A randomized controlled trial to improve social skills in young adults with autism spectrum disorder: The UCLA PEERS program. *Journal of Autism and Developmental Disorders*, *45*, 3978–3989. https://doi.org/10.1007/s10803-015-2504-8.

Linehan, M. M. (2015). *DBT skills training manual* (2nd ed.). New York: Guilford Press.

Linehan, M. M., Comtois, K. A., Murray, A. M., Brown, M. Z., Gallop, R. J., Heard, H. L., … Lindenboim, N. (2006). Two-year randomized controlled trial and follow-up of dialectical behavior therapy vs therapy by experts for suicidal behaviors and borderline personality disorder. *Archives of General Psychiatry*, *63*, 757–766. https://doi.org/10.1001/archpsyc.63.7.757.

Lis, S., & Bohus, M. (2013). Social interaction in borderline personality disorder. *Current Psychiatry Reports*, *15*, 338. https://doi.org/10.1007/s11920-012-0338-z.

Lorenc, T., Rodgers, M., Marshall, D., Melton, H., Rees, R., Wright, K., & Sowden, A. (2018). Support for adults with autism spectrum disorder without intellectual impairment: Systematic review. *Autism*, *22*, 654–668. https://doi.org/10.1177/1362361317698939.

Lovejoy, T. I., & Heckman, T. G. (2014). Telephone-administered motivational interviewing and behavioral skills training to reduce risky sexual behavior in HIV-positive late middle-age and older adults. *Cognitive and Behavioral Practice*, *21*, 224–236. https://doi.org/10.1016/j.cbpra.2013.10.003.

Markman, H. J., Renick, M. J., Floyd, F., Stanley, S., & Clements, M. (1993). Preventing marital distress through communication and conflict management training: A four and five year follow-up. *Journal of Consulting & Clinical Psychology*, *61*, 70–77. https://doi.org/10.1037/0022-006X.61.1.70.

Markman, H. J., Stanley, S. M., & Blumberg, S. L. (2001). *Fighting for your marriage: Positive steps for preventing divorce and preserving a lasting love*. San Francisco: Jossey-Bass.

Mason, G., Rutar Shuman, T., & Cook, K. E. (2013). Comparing the effectiveness of an inverted classroom to a traditional classroom in an upper-division engineering course. *IEEE Transactions on Education*, *56*, 430–435. https://doi.org/10.1109/TE.2013.2249066.

McDougall, C., Perry, A., Clarbour, J., Bowles, R., & Worthy, G. (2009). *Evaluation of HM prison service enhanced thinking skills programme*. London, England: Ministry of Justice.

Miller, E. A., & Rosenheck, R. A. (2006). Risk of nursing home admission in association with mental illness nationally in the Department of Veterans Affairs. *Medical Care*, *44*, 343–351. https://doi.org/10.1097/01.mlr.0000204008.83633.ed.

Miziou, S., Tsitsipa, E., Moysidou, S., Karavelas, V., Dimelis, D., Polyzoidou, V., & Fountoulakis, K. (2015). Psychosocial treatment and interventions for bipolar disorder: A systematic review. *Annals of General Psychiatry*, *14*, 19. https://doi.org/10.1186/s12991-015-0057-z.

Mueser, K. T., Pratt, S. I., Bartels, S. J., Swain, K., Forester, B., Cather, C., & Feldman, J. (2010). Randomized trial of social rehabilitation and integrated health care for older people with severe mental illness. *Journal of Consulting and Clinical Psychology*, *78*, 561–573. https://doi.org/10.1037/a0019629.

Müller, E., Schuler, A., & Yates, G. B. (2008). Social challenges and supports from the perspective of individuals with Asperger syndrome and other autism spectrum disabilities. *Autism*, *12*, 173–190. https://doi.org/10.1177/1362361307086664.

Mynors-Wallis, L., Davies, I., Gray, A., Barbour, F., & Gath, D. (1997). A randomised controlled trial and cost analysis of problem-solving treatment for emotional disorders given by community nurses in primary care. *The British Journal of Psychiatry*, *170*, 113–119. https://doi.org/10.1192/bjp.170.2.113.

Mynors-Wallis, L. M., Gath, D. H., Day, A., & Baker, F. (2000). Randomised controlled trial of problem solving treatment, antidepressant medication, and combined treatment for major depression in primary care. *BMJ (British Medical Journal)*, *320*, 26–30. https://doi.org/10.1136/bmj.320.7226.26.

Mynors-Wallis, L. M., Gath, D. H., Lloyd-Thomas, A. R., & Tomlinson, D.B.M.J. (1995). Randomised controlled trial comparing problem solving treatment with amitriptyline and placebo for major depression in primary care. *BMJ*, *310*, 441–445. https://doi.org/10.1136/bmj.310.6977.441.

Nangle, D. W., Hansen, D. J., Erdley, C. A., & Norton, P. J. (2010). In D. W. Nangle, D. J. Hansen, C. A. Erdley, & P. J. Norton (Eds.), *Practitioner's guide to empirically based measures of social skills*. https://doi.org/10.1007/978-1-4419-0609-0.

National Institute of Health Care Excellence (NICE). (2016). *Autism spectrum disorder in adults: Diagnosis and management*. Clinical Guideline [CG142]. Retrieved from: https://www.nice.org.uk/guidance/CG142.

Nguyen, C. M., Chen, K.-H., & Denburg, N. L. (2018). The use of problem-solving therapy for primary care to enhance complex decision-making in healthy community-dwelling older adults. *Frontiers in Psychology*, *9*, 870. https://doi.org/10.3389/fpsyg.2018.00870.

O'Reilly, M. F., Lancioni, G. E., Sigafoos, J., Green, V. A., Ma, C.-H., & O'Donoghue, D. (2004). A further comparison of external control and problem-solving interventions to teach social skills to adults with intellectual disabilities. *Behavioral Interventions*, *19*, 173–186. https://doi.org/10.1002/bin.163.

Owen, J., Manthos, M., & Quirk, K. (2013). Dismantling study of prevention and relationship education program: The effects of a structured communication intervention. *Journal of Family Psychology*, *27*, 336–341. https://doi.org/10.1037/a0031597.

Panos, P. T., Jackson, J. W., Hasan, O., & Panos, A. (2014). Meta-analysis and systematic review assessing the efficacy of dialectical behavior therapy (DBT). *Research on Social Work Practice*, *24*, 213–223. https://doi.org/10.1177/1049731513503047.

Park, K. M., Ku, J., Choi, S. H., Jang, H. J., Park, J. Y., Kim, S. I., & Kim, J. J. (2011). A virtual reality application in role-plays of social skills training for schizophrenia: A randomized, controlled trial. *Psychiatry Research*, *189*, 166–172. https://doi.org/10.1016/j.psychres.2011.04.003.

Penn, D. L., Corrigan, P. W., Bentall, R. P., Racenstein, J. M., & Newman, L. (1997). Social cognition in schizophrenia. *Psychological Bulletin*, *121*, 114–132. https://doi.org/10.1037/0033-2909.121.1.114.

Pistorello, J., Fruzzetti, A. E., MacLane, C., Gallop, R., & Iverson, K. M. (2012). Dialectical behavior therapy (DBT) applied to college students: A randomized clinical trial. *Journal of Consulting and Clinical Psychology*, *80*, 982. https://doi.org/10.1037/a0029096.

Pratt, S. I., Bartels, S. J., Mueser, K. T., & Forester, B. (2008). Helping older people experience success: An integrated model of psychosocial rehabilitation and health care management for older adults with serious mental illness. *American Journal of Psychiatric Rehabilitation*, *11*, 41–60. https://doi.org/10.1080/15487760701853193.

Pratt, S. I., Mueser, K. T., Wolfe, R., Santos, M. M., & Bartels, S. J. (2017). One size doesn't fit all: A trial of individually tailored skills training. *Psychiatric Rehabilitation Journal*, *40*, 380. https://doi.org/10.1037/prj0000261.

Rapee, R. M., & Lim, L. (1992). Discrepancy between self-and observer ratings of performance in social phobics. *Journal of Abnormal Psychology*, *101*, 728. https://doi.org/10.1037/0021-843X.101.4.728.

Reilly, P. M., & Shopshire, M. S. (2002). *Anger management for substance abuse and mental health clients: Cognitive behavioral therapy manual*. Rockville, MD: Center for Substance Abuse Treatment, Substance Abuse and Mental Health Services Administration, US Department of Health & Human Services.

Roberts, D. L., Combs, D. R., Willoughby, M., Mintz, J., Gibson, C., Rupp, B., & Penn, D. L. (2014). A randomized, controlled trial of social cognition and interaction training (SCIT) for outpatients with schizophrenia spectrum disorders. *British Journal of Clinical Psychology*, *53*, 281–298. https://doi.org/10.1111/bjc.12044.

Roberts, D. L., & Penn, D. L. (2009). Social cognition and interaction training (SCIT) for outpatients with schizophrenia: A preliminary study. *Psychiatry Research*, *166*, 141–147. https://doi.org/10.1016/j.psychres.2008.02.007.

Robinson, P. J., & Reiter, J. T. (2016). *Behavioral consultation and primary care: A guide to integrating services* (2nd ed.). New York: Springer International. https://doi.org/10.1007/978-3-319-13954-8.

Rus-Calafell, M., Gutiérrez-Maldonado, J., & Ribas-Sabaté, J. (2014). A virtual reality-integrated program for improving social skills in patients with schizophrenia: A pilot study. *Journal of Behavior Therapy and Experimental Psychiatry*, *45*, 81–89. https://doi.org/10.1016/j.jbtep.2013.09.002.

Schlegel, K., Vicaria, I. M., Isaacowitz, D. M., & Hall, J. A. (2017). Effectiveness of a short audiovisual emotion recognition training program in adults. *Motivation and Emotion*, *41*, 646–660. https://doi.org/10.1007/s11031-017-9631-9.

Schneider, B. W., & Turk, C. L. (2014). Examining the controversy surrounding social skills in social anxiety disorder. In J. W. Weeks (Ed.), *The Wiley Blackwell handbook of social anxiety disorder* (pp. 366–389). United Kingdom: John Wiley & Sons. https://doi.org/10.1002/9781118653920.ch17.

Segrin, C. (2000). Social skills deficits associated with depression. *Clinical Psychology Review*, *20*, 379–403. https://doi.org/10.1016/S0272-7358(98)00104-4.

Smith, M. J. (1985). *When I say no, I feel guilty*. New York: Bantum Books.

Smith, M. J., Ginger, E. J., Wright, K., Wright, M. A., Taylor, J. L., Humm, L. B., … Fleming, M. F. (2014). Virtual reality job interview training in adults with autism spectrum disorder. *Journal of Autism and Developmental Disorders*, *44*, 2450–2463. https://doi.org/10.1007/s10803-014-2113-y.

Smits, J. A. J., Powers, M. B., Buxkamper, R., & Telch, M. J. (2006). The efficacy of videotape feedback for enhancing the effects of exposure-based treatment for social anxiety disorder: A controlled investigation. *Behaviour Research and Therapy*, *44*, 1773–1785. https://doi.org/10.1016/j.brat.2006.01.001.

Snyder, D. K., Castellani, A. M., & Whisman, M. A. (2006). Current status and future directions in couple therapy. *Annual Review of Psychology*, *57*, 317–344. https://doi.org/10.1146/annurev.psych.56.091103.070154.

Spain, D., & Blainey, S. H. (2015). Group social skills interventions for adults with high-functioning autism spectrum disorders: A systematic review. *Autism*, *19*, 874–886. https://doi.org/10.1177/1362361315587659.

Stanley, S. M., Allen, E. S., Markman, H. J., Rhoades, G. K., & Prentice, D. L. (2010). Decreasing divorce in U.S. Army couples: Results from a randomized controlled trial using PREP for strong bonds. *Journal of Couple & Relationship Therapy*, *9*, 149–160. https://doi.org/10.1080/15332691003694901.

Stanley, S. M., Markman, H. J., St. Peters, M., & Leber, B. D. (1995). Strengthening marriages and preventing divorce: New directions in prevention research. *Family Relations*, 392–401. https://doi.org/10.2307/584995.

Thompson, T., Van Zalk, N., Marshall, C., Sargeant, M., & Stubbs, B. (2019). Social anxiety increases visible anxiety signs during social encounters but does not impair performance. *BMC Psychology*, *7*, 24–33. https://doi.org/10.1186/s40359-019-0300-5.

Tiger, J. H., Hanley, G. P., & Bruzek, J. (2008). Functional communication training: A review and practical guide. *Behavior Analysis in Practice*, *1*, 16–23. https://doi.org/10.1007/BF03391716.

Van Manen, T. G., Prins, P. J. M., & Emmelkamp, P. M. G. (2001). Assessing social cognitive skills in aggressive children from a developmental perspective: The social cognitive skills test. *Clinical Psychology & Psychotherapy*, *8*, 341–351. https://doi.org/10.1002/cpp.319.

Westerhof-Evers, H. J., Visser-Keizer, A. C., Fasotti, L., Schönherr, M. C., Vink, M., van der Naalt, J., & Spikman, J. M. (2017). Effectiveness of a treatment for impairments in social cognition and emotion regulation (T-ScEmo) after traumatic brain injury: A randomized controlled trial. *The Journal of Head Trauma Rehabilitation*, *32*, 296–307. https://doi.org/10.1097/HTR.0000000000000332.

Westerhof-Evers, H. J., Visser-Keizer, A. C., Fasotti, L., & Spikman, J. M. (2019). Social cognition and emotion regulation: A multifaceted treatment (T-ScEmo) for patients with traumatic brain injury. *Clinical Rehabilitation*, *33*, 820–833. https://doi.org/10.1177/0269215519829803.

Zunzunegui, M.-V., Alvarado, B. E., Del Ser, T., & Otero, A. (2003). Social networks, social integration, and social engagement determine cognitive decline in community-dwelling Spanish older adults. *The Journals of Gerontology: Series B: Psychological Sciences and Social Sciences*, *58*, S93–S100. https://doi.org/10.1093/geronb/58.2.S93.

Part III

Social skills interventions

Section A

Children and adolescents

Chapter 8

Play skills for shy preschoolers: A social skills training and facilitated play (SST-FP) early intervention program

Robert J. Coplan
Carleton University, Ottawa, ON, Canada

As detailed in this volume, there are a myriad of social skills training (SST) programs that have been demonstrated to effectively promote the positive development of social, socioemotional, and sociocommunicative competence for young children at risk. However, there are very few such programs that have been specifically designed to target the particular social skills that may be most relevant for young shy children (Coplan, Schneider, Ooi, & Hipson, 2018). This chapter describes the development and ongoing evaluation of the Social Skills Training and Facilitated Play (SST-FP) program, which was created to assist extremely shy preschool-aged children.

Describing shyness in early childhood

Shyness is a temperamental trait characterized by heightened wariness, anxiety, and unease in novel social contexts (e.g., meeting a new child on the playground) and/or feelings of self-consciousness and embarrassment in situations of perceived social evaluation (e.g., speaking in front of the group during "show and tell"; Buss, 1984; Crozier, 1995). From a motivational perspective, shy children are described as experiencing an internal conflict between social approach and social avoidance motivations. In this regard, their desire to interact with peers (i.e., social approach motivation) is simultaneously inhibited by social fear and anxiety (i.e., social avoidance motivation; Asendorpf, 1993; Coplan, Prakash, O'Neil, & Armer, 2004).

Social Skills Across the Life Span. https://doi.org/10.1016/B978-0-12-817752-5.00008-1

Shyness shares considerable conceptual overlap with a number of other constructs that variously represent manifestations of underlying social wariness, reactivity, and anxiety in novel or familiar social situations, including behavioral inhibition (Kagan, 1997), anxious solitude (Gazelle & Shell, 2017), and social reticence (Coplan, Rubin, Fox, Calkins, & Stewart, 1994). A detailed discussion of the similarities and nuanced differences among these constructs is beyond the scope of this chapter (for further discussion, see Rubin, Coplan, & Bowker, 2009), and thus, these terms were deemed functionally equivalent and used interchangeably herein. Importantly, shyness in early childhood is concurrently and predictively associated with a wide range of socioemotional and school-related difficulties (Rubin et al., 2009).

It is also necessary to distinguish shyness from social withdrawal. Social withdrawal refers to the process whereby children remove themselves from opportunities for peer interaction, which can lead to a behavioral pattern of engaging in solitary activities in the presence of available play partners (Rubin et al., 2009). As will be discussed, shy children are prone to displaying socially withdrawn behaviors in peer settings such as preschool (Coplan et al., 2004). However, contemporary conceptualizations of social withdrawal acknowledge that this is a broad and heterogeneous construct. Simply stated, aside from feeling shy, young children may withdraw from opportunities for peer engagement for different reasons. For example, children who appear socially withdrawn at school may retreat to solitude because of a nonfearful preference for playing alone or a desire to avoid unpleasant or unrewarding social interactions (Coplan, Ooi, & Nocita, 2015).

The increased risk for negative consequences associated with early childhood shyness has been demonstrated empirically with both cross-sectional and longitudinal samples and across several domains of maladjustment. For example, shyness in preschool and kindergarten-aged children is associated with undesirable peer experiences, including rejection, exclusion, and victimization (Coplan, Arbeau, & Armer, 2008; Gazelle & Shell, 2017; Sette, Baumgartner, Laghi, & Coplan, 2016). Shy children are also prone to internalizing difficulties, including negative and self-conscious affect (Coplan, Ooi, Xiao, & Rose-Krasnor, 2018; Sette, Baldwin, Zava, Baumgartner, & Coplan, 2019), as well as elevated (but subclinical) symptoms of anxiety (Karevold, Coplan, Stoolmiller, & Mathiesen, 2011; Shamir-Essakow, Ungerer, & Rapee, 2005).

Furthermore, childhood shyness predicts greater risk for the later development of clinical anxiety disorders, particularly social anxiety (Essex, Klein, Slattery, Goldsmith, & Kalin, 2010). Indeed, Clauss and Blackford (2012) concluded from their metaanalysis that childhood shyness was one of the strongest predictors of later anxiety diagnoses. Notwithstanding, it must also be emphasized that many shy children do not experience substantive socioemotional difficulties (Degnan & Fox, 2007). Indeed, as will be discussed, it is this heterogeneity of outcomes associated with shyness that makes it a promising target construct for early intervention.

Connecting shyness to SST

In many ways, shyness is an ideal target for social skills training (SST). Most prominently, shy children are prone to maladaptive peer experiences, and several processes have been suggested to account for why shy children are more likely to evoke negative responses from peers (Coplan et al., 2013). For example, in both novel (e.g., laboratory playroom) and familiar (e.g., preschool/kindergarten classroom) social contexts, shy children tend to withdraw from social interaction with peers, are less likely to initiate social interactions with peers, and speak less (Coplan et al., 1994, 2004, 2008). There is also at least some evidence to suggest that this pattern of behavior persists in peer contexts outside of schools (Coplan, DeBow, Schneider, & Graham, 2009; Coplan, Ooi, et al., 2018). Young children who refrain from peer interaction may miss out on the important and unique opportunities afforded by the peer group for positive social, emotional, cognitive, and moral development (Rubin, Bukowski, & Bowker, 2015). Accordingly, it is not surprising that the primary goals of many intervention programs for shy and socially withdrawn children have been to increase both the quality and frequency of social interactions with peers (Greco & Morris, 2001).

Even in early childhood, peers tend to respond to socially withdrawn behaviors with exclusion and rejection (Coplan et al., 2008; Coplan, Ooi, et al., 2018). Notwithstanding, even when controlling for socially withdrawn behaviors, shyness maintains a significant association with peer problems (Coplan et al., 2013). This is likely because even when shy children do interact with peers, they display a lack of social and sociocommunicative competence (Bohlin, Hagekull, & Andersson, 2005; Karevold, Ystrøm, Coplan, Sanson, & Mathiesen, 2012).

There is already accumulating evidence that naturally occurring variations in socioemotional, sociocommunicative, and social cognitive skills moderate links between shyness and adjustment outcomes (see Coplan, Baldwin, & Wood, in press, for a recent review). More specifically, increased competencies in social domains buffer shy children against negative outcomes (e.g., Coplan & Weeks, 2009; Gazelle & Shell, 2017; Sette et al., 2016). Moreover, children who display competence in social behaviors will likely have better social standing among peers (Rubin et al., 2015), and there is evidence to specifically suggest that more positive peer experiences also serve to reduce shy children's risk for negative outcomes (Baardstu, Coplan, Karevold, Laceulle, & von Soest, 2019; Sette, Zava, Baumgartner, Baiocco, & Coplan, 2017). Taken together, this provides a compelling rationale for incorporating SST into early intervention and prevention programs for shy children.

Highlighting context and particular considerations

There are several issues that should be considered in the context of administering SST programs to shy children. The first pertains to assessments of shyness, most germanely to appropriately identifying shy children who may benefit from ameliorative intervention. Historically, studies of intervention programs purporting to assist shy and socially withdrawn children have suffered from methodological and theoretical shortcomings. These include the use of single-subject designs or treatment groups of less than 5 participants (e.g., Hodges & McCoy, 1990; Sheridan, Kratochwill, & Elliott, 1990); the lack of any control group (e.g., Lewis & Sugai, 1993; Lindeman, Fox, & Redelheim, 1993); or a failure to include an appropriate control group of withdrawn children (Hodges & McCoy, 1990; Storey, Smith, & Strain, 1993). Importantly, there also appears to have been ambiguity in the definitions of social withdrawal, which likely resulted in the selection of a heterogeneous treatment group (Greco & Morris, 2001; Schneider, Coplan, & DeBow, 2008). As mentioned previously, it is now widely acknowledged that children may withdraw from opportunities for social interaction for different reasons (Coplan et al., 2015).

It is also important during the identification phase to distinguish between the temperamental trait of shyness and the clinical diagnosis of social anxiety disorder (SAD). Childhood SAD is a debilitating psychological disorder characterized by an intense and persistent fear or anxiety of one or more social situations in which a person is exposed to unfamiliar people or possible scrutiny by others (American Psychiatric Association, 2013). Although there is continued debate in the literature about the theoretical and empirical distinctions between shyness and social anxiety (Heiser, Turner, Beidel, & Roberson-Nay, 2009; Lemery, Essex, & Smider, 2002), shyness is now widely conceptualized as a temperamental vulnerability toward the development of later anxiety (Rapee & Coplan, 2010).

A second issue pertains to the specificity of the repertoire of social skills that comprise the training program. SST programs are designed to target deficiencies in children's behavioral repertoires, with the underlying presumption that learning and engaging in these specific skills will result in improvements in the quality and quantity of social interactions (Farmer & Chapman, 2009). As evidenced in this volume, there are a myriad of SST programs designed to assist children and adolescents who display externalizing problems (e.g., aggression, conduct disorder, impulsivity, deficits of attention; see Magg (2006) for a "review of reviews"). However, many of the skills that are the focus of such interventions are less relevant and applicable to shy children (Bienert & Schneider, 1995). For example, young shy children do not need to learn how to "not punch" someone when they are angry or how to "stop interrupting" others when they trying to speak. As will be described in more detail in a later section, shy children are more likely to benefit from learning skills that are specific to their domains of deficits (e.g., initiating a social exchange, politely refusing a social invitation when feeling too scared in a way that will not discourage a future invitation).

A third issue relates to the inclusion of additional nonshy peers in the interventions for the purposes of peer pairing. The rationale for this approach is that children participating in an intervention should be provided with opportunities to enhance their social interactions and learn new social skills in a normative and developmentally typical manner (i.e., interacting with other peers). For example, some previous interventions have partnered shy and socially withdrawn children with a more socially competent counterpart, who serves as a model and a facilitator of appropriate social behaviors (Strain & Fox, 1981). Of note, Furman, Rahe, and Hartup (1979) demonstrated an increase in post-treatment observed social interaction as compared to controls for socially withdrawn preschoolers who participated in a series of play sessions with younger peers. These authors suggested that interacting with younger peers helped withdrawn children gain confidence by experiencing a (relatively unfamiliar) leadership role during play. It has been similarly argued that shy children are often overshadowed by their more exuberant, sociable, and talkative counterparts at school (Coplan, Hughes, Bosacki, & Rose-Krasnor, 2011). Taken together, this suggests that shy children may benefit from learning and practicing social skills in a social context that represents an even playing field (i.e., in a group that comprises only shy children).

The final issue concerns a longstanding debate as to whether shy children's observed display of maladaptive social behaviors is more reflective of deficits in performance versus competence (Coplan, Schneider, et al., 2018). In this regard, it has been argued that despite being aware of potential adaptive responses, shy children are unable or unwilling to competently enact behavioral strategies and achieve social goals because of their social fears and social-evaluative concerns (Alfano, Beidel, & Turner, 2006). There is some empirical support for this notion from studies examining links between shyness and indices of linguistic and sociocommunicative competence (Coplan & Evans, 2009). For example, results from some studies have indicated that shy children tend to perform better on tests of receptive (i.e., knowledge-based) as opposed to expressive (i.e., performance-based) language (Crozier & Perkins, 2002; Spere, Schmidt, Theall-Honey, & Martin-Chang, 2004). Similarly, aspects of the testing environment may exacerbate shy children's feelings of social unease, further hindering performance (Crozier & Hostettler, 2003). Accordingly, successful SST interventions should not only include direct social skills training, but also focus on emotional regulation/coping strategies, as well as providing shy children with opportunities to gradually overcome barriers in demonstrating positive social behaviors in the peer context (accompanied by appropriately scaffolded support from trained adults).

Social skills training and facilitated play program for shy preschoolers (SST-FP)

Previous SST programs for shy and socially withdrawn children have typically involved training in both verbal and nonverbal communication skills, as well as incorporating components of coaching, modeling, and social-problem-solving training (Greco & Morris, 2001; Schneider, 1992). There is some preliminary evidence to suggest that such programs can improve social outcomes among shy and withdrawn children, at least in the short term (e.g., Bienert & Schneider, 1995; Christoff et al., 1985; Jupp & Griffiths, 1990). Findings, however, have been inconsistent, and treatment effects do not typically generalize beyond the SST setting (Coplan, Schneider, et al., 2018). With these issues in mind, we developed the Social Skills Training-Facilitated Play (SST-FP, Coplan, Schneider, Matheson, & Graham, 2010) program as an early intervention for preschool-aged shy children. The structure, protocols, and content of this intervention were derived from an extensive review of previous interventions that had shown at least some evidence of success with shy and socially withdrawn children and adolescents (Coplan, Schneider, et al., 2018; Greco & Morris, 2001; Schneider, 1992).

Program description

The SST-FP program is a targeted intervention, intended for preschool-aged children (e.g., aged 48–66 months) who have been identified as "extremely shy." Although there is standard "cut off" for identifying children as extremely shy, Kagan (1997) has argued that children in the top 15% of the distribution in shyness should be considered as a qualitatively distinct subgroup. We have adopted this approach in practice, using a combination of parental and teacher ratings to identify target children based on shyness scores that fall in the top 15% of an unselected sample (e.g., Coplan et al., 2009).

Ideally, SST-FP sessions should be run with mixed-gender groups of between 5 and 7 shy children. The primary intention of this program is to increase social interaction and promote social competence and adaptive coping styles specifically among young shy children—such that they do not go on to develop later more serious problems with anxiety. In this regard, the intervention could be construed as a targeted prevention program. It must also be noted that some young children who are recruited in this manner may also already meet criteria for an anxiety disorder (Rapee, Kennedy, Ingram, Edwards, & Sweeney, 2005). Finally, drawing upon past research (Coplan et al., 2011; Furman et al., 1979), nonshy children were not included in the intervention (as described earlier, shy children may be overwhelmed by more sociable peers and will be more likely to defer opportunities to speak/interact).

The structure of the SST-FP program includes seven weekly sessions with trained group leaders, as well as an eighth booster session 1 month later. Groups are meant to be led by individuals with previous education and working backgrounds in early childhood education and who received additional training specific to the intervention. Sessions are held in a playroom equipped with age-appropriate toys and materials as would typically be found in the early child education context. The general purpose of these sessions is to provide an opportunity for the children to initiate skilled social contact in an unthreatening setting. The format of the hour-long weekly intervention groups consists of: (1) 5 min of unstructured free play; (2) 10 min of "circle time"; (3) 40 min of leader-facilitated free play; and (4) 5 min of a structured positive social activity. A detailed procedure manual for this intervention is available upon request from the authors.

The initial free play period was designed to serve as a brief warm-up time for children (and parents). Children are not guaranteed to arrive for the sessions at the same time. Thus, during this transitory period, children are given time to slowly become accustomed to the novel setting of the playroom, as well as the presence of other initially unfamiliar children. Given shy children's high level of reactivity to social novelty (Kagan, 1997), it should be expected that many of them will be initially resistant to parental separation, particularly during the first few sessions. Parents of shy children are prone to respond to shy behaviors with overprotectiveness, particularly when they perceive their shy child as vulnerable (Coplan et al., 2008). Accordingly, this warm-up period can also be used to gently coax accompanying parents to a waiting area located outside of the playroom.

Circle time sessions are used to provide didactic content. Group leaders focus on a specific set of targeted social skills each week. Songs and games are used as age-appropriate ways of conveying the content, minimizing didactic lessons to the extent possible. Puppets are used by both group leaders and children to facilitate social interaction during circle time (e.g., progressing from social exchanges between puppets to exchanges between puppets and children and eventually to exchanges between children). The circle time sessions are intentionally kept very brief (i.e., not more than 5 min) in order not to tax young children's attention.

The sessions include systematic modeling of social skills, training in social problem solving, emotion-regulation strategies, and relaxation techniques. All of these techniques have been previously demonstrated to be effective components of childhood intervention for young children at heightened risk for developing anxiety disorders (Hirschfeld-Becker & Biederman, 2002). In contrast with many general and global social-skills training programs, a limited number of social skills were selected for their specific appropriateness in facilitating social interactions for young shy children. For example, the first three sessions focus on skills related to initiating and maintaining peer interactions (e.g., introducing yourself, asking someone to play, saying something nice about someone, sharing likes and dislikes, making eye contact during conversations). The next three sessions shift the content to understanding and expressing feelings and the regulation of affect, particularly fear and anxiety. Various age-appropriate strategies for coping with disappointment (i.e., when someone does not want to play) are also discussed. As well, children are taught and practice a simple relaxation breathing technique ("blowing up a balloon with your tummy") to use when they feel nervous or scared. The last two sessions are used for review and practice, with the final session scheduled 1 month after the previous session.

The leader-facilitated free play component was designed to encourage positive social interactions, so as to provide extensive opportunities for leaders to coach, prompt, and reinforce in vivo use of targeted skills (Hodges & McCoy, 1990). This context is meant to mirror free play sessions in childcare settings and preschools. Children are generally free to play with the available materials and people as they see fit. Leaders are interspersed into the sessions to guide and facilitate social participation. For example, a session leader might approach a child playing alone and gently prompt interaction (e.g., "Is there someone you might like to build a building with?").

Leaders are also trained to prompt, model, and reinforce the specific social skills that have been previously discussed during circle time. For example, when witnessing a child making eye contact during a conversation with a peer, the leader might say, "[Child's name], it is good to see you looking right into [Peer's name]'s eyes while you are talking to him." If a child was looking at a peer but not joining in, the leader might say, "[Child's name], do you remember how to ask someone to let you play with them?" Importantly, group leaders are trained to *scaffold* (Vygotsky, 1978) the support they provide to facilitate children's social exchanges (i.e., initially providing considerable support and structure, but gradually dialing back their contributions in order to allow children to act more independently).

As well, leaders are trained to provide individual support and reassurance to children when they display signs of anxiety and social fear. For example, when intervening with a child who appears frightened, the leader might acknowledge the child's feelings (e.g., "I see that you are feeling a little scared now"), provide reassurance (e.g., "It's ok to be scared sometimes"), and then spend a few minutes with the child providing comfort and reviewing relevant techniques learned in circle time (e.g., relaxation breathing).

Finally, the last few minutes of each session are spent with all children engaged in a structured positive social activity. The purpose of this activity is to provide children with a fun social experience before leaving each week. Results from pilot testing indicated that "parachute games" (e.g., children work cooperatively to bounce a ball into the middle hole of a parachute) represented a good choice, as this activity was demonstrated to be both socially interactive and also generated frequent expressions of positive affect among the children.

Evaluation studies

Coplan et al. (2010) provided the first preliminary evidence of the efficacy of the SST-FP program. Participants were $n = 28$ (14 boys, 14 girls) extremely shy preschool-aged children (ages 48–66 months). The primary inclusion criterion for target participants in this initial study was scoring in the top 15% of the distribution on a parental rating of shyness (*Behavioral Inhibition Questionnaire*, BIQ; Bishop, Spence, & McDonald, 2003). The cut-off score was established from a previously recruited unselected sample of 304 preschool children.

Children were randomly assigned to either the Social Skills Facilitated Play (SST-FP) or Waitlist Control (WLC) condition. The intervention was run in two cohorts, and after some participant attrition the final sample consisted of $n=11$ children (7 boys, 4 girls) in the SST groups and $n=11$ children (4 boys, 7 girls) in the WLC group.

Participants were observed during unstructured free play at preschool pre- and postintervention. As compared to their counterparts in the WLC group, shy children who participated in the SST-FP intervention displayed a significantly greater postintervention decrease in observed socially wary behaviors (e.g., watching other children but not joining in, overt displays of anxiety), as well as a significantly greater increase in social interaction and in observed social competencies (e.g., group play, peer conversation, social initiations made to peers, positive affect during peer interaction). Although these results pertain to a small sample and must be considered preliminary in nature, the apparent generalization (at least in the short term) of SST-FP program gains to the naturalistic setting of the preschool playroom—with different peers—is certainly an encouraging initial finding.

In a follow-up study, Li et al. (2016) replicated and extended these finding in a sample of preschool children from mainland China. Target children (similarly identified via parental ratings) were randomly assigned within gender to the SST-FP ($n=8$; 4 boys, 4 girls) or WLC group ($n=8$; 4 boys, 4 girls). The SST-FP program was translated and culturally adapted for administration in China. Baseline, postintervention, and 2-month follow-up measures included observations of children's social behaviors in quartets of novel peers, as well as performance during a "show and tell" speech task postintervention. Among the results, as compared to shy children in the WLC group, shy children who participated in the STT-FP intervention were observed to demonstrate significantly greater postintervention frequencies of group play and peer conversations, as well as greater prosocial behaviors (e.g., cooperation, sharing) during free play with novel peers. The SST-FP group also displayed significantly better speech performance postintervention (e.g., more eye contact, less nervous affect). Of note, the significant gains made by the SST-FP group in peer interactive and prosocial behaviors (but not speech performance) were maintained during follow-up observational assessments 2-months postintervention.

Most recently, Lau, Rapee, and Coplan (2017) assessed the effects of an intervention that combined SST-FP with *Cool Little Kids* (CLK; Rapee et al., 2005) a psychoeducation and training program for parents of young Australian children at risk for anxiety. Results from several studies have established the efficacy of Cool Little Kids (CLK) in reducing anxiety disorders (and symptoms) and life impairment from early-to-middle childhood (Rapee et al., 2005; Rapee, Kennedy, Ingram, Edwards, & Sweeney, 2010) and even into adolescence (Rapee, 2013).

Lau et al. (2017) randomly assigned $n=72$ extremely shy preschoolers to either the intervention group (SST-FP + CLK) or waitlist control group (WLC).

A quasiexperimental design was incorporated such that after 6 months, families in the WLC were offered treatment consisting of parent-education only (CLK). As compared to their counterparts in the WLC, children in the combined intervention condition showed significantly fewer anxiety disorders, severity of symptoms, and life interference at 6 months postintervention. Moreover, these gains were maintained at 12-month postintervention follow up. The WLC children whose parents received CLK following waitlist also demonstrated improvements among children. However, a quasiexperimental comparison between combined and parent-only (CLK) interventions indicated greater reductions from combined intervention (SST-FP + CLK) according to clinician reports, but there were no significant differences in maternal reports. These findings provide at least some evidence to suggest that the inclusion of a child SST-FP component has potential to increase overall treatment gains as compared to parent-only intervention. Given the quasiexperimental design, these findings should be considered as preliminary until randomized controlled trials are conducted that directly compare different combinations of these treatment components.

The three studies just described provide converging evidence in support of the efficacy of SST-FP for reducing social wariness and anxiety, as well increasing positive peer interactions among extremely shy young children. The SST-FP has also been adapted, expanded, and integrated into the Turtle Program, a multicomponent intervention program for extremely shy young children developed by Chronis-Tuscano et al. (2015) and Chronis-Tuscano, Danko, Rubin, Coplan, and Novick (2018). This comprehensive program includes SST-FP, parental psychoeducation, and parent-child interaction therapy (PCIT; Danko, O'Brien, Rubin, & Chronis-Tuscano, 2018).

Results from two preliminary studies have provided some encouraging findings. Chronis-Tuscano et al. (2015) reported that extremely shy children randomly assigned to the treatment condition ($n = 18$) demonstrated significant improvements in maternal-reported anxiety symptoms, teacher-rated school anxiety symptoms, and observed maternal positive affect/sensitivity as compared to shy children in WLC ($n = 22$). Barstead et al. (2018) reported the results pertaining to observations of children's behaviors with peers at school. From pre- to postintervention, shy children who received the intervention demonstrated greater increases in the frequency of observed peer play and social initiations to peers as compared to a waitlist control group.

Conclusions and future directions

Although evaluation is still ongoing, results from initial studies have provided promising support for the efficacy of SST-FP in ameliorating outcomes for young extremely shy children. As a standalone intervention, SST-FP has been demonstrated to reduce social wariness and increase positive peer interactions (as compared to waitlist controls), and these gains appear to generalize to the preschool setting. As a component of more comprehensive multimodal interventions, SST-FP also appears to contribute to the reduction of anxiety disorders, severity of symptoms, and life interference.

There is still much more to be done in order to establish the efficacy of this intervention. For example, larger samples are required to more robustly assess treatment effects—and the size of those effects. Additional longitudinal follow-up studies also need to be conducted in order to establish the longer-term maintenance of treatment effects. As well, a wider range of outcomes that might be impacted by the intervention (e.g., self-esteem, loneliness, aspects of academic functioning) need to be investigated.

To date, preliminary evidence for the efficacy of SST-FP has been reported in samples of children from Canada (Coplan et al., 2010), the United States (Chronis-Tuscano et al., 2015), Australia (Lau et al., 2017), and China (Li et al., 2016). Pilot work has also been conducted in Norway integrating the SST-FP program into the kindergarten classroom (Kjeilen & Flaten, 2015). Evaluation across cultures needs to be continued and expanded.

Finally, multimodal interventions that include components related to SST-FP have demonstrated particularly promising results in terms of efficacy (Barstead et al., 2018; Chronis-Tuscano et al., 2015). However, such comprehensive and intensive programs require substantive resources in terms of both time and costs. A critical question for future research is to determine who (and under what circumstances) might benefit most from the full program (i.e., SST-FP + Parental Education + PCIT) versus a combination of components or simply a single component. Moreover, it may turn out to be the case that adapting the program to be delivered by teachers in preschools or kindergartens would allow for the extension of benefits to the largest number of children.

References

Alfano, C. A., Beidel, D. C., & Turner, S. M. (2006). Cognitive correlates of social phobia among children and adolescents. *Journal of Abnormal Child Psychology*, *34*, 182–194.

American Psychiatric Association. (2013). *Diagnostic and statistical manual of mental disorders* (5th ed.). Washington, DC: American Psychiatric Press.

Asendorpf, J. B. (1993). Abnormal shyness in children. *Journal of Child Psychology and Psychiatry*, *34*, 1069–1081.

Baardstu, S., Coplan, R. J., Karevold, E. B., Laceulle, O. M., & von Soest, T. (2019). Longitudinal pathways from shyness in early childhood to personality in adolescence: Do peers matter? *Journal of Research on Adolescence*. Advance online publication.

Barstead, M. G., Danko, C. M., Chronis-Tuscano, A., O'Brien, K. A., Coplan, R. J., & Rubin, K. H. (2018). Generalization of an early intervention for inhibited preschoolers to the classroom setting. *Journal of Child and Family Studies*, *27*, 2943–2953.

Bienert, H., & Schneider, B. H. (1995). Deficit-specific social skills training with peer-nominated aggressive-disruptive and sensitive-isolated preadolescents. *Journal of Clinical Child Psychology*, *24*, 287–299.

Bishop, G., Spence, S. H., & McDonald, C. (2003). Can parents and teachers provide a reliable and valid report of behavioral inhibition? *Child Development*, *74*, 1899–1917.

Bohlin, G., Hagekull, B., & Andersson, K. (2005). Behavioral inhibition as a precursor of peer social competence in early school age: The interplay with attachment and nonparental care. *Merrill-Palmer Quarterly*, *51*, 1–19.

Buss, A. H. (1984). A conception of shyness. In J. A. Daly & J. C. McCroskey (Eds.), *Avoiding communication: Shyness, reticence, and communication apprehension* (pp. 39–50). Beverly Hills, CA: Sage.

Christoff, K. A., Scott, W. O. N., Kelley, M. L., Schlundt, D., Baer, G., & Kelly, J. A. (1985). Social skills and social problem-solving training for shy young adolescents. *Behavior Therapy*, *16*, 468–477.

Chronis-Tuscano, A., Danko, C. M., Rubin, K. H., Coplan, R. J., & Novick, D. R. (2018). Developmentally-grounded early interventions for young at risk for the development of social anxiety: Review and directions for future research. *Journal of Clinical Child and Adolescent Psychology*, *47*, 655–667.

Chronis-Tuscano, A., Rubin, K. H., O'Brien, K. A., Coplan, R. J., Thomas, S. R., Dougherty, L. R., … Wimsatt, M. (2015). Preliminary evaluation of a multimodal early intervention program for behaviorally inhibited preschoolers. *Journal of Consulting and Clinical Psychology*, *83*, 534–540.

Clauss, J. A., & Blackford, J. U. (2012). Behavioral inhibition and risk for developing social anxiety disorder: A meta-analytic study. *Journal of the American Academy of Child & Adolescent Psychiatry*, *51*(10), 1066–1075.

Coplan, R. J., Arbeau, K. A., & Armer, M. (2008). Don't fret, be supportive! Maternal characteristics linking child shyness to psychosocial and school adjustment in kindergarten. *Journal of Abnormal Child Psychology*, *36*(3), 359–371.

Coplan, R.J., Baldwin, D., & Wood, K.R. (in press). Shy but getting by: Protective factors in the links between childhood shyness and indices of socio-emotional functioning. In L.A. Schmidt & K.L. Poole (Eds.), Adaptive shyness: Developmental, comparative, and cultural perspectives. New York: Springer.

Coplan, R. J., DeBow, A., Schneider, B. H., & Graham, A. A. (2009). The social behaviors of inhibited children in and out of preschool. *British Journal of Developmental Psychology*, *27*, 891–905.

Coplan, R. J., & Evans, M. A. (2009). At a loss for words? Introduction to the special issue on shyness and language in childhood. *Infant and Child Development: An International Journal of Research and Practice*, *18*, 211–215.

Coplan, R. J., Hughes, K., Bosacki, S. L., & Rose-Krasnor, L. (2011). Is silence golden? Elementary school teachers' strategies and beliefs towards hypothetical shy-quiet and talkative-exuberant children. *Journal of Educational Psychology*, *103*, 939–951.

Coplan, R. J., Ooi, L. L., & Nocita, G. (2015). When one is company and two is a crowd: Why some children prefer solitude. *Child Development Perspectives*, *9*, 133–137.

Coplan, R. J., Ooi, L. L., Xiao, B., & Rose-Krasnor, L. (2018). Assessment and implications of multiple forms of social withdrawal in early childhood: A first look at social avoidance. *Social Development*, *27*, 125–139.

Coplan, R. J., Prakash, K., O'Neil, K., & Armer, M. (2004). Do you "want" to play? Distinguishing between conflicted shyness and social disinterest in early childhood. *Developmental Psychology*, *40*, 244–258.

Coplan, R. J., Rose-Krasnor, L., Weeks, M., Kingsbury, A., Kingsbury, M., & Bullock, A. (2013). Alone is a crowd: Social motivations, social withdrawal, and socio-emotional functioning in later childhood. *Developmental Psychology*, *49*, 861–875.

Coplan, R. J., Rubin, K. H., Fox, N. A., Calkins, S. D., & Stewart, S. (1994). Being alone, playing alone, and acting alone: Distinguishing among reticence and passive and active solitude in young children. *Child Development, 65*, 129–137.

Coplan, R. J., Schneider, B. H., Matheson, A., & Graham, A. A. (2010). "Play skills" for shy children: Development of a social skills-facilitated play early intervention program for extremely inhibited preschoolers. *Infant and Child Development, 19*, 223–237.

Coplan, R. J., Schneider, B. H., Ooi, L. L., & Hipson, W. E. (2018). Peer-based interventions for behaviorally inhibited, socially withdrawn, and socially anxious children. In W. Bukowski, B. Laursen, & K. H. Rubin (Eds.), *Handbook of peer interactions, relationships, and groups* (2nd ed., pp. 657–675). New York: Guilford.

Coplan, R. J., & Weeks, M. (2009). Shy and soft-spoken? Shyness, pragmatic language, and socio-emotional adjustment in early childhood. *Infant and Child Development, 18*(3), 238–254.

Crozier, W. R. (1995). Shyness and self-esteem in middle childhood. *British Journal of Educational Psychology, 65*, 85–95.

Crozier, W. R., & Hostettler, K. (2003). The influence of shyness on children's test performance. *British Journal of Educational Psychology, 73*, 317–328.

Crozier, W. R., & Perkins, P. (2002). Shyness as a factor when assessing children. *Educational Psychology in Practice, 18*, 239–244.

Danko, C. M., O'Brien, K. A., Rubin, K. H., & Chronis-Tuscano, A. (2018). The turtle program: PCIT for young children displaying behavioral inhibition. In L. N. Niec (Ed.), *Handbook of parent-child interaction therapy: Innovations and applications for research and practice* (pp. 85–98). New York: Springer.

Degnan, K. A., & Fox, N. A. (2007). Behavioral inhibition and anxiety disorders: Multiple levels of a resilience process. *Development and Psychopathology, 19*, 729–746.

Essex, M. J., Klein, M. H., Slattery, M. J., Goldsmith, H. H., & Kalin, N. H. (2010). Early risk factors and developmental pathways to chronic high inhibition and social anxiety disorder in adolescence. *American Journal of Psychiatry, 167*, 40–46.

Farmer, R. F., & Chapman, A. L. (2009). Changing behavior by building skills. In R. F. Farmer & A. L. Chapman (Eds.), *Behavioral interventions in cognitive-behavior therapy: Practical guidance for putting theory into action* (pp. 177–201). Washington, DC: American Psychological Association.

Furman, W., Rahe, D. F., & Hartup, W. W. (1979). Rehabilitation of socially withdrawn preschool children through mixed-age and same-age socialization. *Child Development, 50*, 915–922.

Gazelle, H., & Shell, M. D. (2017). Behavioral profiles of anxious solitary children: Predicting peer relations trajectories from third to fifth grade. *Merrill-Palmer Quarterly, 63*, 237–281.

Greco, L. A., & Morris, T. L. (2001). Treating childhood shyness and related behavior: Empirically evaluated approaches to promote positive social interactions. *Clinical Child and Family Psychology Review, 4*, 299–318.

Heiser, N. A., Turner, S. M., Beidel, D. C., & Roberson-Nay, R. (2009). Differentiating social phobia from shyness. *Journal of Anxiety Disorders, 23*, 469–476.

Hirschfeld-Becker, D. R., & Biederman, J. (2002). Rationale and principles for early intervention with young children at risk for anxiety disorders. *Clinical Child and Family Psychology Review, 5*, 161–172.

Hodges, J. B., & McCoy, J. F. (1990). Effects of coaching and per utilization procedures on the withdrawn behaviors of preschoolers. *Child and Family Behavior Therapy, 12*, 25–47.

Jupp, J. J., & Griffiths, M. D. (1990). Self-concept changes in shy, socially isolated adolescents following social skills training emphasizing role-plays. *Australian Psychologist, 25*, 165–177.

Kagan, J. (1997). Temperament and the reactions to the unfamiliarity. *Child Development, 68*, 139–143.

Karevold, E., Coplan, R. J., Stoolmiller, M., & Mathiesen, K. S. (2011). A longitudinal study of the links between temperamental shyness, activity, and trajectories of internalizing problems from infancy to middle childhood. *Australian Journal of Psychology, 63*, 36–43.

Karevold, E., Ystrøm, E., Coplan, R. J., Sanson, A., & Mathiesen, K. S. (2012). A prospective longitudinal study of shyness from infancy to adolescence: Stability, age-related changes, and prediction of socio-emotional functioning. *Journal of Abnormal Child Psychology, 40*, 1167–1177.

Kjeilen, H. H., & Flaten, K. (2015). Kule krabatar leikar i barnehagen [Cool crabs play in the kindergarten]. *Spesialpedagogikk, 6*, 23–27.

Lau, E. X., Rapee, R. M., & Coplan, R. J. (2017). Combining child social skills training with a parent early intervention program for inhibited preschool children. *Journal of Anxiety Disorders, 51*, 32–38.

Lemery, K., Essex, M. J., & Smider, N. A. (2002). Revealing the relation between temperament and behavior problem symptoms by eliminating measurement confounding: Expert ratings and factor analyses. *Child Development, 73*, 867–882.

Lewis, T. J., & Sugai, G. (1993). Teaching communicative alternatives to socially withdrawn behavior: An investigation in maintaining treatment effects. *Journal of Behavioral Education, 3*, 61–75.

Li, Y., Coplan, R. J., Wang, Y., Yin, J., Zhu, J., Gao, Z., & Li, L. (2016). Preliminary evaluation of a social skills training and facilitated play early intervention program for extremely shy young children in China. *Infant and Child Development, 5*, 565–574.

Lindeman, D. P., Fox, J. J., & Redelheim, P. S. (1993). Increasing and maintaining withdrawn preschoolers' peer interactions: Effects of double prompting and booster session procedures. *Behavioral Disorders, 11*, 54–66.

Magg, J. W. (2006). Social skills training for students with emotional and behavioral disorders: A review of reviews. *Behavioral Disorders, 32*, 4–17.

Rapee, R. M. (2013). The preventative effects of a brief, early intervention for preschool-aged children at risk for internalising: Follow-up into middle adolescence. *Journal of Child Psychology and Psychiatry, 54*, 780–788.

Rapee, R. M., & Coplan, R. J. (2010). Conceptual relations between anxiety disorder and fearful temperament. *New Directions for Child and Adolescent Development, 127*, 17–31.

Rapee, R. M., Kennedy, S., Ingram, M., Edwards, S., & Sweeney, L. (2005). Prevention and early intervention of anxiety disorders in inhibited preschool children. *Journal of Consulting and Clinical Psychology, 73*, 488–497.

Rapee, R. M., Kennedy, S., Ingram, M., Edwards, S. L., & Sweeney, L. (2010). Altering the trajectory of anxiety in at-risk young children. *American Journal of Psychiatry, 167*, 1518–1525.

Rubin, K. H., Bukowski, W. M., & Bowker, J. C. (2015). Children in peer groups. In R. M. Lerner (Series Ed.), M. H. Bornstein & T. Leventhal (Vol. Eds.), *Handbook of child psychology and developmental science, Vol. 4: Ecological settings and processes in developmental systems.* (7th ed., pp. 175–222). New York: Wiley-Blackwell.

Rubin, K. H., Coplan, R. J., & Bowker, J. (2009). Social withdrawal in childhood. *Annual Review of Psychology, 60*, 141–171.

Schneider, B. H. (1992). Didactic methods for enhancing children's peer relations: A quantitative review. *Clinical Psychology Review, 12*, 363–382.

Schneider, B. H., Coplan, R. J., & DeBow, A. (2008). Clinical diagnosis, prevention, and intervention. In A. L. Coco, K. H. Rubin, & C. Zappulla (Eds.), *L'isolamento sociale durante l'infanzia.* [Social withdrawal in childhood] (pp. 121–141). Milan, Italy: Unicopli.

Sette, S., Baldwin, D., Zava, F., Baumgartner, E., & Coplan, R. J. (2019). Shame on me? Shyness, social experiences at preschool, and young children's self-conscious emotions. *Early Childhood Research Quarterly*, *47*, 229–238.

Sette, S., Baumgartner, E., Laghi, F., & Coplan, R. J. (2016). The role of emotion knowledge in the links between shyness and children's socio-emotional functioning at preschool. *British Journal of Developmental Psychology*, *34*, 471–488.

Sette, S., Zava, F., Baumgartner, E., Baiocco, R., & Coplan, R. J. (2017). Links between social withdrawal and socio-emotional functioning at preschool: The protective role of peer liking. *Journal of Child and Family Studies*, *26*, 1196–1205.

Shamir-Essakow, G., Ungerer, J. A., & Rapee, R. M. (2005). Attachment, behavioral inhibition, and anxiety in preschool children. *Journal of Abnormal Child Psychology*, *33*, 131–143.

Sheridan, S. M., Kratochwill, T. R., & Elliott, S. N. (1990). Behavioral consultation with parents and teachers: Delivering treatment for socially withdrawn children at home and school. *School Psychology Review*, *19*, 33–52.

Spere, K. A., Schmidt, L. A., Theall-Honey, L. A., & Martin-Chang, S. (2004). Expressive and receptive language skills of temperamentally shy preschoolers. *Infant and Child Development*, *13*, 123–133.

Storey, K., Smith, D. J., & Strain, P. S. (1993). Use of classroom assistants and peer-mediated intervention to increase integration in preschool settings. *Exceptionality*, *4*, 1–16.

Strain, P. S., & Fox, J. J. (1981). Peers as behavior change agents for withdrawn classmates. In A. E. Kazdin & B. B. Lahey (Eds.), *Advances in child clinical psychology* (pp. 167–198). New York: Plenum.

Vygotsky, L. S. (1978). *Mind in society: The development of higher psychological processes*. Cambridge, MA: Harvard University Press.

Chapter 9

The Fast Track Friendship Group program

Karen L. Bierman
The Pennsylvania State University, University Park, PA, United States

The developmental dynamics of peer rejection

Ten to fifteen percent of elementary school children experience serious and chronic peer difficulties, including peer rejection, social exclusion, friendlessness, and victimization (Bierman, 2004; Gresham, Elliott, & Kettler, 2010). For most of these children, difficulties start with awkward, insensitive, or aggressive social behavior that is off-putting to peers and leads to peer disliking. Deficits in key social-emotional skills that underlie these behaviors make it hard for children to make friends or elicit peer liking. Children who are disliked by many classmates and liked by few classmates are identified as peer-rejected, and this social status confers significant developmental risk. The peer difficulties of chronically rejected children undergo a negative developmental cascade due in part to their social-emotional skill deficits and in part to the hostile treatment they receive from peers. Peer-rejected children have fewer friends than other children, and their friendships are of lower quality. This social isolation reduces their access to the positive peer experiences that contribute normatively to the development of social skills (Bierman, 2004) and increases their vulnerability to peer victimization (Boivin, Hymel, & Hodges, 2001). Peer victimization, in turn, makes their social vulnerability more obvious to peers, solidifying negative social reputations. In addition, being the target of peer mistreatment leads to increases in social withdrawal and, in some cases, counters aggression (Mayeux, Bellmore, & Cillessen, 2007).

The skill deficits and the associated negative dynamics related to peer rejection disrupt children's functioning at school, impairing social, behavioral, and academic performance. Peer rejection makes school highly stressful, as children often cannot escape negative peer exchanges, fueling negative attitudes about school, and resulting in frequent absenteeism and truancy and lower high school graduation rates (Buhs, Ladd, & Herald, 2006). Chronic peer rejection is also associated with heightened feelings of emotional distress, including low perceived

Social Skills Across the Life Span. https://doi.org/10.1016/B978-0-12-817752-5.00009-3

competence, social anxiety, loneliness, and depression (Fite, Wimsatt, Vitulano, Rathert, & Schwartz, 2012). The negative developmental cascade associated with chronic peer rejection in elementary school contributes to an increased likelihood of future social alienation, risky adolescent behavior, and lifelong mental health issues (McDougall, Hymel, Vaillancourt, & Mercer, 2001).

Common social-emotional skill deficits among peer-rejected children

Behaviorally, peer-rejected children are a heterogeneous group. About half of the children who are chronically rejected display disruptive, oppositional, or aggressive behaviors (Waas, 2006). Many also experience attention problems and learning disabilities (Farmer et al., 2008). For example, over 50% of children diagnosed with attention-deficit/hyperactivity disorder experience chronic peer rejection (Mikami & Hinshaw, 2006). Internalizing problems, particularly social anxiety and withdrawal, are associated with peer rejection, both as causes and consequences of rejection processes (La Greca & Landoll, 2011). In addition, children with autism spectrum disorder who display awkward and atypical social behavior are at high risk for peer rejection (Ratcliffe, Wong, Dossetor, & Hayes, 2014).

The common link among rejected children who show diverse behavior problems is a set of social-emotional skill deficits that impede their ability to interact comfortably and effectively with their peers (Farmer et al., 2008). These skill deficits include strategies needed to effectively initiate and maintain positive peer interactions, such as prosocial behaviors, entry skills, and communication skills (Bierman, 2004). They also include self-control skills, reflecting the capacity to inhibit impulses, control behavior, manage emotions, cope with social stressors, and resolve conflicts peacefully (Gresham et al., 2010). This set of social-emotional skills provides the foundation that supports socially competent interactions in childhood, as well as being fundamental to individuals' capacities to navigate interpersonal relationships effectively throughout life (Domitrovich, Durlak, Staley, & Weissberg, 2017; Dusenbury & Weissberg, 2016). Reflecting the critical importance of these social-emotional skills, Jones, Greenberg, and Crowley (2015) found that teacher ratings of social competence completed when children were in kindergarten predicted a wide range of outcomes 20 years later, including high school graduation, employment status, mental health, and reduced rates of criminal arrests.

Peer-rejected children who exhibit high rates of aggressive-disruptive behavior in elementary school often receive interventions that focus solely or primarily on managing their classroom behavior. While important, a narrow intervention focus on reducing problem behaviors does not adequately address the complex social-emotional skill deficits that underlie and contribute to dysfunctional social behavior. A majority of children who exhibit high rates of aggressive-disruptive behavior problems also have deficits in areas of prosocial skills, communication skills, impulse control, and emotion regulation, as well as biased social-cognitions that contribute to inaccurate social perceptions and aggression-prone problem-solving skills (Bierman, 2004; Farmer et al., 2008; Fite et al., 2012). These skill deficits, in addition to their aggressive and disruptive behaviors, impair peer relationships and hence deserve focused intervention support.

Recent developmental research has led to new insights regarding the factors contributing to behavioral and social-emotional maladjustment in elementary school. In particular, this research has identified exposure to adverse events as a common precursor to behavior and social-emotional difficulties (Hunt, Slack, & Berger, 2017; Niles, Reynolds, & Roe-Sepowitz, 2008). Adverse events involve family and community factors that increase child exposure to stressful, threatening, and unpredictable socialization experiences, such as neglect, abuse, parental substance use, parental antisocial behavior, family instability, and exposure to violence. Trauma exposure has been linked with emotional reactivity (e.g., easily aroused feelings of anxiety, anger, or ambivalence in interpersonal contexts) and difficulties with self-control, including both emotion regulation and behavioral control (Shin, McDonald, & Conley, 2018).

Many peer-rejected children have experienced early adversity, and their trauma exposure is often compounded by peer experiences of social exclusion and victimization. Recent research on trauma-informed intervention approaches has been instrumental in refocusing attention away from the single goal of managing behavior, to the broader goal of fostering the social-emotional and self-regulation skills that children need to effectively navigate social (and school) environments (Greenberg et al., 2003; Shantel, 2015). This is a primary focus of the Fast Track Friendship Group intervention approach. By building prosocial interaction and self-regulatory skills, the Friendship Group program seeks to empower peer-rejected children, enhancing their capacity and motivating their efforts to improve their social decision-making and interpersonal relationships.

Peer group and school context dynamics that affect peer rejection processes

Although awkward, intrusive, and aggressive-disruptive social behaviors play a central role in alienating peers and generating peer dislike, it is important to recognize that peer rejection is a social process and not a trait or disorder that exists within a child. Peers react negatively to children who exhibit socially unskilled behavior, actively avoiding or excluding them from social interactions and sometimes directing aggression toward them. Peer responses contribute in critical ways to the negative developmental cascade associated with peer rejection, when peers act in ways that exacerbate emotional distress, elicit behavioral reactivity, and reduce opportunities for positive interaction (DeRosier & Mercer, 2009; Mikami & Hinshaw, 2006). Negative peer experiences predict diminished classroom participation and learning engagement (Buhs et al., 2006), contributing to declines in future academic performance (Ve'ronneau, Vitaro, Brendgen, Dishion, & Tremblay, 2010).

Peer responses to dysfunctional social behavior can also exacerbate social difficulties. Researchers have identified social processes referred to as peer contagion or deviancy training, in which peers encourage deviant behaviors by laughing at, copying, or otherwise responding in positive ways to inappropriate or antisocial behavior (Dodge, Lansford, & Dishion, 2006). Partnerships between rejected children sometimes form around their joint engagement in inappropriate or antisocial behavior, serving as low-quality friendships that provide companionship and entertainment, but ultimately create negative socialization influences that distance children from normative social values and positive social integration.

Thus, peers contribute to rejection processes in multiple ways. They exclude children from positive peer experiences and high-quality friendships with socially skilled peers who could support normative social-emotional skill development. They direct negative comments and actions toward disliked children that elicit emotional distress and angry resentment. For some children, they contribute to deviancy training, encouraging negative social behavior. In these ways, peer responses amplify the internalizing and externalizing problems of rejected children in elementary school, increasing risk for psychopathology, antisocial activity, and substance use in adolescence (Dishion & Tipsord, 2011).

Correspondingly, effective interventions for peer-rejected children need to address the peer and school contexts in which problematic peer interactions take place. The Friendship Group program encourages the inclusion of classmates in intervention sessions and incorporates a set of therapeutic strategies used to create a positive peer context during group sessions to support positive changes in peer responses as well as promote child prosocial interaction and self-control skills.

The Fast Track Friendship Group program

The Fast Track Friendship Group program is a small group intervention for children experiencing significant peer difficulties. This program is designed to address these children's social-emotional skill deficits, improve social behavior and peer responding, reduce distress, and thereby foster improved peer relationships and enhanced school adjustment. In an ideal multitiered system of positive behavioral supports, schools offer classroom-level curriculum-based efforts to promote social-emotional skills, and more intensive supports to remediate social skill deficits, matched to the level of student need (Gresham, Cook, Crews, & Kern, 2004). It is generally expected that approximately 15% of students need additional support beyond tier one (universal) classroom programming in order to address their social skill deficits and peer difficulties (Sugai & Horner, 2002). The Fast Track Friendship Group program is designed for these children, representing a tier two program for children experiencing peer rejection or other significant peer difficulties. The Friendship Group program is research-based; its design was informed by research on the effectiveness of different social skill training approaches (see Bierman & Powers, 2009, for a review).

Social-emotional skill training

The Friendship Group program provides social-emotional skill training in small groups of 3–6 children. Sessions are designed to: (1) promote skill acquisition by presenting models (e.g., using stories, discussions, examples, modeling videotapes) that define, explain, and illustrate the target skill, and (2) enhance skill performance by providing opportunities to practice the skills in the context of positive reinforcement and corrective performance feedback (Bierman & Powers, 2009).

This intervention approach has been well validated in prior studies. For example, Gresham et al. (2004) examined 6 metaanalyses conducted between 1987 and 2003, involving 338 studies and more than 25,000 children between 3 and 18 years of age. Social skill training emerged as an effective intervention strategy for students with emotional and behavioral problems, with an overall mean effect size of 0.29 (range = 0.19–0.40), corresponding to an improvement rate of 65% among the children who received social skill training compared to 35% among children in the control groups. On the basis of these studies, Gresham et al. (2004) further concluded that social skill training was effective for children who varied substantially in terms of their specific emotional and behavioral problems, including a wide range of externalizing and internalizing problems.

The Friendship Group program focuses on the social and emotional skills that play a central role in effective social interaction and are common deficits among peer-rejected children. These include: (1) prosocial engagement (social participation and cooperation), (2) communication skills (self-expression, asking questions, listening skills), (3) emotion regulation and behavioral self-control (understanding and managing strong feelings; impulse control), (4) responsible social behavior (fair play, respecting others, good sportsmanship), (5) social problem-solving skills (negotiation, conflict resolution, and collaborative planning), and (6) managing stress (coping effectively with bullying, teasing, and disappointment). Skills are arranged in a developmental sequence, with initial groups emphasizing participation, communication, and emotional expression to build group cohesion, and provide a foundation for discussing more difficult issues. A focus on emotion regulation and self-control follows, along with responsible social behavior in the context of competitive play. Problem solving, conflict resolution, and negotiation skills are taught after the foundation of emotion regulation and behavioral self-control skills has been established. Sessions on coping skills for social stressors such as bullying and social exclusion are provided in the later sessions. Skills are organized in modules, so that it is possible to increase or reduce emphasis and practice in specific skill domains depending upon the needs of the children in each group (see Table 1).

The specific content used in the Friendship Group program was developed and refined in a series of randomized trials with different elementary school populations of peer-rejected children. The program includes a total of 36 lessons (22 lessons for children in the younger elementary grades, kindergarten through

TABLE 1 Friendship Group unit organization and targeted skills.

Unit focus	Targeted skills
Early elementary sessions: (grades K-2; ages 5–8)	
Unit 1: establishing common ground	Social entry and friendship initiation skills, including establishing common ground via self-disclosure, asking questions, and listening. Also includes lessons on sharing feelings
Unit 2: caring and controlled behavior	Cooperation skills, including helping others and sharing. Self-control skills, including inhibiting impulsive behavior, and calming down when distressed. Fair play skills, including following rules and taking turns
Unit 3: negotiating with friends	Making plans and problem solving. Resolving conflicts peacefully by identifying the problem, listening to others' perspectives, suggesting solutions, compromising
Unit 4: handling competitive play	Good sportsmanship, including being a good winner and a good loser. Treating others with respect
Unit 5: communicating effectively	Communicating with others by sharing your feelings and point of view, listening to and respecting the other's perspective, noticing your friends' feelings, and working together as a team
Unit 6: sustaining friendships	Coping effectively with teasing or bullying and managing disappointments. Sustaining friendships over time
Advanced elementary sessions (grades 3–5; ages 8–11)	
Unit 1: cooperation and conversation skills	Social entry and friendship initiation skills, including meeting and greeting others, initiating conversation, inviting others to join in, and sustaining conversations and interactions
Unit 2: understanding and respecting others	Good sportsmanship, including a review of the Golden Rule (treat others as you wish to be treated), cooperation skills, managing conflicts by expressing concerns, listening to others, generating ideas, and compromising or negotiating to reach a fair decision
Unit 3: coping with social stress	Managing stress and staying calm when distressed. Considering multiple perspectives on a problem. Coping effectively with teasing and bullying. Sustaining friendships over time

grade 2; 14 lessons for children in the older grades 3 to 5). The length of total Friendship Group intervention (14–22 weeks) follows the recommendation of McIntosh, Vaughn, and Zaragoza (1991) and Gresham, Van, and Cook (2006). Their research suggests that the length of social skill training programs is one factor affecting impact; for example, in a review of 22 social skill training programs, McIntosh et al. (1991) found that the highest impact programs provided over three times more social skill training than programs that did not produce significant effects. Similarly, Gresham et al. (2006) noted that the typical social skills intervention lasts for 10–12 weeks but argued that students with severe skill deficits typically need twice that amount. Studies that provided the basis for selecting the particular skills and strategies included in Friendship Group lessons included rigorous randomized trials that evaluated social skill training for disliked, withdrawn students in grades 5 and 6 (Bierman, 1986; Bierman & Furman, 1984), rejected-aggressive students in grades 2 and 3 (Bierman, Miller, & Stabb, 1987), and aggressive students in grades 1–4 (Bierman, Greenberg, and Conduct Problems Prevention Research Group (CPPRG), 1996; CPPRG, 1999, 2002). Each of these studies documented the efficacy of the Friendship Group approach to improve social skills and social behaviors and to increase peer acceptance.

Each Friendship Group session includes a manualized guide for group leaders, identifying target skills, and providing skill presentation materials, specific practice activities and games, guidelines for implementation, and information sheets for parents. There are also additional practice activities, which allow group leaders to extend practice on particular skills, as needed. Following a standard format for coaching programs (Bierman, 2004; Gresham et al., 2006), each session is focused on a set of target skills. The first step in skill training involves the presentation of the target skill, when instructions, modeling, and discussion are used to explain and clarify skill concepts and provide exemplars of positive and negative skill performance. Each Friendship Group program session begins with a Friendship Circle that includes greeting, recap of prior skills, and the presentation of the target skill for the day. Skills are introduced using a story, role play, game, or other discussion starter. The goal is to illustrate positive and negative examples of the skill (e.g., what to do and what not to do), and encourage active child discussion of the skills in a fun and engaging manner.

The second step in the skill training process is the provision of structured and supportive opportunities to practice targeted skills. To do so, the second phase of each Friendship Group program session occurs at a Construction Station where children are led in table-top activities or structured games or role plays that provide them with specific opportunities to practice the target skills. For the younger children, the construction station activities usually include manipulatives (e.g., arts & crafts, blocks). In the advanced elementary sessions, the activities more often involve role-play challenges. Friendship Group sessions also incorporate less structured and more naturalistic opportunities to practice targeted skills. Each session includes a third phase involving Collaborative Challenges, which are physically active games or team challenges that require the more general use of target skills. These challenges foster the practice of impulse control, motivate group engagement, and encourage practice in planning, communication skills, and group problem solving. Whereas the goal of Construction Station activities is to practice new skills in a structured setting that maximizes support for positive skill performance, the goal of the Collaborative Challenges is to provide an opportunity for the generalized use of skills in more naturalistic peer interactions. For groups that are held outside of the school setting, guidelines for optional snack activities are also included. Snack is organized to provide additional support for skill acquisition and practice. For example, snack provides an opportunity for cooperative planning (e.g., sharing snack jobs, such as passing out cups and napkins). In later sessions, "sharing snacks" are introduced, which foster practice in problem solving and negotiation skills, as group members must decide how to divide snack materials fairly and work together to distribute them.

A third, critically important element of effective coaching sessions is the provision of performance feedback, to help children recognize when they are demonstrating skillful behavior and when they need to adjust, redirect, or refine their skill performance. During initial sessions, group leaders provide performance feedback in the form of specific praise to reinforce positive efforts and accomplishments and noncritical redirection or corrective input that allows children to adjust and improve skill performance. Increasingly over time, the goal is to improve children's abilities to self-monitor their own behavior and self-correct based upon their self-reflections and responses of their social partners. Friendship Group includes the use of a set of therapeutic strategies including positive support, emotion coaching, induction strategies, and problem-solving dialog (described in a later section of this chapter) to increase children's self- and social awareness and promote self-regulation. In addition, in the advanced elementary program, there are also three sessions in which "friendship movies" are taped and reviewed by the group to elicit self-reflection and peer feedback. Each session ends with a Closing Circle when group members share compliments. Closing circle provides the opportunity to highlight positive skill performance to strengthen feelings of efficacy and motivate future efforts.

An important element of effective skill training programs is generalization programming, which involves efforts to help children generalize the skills they learn in group sessions to "real-life" interactions outside of group. The Friendship Group program activities are designed to create a foundation for generalization by incorporating extended practice in multiple play and conversation contexts that increase in complexity over the course of the year. To more explicitly encourage and support generalization, each session includes a "Friendship Tips" handout to be shared with teachers and parents to keep them informed about the focus of the group session and provide ideas for follow-up practice opportunities. Periodic meetings with parents and teachers are encouraged to review each child's progress and discuss specific positive peer interaction opportunities that they might support outside of the group context.

Including peer partners

The Friendship Group program advocates the inclusion of peer partners in small group sessions. Although social skill training can be done in individual sessions that rely on role-play practice, an extensive research base suggests that including peer partners in social skill training sessions and using naturalistic peer activities and games for skill practice increases intervention impact (Bierman, 2004; Pelham & Fabiano, 2008; Troop & Asher, 1999). For example, Bierman and Furman (1984) found that including normative classmates as peer partners in social skill training sessions improved program impact on peer acceptance and enhanced the sustainability of program gains over time, relative to an individual social skill training condition. This is probably because social skills are more difficult to perform in the context of naturalistic social interaction that can be more emotionally challenging, socially ambiguous, and fast paced than a typical role play. Including peer partners and active play activities in social skill training sessions gives children more opportunity to practice skills in a context similar to the naturalistic peer interaction context of the classroom and playground (Haring, 1992).

In the Fast Track Program trial, Friendship Group was implemented as an extracurricular school-based program with sessions held after school or on the weekend. Friendship Groups included 6 aggressive children and were run by a group leader and coleader. Implementing Friendship Group as an extracurricular program (rather than in-school program) had two major advantages. First, it was possible to hold long sessions (60–90 min) without interfering with academic activities. Second, it made it possible to run concurrent, collateral programs for parents and include parent-child sessions after the group programs (see CPPRG, 2019). However, groups that are comprised of children who all exhibit elevated aggression require extensive attention to behavior management. Iatrogenic processes can emerge in such groups, when group members reinforce each other for negative behavior (Dodge et al., 2006). With trained professional leaders and behavior management systems in place, problems with negative peer dynamics were not prevalent in the Fast Track Friendship Group program. However, management difficulties emerged in 25% of the groups and were a significant problem in 5% of the groups (Lavallee, Bierman, Nix, & CPPRG, 2005). Hence, we do not recommend homogeneous grouping of children who all struggle with aggressive impulse control. After the Fast Track Program, we worked with organizations providing Friendship Group as an after-school program and mental health service, with sessions held in an office location or community-based center. In these contexts, we recommended heterogeneous grouping, combining children with similar social skill deficits who had complementary behavioral difficulties and balancing groups with members who were aggressive versus withdrawn. Groups that include a mix of aggressive and withdrawn peers are often easier to manage than groups that contain only aggressive children and thereby facilitate the creation of a therapeutic milieu. Indeed, metaanalyses suggest that social skill training interventions that use heterogeneous grouping are more beneficial for aggressive children than grouping aggressive children together (Ang & Hughes, 2001).

In other studies of the Friendship Group program, we have implemented sessions as a pull-out program during school time. In this implementation context, we have often run smaller groups (3–4 children) with one group leader and rotated normative classmates as peer partners so that small groups include both children experiencing peer difficulties and some classmates who have age-appropriate social skills and are accepted by peers. Including classmates as rotating peer partners provides more positive peer models in the group context and increases the likelihood of generalization of positive peer interactions for group members outside of the group setting. In addition, two separate studies have shown that when classroom peers rotate as partners in social skill training sessions, they are positively affected themselves—becoming more positively responsive socially and increasing their liking for the target child (Bierman, 1986; Bierman et al., 1987). School-based sessions must be shorter (no longer than 45 min) in order to avoid conflicts with academic activities, but have the advantage of increasing generalization opportunities from group sessions to peer interactions in the classroom and on the playground. Using classmates as group partners supports this kind of generalization.

Therapeutic strategies

The way that group leaders organize their behavior management and respond to child misbehavior and peer conflicts during group sessions has an important impact on child skill acquisition (Lavallee et al., 2005). The Friendship Group program encourages the use of a set of therapeutic management strategies that are designed to increase opportunities and support for the development of self-regulation skills, create a positive peer socializing environment, and elicit positive peer responding during sessions (see also Bierman, 1986, 2004). To maximize skill acquisition and generalization, it is important for children to feel effective when they use the targeted social-emotional skills during group sessions and to receive peer reinforcement for these skills. One way to do this is with adult direction and reinforcement. For example, the adult leader could manage the group by providing specific instructions and differential reinforcement to children who exhibit the targeted social skills. However, a limitation of relying on the adult leader to elicit and reinforce desired behavior is that adults are often not present during peer interactions. Hence, ideally, children learn to self-regulate their social behavior and attend to peer responses to adjust their skill performance. The Friendship Group therapeutic processes are designed to foster self-regulated behavior, attention to social impact, and positive responsiveness among all group members.

To create this kind of therapeutic climate in the Friendship Group, group leaders are encouraged to use four kinds of therapeutic strategies to manage and process group interactions (see Table 2). *Positive support strategies* are

TABLE 2 Therapeutic processes used in Friendship Group.

Positive support strategies	
Friendly narration	Make frequent warm and friendly comments that describe what is going on, identify common ground, and encourage child-to-child conversation
Positive guidance	Provide guidance for expected behavior. Include specific entry and closure transition activities. Offer restless children specific roles as helpers or assistants
Make a connection	Use social referencing (eye contact, nodding, reassuring gesture) and a warm voice tone to support felt security and engagement
Emotion coaching	
Talk about feelings	Throughout the session, describe your own feelings and encourage children to describe and discuss their feelings
Reflect feelings	Use varied feeling labels to describe a child's experience
Reframe feelings	When children are upset and angry, de-escalate emotional arousal and reorient threat appraisals with a calm demeanor and the selective use of a modulated feeling label
Induction strategies	
Clarify desired behaviors	Praise children who are exhibiting desired behaviors. State positive hopes and expectations
Identify the impact of problem behaviors	In a neutral tone, use I-statements to explain the negative impact of a behavior on yourself, or elicit feedback from peers
Focusing on consequences that matter for the child	In a neutral tone, describe the impact of a problem on social outcomes the child cares about (playing the game, having a friend)
Give choices; offer constructive alternatives	Provide choices that indicate appropriate behavioral options; redirect children into positive roles or activities
De-escalate power struggles	Use a soft, neutral tone to express concerns about the child's difficulties and negative consequences for the child; align with the child to facilitate coping and problem-solving efforts
Social problem-solving dialog	
Stop the action	Intervene to stop conflicts. Have children "take five" to calm down
Clarify the problem	Use active listening to help each child share feelings and explain his or her perspective on the problem
Generate solutions and plan	Elicit solutions and support decision making to select a plan of action
Try it out	Support implementation of the plan; reinforce children for their problem-solving efforts

designed to increase children's comfort in social interaction and reduce anxiety. *Emotion coaching* fosters emotional awareness of one's own feelings and of the feelings of others in the group, supporting empathy and emotion regulation skills. *Induction strategies* elicit and support self-regulation by providing children with information that allows them to reflect on (and, if needed, reconsider) their behavioral choices, in order to decrease adult directive control and encourage self-management. Finally, *social problem-solving dialog* is used to enhance flexible thinking and conflict management skills. These strategies are designed to promote a positive climate within the group, increase positive responding, enhance positive control beliefs, and encourage self-regulation. Friendship Group also includes group planning and reflection discussions to help children consider the behaviors that helped them have fun together (and those that interfered with group success).

Evidence supporting the efficacy of the Friendship Group program

Friendship Group was developed and refined in the context of the Fast Track Program, a multicomponent prevention program designed to promote the social-emotional skills of children at risk for conduct disorders and increase home and school supports for positive behavioral control (CPPRG, 2019). Fast Track involved a multisite randomized-controlled efficacy trial conducted at four geographically and demographically diverse areas of the United States—rural Pennsylvania; Seattle, Washington; Durham, North Carolina; and Nashville, Tennessee. In this study, children were identified for intervention based on teacher and parent ratings of aggressive-disruptive behavior. To address these behaviors, promote social-emotional competencies, and reduce risk for future antisocial and violent behavior, Fast Track involved a set of interventions, including a classroom-level (tier one) social-emotional learning program, academic tutoring, parent groups, and home visits, as well as the Friendship Group program. Friendship Group sessions were held after school or on a weekend, in small groups of six aggressive-disruptive children led by two group leaders, concurrent with parent group sessions. The design compared the outcomes of aggressive-disruptive children who received this entire set of interventions with aggressive-disruptive children in control schools who did not receive any of these extra interventions. Hence, the findings from Fast Track are not specific to the Friendship Group program, but they suggest its efficacy.

Fast Track demonstrated that, compared to children in the control group, children who received the Fast Track intervention during the elementary school years showed improved social-cognitive skills (including improved emotion recognition, emotion coping, and social problem-solving skills), more positive peer interaction, improved peer sociometrics (more often nominated as "most liked" and less often nominated as "least liked" by classmates), and reduced aggressive-disruptive behavior (CPPRG, 1999, 2002). Fast Track youth were followed into adulthood, where they showed reduced rates of antisocial behavior and arrest, along with significantly lower levels of internalizing and externalizing behavior problems and lower rates of substance abuse relative to youth in the control group (CPPRG, 2015). These adult Fast Track outcomes no doubt reflect the impact of multiple Fast Track intervention components. In addition, one cannot determine the degree to which the value of the Friendship Group program was amplified by situating it in the context of additional intervention supports that targeted parenting skills, parent-child relationship quality, and academic difficulties. Of note, however, was a study examining the association between intervention effects in elementary school and later adult benefits. Analyses identified gains in social-emotional skills during childhood, especially improvements in self-regulation and social functioning, as key mediators of later Fast Track effects on reductions in adolescent and young adult criminal activity and problem behaviors (Sorensen, Dodge, & Conduct Problems Prevention Research Group, 2016).

The Fast Track Friendship Group program was also evaluated in a randomized trial of the PATHS to Success program, designed to promote the social-emotional and self-regulatory skills of kindergarten and first-grade children screened for elevated aggressive behavior at school entry (Greenberg & Bierman, 2011). All children in the PATHS to Success program received tier one social-emotional support via the PATHS Curriculum implemented in their classrooms. Children with identified elevations in aggressive behavior based on teacher ratings were randomly assigned to receive Friendship Group and additional parent training or to receive PATHS alone; hence this study compared the outcomes of children who received a universal intervention and parent training plus Friendship Group with children who received the universal intervention alone. Friendship Group sessions were held during school time as a pull-out program, and groups included two aggressive children and two rotating classroom partners with one group leader. All classroom members with parent permission to participate took turns as rotating partners. Likely as a function of the provision of PATHS in the classroom, children in both the intervention and control groups in this study showed decreases over time in aggressive behavior and increases over time in social competence. However, compared with the control group who received PATHS alone, children in the intervention group who received Friendship Group as well as PATHS showed significantly more growth in emotion recognition skills, demonstrated improvements in attention skills in the classroom, and were rated by teachers as higher in school readiness. The school readiness measure included adaptive approaches to learning and the skills necessary to succeed in school, such as the ability and willingness to follow classroom routines and complete tasks. One year later, follow-up analyses showed that children who received Friendship Group sustained gains in adaptive learning engagement and school readiness and also showed enhanced empathy and kindness toward others.

In both the Fast Track Program and the Paths to Success program, Friendship Group was delivered as a tier two intervention for high-risk aggressive children in the context of a universal intervention supporting the social-emotional learning of all children in the classroom. In a more recent randomized trial, the Friendship Connections Project, the Friendship Group program is being implemented as a standalone program. In this project, children are identified as peer-rejected using classroom sociometric nominations, and then randomly assigned to receive the Friendship Group program or to be part of a "usual practice" control group. The children being served in this study are all peer-rejected but vary considerably in the nature of their behavior problems, with about half demonstrating elevated aggressive or impulsive-inattentive behaviors and others displaying socially withdrawn or socially awkward social behaviors. Friendship Group sessions are held during school (as a pullout program) with small groups, including one rejected child and 2–3 rotating peer partners recommended by teachers. This trial is currently underway, but preliminary findings document the efficacy of the Friendship Group program when implemented as a "standalone" intervention for children who are peer-rejected for a variety of reasons. Positive effects include significant increases in directly assessed and teacher-rated social-emotional skills, along with improvements in observed learning engagement and peer acceptance assessed with sociometric nominations (Bierman, 2019).

The logic model describing the program components and modalities used in the Friendship Group program, along with the targeted risk and protective factors, proximal outcomes, and distal outcomes is illustrated in Fig. 1.

Summary

Elementary school students with significant peer difficulties and associated social skill deficits and behavior problems are at high risk of developing long-term pervasive behavioral and academic problems. The Fast Track Friendship Group program is a small group, evidence-based tier two intervention designed for children struggling with peer rejection and related peer difficulties. The Friendship Group manual (Bierman et al., 2017) provides detailed plans for 36 lessons, covering a developmental progression of social-emotional skills for children in the early elementary grades (kindergarten to second grade) and the later elementary grades (third to fifth grade). A set of therapeutic strategies is used to maximize skill learning opportunities during group sessions and to support positive peer responding. Lesson-specific Friendship Tips are provided to children to share with their teachers and parents to encourage generalization support outside of the group context. Well-controlled evaluation studies validate the power of the Friendship Group intervention to boost children's social-emotional skills, reduce aggressive behavior, and improve peer relations.

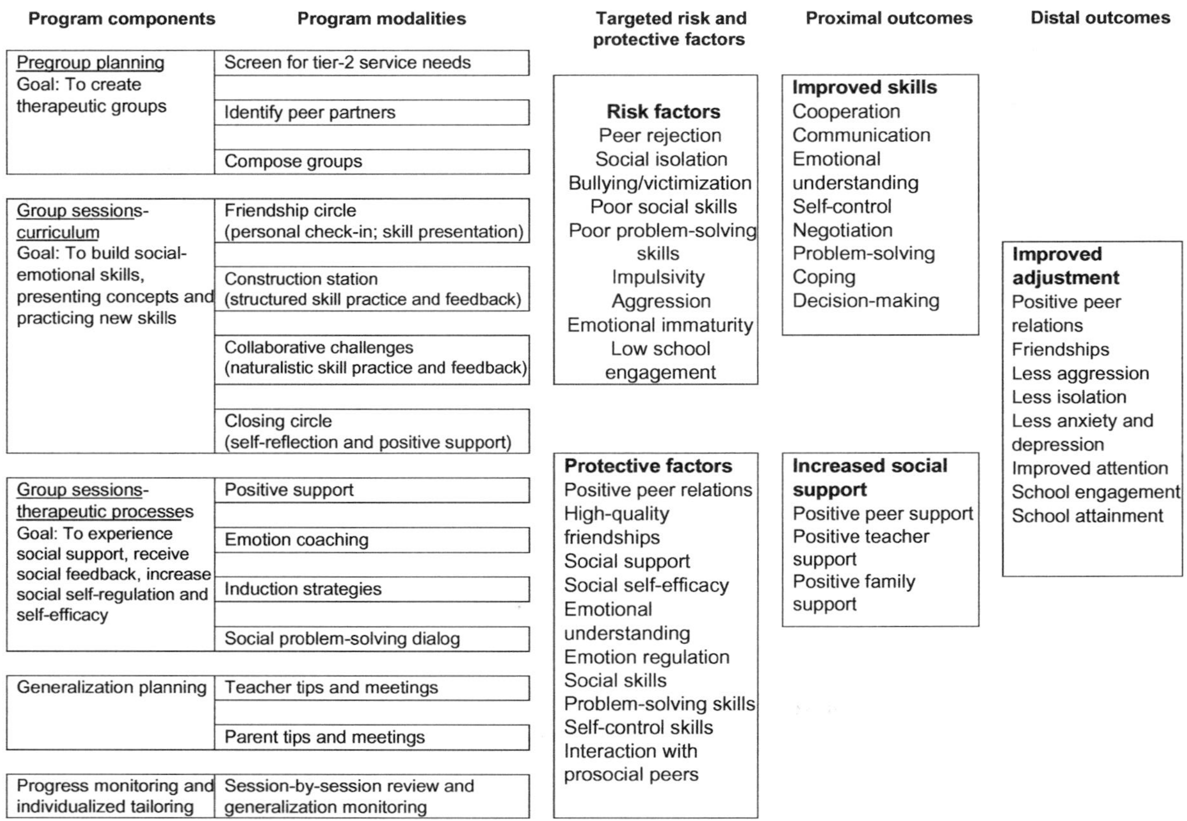

FIG. 1 Logic model for the Fast Track Friendship Group.

Acknowledgments

The development of the original Fast Track Friendship Group program was supported by National Institute of Mental Health (NIMH) Grants R18MH48043, R18MH50951, R18MH50952, R18MH50953, K05MH00797, and K05MH01027; National Institute on Drug Abuse (NIDA) Grants DA016903, K05DA15226, RC1DA028248, and P30DA023026; and Department of Education Grant S184U30002. The Center for Substance Abuse Prevention also provided support through a memorandum of agreement with the NIMH. In addition, the Friendship Group program was further developed and refined in the context of projects funded by the NIMH R34MH085889, the Pennsylvania Department of Health, and R305A150488 funded by the Institute of Educational Sciences.

In developing this program, we are grateful for the close collaboration of the Altoona Area School District, Bellefonte Area School District, Durham Public Schools, Harrisburg School District, Highline Public Schools, Juniata County School District, Middletown Area School District, Mifflin County School District, Metropolitan Nashville Public Schools, State College Area School District, Seattle Public Schools, Steelton-Highspire School District, Tyrone Area School District, York City School District, Barnardos Children's Charity of Ireland, and Barnardos Children's Charity of the United Kingdom. We greatly appreciate the hard work and dedication of the many staff members who implemented the project, provided feedback and suggestions, collected the evaluation data, and assisted with data management and analyses.

References

Ang, R., & Hughes, J. (2001). Differential benefits of skills training with antisocial youth based on group composition: A meta-analytic investigation. *School Psychology Review, 31*, 164–185.

Bierman, K. L. (1986). Process of change during social skills training with preadolescents and its relation to treatment outcome. *Child Development, 57*, 230–240.

Bierman, K. L. (2004). *Peer rejection: Developmental processes and intervention strategies*. New York: Guilford.

Bierman, K. L. (2019). *Friendship connections project annual progress report*. [Unpublished manuscript].

Bierman, K. L., & Furman, W. (1984). The effects of social skills training and peer involvement on the social adjustment of preadolescents. *Child Development, 55*, 151–162.

Bierman, K. L., Greenberg, M. T., Coie, J. D., Dodge, K. A., Lochman, J. E., & McMahon, R. J. (2017). *Social and emotional skills training for children: The Fast Track Friendship Group manual*. New York, NY: Guilford Press.

Bierman, K., Greenberg, M. T., & Conduct Problems Prevention Research Group. (1996). Social skill training in the FAST Track Program. In R. D. V. Peters & R. J. McMahon (Eds.), *Prevention and early intervention: Childhood disorders, substance abuse, and delinquency* (pp. 65–89). Newbury Park, CA: Sage.

Bierman, K. L., Miller, C. L., & Stabb, S. D. (1987). Improving the social behavior and peer acceptance of rejected boys: Effects of social skill training with instructions and prohibitions. *Journal of Consulting and Clinical Psychology, 55*, 194–200.

Bierman, K. L., & Powers, C. J. (2009). Social skills training to improve peer relations. In K. H. Rubin, W. Bukowski, & B. Laursen (Eds.), *Handbook of peer interactions, relationships, and groups* (pp. 603–621). New York, NY: Guilford.

Boivin, M., Hymel, S., & Hodges, E. V. E. (2001). Toward a process view of peer rejection and harassment. In M. Boivin, S. Hymel, & E. Hodges (Eds.), *Peer harassment in school: The plight of the vulnerable and victimized* (pp. 265–289). New York: Guildford Press.

Buhs, E. S., Ladd, G. W., & Herald, S. L. (2006). Peer exclusion and victimization: Processes that mediate the relation between peer group rejection and children's classroom engagement and achievement? *Journal of Educational Psychology, 98*, 1–13.

Conduct Problems Prevention Research Group. (1999). Initial impact of the Fast Track prevention trial for conduct problems: I. The high-risk sample. *Journal of Consulting and Clinical Psychology, 67*, 631–647.

Conduct Problems Prevention Research Group. (2002). Evaluation of the first 3 years of the Fast Track prevention trial with children at high risk for adolescent conduct problems. *Journal of Abnormal Child Psychology, 30*, 19–35.

Conduct Problems Prevention Research Group. (2015). Impact of early intervention on psychopathology, crime, and well-being at age 25. *American Journal of Psychiatry, 172*, 59–70.

Conduct Problems Prevention Research Group. (2019). *The Fast Track Program for children at risk: Preventing antisocial behavior*. New York, NY: Guilford.

DeRosier, M. E., & Mercer, S. (2009). Perceived behavioral atypicality as a predictor of social rejection and peer victimization: Implications for emotional adjustment and academic achievement. *Psychology in the Schools, 46*, 375–387.

Dishion, T. J., & Tipsord, J. M. (2011). Peer contagion in child and adolescent social and emotional development. *Annual Review of Psychology, 62*, 189–214.

Dodge, K., Lansford, J. E., & Dishion, T. J. (2006). The problem of deviant peer influences in intervention programs. In K. A. Dodge, T. J. Dishion, & J. E. Lansford (Eds.), *Deviant peer influences in programs for youth* (pp. 3–13). New York: Guilford Press.

Domitrovich, C. E., Durlak, J. A., Staley, K. C., & Weissberg, R. P. (2017). Social-emotional competence: An essential factor for promoting positive adjustment and reducing risk in schoolchildren. *Child Development, 88*, 408–416.

Dusenbury, L., & Weissberg, R. P. (2016). *Social and emotional learning for elementary-school children: Finding from research and implications for policy*. Chicago, IL: Collaborative for Academic, Social, and Emotional Learning.

Farmer, T. W., Estell, D. B., Hall, C. M., Pearl, R., Rodkin, P., & Van Acker, R. M. (2008). Interpersonal competence configurations, behavior problems, and social adjustment in preadolescence. *Journal of Emotional and Behavioral Disorders, 16*, 195–212.

Fite, P. J., Wimsatt, A. R., Vitulano, M. L., Rathert, J. L., & Schwartz, S. (2012). Examination of peer rejection and depressive symptoms as mediators of the link between rule-breaking behavior and poor academic performance. *Journal of Psychopathology and Behavioral Assessment, 34*, 164–171.

Greenberg, M. T., & Bierman, K. (2011). *Report on the PATHS to success trial*. Unpublished grant report to Pennsylvania Department of Health.

Greenberg, M. T., Weissberg, R. P., O'Brien, M. U., Zins, J. E., Fredericks, L., Resnik, H., & Elias, M. J. (2003). Enhancing school-based prevention and youth development through coordinated social, emotional, and academic learning. *American Psychologist, 58*, 466–474.

Gresham, F. M., Cook, C., Crews, S., & Kern, L. (2004). Social skills training for children and youth with emotional and behavioral disorders: Validity considerations and future directions. *Behavioral Disorders, 30*, 32–46.

Gresham, F. M., Elliott, S. N., & Kettler, R. J. (2010). Base rates of social skills acquisition/performance deficits, strengths, and problem behaviors: An analysis of the social skills improvement system—Rating scales. *Journal of Psychological Assessment, 22*(4), 809–815.

Gresham, F. M., Van, M. B., & Cook, C. R. (2006). Social skills training for teaching replacement behaviors: Remediating acquisition deficits in at-risk students. *Behavioral Disorders*, *31*, 363–377.

Haring, N. (1992). The context of social competence: Relations, relationships, and generalization. In S. Odom, S. McConnell, & M. McEvoy (Eds.), *Social competence of young children with disabilities: Issues and strategies for intervention* (pp. 307–320). Baltimore: Paul H. Brookes.

Hunt, T. K. A., Slack, K. S., & Berger, L. M. (2017). Adverse childhood experiences and behavioral problems in middle childhood. *Child Abuse and Neglect*, *67*, 391–402.

Jones, D. E., Greenberg, M., & Crowley, M. (2015). Early social-emotional functioning and public health: The relationship between kindergarten social competence and future wellness. *American Journal of Public Health*, *105*(11), 2283–2290.

La Greca, A. M., & Landoll, R. R. (2011). Peer influences in the development and maintenance of anxiety disorders. In W. K. Silverman & A. Field (Eds.), *Anxiety disorders in children and adolescents: Research, assessment, and intervention* (2nd ed.). London: Cambridge University Press.

Lavallee, K. L., Bierman, K. L., Nix, R. L., & CPPRG. (2005). The impact of first-grade "friendship group" experiences on child social outcomes in the Fast Track Program. *Journal of Abnormal Child Psychology*, *33*, 307–324.

Mayeux, L., Bellmore, A. D., & Cillessen, A. H. (2007). Predicting changes in adjustment using repeated measures of sociometric status. *Journal of Genetic Psychology*, *168*, 401–424.

McDougall, P., Hymel, S., Vaillancourt, T., & Mercer, L. (2001). The consequences of childhood peer rejection. In P. McDougall, S. Hymel, T. Vaillancourt, & L. Mercer (Eds.), *Interpersonal rejection* (pp. 213–247). New York: Oxford University Press.

McIntosh, R., Vaughn, S., & Zaragoza, N. (1991). A review of social interventions for students with learning disabilities. *Journal of Learning Disabilities*, *24*, 451–458.

Mikami, A. Y., & Hinshaw, S. P. (2006). Resilient adolescent adjustment among girls: Buffers of childhood peer rejection and attention-deficit/hyperactivity disorder. *Journal of Abnormal Child Psychology*, *34*, 825–839.

Niles, M. D., Reynolds, A. J., & Roe-Sepowitz, D. (2008). Early childhood intervention and early adolescent social and emotional competence: Second-generation evaluation evidence from the Chicago Longitudinal Study. *Educational Research*, *50*, 55–73.

Pelham, W. E., & Fabiano, G. A. (2008). Evidence-based psychosocial treatment for attention deficit/hyperactivity disorder: An update. *Journal of Clinical Child and Adolescent Psychology*, *37*, 185–214.

Ratcliffe, B., Wong, M., Dossetor, D., & Hayes, S. (2014). Teaching social-emotional skills to school-age children with Autism Spectrum Disorder: A treatment versus control trial in 41 mainstream schools. *Research in Autism Spectrum Disorders*, *8*, 1722–1733.

Shantel, D. C. (2015). An ecological perspective on emerging trauma-informed teaching practices. *Children & Schools*, *37*, 223–230.

Shin, S. S., McDonald, S. E., & Conley, D. (2018). Profiles of adverse childhood experiences and impulsivity. *Child Abuse and Neglect*, *85*, 118–126.

Sorensen, L. C., Dodge, K. A., & Conduct Problems Prevention Research Group. (2016). How does the fast track intervention prevent adverse outcomes in young adulthood? *Child Development*, *87*(2), 429–445.

Sugai, G., & Horner, R. (2002). The evolution of discipline practices: School-wide positive behavior supports. *Child and Family Behavior Therapy*, *24*, 23–50.

Troop, W. P., & Asher, S. R. (1999). Teaching peer relationship competence in schools. In R. J. Stevens (Ed.), *Teaching in American schools* (pp. 141–171). Columbus, Ohio: Merrill.

Ve'ronneau, M., Vitaro, F., Brendgen, M., Dishion, T. J., & Tremblay, R. E. (2010). Transactional analysis of the reciprocal links between peer experiences and academic achievement from middle childhood to early adolescence. *Developmental Psychology*, *46*, 773–790.

Waas, G. A. (2006). Peer relationships. In G. A. Waas (Ed.), *Children's needs III: Development, prevention, and intervention* (pp. 325–340). Washington, DC: National Association of School Psychologists.

Further reading

Conduct Problems Prevention Research Group. (1992). A developmental and clinical model for the prevention of conduct disorders: The Fast Track Program. *Development and Psychopathology*, *4*, 509–528.

Chapter 10

The *PATHS* curriculum: Thirty-five years and counting

Carol A. Kusché
Seattle Psychoanalytic Society and Institute, Seattle, WA, United States; University of Washington, Seattle, WA, United States; PATHS® Training LLC, Seattle, WA, United States

Prior to the 1980s, teaching social skills and emotional literacy in the classroom was virtually unheard of in elementary education. In fact, the acronym SEL (Social-Emotional Learning) had not yet been coined. Education focused on cognition, and students were expected to leave their feelings at the door. Unfortunately, this was untenable, as many students, especially those experiencing emotional distress, were unable to comply. Many teachers in the educational trenches knew that we badly needed something to help with children's emotional dysregulation, and although behavioral reinforcement paradigms and cognitive problem solving (e.g., Shure & Spivak, 1979) were available, these did not fully address children's emotions. For further context, it is important to note that children's social and emotional development had not really gained traction in the field at this time and was not included in child development textbooks. As Masters et al. (1981) noted, "The experimental literature on affective states in children…is an area that has little, if any, clinical or applicational work…It is an area that is quite young, with less than a decade of research effort to be summarized" (p. 91).

This was the state of the field in the early 1980s when our research group at the University of Washington, including myself, Mark Greenberg, and others, began to develop the stone soup we called the PATHS (Promoting Alternative Thinking Strategies) curriculum. The name PATHS reflected our model of educating the whole child (ABCD Model of Development; Kusché & Greenberg, 2011) through the integration of affect (A), behavior (B), cognition (C), and (D) the dynamic process of development. More specifically, because emotional development is an important precursor to other ways of thinking, for optimal brain development, it needs to be integrated with cognitive and linguistic abilities, which are slower to develop. Other subfields and theories utilized in developing the PATHS program included social cognitive neuroscience, psychoanalytic

Social Skills Across the Life Span. https://doi.org/10.1016/B978-0-12-817752-5.00010-X

developmental neuroscience, attachment theory, and relevant research in psychology, anthropology, and sociology.

Our first research application of the PATHS curriculum was with elementary students who were deaf or hard of hearing. Results obtained (reported later in this chapter) were positive and far beyond what we had expected. Use of the program quickly spread. Teachers in regular and special education who had observed our research also showed great interest in using PATHS with their students. "Why can't we use it too?" they would ask us. As a result, our next projects focused on the use of PATHS with students in regular and special education. We learned in real time how powerful emotional literacy and social skills instruction (later called SEL) could be.

Over the next 30 years, use of PATHS spread across the United States and to other countries. At the same time, appreciation for SEL was evolving, and SEL programs began to proliferate. However, all SEL is not the same. As Shriver (CASEL, 2017) noted, "Too many policies and programs are still fragmented, funded separately, and not integrated. We need to stop doing what doesn't work and redirect resources in a more integrated way." In addition, very few programs have been extensively evaluated for effectiveness. After rigorously reviewing hundreds of programs for research-based effectiveness, Blueprints for Healthy Youth Development (formerly Blueprints for Violence Prevention) gave the designation of Model Program to only two SEL programs for preschool and elementary education, with PATHS being one: https://www.blueprintsprograms.org/programs/promoting-alternative-thinking-strategies-paths/.

The PATHS curriculum: An overview

The PATHS curriculum is a research-based, multiyear, universal SEL program designed to promote prevention and intervention for students in preschool through grades 5/6. The overarching goals of PATHS are to increase emotional and social competence and reduce aggression and behavior problems while simultaneously enhancing the educational process in the classroom. Among other things, the PATHS program helps children handle emotions effectively, empathize, resolve conflicts peacefully, and make responsible decisions, including enacting prosocial solutions to problems. Use of PATHS also improves classroom and school atmosphere.

The original PATHS curriculum consisted of an instruction manual and five volumes of developmentally sequenced lessons (Kusché & Greenberg, 1994). Preschool PATHS (Domitrovich, Greenberg, Kusché, & Cortes, 2005) was later added to the program. The original curriculum and Preschool PATHS were subsequently reorganized and expanded into a grade-level version of PATHS where new learning builds on previous learning (Greenberg, Kusché, & CPPRG, 2011, 2012; Kusché, Greenberg, & CPPRG, 2011). Grade-level PATHS is organized according to conceptual units differentiated by grade, with integration of concepts within and between lessons. Detailed lessons address multiple goals such as group bonding, attachment to teacher and school, emotional literacy, empathy/perspective taking, self-control, anger management, conflict resolution, healthy decision making, problem solving, and healthy relationships.

PATHS lessons are provided in complete classroom kits for each grade level (PreK—Grade 5/6). An instructional manual and one or two binders of lessons are included in each kit. Teacher-friendly lessons include complete scripts (in bold red italics) with instructions and notes (in bold black print) to facilitate implementation, but teachers are encouraged to adapt lessons as needed for their particular classrooms and to add their own material if desired. Miniature pictures and icons are placed in the margins to provide visual cues. General and specific objectives are provided at the beginning of each lesson to assist with organization and lesson plans, and most materials are included in the kits (posters, feeling faces, pictures, photographs, puppets, stickers, story books, novels, etc.). Example lessons can be found at: https://pathsprogram.com/program-and-components. Supplementary activities are included for most lessons, including extensive lists and synopses for high-quality books for children in grades 1–3. Parent letters and handouts are available online for all grade levels to encourage use of PATHS concepts at home. Optional lessons, reviews, and an optional evaluation package are also provided.

In PATHS, learning is promoted in a multimethod manner through the use of didactics and interactive activities, such as dialoguing, role playing, stories, graphics, writing, art, and music. Role playing is especially important for improving perspective-taking skills and empathy. When students reverse roles with a partner, they learn to think about and identify the perceptions of others. This perspective taking, in turn, has been found to be important for decreasing antisocial behaviors (e.g., significantly lower delinquency recidivism rates; Chandler, 1973).

Educators or counselors teach PATHS lessons in the classroom for a *minimum* of two to three times a week for at least 30 min. However, more frequent sessions are recommended. As will be reviewed later, the more PATHS is used, the stronger the results are likely to be. It should also be noted that one lesson does not necessarily equate to one session. Teachers are encouraged to break lessons into smaller segments according to student need or if a particular concept is of special interest. Thus, one lesson can require one to five or even more sessions.

Ideally, the teaching style of educators and counselors who learn PATHS material and teach PATHS lessons is enhanced (e.g., becomes more engaging, interactive, empathic, etc.). While PATHS is not intended to change the way teachers teach, we have observed that teaching style does often improve in these ways. As one teacher described it, PATHS is "becoming a part of the fabric of the school." PATHS training workshops with certified PATHS trainers are optional, but teachers tell us that workshops make implementation much easier. Our workshops include such components as an overview of the program, description of concepts, information on brain development, and practice with teaching lessons. Online, self-paced training is also available, as is optional coaching to support ongoing implementation.

Since 1982, PATHS has been successfully used in thousands of schools in diverse cultures and settings (e.g., regular education, special education, rural, urban, low SES, high SES). It has been translated into numerous foreign languages (e.g., Belgian, Croatian, Dutch, French, German, Greek, Hebrew, Mandarin, Norwegian, Pakistani, Portuguese, Polish, Swedish, and Turkish). A Spanish adaptation of Preschool PATHS is available for use with children in migrant and seasonal families (Fishman & Wille, 2014). An unpublished version of PATHS is available for use in aftercare programs. PATHS has also been used in outpatient clinics, inpatient hospitals, and homeless shelters.

The PATHS program has consistently received top ratings as a strong evidence-based program from numerous entities [e.g., CASEL (Collaborative for Academic, Social, and Emotional Learning), Blueprints for Healthy Development, US Dept. of Education, SAMHSA's National Registry, US Dept. of Justice, The California Evidence-Based Clearinghouse for Child Welfare, KidsMatter Australian Primary Schools Mental Health Initiative, Early Intervention: The Next Steps: A Report for Her Majesty's Government, Early Intervention Foundation Handbook, Mentally Healthy Schools UK, Canadian Prevention Science, etc.]. The PATHS program has also been determined to be cost effective, as most of the materials can be reused each year. Washington State Institute for Public Policy (2018) estimated a benefit-cost ratio of $22.22 for each dollar invested.

Major concepts in PATHS

Classroom cohesion and group bonding

PATHS begins with a focus on classroom cohesion and group bonding. Our social brains are wired from evolution with a need to belong to a group and a desire to work for the best interests of one's group (Lieberman, 2013). Promoting a sense of group attachment (e.g., to teachers, other students, classroom, school) increases opportunities for social support and decreases classroom disruption. Group cohesion and classroom discipline are emphasized in the first lesson, when students are taught why rules are important and then work as a group to formulate a set of rules for their classroom. This facilitates students' willingness to internalize the rules and emotional investment in following them.

Complimenting

During the second lesson, students learn about complimenting, and the PATHS Kid for Today paradigm is introduced. A different PATHS Kid is randomly selected for each lesson to be the teacher's assistant. At the end of the lesson, a Compliment List is made for the PATHS Kid, including compliments from other students, the teacher, and him/herself. This list is then taken home so family members can add their compliments. This routine is included at the end of every lesson so that it becomes a tradition, one that becomes extremely important to the students. Visitors to classrooms are given their own compliment lists, which extends the sense of belonging to the larger community.

Self-control, attention, and listening skills

The ability to control one's behavior and to regulate one's affect can facilitate concentration, attention, and listening, each of which are crucial for learning. Self-control is also instrumental for the first step of problem solving (i.e., Stop and calm down). Different paradigms for self-control and self-management of dysregulated affect are employed in PATHS as developmentally appropriate. In PreK/K, students hear a story about Twiggle the Turtle who learns to calm down by going inside of his shell and using Three Steps for Calming Down. This paradigm is utilized by students throughout the day as needed, with a reinforcement system in place for the teacher to use. The Turtle Technique and Three Steps for Calming Down are reintroduced in first grade with a different story and reinforcement paradigm. In first and second grades, the Three Steps are incorporated into The Control Signals Poster (CSP) as the red light, followed by the yellow light, (Make a plan—Think), and the green light (Try your plan—Go). In the older grades, self-control and self-management strategies include relaxation techniques, meditation, and other strategies to promote cortical control over limbic processes.

Emotional literacy

Emotional literacy (understanding, recognizing, and labeling feelings) is a keystone of the PATHS curriculum. Emotions are of central importance for almost all aspects of life (e.g., attention, memory, learning, motivation, interpersonal relations, verbal communication, written communication, internal communication, optimal information processing, creativity, critical thinking, etc.; Kusché & Greenberg, 1998). Furthermore, emotional literacy is important for all of the other conceptual units in PATHS (e.g., self-control, problem solving, relationships, etc.).

Emotion concepts

In PATHS, students are not taught how to feel about things; rather, students are taught general principles regarding emotions (e.g., everyone has the same feelings, but different people can feel differently about different things; emotions are signals that give us important information about ourselves and our environment; all feelings are OK to have, but behaviors can be OK or not OK; feelings can be comfortable or uncomfortable; feelings are processed by the brain; etc.). In each feelings lesson, specific emotions are defined, and examples of situations are reviewed. Stories and activities are used to further illustrate emotion concepts. Students are shown pictures and photographs of facial expressions, which they practice replicating. Students also volunteer to talk about times when they have felt various feelings.

Emotion recognition and labeling

The recognition and labeling of feelings is a major focus of the PATHS program. Research has shown that labeling painful feelings (e.g., anger) activates the right ventrolateral prefrontal cortex (rVLPFC), which in turn, decreases the intensity of firing of the amygdala (Lieberman et al., 2007); this prefrontal control over limbic functioning helps children regulate emotions and reduce distress. Labeling painful feelings through verbal mediation also brings unconscious processing (in the right hemisphere) to conscious awareness (in the left), which increases the capacity for self-control (Kusché & Greenberg, 2006). Recognizing and labeling the feelings of others facilitates perspective taking, empathy, and improved relationships.

In PreK—Grade 2, students collect a set of feeling face cards (yellow for comfortable, blue for uncomfortable) with emotional expressions and labels. Students use these cards throughout the day for a variety of purposes (e.g., to practice emotion recognition; show others how they are feeling; assist with self-control and communication; identify how characters in stories are feeling; etc.). Teachers use their own sets of Feeling Faces, which assists with dialoguing. In Grades 3 and 4, students use a Feelings Dictionary with writing activities, while in Grades 5 and 6, students utilize a Feelings Thesaurus.

Problem solving

Problem-solving skills begin in PreK/K with the Three Steps for Calming Down and continue with the CSP in grades 1–3. The red, yellow, and green lights are then expanded into more explicit steps to form an 11-step problem-solving model. In Grade 3, students learn a subset of these steps (problem identification, goal setting, and generating solutions), while the full model is taught in Grade 4 with review in Grade 5/6. It should be noted that the first and third steps of our problem-solving model are "Stop and calm down" and "Identify the feelings," which integrates previous instruction in self-control and emotional literacy.

Problem-Solving Meetings are an important component implemented in all grades. Students and teachers, anonymously if desired, write down problems they would like to have addressed by the class and put them in a Problem Solving Box. Another application involves group problem-solving meetings in teachable moments when problems actually arise (e.g., problems on the playground, problems on the bus). Students are very earnest during these meetings and sincerely try to help their peers (and teacher) to successfully solve problems. An additional application involves a go-to paradigm for unexpected trauma (e.g., a school shooting in the news), with the goal of working together as a class to cope with the concomitant feelings.

Interpersonal relationships

Social skills related to interpersonal relationships are interspersed throughout the curriculum (e.g., making friends, repairing friendships, joining a group, getting along with others, bullying, teasing, gossip, apologizing, diversity, respect, different perspectives, rejected/included, discrimination, privacy, etc.). Students learn why manners and respect are important (e.g., the way we act affects how other people feel), as well as the skills to promote internalization and motivation to use them.

Classroom atmosphere

Classroom atmosphere improves with PATHS when students identify with being part of the group, learn to handle emotions positively, empathize with others, resolve conflicts peacefully, and make responsible decisions. When students are listened to and respected by their teachers and peers, students feel valued, supported, and like important members of the classroom. This promotes respect and prosocial behaviors on the part of the students, which greatly improves classroom atmosphere and school climate. As students become more attentive and self-motivated, time is saved that otherwise may have been taken away from teaching to focus on disciplinary issues. In addition, instruction is included to integrate PATHS concepts into general classroom management. The goal is for PATHS to become embedded in the classroom routine. Moreover, improvements in classroom atmosphere have positive repercussions for the overall school climate.

Generalization: Using what is learned and improving academic achievement

Transferring classroom learning to everyday life is crucial for educational success. In order for students to effectively transfer SEL from classroom lessons to daily life, they need a variety of opportunities to practice what they have learned, especially when emotions are strong. To this end, generalization techniques such as feeling faces, problem-solving meetings, and dialoguing are used between lessons to allow for practice and use of new skills in teachable moments. Posters are included with the kits so that students can reference them when needed. In addition, staff outside of the classroom can use PATHS concepts as needed (e.g., problem-solving sheets in the principal's office, CSPs in the cafeteria and hallways, a CSP painted on the playground, community projects, etc.).

Lessons that promote academic improvement include topics such as motivation, perseverance, organization, and attributions for success. Lessons on the concepts of fairness and logic increase ethical understanding and analytic thinking. Further, instruction is included to integrate PATHS concepts into academics, an especially important domain for generalization.

Academic material is already integrated into many of the lessons (e.g., reading, oral presentations, writing exercises, logical thinking, art). Original children's stories are included in the lower grades, while Newbery Medal award-winning novels are included in grades 4 and 5/6. Students utilize emotion vocabulary to enhance writing prose and poetry. Comprehensive alignment reports to Common Core State Standards (CCSS) for English language arts, by standard and by resource, are available for each grade level. In fact, most language arts requirements for CCSS are met when teaching PATHS. However, teachers can extend this even further. For example, recognition of the emotional states of characters and empathic identification are important for comprehension and enjoyment when reading; as such, emotional literacy can be extended to reading and language arts. PATHS skills such as problem solving can be incorporated during social studies, citizenship, and science lessons. Hopefully this helps teachers to see PATHS as not another "add-on" to squeeze into the day, but rather as something that enhances their teaching process.

The more familiar teachers become with the program, the more they automatically utilize PATHS concepts throughout the day. When implemented well, the program becomes part of the entire classroom day and overall school culture. This integration is exemplified by Lee Clinton Buddy Jr., Principal of Wade Elementary, a PATHS school in Cleveland: "Social and emotional learning is really at the heart of everything we do at Wade Park" (quoted by Camera, 2018).

PATHS research

The PATHS curriculum is the most thoroughly researched SEL program available. As Gershon and Pellitteri (2018) noted, "PATHS (Preschool and School-age) appears to have been adapted and studied internationally more frequently than other SEL programs" (p. 33). To date there are over 45 peer-reviewed published studies documenting the effectiveness of PATHS in significantly reducing risk factors and increasing protective factors in a variety of domains (e.g., behavior, self-control, emotional literacy, problem-solving skills, prosocial relationships, executive brain functioning, and academics). In most of these studies, intervention teachers received two (or three) days of in-service PATHS training and ongoing coaching.

Initial PATHS studies

The first three studies of the PATHS curriculum involved three different child populations: Deaf/hard-of-hearing, regular education, and special education. All of these studies utilized the original version of the program (Kusché & Greenberg, 1994).

Our first randomized controlled study of PATHS (Greenberg & Kusché, 1993, 1998; Kusché, 1984) involved pre-, post-, and follow-up testing with deaf/hearing impaired children, with a wait-list control group design. A total of 57 deaf children in 11 self-contained classrooms (grades 1–6) in six elementary schools were randomly assigned to 1 year intervention or wait-listed no-treatment control groups at the school level. A large battery of measures was utilized, included parent and teacher ratings, self-ratings, and one-on-one testing. One of these measures, the Kusché Emotional Inventory (KEI; Kusché, 1984), was developed with extensive testing for validity and reliability for this project.

Findings after 1 year showed significant improvements for intervention students as compared to control students with regard to emotional recognition and understanding, emotion fluency, social problem-solving skills, self-control, ability to tolerate frustration, decreased impulsivity, cognitive flexibility, and reading achievement. Deaf children who showed greater improvement in emotional understanding and problem-solving skills also showed greater improvement in behavior according to parent and teacher reports (Greenberg & Kusché, 1993). All intervention gains were maintained or increased 1 and 2 years after PATHS intervention. Results from the KEI were markedly strong with both younger (grades 1–3) and older (grades 4–6) intervention students for both recognizing and labeling emotions (Kusché, 1984). This was also the first published study to document the effectiveness of teacher instruction for emotional literacy. Findings with the replication sample showed significant improvement with all domains, including decreased behavior problems.

Our next two studies (Greenberg & Kusché, 1998; Greenberg, Kusché, Cook, & Quamma, 1995; Riggs, Greenberg, Kusché, & Pentz, 2006) involved students in regular education ($N=192$ in 2nd and 3rd grades) and students in self-contained special education classrooms ($N=94$ in 1st through 3rd grades). Both studies employed a pre-, post (1 year)-, and follow-up (each year for the following 2 years) test design, and random assignment was done at the school level. Measures included parent and teacher ratings, self-ratings, and one-on-one testing. Two new measures were developed for this study, the Kusché Affective Interview—Revised (KAI-R; Kusché, Greenberg, & Beilke, 1988) and the Social Problem Solving Interview (SPSI; Greenberg & Kusché, 1988).

Posttest findings for regular education after 1 year showed significant improvements for intervention students with emotional recognition and understanding, emotion fluency, social problem-solving skills, self-control, ability to tolerate frustration, decreased impulsivity, improved working memory, and increased ability to integrate information and plan ahead when solving complex tasks. Significant reductions in aggressive and disruptive behaviors were found at 1-year follow-up.

Similar results were found with special education students. In addition, significant reductions in conduct problems were found at posttest with a decreased trajectory for problem behavior continuing after 3 years. Significant decreases in depressive symptoms were found at posttest in special education students who had high levels of depression at pretest. Growth curve analyses showed sustained reduction in self-reported depressive symptoms, as well as sustained decreases in teacher-reported internalizing and externalizing behaviors 2 years after the intervention with further decline at 3-year follow-up.

Preschool PATHS

The first research study with Preschool PATHS involved a randomized controlled trial with 248 preschoolers in 20 Head Start Classrooms (Domitrovich, Cortes, & Greenberg, 2007). After 1 year of implementation, intervention preschoolers showed significant improvements in identifying emotions, both expressively and receptively, and better social skills. In a later study, intervention preschoolers described relationships with teachers significantly more positively than matched controls (Greenberg et al., 2018).

In a large independent study involving 104 Head Start Centers (307 classrooms) in four different locations in the United States, centers were randomly assigned to one of three different interventions (Preschool PATHS being one of these) or to a no-treatment control group (Morris et al., 2014). After 1 year of implementation, significant improvements were found in children's social and learning behaviors, knowledge of emotions, and social problem-solving skills. At follow-up, former PATHS preschoolers had significantly lower levels of expected grade retention in kindergarten ($<1\%$ compared to 7% of control children). Several foreign replications of translated versions of Preschool PATHS have shown significant results in multiple domains (Croatia—Mihic, Novak, Basic, & Nix, 2016; Hong Kong—Kam, Wong, & Fung, 2011; Turkey—Burcu, 2012; Seyhan, Karabay, Tuncdemir, Greenberg, & Domitrovich, 2017). Research is currently underway in Sweden (Ferrer-Wreder et al., in press).

Head Start REDI combined language/emergent literacy skills (dialogic reading, phonological awareness training, letter knowledge acquisition) with the use of Preschool PATHS in a cluster-randomized clinical trial (20 randomly assigned Head Start Centers; $N=250$ 4-year-old children in 2 cohorts; Bierman, Domitrovich, et al., 2008; Bierman, Nix, Greenberg, Blair, & Domitrovich, 2008). Significantly greater gains in social knowledge, problem solving, self-control, and emotional regulation, and lower levels of anxious/withdrawn and aggressive behaviors and off-task behavior were found at post-test for intervention children. Sustained effects were found in kindergarten 1 year later with learning engagement, competent social problem-solving skills, reduced aggressive-disruptive behavior, and phonemic decoding skills (Bierman et al., 2014), which promoted school readiness (Nix, Bierman, Domitrovich, & Gill, 2013). In Grade 3, implementation children showed a lower decreasing developmental trajectory of aggressive-oppositional behavior, a high-stable developmental trajectory of student-teacher closeness, and a high-stable developmental trajectory of learning engagement (Nix et al., 2016).

Fast Track project

Fast Track was a large implementation conducted in four American cities with randomly assigned elementary schools in high crime neighborhoods. Three cohorts of students received PATHS in first grade over three successive years ($N=198$ classrooms) and were compared with three cohorts of no-treatment matched control classrooms ($N = 180$). PATHS served as the universal component for all students in intervention classrooms. Five programs (small friendship groups, child friendship enhancement, parent training, home visits, and academic tutoring) plus PATHS were implemented with high-risk students. Thus, two different populations with two different intervention paradigms are represented in the published studies of the Conduct Problems Prevention Research Group (CPPRG): (1) Analyses of nonrisk students, half of whom received PATHS (universal component) and (2) analyses of high-risk students, half of whom received PATHS and five additional programs (intervention component).

Since no component analyses were undertaken with the intervention component, it is not possible to determine the exact role of PATHS in the outcomes of the high-risk cohort. However, a decomposition of treatment effects with the high-risk cohort 20 years after first grade indicated that improvements in self-regulation and social skills during childhood (e.g., prosocial behavior, emotion regulation, and problem solving) accounted for roughly one-third of Fast Track's impact on later crime outcomes in early adulthood (Sorensen, Dodge, & CPPRG, 2016).

At the end of the first year of Fast Track, multilevel, hierarchical, linear analyses conducted at the classroom and school levels showed significantly lower levels of peer-nominated aggression, hyperactivity, and disruptive behavior, higher numbers of prosocial peer nominations, lower teacher ratings of disruptive behavior, and more positive ratings of classroom atmosphere in PATHS classrooms (CPPRG, 1999). At the end of third grade, significant positive effects were found for PATHS classrooms with regard to reduced aggression, increased prosocial behavior, authority acceptance, concentration, social competence, and academic engagement (CPPRG, 2010). In addition, intervention students showed significantly lower problem levels, while control students showed an increase in problem levels, thus demonstrating both intervention and prevention effects.

Numerous studies of the high-risk cohort from Grade 1 to adulthood (age 25) have shown significant results with regard to both intervention and prevention. Significant effects for prevention of antisocial behavior and externalizing psychiatric disorders were found by grade 3 (CPPRG, 2007); by grade 9, intervention had reduced the risk of conduct disorder by 75%, ADHD by 53%, and all externalizing psychiatric disorder cases by 43%; intervention students were also far less likely to use pediatric, general health, and emergency department services (Jones, Greenberg, & Crowley, 2015). In a 20-year longitudinal study, former high-risk intervention students at age 25 had significantly higher well-being scores, fewer internalizing problems, less externalizing problems, fewer violent and drug crime conviction scores, less substance abuse problems, and lower risky sexual behavior scores compared to nonintervention controls (CPPRG, 2015). A complete list of Fast Track research is available at: https://fasttrackproject.org/publications.php.

Cultural adaptations

In writing PATHS, we endeavored to keep the lessons as universal as possible, and it has been used successfully in many different cultures (e.g., a Mandarin translation was well received in mainland China). But our cultural blinders also resulted in some surprises. In developing a Pakistani version, Inam, Tariq, and Zaman (2015) noted the universality of most core program components. One exception, however, involved complimenting, which "in eastern cultures…is perceived as negative politeness" (p. 236).

The United Kingdom felt a need to make PATHS more culturally relevant (no changes were requested for Canada or Australia). This resulted in the Together 4 All Programme, which was later renamed the PATHS Programme (UK version), adapted from the original version of PATHS (Kusché & Greenberg, 1994). No comparison studies between the United States and United Kingdom versions have been undertaken, but research studies from the United Kingdom appear to regard their version as comparable to the US program.

An independent randomized control study of the PATHS Programme with 12 schools was conducted in 2008–10 in Northern Ireland (Ross, Sheard, Cheung, Elliott, & Slavin, 2011). Younger and older PATHS pupils exhibited significant improvements in prosocial skills, cooperation, emotion recognition, and social problem-solving skills after 18 months. Older students also showed significant reductions in aggression. Between 2014 and 2018, 40 additional schools in N. Ireland (over 12,270 students) implemented the PATHS Programme (In Focus, 2018), but no control schools were used. Student responses ($N=6582$) showed improvement with all pre/post measures. Almost all children (96%) enjoyed PATHS lessons, while 95% of teachers and 97% of principals said they would recommend PATHS to other schools.

In a large study in Manchester, England, 45 schools were randomly assigned to PATHS or no-PATHS conditions (4516 students, ages 7–9 at pretest). At the end of 2 years, significant improvement in social-emotional competence and prosocial behavior was found with PATHS students, in addition to significant reductions in emotional symptoms with at-risk students (Humphrey et al., 2016). Significant improvement was also found with psychological wellbeing after 2 years, but not with peer social support or school connectedness (Panayiotou, Humphrey, & Hennessey, 2019). However, when multilevel complier average causal effect estimation (using dosage as a compliance marker) was applied, intervention effect size for psychological wellbeing increased and medium-to-large significant effects were found for both peer social support and school connectedness. Since 2013, PATHS Plus (PATHS Programme plus Friendship Groups; Bierman et al., 2017) has been implemented in 126 schools (23,646 students aged 8–11) in England, Ireland, Scotland, and Wales. Improvement has been reported with a wide variety of measures, but no control groups were used.

Other replications

Additional published research studies of PATHS implementations in the United States and other countries have similarly reported significant increases in protective factors (e.g., emotional understanding, recognition and labeling feelings, emotional fluency, self-control, problem-solving) and decreases in maladaptive outcomes (e.g., externalizing problems, disruptive behaviors; depression). A bibliography containing many of these citations can be found at: https://pathsprogram.com/further-research.

Conceptual findings

Prefrontal cortical mediation of limbic functioning

When developing PATHS, we hypothesized that strengthening neural pathways from the prefrontal cortex to the limbic areas (e.g., amygdala) through verbal mediation (e.g., labeling feelings) and other executive functions could facilitate higher order affect regulation and inhibitory control (Kusché, 1984; Kusché & Greenberg, 2006). Neuroimaging suggests that although several areas of the brain contribute to self-control, the right ventrolateral prefrontal cortex (rVLPFC) reliably activates with all types of self-control, as well as with perspective taking (Lieberman, 2013), and labeling feelings activates the rVLPFC and decreases intensity of firing of the amygdala, thus decreasing painful affect (Lieberman et al., 2007).

A mediation test supporting this pathway theory was conducted as part of a randomized controlled study of 318 second- and third-grade students (Riggs et al., 2006). Half of the students received 1 year of PATHS implementation. Students were individually tested at pre- and posttest for inhibitory control (Stroop Test) and verbal fluency (McCarthy Scales subtest), two well-known measures that have been shown through neuroimaging to activate the rVLPFC (Todorov, Fiske, & Prentice, 2011) and the dorsolateral cortex and anterior cingulate (Ravnkilde, Videbech, Rosenberg, Gjeede, & Gade, 2002). Teachers rated students on externalizing and internalizing behaviors at pretest and 1 year follow-up. Findings showed that the significant improvements in inhibitory control with PATHS students at posttest significantly mediated improvement in teacher ratings of internalizing and externalizing behaviors for these same PATHS students at follow-up. This same significant mediation pattern was found for verbal fluency and internalizing problems. Although imaging was not conducted with the youth in this study, these findings provide some empirical support for the theory that prefrontal cortical neurocognitive functioning plays a crucial role in social-emotional functioning, and that PATHS instruction results in changes in executive functioning that directly relate to reductions in behavioral problems.

Academic improvement

As noted, lessons promoting academic improvement focus on concepts such as motivation, perseverance, and organization, and improved classroom functioning and atmosphere are purported to have positive impacts on all learners. Several researchers have reported significant improvements in academic achievement scores following implementation of PATHS. Using a cluster-randomized design with 24 elementary schools in a large, high-risk, urban school district, Schonfeld et al. (2015) followed 705 students from 3rd to 6th grade, with roughly half receiving PATHS. Analyses of odds ratios showed that PATHS students had significantly higher test scores on reading and math in 4th grade and higher scores in writing in 5th and 6th grades. In addition, higher dosage was related to higher probability for PATHS students to achieve basic proficiency on reading, writing, and math test scores. In another study with Canadian students, half of whom received PATHS, Rahbari, Jacques, and Hughes (2014) found that PATHS students evidenced significantly higher reading and receptive language achievement in grade 1 and significantly higher math scores in grades 2 and 3.

Panayiotou, Humphrey, and Wigelsworth (2019) also found academic improvement with a sample of 1626 students from 45 English elementary schools who had received a 2-year PATHS implementation. These students had been 7–9 at pretest and had shown significant improvement in social-emotional competence, compared to controls, after 2 years at the ages of 9–12. This score was labeled Time 1 in a 3-wave integrated annual assessment (Time 1 = social-emotional competence, Time 2 = mental health difficulties/school connectedness, Time 3 = academic assessment). Panayiotou and colleagues found that social-emotional competence at Time 1 had a significant effect at Time 2 on mental health difficulties and school connectedness, and that mental health difficulties at Time 2 were a significant mediator and predictor of academic achievement at Time 3. The researchers suggested that social-emotional competence may act as a protective factor for later mental health difficulties and/or may serve as a buffer for the adverse effects of mental health problems, which in turn, predict future improvement in academic achievement.

Observations and recommendations

(1) Significant results for behavioral improvement (e.g., disruptive behavior) often take longer to find than acquisition of skills (e.g., emotional fluency). Follow-up assessments are recommended when doing research, especially when testing for behavioral change. In addition, behavioral improvement is not possible if children do not have problems in the first place. In other words, behavioral improvement is only possible when children have problems at pretest.

(2) When we first began our research, virtually all other classrooms qualified as no treatment controls. Because of the success of SEL, however, this is no longer the case. In the United Kingdom, for example, SEL is mandatory in all classrooms, so all research there is actually a comparison of PATHS versus other SEL programs.

(3) Several researchers have found that the number of lessons taught each week (i.e., dosage) makes a significant difference with regard to outcomes (e.g., Panayiotou, Humphrey, & Hennessey, 2019; Schonfeld et al., 2015). In general, it appears that the more frequently PATHS is taught, the stronger the results. Teachers typically report reasons for reduced dosage as being due to academic pressures and lack of time (Dariotis, Bumbarger, Duncan, & Greenberg, 2008), and average estimates of omission are high (between 23% and 81%; Durlak, 1998). Ideally, we would like to see PATHS taught every day, but if the curriculum is taught once a week or less, teachers will likely see weaker results.

(4) In the past decade, SEL programs have multiplied rapidly, but few are comprehensive or well researched. As Matthews et al. (2002) noted, "very few currently implemented programs were specifically designed to serve as primary prevention….[A]side from perhaps the PATHS program, none of the others specifically addresses all major factors of EI [Emotional Intelligence]. In most cases, only one or two facets of emotional competency are actually addressed per program" (p. 457). Although numerous SEL programs have been developed since that time, this continues to be the case. Although easy to implement can seem attractive, it is a waste of time if it does not work.

(5) Longitudinal research of PATHS implementations would be very beneficial to ascertain potential long-term benefits in adolescence and adulthood.

Conclusion

Happily, things have changed markedly since we first started our work with PATHS in the early 1980s. As Faria, Kendziora, Brown, O'Brien, and Osher (2013) noted, "The debate over whether schools should attend to the social and emotional aspects of learning is increasingly settled" (p. 1). Advances in neuroscience such as functional magnetic resonance imaging have greatly increased our understanding of how the brain functions and develops in general and with regard to emotional and social domains in particular. Basic and applied research in emotion are not only legitimate now in the field of psychology, but they are also proliferating. Emotional development is a core topic in child development textbooks, and entire institutions are currently dedicated to the study of emotion (e.g., The Swiss Center for Affective Sciences established in 2005). It is gratifying to think that our work has not only helped many children and teachers over the past three decades, but perhaps has also contributed to this important evolution.

References

Bierman, K., Domitrovich, C., Nix, R., Gest, S., Welsh, J., Greenberg, M., & Gill, S. (2008). Promoting academic and social-emotional school readiness: The head start REDI program. *Child Development, 79*(6), 1802–1817.

Bierman, K. L., Greenberg, M. T., Coie, J. D., Dodge, K. A., Lochman, J. E., & McMahon, R. J. (2017). *Social and emotional skills training for children: The Fast Track Friendship Group manual*. New York: Guilford Press.

Bierman, K. L., Nix, R. L., Greenberg, M. T., Blair, C., & Domitrovich, C. E. (2008). Executive functions and school readiness intervention: Impact, moderation, and mediation in the Head Start REDI program. *Developmental Psychology*, *20*(3), 821–843.

Bierman, K. L., Nix, R. L., Heinrichs, B. S., Domitrovich, C. E., Gest, S. D., Welsh, J. A., & Gill, S. (2014). Effects of Head Start REDI on children's outcomes 1 year later in different kindergarten contexts. *Child Development*, *85*(1), 140–159.

Burcu, T. (2012). Social competence and promoting alternative thinking strategies—PATHS® preschool curriculum educational sciences. *Theory & Practice*, *12*, 2691–2698.

Camera, L. (2018). The kids are not all right. *US News & World Report*. Retrieved from: https://www.usnews.com/news/education-news/articles/2018-01-26/the-kids-are-not-alright-the-push-for-social-and-emotional-learning.

CASEL. (2017). *What the experts are saying*. Q&A Tim Shriver. Retrieved from: https://www.casel.org/wp-content/uploads/2017/04/SHRIVER-Q-A-1-12-17.pdf.

Chandler, M. J. (1973). Egocentrism and antisocial behavior: The assessment and training of social perspective-taking skills. *Developmental Psychology*, *9*(3), 326–332. https://doi.org/10.1037/h0034974.

CPPRG. (1999). Initial impact of the Fast Track prevention trial for conduct problems: II. Classroom effects. *Journal of Consulting and Clinical Psychology*, *67*, 648–657.

CPPRG. (2007). Fast Track randomized controlled trial to prevent externalizing psychiatric disorders: Findings from grades 3 to 9. *Journal of the American Academy of Child & Adolescent Psychiatry*, *46*(10), 1250–1262.

CPPRG. (2010). The effects of a multiyear universal social-emotional learning program: The role of student and school characteristics. *Journal of Consulting and Clinical Psychology*, *78*(2), 156–168. https://doi.org/10.1037/a0018607.

CPPRG. (2015). Impact of early intervention on psychopathology, crime, and well-being at age 25. *American Journal of Psychiatry*, *172*, 59–70.

Dariotis, J. K., Bumbarger, B. K., Duncan, L. G., & Greenberg, M. T. (2008). How do implementation efforts relate to program adherence? Examining the role of organizational, implementer, and program factors. *Journal of Community Psychology*, *36*, 744–760. https://doi.org/10.1002/jcop.20255.

Domitrovich, C. E., Cortes, R., & Greenberg, M. T. (2007). Improving young children's social and emotional competence: A randomized trial of the Preschool PATHS program. *Journal of Primary Prevention*, *28*(2), 67–91.

Domitrovich, C. E., Greenberg, M. T., Kusché, C. A., & Cortes, R. (2005). *The PATHS® program (preschool/kindergarten level)*. Avondale, AZ: PATHS® Program LLC.

Durlak, J. A. (1998). Why program implementation is important. *Journal of Prevention & Intervention in the Community*, *17*, 5–18. https://doi.org/10.1300/J005v17n02_02.

Faria, A.-M., Kendziora, K., Brown, L., O'Brien, B., & Osher, D. (2013). *PATHS implementation and outcome study in the Cleveland Metropolitan School District: Final report*. American Institutes for Research. Retrieved 7/26/19 at: https://www.air.org/sites/default/files/downloads/report/Evaluation_of_PATHS_in_CMSD_final_report_6_2413_0.pdf.

Ferrer-Wreder, L., Eninger, L., Olsson, T. M., Sedem, M., & Allodi Westling, M. (in press). The cultural adaptation of interventions to promote positive development: The preschool edition of PATHS in Sweden. In R. Dimitrova & N. Wiium (Eds)., Handbook of positive youth development in a global context. Research, policy and practice applications. New York, Springer.

Fishman, M., & Wille, J. (2014). *Head start CARES for migrant and seasonal families: Adapting a preschool social-emotional curriculum*. OPRE report 2014-43. MDRC: Head Start Cares. Retrieved from: https://www.mdrc.org/sites/default/files/HS_CARES_Migrant%20Report%20 2014.pdf.

Gershon, P., & Pellitteri, J. (2018). Promoting emotional intelligence in preschool education: A review of programs. *The International Journal of Emotional Education*, *10*(2), 26–41.

Greenberg, M., Domitrovich, C., Ocak Karabay, S., Tuncdemir, A., Tugce, B., & Gest, S. D. (2018). Focusing on teacher-children relationship perception and children's social emotional behaviors—The PATHS preschool program. *International Journal of Educational Research Review*, *3*, 8–20.

Greenberg, M. T., & Kusché, C. A. (1988). *Social problem solving interview (SPSI)* [Unpublished manuscript]. Department of Psychology, University of Washington.

Greenberg, M. T., & Kusché, C. A. (1993). *Promoting social and emotional development in deaf children: The PATHS® project*. Seattle: University of Washington Press.

Greenberg, M. T., & Kusché, C. A. (1998). Preventive intervention for school-age deaf children: The PATHS® curriculum. *Journal of Deaf Studies and Deaf Education*, *3*, 49–63.

Greenberg, M. T., Kusché, C. A., Cook, E. T., & Quamma, J. P. (1995). Promoting emotional competence in school-aged children: The effects of the PATHS® curriculum. *Development and Psychopathology*, *7*, 117–136.

Greenberg, M. T., Kusché, C. A., & CPPRG. (2011, 2012). *The PATHS® program* (grades 3–5). Avondale, AZ: PATHS® Program LLC.

Humphrey, N., Barlow, A., Wigelsworth, M., Lendrum, A., Pert, K., Joyce, C., … Turner, A. (2016). A cluster randomized controlled trial of the promoting alternative thinking strategies (PATHS) curriculum. *Journal of School Psychology*, *58*, 73–89. https://doi.org/10.1016/j.jsp.2016.07.002.

In Focus. (2018). *The PATHS® programme for schools (UK version): Findings from the implementation of The PATHS® Programme for Schools (UK version) in N. Ireland (2014–2018)*. http://www.barnardos.org.uk/paths_in_focus_report.pdf.

Inam, A., Tariq, P. N., & Zaman, S. (2015). Cultural adaptation of preschool PATHS (promoting alternative thinking strategies) curriculum for Pakistani children. *International Journal of Psychology*, *50*, 232–239.

Jones, D. E., Greenberg, M., & Crowley, M. (2015). Early social-emotional functioning and … public health: The relationship between kindergarten social competence and future wellness. *American Journal of Public Health*, *105*, 2283–2290. https://doi.org/10.2105/AJPH.2015302630.

Kam, C., Wong, L. W., & Fung, K. M. (2011). Promoting social-emotional learning in Chinese schools: A feasibility study of PATHS implementation in Hong Kong. *The International Journal of Emotional Education*, *3*(1), 30–47.

Kusché, C. A. (1984). *The understanding of emotion concepts by deaf children: An assessment of an affective curriculum* [Doctoral dissertation]. DAO. 56952.

Kusché, C. A., & Greenberg, M. T. (1994). *The PATHS curriculum*. Seattle: Developmental Research & Programs.

Kusché, C. A., & Greenberg, M. T. (1998). Integrating emotions and thinking in the classroom. *THINK*, *9*, 32–34.

Kusché, C. A., & Greenberg, M. T. (2006). Brain development and social-emotional learning: An introduction for educators. In M. J. Elias & H. Arnold (Eds.), *The educator's guide to emotional intelligence and academic achievement: Social emotional learning in the classroom* (pp. 15–34). Thousand Oaks, CA: Corwin Press.

Kusché, C. A., Greenberg, M. T., & CPPRG. (2011). *The PATHS® program* (grades 1–2). Avondale, AZ: PATHS® Program LLC.

Kusché, C. A., & Greenberg, M. T. (2011). *PATHS: An introduction to the curriculum*. Avondale, AZ: PATHS® Program LLC.

Kusché, C. A., Greenberg, M. T., & Beilke, B. (1988). *The Kusche affective interview—Revised* [Unpublished manuscript]. Department of Psychology, University of Washington.

Lieberman, M. D. (2013). *Social: Why our brains are wired to connect*. NY: Broadway Books.

Lieberman, M. D., Eisenberger, N. I., Crockett, M. J., Tom, S. M., Pfeifer, J. H., & Way, B. M. (2007). Putting feelings into words: Affect labeling disrupts amygdala activity in response to affective stimuli. *Psychological Science*, *18*(5), 421–428.

Masters, J. C., Felleman, E. S., & Barden, R. C. (1981). Experimental studies of affective states in children. In B. B. Lahey & A. E. Kazdin (Eds.), Vol. 4. *Advances in clinical child psychology & behavior* (pp. 91–118). Boston: Springer.

Matthews, G., Zeidner, M., & Roberts, R. D. (2002). *Emotional intelligence: Science and myth*. Cambridge: MIT Press.

Mihic, J., Novak, M., Basic, J., & Nix, R. L. (2016). Promoting social and emotional competencies among young children in Croatia with preschool PATHS®. *The International Journal of Emotional Education*, *8*(2), 45–59. www.um.edu.mt/cres/ijee4.

Morris, P., Mattera, S. K., Castells, N., Bangser, M., Bierman, K., & Raver, C. (2014). *Impact findings from the Head Start CARES demonstration: National evaluation of three approaches to improving preschoolers' social and emotional competence*. OPRE report 2014-44 Washington, DC: Office of Planning, research and evaluation, Administration for Children and Families, US Department of Health and Human Services.

Nix, R. L., Bierman, K. L., Domitrovich, C. E., & Gill, S. (2013). Promoting children's social-emotional skills in preschool can enhance academic and behavioral functioning in kindergarten: Findings from Head Start REDI. *Early Education & Development*, *24*, 1000–1019.

Nix, R. L., Bierman, K. L., Heinrichs, B. S., Gest, S. D., Welsh, J. A., & Domitrovich, C. E. (2016). The randomized-controlled trial of Head Start REDI: Sustained effects on developmental trajectories of social-emotional functioning. *Journal of Consulting and Clinical Psychology*, *84*(4), 310–322.

Panayiotou, M., Humphrey, N., & Hennessey, A. (2019). Implementation matters: Using complier average causal effect estimation to determine the impact of the promoting alternative thinking strategies (PATHS) curriculum on children's quality of life. *Journal of Educational Psychology*, https://doi.org/10.1037/edu0000360. Advance online publication.

Panayiotou, M., Humphrey, N., & Wigelsworth, M. (2019). An empirical basis for linking social and emotional learning to academic performance. *Contemporary Educational Psychology*, *56*, 193–204.

Rahbari, N., Jacques, S., & Hughes, J. (2014). *The effect of the PATHS® curriculum on school- aged children's academic performance across development*. In *Presented at development 2014: A Canadian conference on developmental psychology, Ottawa, Canada*.

Ravnkilde, B., Videbech, P., Rosenberg, R., Gjeede, A., & Gade, A. (2002). Putative tests of frontal lobe function: A PET-study of brain activation during Stroop's test and verbal fluency. *Journal of Clinical and Experimental Neuropsychology*, *24*(4), 534–547.

Riggs, N. R., Greenberg, M. T., Kusché, C. A., & Pentz, M. A. (2006). The mediational role of neuro-cognition in the behavioral outcomes of a social-emotional prevention program in elementary school students: Effects of the PATHS® curriculum. *Prevention Science*, *7*, 91–102.

Ross, S. M., Sheard, M. K., Cheung, A., Elliott, L., & Slavin, R. (2011). Promoting primary pupils' social-emotional learning and pro-social behaviour: Longitudinal evaluation of the Together 4 All Programme in Northern Ireland. *Effective Education*, *3*, 61–81, https://doi.org/10.1080/19415532.2012.665773.

Schonfeld, D. J., Adams, R. E., Fredstrom, B. K., Weissberg, R. P., Gilman, R., Voyce, C., … Speese-Linehan, D. (2015). Cluster-randomized trial demonstrating impact on academic achievement of elementary social-emotional learning. *School Psychology Quarterly*, *30*(3), 406–420. https://doi.org/10.1037/spq0000099.

Seyhan, G. B., Karabay, S. O., Tuncdemir, T. B., Greenberg, M. T., & Domitrovich, C. (2017). The effects of promoting alternative thinking strategies preschool program on teacher-children relationships and children's social competence in Turkey. *International Journal of Psychology*, https://doi.org/10.1002/ijop.12426.

Shure, M. B., & Spivak, G. (1979). Interpersonal cognitive problem solving and primary prevention: Programming for preschool and kindergarten children. *Journal of Clinical Child Psychology*, *2*, 89–94.

Sorensen, L. C., Dodge, K. A., & CPPRG (2016). How does the Fast Track intervention prevent adverse outcomes in young adulthood? *Child Development*, *87*, 429–445.

Todorov, A., Fiske, S. T., & Prentice, D. (2011). *Neuroscience: Toward understanding the underpinnings of the social mind*. Oxford: Oxford University Press.

Washington State Institute for Public Policy: Benefit-Cost Analysis. (2018). *Promoting alternative thinking strategies (PATHS)*. https://www.wsipp.wa.gov/BenefitCost/Program/94.

Chapter 11

Superheroes social skills

Keith C. Radley[a] and Kate A. Helbig[b]
[a]*University of Utah, Salt Lake City, UT, United States,* [b]*University of South Dakota, Vermillion, SD, United States*

Deficits in social communication, as well as restrictive interests and repetitive behaviors, are defining characteristics of individuals with autism spectrum disorder (ASD; American Psychiatric Association, 2013). Impairments in social communication may be present in both verbal and nonverbal communication skills. Verbally, communication deficits may include prolonged social interactions, difficulty initiating and maintaining conversations, and problems understanding others' perspectives and emotions. Examples of deficits in nonverbal behavior may include poorly modulated eye contact and proximity (i.e., standing too far or too close to others), and facial expressions and gestures that do not fit the topic of conversation. Restrictive interests and repetitive behaviors can further hinder social interactions. Individuals with ASD are often fixated on certain topics, activities, or objects. During conversation, individuals with ASD may have difficulties responding to topics outside of their restricted interests. For example, an individual with a restricted interest in dinosaurs may find it difficult to discuss topics outside of dinosaurs, despite others' lack of interest in the topic.

Although individuals with ASD may present with a range of deficits related to social communication and restricted and repetitive behaviors, common areas of deficit include nonverbal communication, joint attention, initiating conversations, cooperation, self-control, and recognizing and expressing emotions (Rankin, Weber, Kang, & Lerner, 2016; Sperry, Neitzel, & Engelhardt-Wells, 2010). Given weaknesses in these areas, it is not surprising that children with ASD experience negative outcomes related to social skills (e.g., Friedman, Warfield, & Parish, 2013). Peers may be unable to relate to children with ASD, as they may not share the same interests and may be disinterested in engaging in conversation about the restricted interests of an individual with ASD. Additionally, poor nonverbal communication skills, such as individuals standing too closely or looking away from the speaker, may make others feel uncomfortable in conversation. Experiencing rejection from peers can lead to feelings

Social Skills Across the Life Span. https://doi.org/10.1016/B978-0-12-817752-5.00011-1

of loneliness and isolation and contribute to symptoms of anxiety and depression in individuals with ASD (Guarlnick, 1999; Howlin, Mawhood, & Rutter, 2000). Furthermore, impairments in social communication skills can contribute to poor academic achievement and difficulties obtaining employment (Bush & Tassé, 2017). Challenges with asking for help, perspective taking, and interacting with peers can deter individuals with ASD from succeeding in the classroom and in the workplace. Because these negative outcomes are largely related to deficits in social communication skills, it is imperative that individuals with ASD have access to social skills training strategies that have been found to be effective in promoting social success.

Efficacy of social skills training

Social skills training is one of the most frequently implemented interventions for individuals with ASD (Goin-Kochel, Myers, & Mackintosh, 2007). Although a wide variety of procedures is utilized, interventions are generally identified as being evidence-based (e.g., Griffin, Sam, and AFIRM Team, 2016). For example, Wolstencroft et al. (2018) found social skill groups for children with ASD to result in large effects on parent ratings of child social skills, as well as on restricted and repetitive behaviors or these individuals. Considering individual social skills training strategies, widely utilized interventions, such as video modeling, self-management, and peer-mediated intervention, have strong empirical support for promoting social development (Lee, Simpson, & Shogren, 2007; Wang, Parilla, & Cui, 2013).

Although several meta-analyses and systematic reviews indicate that social skills training is effective for individuals with ASD (e.g., Reichow & Volkmar, 2010; Wang et al., 2013; Wolstencroft et al., 2018), other researchers have found less positive outcomes. For instance, Gates, Kang, and Lerner (2017) meta-analysis of social skills groups for individuals with ASD revealed that these interventions may produce moderate overall effects, but effects are primarily limited to social skills knowledge and not participant behavior. Specifically, evaluations using observations by those outside of the training settings (i.e., parents, teachers) often yield null to small effects. In fact, challenges of producing generalized behavior change have regularly been documented (e.g., Bellini, Peters, Benner, & Hopf, 2007; Bowker, D'Angelo, Hicks, & Wells, 2011; Hume, Campbell, & Reschly, 2019). According to Stokes and Baer (1977), generalization may be defined as "the occurrence of relevant behavior under different, nontraining conditions (i.e., across subjects, settings, people, behaviors, and/or time) without the scheduling of the same events in those conditions as had been scheduled in the training conditions" (p. 350). Specifically, generalization of social skills training can be conceptualized as an individual's performance of the targeted skill within an environment that is novel (i.e., not the training setting) or demonstration of the social skill during an interaction with an individual that was not present during the training session.

Stokes and Baer (1977) proposed nine strategies that practitioners may consider as means of promoting social skill use to nontraining contexts. The first and oft-implemented strategy, train and hope, describes a lack of generalization supports. More specifically, individuals receive training in a decontextualized setting, and practitioners then hope that they use the learned skills in novel contexts. The remaining eight strategies described by Stokes and Baer involve active efforts by practitioners to encourage skill use in nontraining settings. These strategies include: (1) implementing social skills training in naturalistic settings (i.e., sequential modification); (2) exposing social skills trainees to natural contingencies that will maintain skill use; (3) training a large number of exemplars of social skill use; (4) allowing for informal and "loose" training; (5) preventing the easy discrimination of the availability of reinforcement; (6) incorporating stimuli from the natural environment into the training environment; (7) encouraging self-control and self-management of social skill use; and lastly, (8) instructing the individual to use the skill in nontraining settings (e.g., "I want to see you use this skill in the classroom"). Historically, these active generalization promoting strategies have not been incorporated into social skills training programs (Bellini et al., 2007). By actively incorporating generalization strategies within training and intervention provision, practitioners are more likely to promote social skill use in both training and nontraining settings.

Superheroes Social Skills

The Superheroes Social Skills program is a manualized social skills training program developed to address problems of generalization previously noted. The program was originally intended for use with elementary-age children with ASD in school settings by school psychologists and special educators, but has subsequently been utilized in a wider range of settings (e.g., clinics, summer camps). The program is available commercially through Ancora Publishing and can be purchased through the publisher's website (https://www.ancorapublishing.com/product/superheroes-social-skills/). As the program was originally developed as a collaboration between the School Psychology program at the University of Utah and the Utah Board of Education, a prepublication version is available through the Utah Board of Education for educators with an active license in Utah. The Superheroes Social Skills program, as distributed by both Ancora Publishing and the Utah Board of Education, consists of an intervention manual with instructions for implementing lessons, as well as all other materials needed for intervention. The manual included describes step-by-step implementation for all social skills lessons.

The program was developed with an emphasis on efficacy, generalizability, and practicality. Regarding efficacy, the program incorporates several practices with strong empirical support for promoting social skill acquisition. Specifically, the program includes video modeling, behavioral skills training, self-monitoring, social stories, and inclusion of peers as means of promoting behavior change—all of which have received support in individual studies or metaanalyses as strategies for social skills training (e.g., Acar, Tekin-Iftar, & Yimis, 2017; Bellini & Akullian, 2007; Davis, Mason, Davis, Rose, & Crutchfield, 2016; Neumberger, Ringdahl, Vargo, Crumpecker, & Gunnarsson, 2013).

The included practices were also selected due to their ability to promote generalization of learned skills to novel settings and persons. Utilization of video models, behavioral skills training, and social stories allows for the presentation of multiple exemplars' skill use, meeting Stokes and Baer's (1977) definition of training a large number of exemplars. The use of video models and social stories also exposes participants to varied skill use in diverse settings, allowing for training loosely. The inclusion of typically developing peers allows for the incorporation of stimuli from naturalistic settings that may later serve as cues for skill use in generalization settings, whereas self-monitoring promotes self-control and self-management of social skills. In addition to promoting generalization through these practices, generalization is further emphasized through the provision of homework assignments in which participants are encouraged to practice target skills outside of the training setting.

Although any of the aforementioned practices may be implemented individually by practitioners, the Superheroes Social Skills program was designed to reduce logistical demands associated with use of these training strategies in several ways. First, the manualized nature of the program eliminates the need for practitioners to develop their own intervention materials—as practitioners are provided with practice-ready video models, social stories, and self-monitoring materials. Logistical demands are also reduced by including the same elements in each lesson, with each lesson comprising a two-page, stepwise lesson plan. Consistent use of intervention strategies and lesson formatting may assist practitioners in quickly mastering preparation and delivery of social skills training. Finally, much of the instruction is delivered by animated superheroes via video. Presentation of instruction via video ensures that the skill rationales and steps are presented consistently and with integrity and further reduces implementation demands on practitioners utilizing the intervention.

Previous research has highlighted skills essential for improving both proximal and distal outcomes of individuals with ASD. Of particular importance are skills related to nonverbal communication, joint attention, initiating conversations, cooperation, self-control, and recognizing and expressing emotions (Rankin et al., 2016; Toth, Munson, Meltzhoff, & Dawson, 2006; White, Keonig, & Scahill, 2007). The skills targeted within Superheroes Social Skills were intended to align with those identified as critical for individuals with ASD. Another goal is that participants in the program will not only improve in the skills taught, but also acquire additional skills that may result in improved developmental trajectories.

A total of 17 different discrete social skills are taught within the curriculum that are classified as Foundational, Intermediate, or Advanced. Skills targeted within the Foundational section are Get Ready and Following Directions, skills included as a means of establishing an instructional context wherein social skills may be learned. These first two skills taught are then utilized as rules for the group throughout the remainder of the intervention. Moving on from those skills related to instructional context, training then shifts to skills that are important for social interaction. Instruction begins with skills associated with managing anxiety during social situations. Following, skills related to participating in a group, imitating a model, engaging in nonverbal communication, expressing wants and needs, and showing joint attention are then taught.

The Intermediate Skills build upon those presented in the Foundational section, and provide participants with additional skills related to social interactions. Specifically, all skills in this section include the nonverbal communication skills learned in the Foundational section as the first steps of the skills. Three skills are targeted in the Intermediate section. Turn Taking is introduced first and aims to promote cooperative play behaviors. Next, a lesson in responding to questions and requests from others is presented. Finally, skills related to maintaining a conversation—particularly regarding topics that may not be of interest to participants—are taught.

The Advanced Skills extend training to additional critical social skills. Within this section, substantial attention is given to skills related to perspective taking and problem solving. The first skill in this section entails recognizing emotions by using facial expressions, posture, and tone of voice. Skills related to understanding others' feelings are then presented. Finally, problem-solving skills are taught across four skills: reporting problems, recognizing and reporting bulling, responding to bullying, and solving novel problems while staying safe. It is important to note that the skills that comprise the Advanced Skills rely less on skills previously taught, with only one of the skills referencing a skill taught in either the Foundational or Intermediate sections.

Structure

As previously described, lessons contained within the Superheroes Social Skills program consist of the same lesson structure irrespective of the skill being taught or the location of the skill within the program. The Superheroes Social Skills manual suggests that groups have between three and eight participants. Further, it is recommended that groups comprise individuals within 2 to 3 years of age of each other. Finally, ideal group composition is proposed to be one typically developing individual to every target participant. However, research has often been conducted with no typically developing individuals in the group (e.g., Murphy, Radley, & Helbig, 2018).

Social skill lessons begin with a check-in (see Table 1). During this time, the skill previously taught is reviewed. Participants are then asked to describe a time in which they utilized the previously learned skill outside of the training setting. If participants do not report utilizing the skill, they are provided with opportunities to rehearse the skill. As the final component of check-in, self-monitoring

TABLE 1 Superheroes Social Skills lesson steps.

Step	Description
1	Check-in. Have materials placed in front of the group; children are seated; brief review of prior session (when applicable)
2	Review Rules and Purpose of session
3	Introduce or review target skill and rationale
4	Watch corresponding Fast Hands animation and video models
5	Facilitator role plays both a positive and a negative example of the skill
6	Participants engage in role plays of target skill. Facilitator distributes Power Charges during role plays
7	Watch Digital Comic
8	Play social game
9	Record Power Charges
10	Explain Homework to group (i.e., read comic at home, practice skill and self-monitor skill use)
11	Scooter cards distributed throughout session. Superhero of the Day selected at end of group; reinforcers delivered

cards for the skill previously taught are collected, and participants' recording of skill use is documented.

Following check-in, the facilitator reviews the daily schedule with participants. Next, the facilitator reviews the group rules and describes a group contingency that is utilized to encourage demonstration of group rules. Specifically, the facilitator states that participants will earn "Scooter Cards," cards that depict a robot character from the animated videos, if observed demonstrating the group rules. Participants are also informed that "Black Hole Cards" will be received if participants are caught violating group rules (see Fig. 1). Any Scooter Cards or Black Hole Cards earned by participants during the group are placed in a bag or other container for use in a lottery-style drawing at the conclusion of the group. Together, the check-in and review of group rules should take approximately 4 to 7 min.

Next, the skill to be learned is introduced. To do so, the facilitator states the name of the skill and provides a rationale for skill use. Using the Body Basics skill as an example, the facilitator would state the following: "Today we'll be learning a new skill—Body Basics. If you use Body Basics, you let other people know you are listening and paying attention to them. They will be more likely to continue talking with you." Once the facilitator has introduced the skill and the rationale for use, a self-monitoring card is distributed to all participants. On one

FIG. 1 Scooter and Black Hole cards.

side of the self-monitoring card, the target skill is identified and one of the superhero characters is depicted. Around the border of the card, there are 30 empty circles to be filled by the participants when they demonstrate the target skill. The steps to performance of the target skill are presented on the other side of the card. The introduction of the new skill is intended to take approximately 1 min.

Instruction in the target social skill is then provided by the superhero characters via video. Superhero characters are presented in what is termed "Fast Hands Animation." These animations depict an artist's hand as he draws the superhero characters, with the video of the drawing being highly accelerated. As the artist completes a picture of the superhero, a voiceover describing the steps to the skill is provided in the voice of the character. Each skill in the program is explained in three to five steps. After all the skill steps have been described, the superhero character then invites the participants to watch as other children demonstrate the target skill. The participants then watch three to five video models of unknown peers as they engage in the target skill. Unknown peers represent children of diverse ages, races, and genders, and unknown peers appear in a variety of contexts (e.g., home, community, school). As the video models demonstrate each skill step, the video pauses, and voice and text over indicate the skill step that has just been demonstrated. Again, using the Body Basics skill as an example, the video would pause as the model turns to face a communication partner while a voice and text over would state the step that has just been completed (i.e., "Face the Person"). The description of skill steps and video models typically lasts between 6 and 10 min.

Once the superhero characters have presented the steps for the target skill and participants have viewed the video models of target skills, the facilitator of the group provides models of the target skill. The facilitator first describes a nonexample of the target skill (e.g., interrupting someone's turn for the Turn Taking lesson). After offering the nonexample, the facilitator asks participants to identify which of the skill steps was skipped or not performed correctly. If the participants have difficulty identifying errors in skill demonstration, the facilitator provides corrective feedback. An accurate model of skill use is then presented by the facilitator, following which the participants are again asked to identify whether any skill steps were skipped or not performed correctly.

The participants then engage in role plays of the target skill. The facilitator pairs up participants, ideally pairing a participant with ASD and a typically developing peer. The facilitator then provides participants with a scenario in which to practice the target skill, and encourages each participant in the pair to take a turn demonstrating the skill. As participants are practicing the skill, the facilitator provides performance feedback and reminds participants to use the self-monitoring card when the skill is demonstrated correctly. The participants continue to engage in role play until all participants have demonstrated accurate use of all skill steps. Facilitator modeling and participant role playing are expected to last between 6 and 10 min.

Once participants have completed role plays, instruction is again presented via video in the form of an animated social story. The social story takes the form of a comic book, with the video panning across frames of the comic as text is presented in character voices. Each animated social story depicts the superhero characters using the target social skill in novel situations. After demonstrating use of the target skill, the superhero characters provide an opportunity for the participants to recall the steps to the target skill—accomplished through presenting an empty thought or dialog bubble. If the participants inaccurately describe the skill steps at this time, the facilitator provides feedback. The total duration of animated social stories is 3 to 4 min.

Next, participants engage in a social game that requires use of the target skill. The games played are unique to each skill, and are often already familiar to facilitators and participants. For example, a modified version of Follow the Leader in which participants hide around the room, only to join in a line after making eye contact with the line leader, is played during Body Basics lessons. As participants play the game, the facilitator continues to encourage participants to utilize the self-monitoring card when skill steps are demonstrated. Time spent playing the social game is typically between 4 and 5 min.

Following the social game, the Superheroes Social Skills manual describes an optional free time or snack break. If utilized, the facilitator may allow the participants to interact freely while playing games or eating a snack for a relatively brief time (i.e., 3 to 5 min). It should be noted that research utilizing the Superheroes Social Skills program has excluded the optional free time (e.g., Radley, McHugh, Taber, Battaglia, & Ford, 2017).

The facilitator then begins to conclude the group. First, the facilitator records how many bubbles each participant has filled in on his or her self-monitoring card. Recording of in-group self-monitoring is performed as a means of collecting data on accurate demonstrations of the skill, as well as ascertaining how frequently participants engage in skill practice outside of the group. Next, the facilitator describes homework to be completed by participants outside of the group. Each homework assignment consists of the same elements: engage in practice of the skill, self-monitor skill use, and read a paper copy of the social story. As an additional means of promoting skill use outside of the training setting, parents and teachers of participants are provided with a note describing the skill learned, and they are asked to watch for and encourage use of the skill. No consequences are provided to participants based on completion or lack of completion of homework activities. These components of the lesson may last from 3 to 5 min.

The final component of the lesson involves drawing a card from the container or bag holding earned Scooter Cards and Black Hole Cards. The facilitator draws one card at random from the container or bag. If a Scooter Card is drawn, all participants earn access to a reward. Should a Black Hole Card be drawn, the facilitator reviews the group rules—providing particular emphasis on the group rules that were most problematic during the lesson.

Research evaluating Superheroes Social Skills

The Superheroes Social Skills program has been implemented in a variety of applied settings and populations, with a total of 19 peer-reviewed published evaluations of the intervention. Although each evaluation of the Superheroes Social Skills program will not be reviewed in this section, an overview of empirical evidence will be described with respect to the effectiveness of the program for individuals with developmental disabilities, as well as across disability status. Generally, results of these studies indicate the effectiveness of the program for participants with ASD. In regard to generalization of skill accuracy to novel settings and people, there are promising preliminary data to suggest that the implementation of the program can help promote generalization of social skills. However, it is important to note that there needs to be much more research, specifically large-scale studies and replication of current studies to strengthen the evidence base of the Superheroes Social Skills program.

The majority of research evaluating the Superheroes Social Skills program has focused on elementary-age children with ASD (e.g., Radley, Hanglein, & Arak, 2016; Radley, McHugh, et al., 2017). Results of these studies have suggested that individuals who participate in the intervention demonstrate increased accuracy of target social skills in both training and nontraining (i.e., generalization) settings (e.g., Radley, Jenson, Clark, & O'Neill, 2014), increases in duration of social engagement during unstructured periods (e.g., Radley, Jenson, et al., 2014), increases in the variety of social skill use (e.g., Radley, Dart, Moore, Battaglia, & LaBrot, 2017), improvements in ratings of social competency by stakeholders (e.g., Radley, McHugh, et al., 2017), and increases in social connectedness of individuals with ASD and their classroom peers (e.g., Radley, Ford, Battaglia, & McHugh, 2014). Although the majority of studies have focused on elementary-age populations, extant data also indicate the utility of the program with middle school-age individuals with ASD (e.g., Murphy, Radley, & Helbig, 2018).

In an example of implementation of Superheroes Social Skills with elementary-age children with ASD, Radley, Ford, et al. (2014) assessed the effects of the program for four male participants (3 Caucasian; 1 African American) with either a diagnosis of ASD or special education classification of Autism. These participants were referred by either teachers or administrators for social skills training, in an inclusive classroom, and demonstrated low levels of social engagement during recess. Three same-aged typically developing peers were nominated by their teachers as they exhibited appropriate social skills and participated in the group; however, skill acquisition data were collected only for the participants with ASD. Sessions were conducted once per week and lasted approximately 30 min. Eight skills from the curriculum, Participate, Imitation, Body Basics, Expressing Wants and Needs, Joint Attention, Turn Taking, Responding to Questions, and Conversation, were selected and targeted during intervention sessions. Following implementation of Superheroes Social Skills, participants were observed to increase in the duration of social engagement during recess periods—suggesting generalization of social skills learned in the training setting to a novel setting.

Although the majority of research has focused on the effect of participation in Superheroes Social Skills on individuals with ASD, several other studies have investigated its efficacy with individuals across disability type. In one example, the intervention was implemented with an elementary-age child with a specific language impairment (O'Handley, Radley, & Lum, 2016). In another study, researchers included high school-age individuals with special education classifications of Intellectual Disability (O'Handley, Ford, Radley, Helbig, & Wimberly, 2016). In that study, participants consisted of four African American males between the ages of 15 and 16 years old, all of whom were educated within a self-contained classroom, with three of the four participants receiving speech and language therapy. Four skills were taught as part of intervention, with assessment of skill accuracy taking place in both the training setting and a generalization setting (i.e., classroom with teacher). Results indicated that after the Superheroes Social Skills program was implemented, increases in skill acquisition were observed across all participants, in both training and generalization settings. More encouraging are findings that skill accuracy and generalized skill accuracy were maintained at both a 3- and 5-week follow up. This study provides initial data regarding the effectiveness of the Superheroes Social Skills program for adolescents within the high school environment.

In a unique application of the program, O'Handley, Radley, and Cavell (2016) investigated the effect of participation in lessons from Superheroes Social Skills on disruptive and aggressive behavior of six African-American children in an alternative school setting. Participants in the study had a range of special education classifications, including Other Health Impairment, Intellectual Disability, Emotional/Behavioral Disorder, and Speech/Language Impairment. Participants were between the ages of 8 and 12 years and consisted of three males and three females. Three skills from Superheroes Social Skills were presented as part of intervention: Get Ready, Following Directions, and Turn Taking. Following implementation of social skills training, disruptive behavior was observed to decrease substantially, participants improved in skill accuracy, and sociometric standing of all participants increased. Other studies have suggested that participants may benefit regardless of disability status, with peers without identified disabilities improving in social skill use (Radley, O'Handley, et al., 2017). Taken together, extant data suggest that participation in the Superheroes Social Skills program may be beneficial for a wide range of individuals.

Although the preliminary evidence regarding the utilization of the Superheroes Social Skills program is promising, it is important to note limitations of the current literature. First, all 19 of the studies that have evaluated the Superheroes Social Skills program have utilized single-case design methodology. Though these studies have met the rigor of single-case design standards, the ability to generalize the results is limited by the small sample sizes. Also contributing to such generalization concerns is the lack of replication of the current studies, leaving just one demonstration of the effectiveness of the program for various populations (e.g., middle-school students with ASD, high-school students with ID). Future researchers evaluating the Superheroes program should consider systematic replications or large randomized control trials to strengthen the current evidence base of the intervention package.

Lessons learned from research

Superheroes Social Skills represents a manualized intervention, with target population and intervention procedures being clearly described within intervention materials. Despite this, empirical evaluations of the program have often modified procedures to adapt to the nature of intervention settings and participants. The following section describes lessons learned across repeated evaluations of the curriculum, as well as strategies that practitioners may consider when adopting the program in order to ensure efficiency and effectiveness.

Research evaluating the Superheroes Social Skills program has not implemented the program in a consecutive manner, beginning with the first lesson and progressing until the final lesson. Instead, evaluations have sampled out skills based on participant need—presenting only skills that were most critical for participants. In applied settings, practitioners may consider a similar practice—particularly as time constraints in these settings may prohibit the implementation of the Superheroes Social Skills curriculum in its entirety. When implementing select lessons instead of the full curriculum, it is extremely important to consider initial assessment of social skills. Though the program does not include a built-in assessment, there are a few strategies to identify the skill deficits most prominent for a particular individual or group of individuals. The Autism Social Skills Profile (ASSP; Bellini & Hopf, 2007) is a freely available rating scale that assesses a wide range of specific social skill deficits for individuals with ASD. This has been utilized in previous studies as an assessment technique to identify discrete social skill deficits (e.g., Radley, O'Handley, et al., 2014). However, if there is limited time, or situational factors restrict the ability to complete such checklists, practitioners may instead present the table of contents of Superheroes Social Skills to a teacher or caregiver and allow them to select skills off of the "menu" or table of contents that would be most important for a participant to acquire. This can also be conducted in an interview format, depending on the consultative relationship between the practitioner and client.

Previous research has also highlighted the potential utility of modification of schedules of reinforcement within the Superheroes Social Skills program (e.g., Radley, Dart, et al., 2017). Deficits in social communication and restrictive and repetitive behaviors, though distinct diagnostic criteria, often comanifest in the form of restricted conversational interests or rote patterns of communication. When conducting social skills training with individuals that are repetitive in their responses or have very restricted interests and consistently talk about one topic, Superheroes Social Skills has been found to be effective when lag schedules of reinforcement are incorporated into the program. Lag schedules of reinforcement describe a procedure in which reinforcement is provided following a response that differs from a predetermined number of previous responses. Within the curriculum, lag schedules of reinforcement have been incorporated into role-play opportunities. This procedure allows facilitators to systematically give reinforcement for both accurate demonstration of target skills, as well as demonstration of a rich and varied repertoire of social skills. This modification has proven effective in addressing both social communication and restricted and repetitive patterns of communication, allowing for the delivery of a more comprehensive social skills training program.

Also related to the provision of reinforcement within the Superheroes Social Skills program, researchers have varied in their utilization of Scooter and Black Hole Cards. In some instances, Scooter and Black Hole Cards have been omitted entirely from the program. When thinking about not using the Scooter and Black Hole Cards, some considerations should be made. First, practitioners should evaluate the amount of time available to implement each social skills lesson. If practitioners are limited in the amount of time available for facilitation of the intervention, it may be most beneficial to maximize the amount of time spent teaching and practicing the target skill—particularly if the group does not demonstrate challenges associated with following group rules. Thus, for participants who demonstrate social deficits but do not exhibit challenges related to following directions and participating in group, use of Scooter and Black Hole Cards may be unnecessary. However, if the participants were referred for demonstrating disruptive behaviors, then it may be important to include the Scooter and Black Hole Cards in order to maintain instructional control in the group. Thus, practitioners should carefully reflect on the behaviors of members of their group when deciding on the inclusion or omission of Scooter and Black Hole Cards.

Another modification that may be beneficial to make with respect to Scooter and Black Hole Cards is reconsidering how group members access rewards at the end of each session. As it is described in the intervention manual, group participants earn access to rewards based on following group rules (i.e., earning Scooter Cards). However, instead of linking access to rewards to receipt of Scooter Cards, rewards can be made contingent upon accurate demonstration of the target skill. In making this modification, members of the group should be informed that they can earn a predetermined reward if they demonstrate the skill accurately a certain number of times. Tracking accurate skill usage may be accomplished using the self-monitoring card. For example, participants may be informed that if they earn five Power Charges, they can access a reward at the end of the lesson. This modification can be helpful in that it is directly linked to the primary concern (i.e., social behavior) and functions as an immediate reinforcer, which increases the likelihood of the students engaging in that specific behavior (i.e., target social skill) in the future.

Conclusion

Social competence plays a critical role in both short- and long-term outcomes of individuals with ASD. Despite the frequency with which interventions are implemented to address social deficits (e.g., Reichow & Volkmar, 2010), social skills interventions often fall short of producing the desired effects (e.g., Bellini et al., 2007; Bowker et al., 2011). Thus, it is critical that social skills training programs be rigorously researched and that practices found to be effective bridge the research-to-practice gap. To date, 19 evaluations of the Superheroes Social Skills program have documented beneficial outcomes for children and adolescents with ASD in a variety of settings—suggesting the efficacy of the program in producing valued social outcomes. Regarding the ability of the program to bridge the research-to-practice gap, evaluations in naturalistic settings (e.g., school), high ratings of participant and stakeholder satisfaction, and the manualized nature of the program indicate that the program may effectively provide practitioners with training materials that can be applied in real-world settings (e.g., Dingfelder & Mandell, 2011). Although additional research is needed to further evaluate for whom participation in the Superheroes Social Skills program may be most beneficial, extant data indicate the potential of the program to produce salient and valuable improvements in the social competence of participants.

References

Acar, C., Tekin-Iftar, E., & Yimis, A. (2017). Effects of mother-delivered social stories and video modeling in teaching social skills to children with autism spectrum disorders. *Journal of Special Education, 50*, 215–226. https://doi.org/10.1177/0022466916649164.

American Psychiatric Association. (2013). *Diagnostic and statistical manual of mental disorders: DSM-5* (5th ed.). Arlington, VA: American Psychiatric Association.

Bellini, S., & Akullian, J. (2007). A meta-analysis of video modeling and video self-modeling interventions for children and adolescents with autism spectrum disorder. *Exceptional Children*, *73*, 264–287. https://doi.org/10.1177/001440290707300001.

Bellini, S., & Hopf, A. (2007). The development of the autism social skills profile: A preliminary analysis of psychometric properties. *Focus on Autism and Other Developmental Disabilities*, *22*, 80–87. https://doi.org/10.1177/10883576060220020801.

Bellini, S., Peters, J. K., Benner, L., & Hopf, A. (2007). A meta-analysis of school-based social skills interventions for children with autism spectrum disorders. *Remedial and Special Education*, *28*, 153–162. https://doi.org/10.1177/07419325070280030401.

Bowker, A., D'Angelo, N. M., Hicks, R., & Wells, K. (2011). Treatments for autism: Parental choices and perceptions of change. *Journal of Autism and Developmental Disorders*, *41*, 1373–1382. https://doi.org/10.1007/s10803-010-1164-y.

Bush, K. L., & Tassé, M. J. (2017). Employment and choice-making for adults with intellectual disability, autism, and down syndrome. *Research in Developmental Disabilities*, *65*, 23–34. https://doi.org/10.1016/j.ridd.2017.04.004.

Davis, J. L., Mason, B. A., Davis, H. S., Rose, A. M., & Crutchfield, S. A. (2016). Self-monitoring interventions for students with ASD: A meta-analysis of school-based research. *Review Journal of Autism and Developmental Disorders*, *3*, 196–208. https://doi.org/10.1007/s40489-016-0076-y.

Dingfelder, H. E., & Mandell, D. S. (2011). Bridging the research-to-practice gap in autism intervention: An application of diffusion of innovation theory. *Journal of Autism and Developmental Disorders*, *41*, 597–609. https://doi.org/10.1007/s10803-010-1081-0.

Friedman, N. D., Warfield, M. E., & Parish, S. L. (2013). Transition to adulthood for individuals with autism spectrum disorder: Current issues and future perspectives. *Neuropsychiatry*, *3*, 181. https://doi.org/10.2217/NPY.13.13.

Gates, J. A., Kang, E., & Lerner, M. D. (2017). Efficacy of group social skills interventions for youth with autism spectrum disorder: A systematic review and meta-analysis. *Clinical Psychology Review*, *52*, 164–181. https://doi.org/10.1016/j.cpr.2017.01.006.

Goin-Kochel, R., Myers, B., & Mackintosh, V. (2007). Parental reports on the use of treatments and therapies for children with autism spectrum disorders. *Research in Autism Spectrum Disorders*, *1*, 195–209. https://doi.org/10.1016/j.rasd.2006.08.006.

Griffin, W., Sam, A., AFIRM Team. (2016). *Social skills training*. Chapel Hill, NC: National Professional Development Center on Autism Spectrum Disorder, FPG Child Development Center, University of North Carolina. Retrieved from: http://afirm.fpg.unc.edu/social-skills-training.

Guarlnick, M. J. (1999). Fanily and child influence on the peer-related social competence of young children with developmental delays. *Mental Retardation and Developmental Disabilities Research Reviews*, *5*, 21–29. https://doi.org/10.1002/(SICI)1098-2779(1999)5:1<21::AID-MRDD3>3.0.CO;2-O.

Howlin, P., Mawhood, L., & Rutter, M. (2000). Autism and developmental receptive language disorder—A follow-up comparison in early adult life. II: Social, behavioural, and psychiatric outcomes. *Journal of Child Psychology and Psychiatry*, *41*, 561–578. https://doi.org/10.1111/1469-7610.00643.

Hume, K., Campbell, J. M., & Reschly, A. (2019). Peer interventions for students with autism spectrum disorder in school settings: Introduction to the special issue. *School Psychology Review*, *48*, 115–122. https://doi.org/10.17105/SPR-2018-0081.V48-2.

Lee, S. H., Simpson, R. L., & Shogren, K. A. (2007). Effects and implications of self-management for students with autism: A meta-analysis. *Focus on Autism and Other Developmental Disabilities*, *22*, 2–13. https://doi.org/10.1177/10883576070220010101.

Murphy, A. N., Radley, K. C., & Helbig, K. A. (2018). Use of superheroes social skills with middle school-age students with autism spectrum disorder. *Psychology in the Schools*, *55*, 323–335. DIUL https://doi.org/10.1002/pits.22104.

Neumberger, J. E., Ringdahl, J. E., Vargo, K. K., Crumpecker, A. C., & Gunnarsson, K. F. (2013). Using a behavioral skills training package to teach conversation skills to young adults with autism spectrum disorders. *Research in Autism Spectrum Disorders*, *7*, 411–417. https://doi.org/10.1016/j.rasd.2012.09.004.

O'Handley, R. D., Ford, W. B., Radley, K. C., Helbig, K. A., & Wimberly, J. K. (2016). Social skills training for adolescents with intellectual disabilities: A school-based evaluation. *Behavior Modification*, *40*, 541–567. https://doi.org/10.1177/0145445516629938.

O'Handley, R. D., Radley, K. C., & Cavell, H. J. (2016). Utilization of superheroes social skills to reduce disruptive and aggressive behavior. *Preventing School Failure*, *60*, 124–132. https://doi.org/10.1080/1045988X.2015.1038775.

O'Handley, R. D., Radley, K. C., & Lum, J. D. K. (2016). Promoting social communication in a child with specific language impairment. *Communication Disorders Quarterly*, *37*, 199–210. https://doi.org/10.1177/1525740115595346.

Radley, K. C., Dart, E. H., Moore, J. W., Battaglia, A. A., & LaBrot, Z. C. (2017). Promoting accurate variability of social skills in children with autism spectrum disorder. *Behavior Modification*, *41*, 84–112. https://doi.org/10.1177/0145445516655428.

Radley, K. C., Ford, W. B., Battaglia, A. A., & McHugh, M. B. (2014). The effects of a social skills training package on social engagement of children with autism spectrum disorders in a generalized recess setting. *Focus on Autism and Other Developmental Disabilities*, *29*, 216–229. https://doi.org/10.1177/1088357614525660.

Radley, K. C., Hanglein, J., & Arak, M. (2016). School-based social skills training for preschool-age children with autism spectrum disorder. *Autism*, *20*, 938–951. https://doi.org/10.1177/1362361315617361.

Radley, K. C., Jenson, W. R., Clark, E., & O'Neill, R. E. (2014). The feasibility and effects of a parent facilitated social skills training program on social engagement of children with autism spectrum disorders. *Psychology in the Schools*, *51*, 241–255. https://doi.org/10.1002/pits.21749.

Radley, K. C., McHugh, M. B., Taber, T., Battaglia, A. A., & Ford, W. B. (2017). School-based social skills training for children with autism spectrum disorder. *Focus on Autism and Other Developmental Disabilities*, *32*, 256–268. https://doi.org/10.1177/1088357615583470.

Radley, K. C., O'Handley, R. D., Battaglia, A. A., Lum, J. D. K., Dadakhodjaeva, K., Ford, W. B., & McHugh, M. B. (2017). Effects of a social skills intervention on children with autism spectrum disorder and peers with shared deficits. *Education and Treatment of Children*, *40*, 233–262. https://doi.org/10.1353/etc.2017.0011.

Radley, K. C., O'Handley, R. D., Ness, E. J., Ford, W. B., Battaglia, A. A., McHugh, M. B., & McLemore, C. E. (2014). Promoting social skill use and generalization in children with autism spectrum disorder. *Research in Autism Spectrum Disorders*, *8*, 669–680. https://doi.org/10.1016/j.rasd.2014.03.012.

Rankin, J. A., Weber, R. J., Kang, E., & Lerner, M. D. (2016). Parent- and self-reported social skills importance in autism spectrum disorder. *Journal of Autism and Developmental Disorders*, *46*, 273–286. https://doi.org/10.1007/s10803-015-2574-7.

Reichow, B., & Volkmar, F. R. (2010). Social skills interventions for individuals with autism: Evaluation for evidence-based practices within a best evidence synthesis framework. *Journal of Autism and Developmental Disorders*, *40*, 149–166. https://doi.org/10.1007/s10803-009-0842-0.

Sperry, L., Neitzel, J., & Engelhardt-Wells, K. (2010). Peer-mediated instruction and intervention strategies for students with autism spectrum disorders. *Preventing School Failure*, *54*, 256–264. https://doi.org/10.1080/10459881003800529.

Stokes, T. F., & Baer, D. M. (1977). An implicit technology of generalization. *Journal of Applied Behavior Analysis*, *10*, 349–367. https://doi.org/10.1901/jaba.1977.10-349.

Toth, K., Munson, J., Meltzhoff, A. N., & Dawson, G. (2006). Early predictors of communication development in young children with autism spectrum disorder: Joint attention, imitation, and toy play. *Journal of Autism and Developmental Disorders*, *36*, 993–1005. https://doi.org/10.1007/s10803-006-0137-7.

Wang, S. Y., Parilla, R., & Cui, Y. (2013). Meta-analysis of social skills interventions of single-case research for individuals with autism spectrum disorders: Results from three-level HLM. *Journal of Autism and Developmental Disorders*, *43*, 1701–1716. https://doi.org/10.1007/s10803-012-1726-2.

White, S. W., Keonig, K., & Scahill, L. (2007). Social skills development in children with autism spectrum disorders: A review of the intervention research. *Journal of Autism and Developmental Disorders*, *37*, 1858–1868. https://doi.org/10.1007/s10803-006-0320-x.

Wolstencroft, J., Robinson, K., Srinivasan, R., Kerry, E., Mandy, W., & Skuse, D. (2018). A systematic reivew of group social skills interventions and meta-analysis of outcomes, for children with high functioning ASD. *Journal of Autism and Developmental Disorders*, *48*, 2293–2307. https://doi.org/10.1007/s10803-018-3485-1.

Further reading

Alberto, P., & Troutman, A. (2008). *Applied behavior analysis for teachers* (8th ed.). Upper Saddle River, NJ: Prentice Hall.

Albin, R. W., Luchyshyn, J. M., Horner, R. H., & Flannery, K. B. (1996). Contextual fit for behavioral support plans: A model for "goodness of fit". In L. Koegel, R. Koegel, & G. Dunlap (Eds.), *Positive behavior support: Including people with difficult behavior in the community*. Baltimore: Paul H. Brookes.

Callahan, K., Hughes, H. L., Mehta, S., Toussaint, K. A., Nichols, S. M., Ma, P. S., … Wang, H. T. (2017). Social validity of evidence-based practices and emerging interventions in autism. *Focus on Autism and Other Developmental Disabilities*, *32*, 188–197. https://doi.org/10.1177/1088357616632446.

Jenson, W. R., Bowen, J., Clark, E., Block, H. M., Gabrielsen, T., Hood, J. A., … Springer, B. (2011). *Superheroes social skills*. Eugene, OR: Pacific Northwest.

Radley, K. C., Ford, W. B., McHugh, M. B., Dadakhodjaeva, K., O'Handley, R. D., Battaglia, A. A., & Lum, J. D. K. (2015). Brief report: Use of superheroes social skills to promote accurate social skill use in children with autism spectrum disorder. *Journal of Autism and Developmental Disorders*, *45*, 3048–3054. https://doi.org/10.1007/s10803-015-2442-5.

Wang, S. Y., Cui, Y., & Parrila, R. (2011). Examining the effectiveness of peer-mediated and video-modeling social skills interventions for children with autism spectrum disorders: A meta-analysis in single-case research using HLM. *Research in Autism Spectrum Disorders*, *5*, 562–569. https://doi.org/10.1016/j.rasd.2010.06.023.

Wolf, M. M. (1978). Social validity: The case for subjective measurement or how applied behavior analysis is finding its heart. *Journal of Applied Behavior Analysis*, *11*, 203–214. https://doi.org/10.1901/jaba.1978.11-203.

Chapter 12

School-based treatment for children and adolescents with social anxiety disorder

Samantha Coyle[a], Farah Mahmud[a], Cody Weeks[a], and Carrie Masia Warner[a,b]

[a]*Montclair State University, Montclair, NJ, United States,* [b]*Nathan Kline Institute for Psychiatric Research, Orangeburg, NY, United States*

Social anxiety disorder (SAD) is a psychological condition characterized by significant fear and avoidance of social and performance situations (American Psychiatric Association, 2013). Anxiety disorders are the most common psychiatric diagnoses in adolescents. Among them, SAD is the second most common (following specific phobia), with a lifetime prevalence rate of about 9.1% before the age of 18 (Merikangas et al., 2010). Commonly feared situations include initiating conversations, speaking up in groups, performing in front of others, asking teachers for help, and spending time with peers (Blöte, Miers, & Westenberg, 2015). As is evident, many of these situations are routine occurrences at school. Thus, it is not surprising that one in five youth with SAD engage in school refusal, with this behavior becoming more common during adolescence (Waite & Creswell, 2014).

The typical developmental challenges of adolescence make this period difficult for socially anxious youth. Unlike during childhood, when their parents typically organize playdates and invite the entire class to birthday parties, teenagers are expected to manage their own social relationships in addition to managing academic, interpersonal, and romantic issues with greater autonomy (Hartup & Stevens, 1999; Spence & Rapee, 2016). SAD onset peaks around age 13 (Kessler et al., 2005) and can cause significant impairment in managing adolescent social stressors. As a result, much research has examined the link between social anxiety and the quality of interpersonal relationships and peer victimization, as well as social skills related to both areas.

Social Skills Across the Life Span. https://doi.org/10.1016/B978-0-12-817752-5.00012-3

Social anxiety and interpersonal relationships

Consistent evidence supports that adolescents with social anxiety have greater difficulty with their interpersonal relationships (Erath, Flanagan, & Bierman, 2007; La Greca & Harrison, 2005). For example, individuals with SAD report more distress and difficulty when establishing friendships (Cohen & Kendall, 2015; Erath et al., 2007). These youth often avoid interacting with classmates and prefer to spend more time alone (Cohen & Kendall, 2015; Schneider, 2009). Socially anxious youth have fewer and less intimate relationships (Tillfors, Persson, Willen, & Burk, 2012). Additionally, research shows that adolescents with social anxiety are less popular and less accepted by peers (Greco & Morris, 2005; Van Zalk, Van Zalk, Kerr, & Stattin, 2011). In fact, when assessing peer acceptance, which involves both social status (e.g., how liked someone is) and social impact (e.g., whether the individual is noticed by one's peers), youth who report more anxiety in social situations are more apt to be disliked and less likely to be noticed by their peers (Greco & Morris, 2005). Relatedly, youth with greater social anxiety often rate their classmates as less supportive of them, providing further evidence of deficits in interpersonal relationships (Coyle & Malecki, 2018). Based on these findings, it is not surprising that youth with SAD experience more loneliness and less satisfaction with the quality of their friendships relative to nonanxious peers (Beidel et al., 2007).

Social anxiety and victimization

In addition to research demonstrating that socially anxious youth struggle to establish *positive* relationships with their peers, there is also a growing body of research that suggests that socially anxious youth are at greater risk of *peer victimization* (Blöte et al., 2015; Ranta, Kaltiala-Heino, Fröjd, & Marttunen, 2013). This link has been found in both self- and peer-reported data (Erath et al., 2007), with greater victimization contributing to increased social anxiety and vice versa (Ranta et al., 2013; Vernberg, Abwender, Ewell, & Beery, 1992). Relational victimization, or acts intended to harm the social status or reputation of others (e.g., rumor starting, exclusion), has demonstrated stronger links with social anxiety symptoms than other forms of victimization, such as physical or direct aggression (i.e., calling someone mean names, hitting, or kicking) (Ranta et al., 2013; Siegel, La Greca, & Harrison, 2009). Some research has found that *perpetration,* or active involvement in bullying another individual, may also be linked with increased social anxiety over time (Pabian & Vandebosch, 2016), suggesting that involvement in bullying across roles (i.e., perpetrator, victim) or social conflict in general may be a risk factor for social anxiety.

In addition, the rise in digital technology has provided a new venue to experience victimization via text messages, email, and social media (Kowalski, Giumetti, Schroeder, & Lattanner, 2014). Cross-sectional and longitudinal studies have found higher occurrences of cybervictimization to be positively linked with social anxiety (Coelho & Romão, 2018; Coyle, Malecki, & Emmons, 2019;

Pabian & Vandebosch, 2016). Researchers have suggested that socially anxious youth may be easy targets for bullies or cyberbullies because they lack the skills to advocate and defend themselves in these situations (Navarro, Yubero, Larranaga, & Martinez, 2011). Repeated victimization experiences may then exacerbate already high levels of social anxiety, contributing to further avoidance and withdrawal from social interactions (Navarro et al., 2011). This seems to be supported in recent studies that suggest that youth who feel capable of coping with bullying experiences, both online and in person, have less social anxiety than those who feel less capable or report avoidance strategies as a coping mechanism (Singh & Bussey, 2011; Trompeter, Bussey, & Fitzpatrick, 2018). Together, these findings suggest that interventions that provide youth with the skills they need to feel equipped to handle interpersonal stressors, such as victimization, while also discouraging avoidance, are ideal interventions for socially anxious youth.

Social anxiety and social skills

Likely due to avoidance of social situations that limits development of social skills, ineffectual social behavior contributes to the compromised social relationships of adolescents with SAD (Alfano, Beidel, & Turner, 2006; Beidel, Turner, & Morris, 1999; Inderbitzen-Nolan, Anderson, & Johnson, 2007; Miers, Blöte, & Westenberg, 2010). The majority of observational research on youth with SAD has supported impairment in social skills (Schneider & Turk, 2014; Spence & Rapee, 2016). For instance, youth with SAD are less likely to initiate interactions and have fewer and less successful interactions with their classmates (Spence, Donovan, & Brechman-Toussaint, 1999). Individuals with SAD are also noted to be less effective in carrying out a conversation and giving or receiving compliments, skills that are essential in establishing new relationships (Alfano et al., 2006; Beidel et al., 1999). Furthermore, youth with SAD are rated as less friendly, less assertive, and lower in leadership qualities than nonanxious peers, perhaps contributing to the increased risk of victimization due to difficulties in their ability to defend or stand up for themselves (Inderbitzen-Nolan et al., 2007; Navarro et al., 2011).

Peer perceptions have further supported inadequacies in adolescents' skills related to interpersonal success. More specifically, unfamiliar same-aged peers rate socially anxious youth as less likeable (Verduin & Kendall, 2008) and less desirable to engage with in the future (Blöte et al., 2015) following social skill performance tasks, compared to control subjects. In a study investigating peer perceptions of social performance on a speech task, peer raters noted that compared to nonanxious peers, youth with SAD demonstrated more deficits in speech content, facial expressions, posture and body movement, and speaking ability (Miers et al., 2010). The rapid judgment of socially anxious youth as impaired in their social skills may explain their frequent unfavorable social experiences and negative evaluations by other students (Greco & Morris, 2005; Miers et al., 2010; Verduin & Kendell, 2008).

In summary, youth with social anxiety experience difficulty in their ability to initiate and maintain interactions with others and are less assertive relative to peers. These impairments impede positive relationships and increase risk for victimization. Youth with SAD often find themselves in a vicious cycle. That is, as negative social encounters increase, so does their social anxiety and social avoidance (Tillfors et al., 2012), further limiting the development of skills necessary to overcome social fears (Spence et al., 1999). This has been supported by longitudinal work that has found that poorer social performance and more social problems in school are linked with greater social anxiety across time (Miers, Blöte, de Rooij, Bokhorst, & Westenberg, 2013). Although a full discussion of this issue is beyond the scope of this chapter, it should be noted that debate exists in the literature as to whether impaired social behavior is due to true skill deficits (i.e., they lack the skills), or anxious inhibition of skills that are present (i.e., performance deficit) (Schneider & Turk, 2014). Regardless, based on the preponderance of social impairment, it is evident that treatments for SAD must improve social skills (both verbal and nonverbal) and reverse social avoidance, a key aspect of dysfunction in SAD. The remainder of this chapter will discuss a school-based group intervention for SAD, referred to as skills for academic and social success (SASS) (Masia Warner, Colognori, & Lynch, 2018), that emphasizes group social skills training and exposure to social and performance situations. The social skills highlighted in SASS target several of the skills identified as areas of deficits within the literature, including initiating and maintaining conversations, increasing awareness of nonverbal behavior during social tasks, and building assertiveness skills.

Considerations for school-based intervention using SASS

Benefits of school-based intervention for SAD

The school setting is ideal for the treatment of SAD for several reasons. First, SAD appears to be less responsive than other anxiety disorders to individual treatment formats (Ginsburg et al., 2011), likely because group intervention creates a practical environment in which to teach and practice social skills (Kendall, Settipani, & Cummings, 2012). Forming groups in clinical settings can be challenging because of variability in client ages, diagnoses, and schedules (Masia Warner et al., 2011). The school environment allows for greater ease in matching students based on developmental level, clinical symptoms, and needs (Masia Warner et al., 2016). In addition, the majority of feared or avoided situations central to SAD occur at school (e.g., talking to peers, eating in the cafeteria, speaking up in class) (Blöte et al., 2015). Thus, the treatment of SAD in schools provides opportunities for real-life exposures (e.g., answering questions in class, joining a group of peers in the library) and for practicing social skills in realistic contexts with various individuals (e.g., teachers, staff, peers). Finally, as schools are the main context where social relationships are established and interpersonal conflicts occur, school counselors are ideally positioned to coach adolescents on an ongoing basis in challenging situations that may arise (Fox, Masia Warner, & Drew, 2018). The group structure and the natural, authentic environment inherent in school-based treatment can increase effectiveness of the intervention and generalization of social skills across social contexts.

Multi-tiered systems of supports (MTSS)

Possibly due to increased and unaddressed mental health needs that cause interference in academic functioning, federal and state legislation, along with professional organizations (e.g., National Association of School Psychologists), have called for extending MTSS, which has mainly been for academic interventions, to include mental health (Kilgus, Reinke, & Jimerson, 2015). The MTSS framework is based on the public health model of prevention and provides a systematic and organizational structure that facilitates the delivery of services within the school setting (Cook et al., 2015). The ultimate goal of MTSS is to promote positive social, emotional, and academic success for all students to reduce barriers to learning and increase access to mental health services (Cook et al., 2015; Strein, Hoagwood, & Cohn, 2003). Through this framework, universal screening is emphasized to identify youth at risk of academic, behavioral, or emotional challenges. Despite the high prevalence of SAD, it remains largely undetected, and the majority of affected adolescents do not receive services until secondary complications arise (e.g., depression, school refusal) (Merikangas et al., 2010). Thus, in line with MTSS, universal screenings of social anxiety using well-validated self-report instruments (e.g., SCARED; Birmaher et al., 1999) can be an effective approach to assess social anxiety in adolescents. Teachers can also be educated during faculty meetings on the behavioral symptoms of social anxiety and asked to refer students to school counselors. Using an MTSS framework, identification of youth requiring more significant supports and early intervention can be accomplished.

In addition to enhancing identification, the MTSS framework includes three "layers" of evidence-based interventions that increase in intensity from one level to the next. The SASS intervention program is ideally suited to align with this tiered model of service delivery. Tier one, or universal intervention, is applied to entire classrooms or all students, such as providing SASS social skills training lessons as part of health education classes. Tier two is the standard SASS delivery, which involves small groups for students with elevated social anxiety that require more targeted support. The SASS program may also be adjusted for Tier three, in which students require more frequent or intensive intervention, such as adding individual sessions or meetings with teachers to address specific classroom situations (see Masia Warner et al., 2018).

Skills for academic and social success

SASS is a group, cognitive-behavioral intervention that incorporates social skills training as part of a multicomponent treatment. SASS consists of psychoeducation and realistic appraisal, while emphasizing social skills training and exposures to overcome social fears. SASS was adapted from social effectiveness therapy for children (SET-C), an evidence-based clinical treatment for SAD in youth, which was modified to be feasibly implemented in schools by school counselors. SASS consists of 12 in-school group sessions that each last about 40 min or one class period, to coincide with the school schedule. It also includes two individual meetings (15 min each), two group booster sessions (40 min each), four weekend social events (approximately 90 min each), two parent meetings (45 min each), and teacher meetings as needed throughout the program. Each group consists of approximately six to eight students. A proactive approach to identifying anxious students is recommended. This might include referrals from teachers and school counselors who have been educated about common anxiety symptoms or routine school screenings using brief self-report measures [e.g., the social anxiety subscale of the screen for child anxiety related emotional disorders (SCARED; Birmaher et al., 1999; Sweeney et al., 2015)]. Given this book's emphasis on social skills, we will primarily describe how we tailor social skills training for socially anxious adolescents. Other components of the SASS intervention (e.g., psychoeducation, parent meetings, etc.) are fully described in Masia Warner et al. (2018) and will be reviewed only briefly.

Social skills training and exposure

Learning and practicing social skills can help increase the likelihood that adolescents will experience success in social situations and encourage them to enter situations they typically avoid. SASS targets four skills that are seen as most essential for enhancing social experiences of adolescents with social anxiety. They are: (1) initiating conversations, (2) maintaining conversations and establishing friendships, (3) listening and remembering, and (4) assertiveness. These skills were chosen based on the specific impairments in socially anxious youth, as mentioned earlier.

For each of the skills, group leaders begin the session by introducing the skill and the rationale as to why it is important, model the skill for students, and have students engage in role-play exercises to allow them to practice the learned skills with the other group members. The purpose of role-play activities is to rehearse the skill and boost confidence interacting in social situations. Each adolescent in the group participates in at least two role plays, which are specifically selected to mirror commonly encountered social experiences for adolescents (e.g., being paired with another student to work on a project, starting a conversation with a classmate). Students are provided with support and individualized feedback during each session. Group leaders also offer suggestions for improvement, such as speaking louder or increasing eye contact. Because socially anxious adolescents often look unfriendly or unapproachable due to anxiety-induced nonverbal behaviors (e.g., frowning, avoiding eye contact), all skills groups emphasize teaching students to become aware of these nonverbal behaviors and messages to others.

Social skill #1: Initiating conversations

To facilitate the development of peer contact, participants are explicitly taught when to start conversations, ways to open conversations, and the role that a friendly, nonthreatening appearance can play in engaging others. Students are instructed to make three main observations when deciding whether to start a conversation: (1) whether the person appears busy, (2) whether the person appears friendly, and (3) whether the person appears receptive to engaging in a conversation. Individuals with social anxiety often worry about saying "just the right thing," or express concerns about sounding boring. Therefore, group leaders stress that conversation starters can be simple and even dull, such as commenting on things happening in the environment or obvious similarities (e.g., they are both on the same soccer team). After reviewing the skill, group leaders ask adolescents for typical scenarios in which they might like to start conversations (e.g., sitting on bench at a team practice), and then students practice initiating conversations in these role-play situations. It is important to note that socially anxious individuals can become dependent on using similar conversation openers and subsequently struggle to start conversations in different contexts. Therefore, it is important to explicitly train flexibility. This can be done by having group members generate varying statements in the same role-play scenarios, as well as taking turns brainstorming statements that can be used across many different role-plays. Group members are assigned homework to practice starting about two conversations daily or possibly more depending on the adolescents' level of impairment.

Social skill #2: Maintaining conversations and establishing friendships

The second session focuses on topic transitions and extending invitations. This session teaches adolescents how to ask open (e.g., what types of music do you like?) rather than close-ended questions (e.g., do you like hip-hop?) that have a greater chance of encouraging discussion rather than eliciting a one-word response. In addition, group leaders discuss appropriate times to switch topics and emphasize that brief pauses in conversation are natural and not always a reason to change the subject. During conversational role plays, group members are instructed to stay on a topic until the group leader tells them to switch. Group leaders discuss the importance of conveying interest in what the other person is saying and following up with questions related to that information. Lastly, because socially anxious teenagers often have difficulty developing friendships outside of school and building supportive relationships with their peers, group leaders explain that extending social invitations is an important next step in making friends and instruct adolescents to practice extending invitations. Group leaders also identify and discuss common reservations that adolescents express about asking others to get together (e.g., the person will think I am weird; it is too soon to ask my friend to get together; he will feel like he has to say yes).

Social skill #3: Listening and remembering

The third social skills session focuses on listening and remembering during social interactions. Group leaders begin the session by introducing how anxiety interferes with performance in structured (e.g., asking questions about material learned in class) and unstructured settings (e.g., having conversations with peers). They also explain that people who listen during conversations, as well as recall what others have said, appear more genuine and have more enjoyable and naturally flowing conversations. Several exercises are used to practice these skills, such as having group members introduce themselves as fictional characters and question each other on the details they present. Next, students present four facts describing themselves (e.g., I have three siblings; I play soccer), and practice initiating and maintaining conversations based on personal details they remember. By practicing active listening techniques, youth appear more engaged and at ease during social interactions.

Social skill #4: Assertiveness

In this session, group leaders emphasize the importance of assertive communication in developing mutually beneficial relationships, dealing with peer conflict, and handling victimization experiences. Adolescents practice using "I" statements to make requests (e.g., I would like to join the yearbook club) and to express opinions and preferences (e.g., I think we can finish this project faster if we divide the work). Group leaders discuss the importance of expressing positive and negative emotions in building relationships, as they make others feel good about friendships and help resolve conflict. Refusing requests is another important assertiveness skill covered in this session. Students are taught to use the phrase, "I'm sorry, but…," repeat the request, and provide a brief and honest reason for refusal (e.g., I'm sorry, but I can't help you with your homework because I need to go to soccer practice). Finally, peer victimization is addressed. Group leaders help students brainstorm possible responses to hypothetical situations or past bullying experiences, while comparing the costs and benefits of each solution. Possible responses might include ignoring the bully, planning to be with a friend during times when the bully might be around, and reporting the bully. Students also determine which adults to confide in when bullying occurs. Providing youth with the skills to actively address victimization experiences is important, given the link between victimization and social anxiety in youth.

Facing your fear exposure sessions

There are five group exposure sessions that alternate with social skills sessions. The group leader presents the rationale for exposure, explaining that social avoidance maintains anxiety and that gradually facing feared situations will reduce anxiety over time. The group leader explains that effective exposure is a gradual process and requires repeatedly entering and remaining in currently avoided situations. Adolescents create fear hierarchies or ladders in which they order anxiety-provoking situations from least to most feared. Hierarchies should include exposures that can be executed in the school environment (e.g., cafeteria, library, classroom) and that represent the core concerns associated with social anxiety (e.g., criticism or rejection experiences). During exposure sessions, students practice entering situations on their fear hierarchy while in the group (e.g., giving a presentation) or around school (e.g., initiating a conversation with a peer in the library, asking a teacher about a disappointing grade).

Additional components of SASS

Psychoeducation

In the first group session, the group leader provides an overview of SASS, the rationale for and general structure of the program, and the group rules/norms. Confidentiality is also addressed. Adolescents learn about the symptoms of social anxiety within a cognitive-behavioral model, with an emphasis on understanding their own emotional, cognitive, and behavioral symptoms and how they interact to increase social anxiety. The role of avoidance in maintaining anxiety is also emphasized. Students are also encouraged to think about their personal motivations for treatment and specific situations that they would like to address.

Realistic thinking

The second group session focuses on cognitive reappraisal or *realistic thinking* (Rapee, Wignall, Spence, Cobham, & Lyneham, 2008). As adolescents with social anxiety often overestimate the likelihood of negative outcomes, students are taught to identify negative expectations and to evaluate them more realistically. They are taught to ask various questions to assess their predictions (e.g., how many times has this happened in the past?). The group leader has the adolescents apply realistic thinking strategies by asking for real examples of feared social situations and practicing identifying and evaluating the negative predictions.

Relapse prevention

The final group session focuses on the maintenance of gains and avoidance of relapse. Each adolescent gives a speech about his or her experience in the program, which serves as an exposure exercise and termination activity. The group leader facilitates a discussion of strategies for continuing progress and handling setbacks to avoid relapse.

Individual sessions

There are two 15-min individual sessions through which the group leader can better understand any personal issues hindering treatment progress. They can also use this time to tailor cognitive restructuring and/or review certain social skills or exposures that are specific to the needs of the adolescent. In addition, adolescents can discuss interpersonal stressors that might be impacting their progress and ability to engage in practice exercises (e.g., victimization experiences, academic challenges) and develop strategies to address these issues.

Social events

There are four 90-min social events throughout the program held on weekends either in community settings or at the school. These are attended by the group leader, program participants, and peer assistants (recruited prosocial peers who may have previously completed the program). Event activities can include bowling, an outdoor picnic, board games, or rollerblading. Their purpose is to provide opportunities to use social skills learned within the program in a supported social environment and gain exposure to situations that are commonly avoided. Across the four social events, group leaders gradually provide less structure and support to adolescents (e.g., starting with a highly structured bowling activity and ending with a less structured picnic), allowing students to use skills more independently and be challenged as they progress.

Peer assistants

Peer assistants are students who assist with the program. It is ideal to have adolescents who previously completed the program serve as peer assistants. Their main role is to attend social events to promote a positive experience and help group members practice social skills at events. Peer assistants may also help program participants practice social skills during school sessions or in other situations around school.

Parent meetings

SASS includes two parent meetings. The first parent meeting provides an overview of the program and general psychoeducation about social anxiety. The second meeting teaches parents helpful strategies to support their children's treatment progress. For example, parents are asked to refrain from helping their children to avoid difficult situations (e.g., speaking to others for them), and rather to encourage them to face their fears and function more independently.

Teacher involvement

One of the advantages of school-based treatment is that group leaders have access to teachers and other staff members who work with students regularly. Group leaders can meet with teachers to educate them about social anxiety, to identify areas of difficulty in the classroom for group members, and to collaborate with teachers to conduct classroom exposures (e.g., have a student walk in late to class). Teachers can also provide updates and feedback about student progress.

Booster sessions

Group follow-up sessions are conducted 1 month and 2 months after termination in order to monitor progress and conduct additional exposure exercises. Students also discuss obstacles to continued improvement and ways to enhance peer relationships and social engagement.

Evaluating SASS effectiveness

One small open trial (Masia, Klein, Storch, & Corda, 2001) and two school-based controlled trials, in which SASS was implemented by doctoral level, study team psychologists in private schools, were conducted to examine the feasibility and potential efficacy of SASS. The first trial compared SASS to a no-treatment condition ($n=35$) (Masia Warner et al., 2005). The second ($n=36$) tested SASS against a credible attention control (Masia Warner, Fisher, Shrout, Rathor, & Klein, 2007). In both trials, SASS was markedly efficacious in reducing social anxiety and avoidance and in enhancing social functioning immediately after treatment and 6 months thereafter. Overall, these results were encouraging, considering the relatively short duration of sessions, a feature essential for school intervention. However, because reliance on specialized mental health professionals would limit dissemination of SASS, Masia Warner and colleagues tested whether trained school counselors could implement SASS effectively in a third randomized controlled trial. One hundred and thirty-eight, ninth through eleventh graders with SAD were randomized to one of three conditions: (a) SASS delivered by school counselors (C-SASS), (b) SASS delivered by psychologists (P-SASS), or (c) a control condition, skills for life (SFL), a general school counseling program. Compared to controls (18.6% and 25.6%), significantly more adolescents treated with C-SASS (65% and 85%) and P-SASS (66% and 72%) were classified as treatment responders following treatment completion and 5 months later. These adolescents experienced greater improvement and reductions in social anxiety after treatment. No significant differences were found in clinical outcomes between SASS delivered by school counselors and clinical psychologists (Masia Warner et al., 2016). This indicates that school-based treatment for social anxiety delivered by school counselors is effective and justifies efforts to broaden its usability.

Future directions

Sustainability of SASS in schools

School counselors are able to implement the SASS program with positive student outcomes when provided with training through a federally funded research study (Masia Warner et al., 2016). However, it is possible that SASS implementation may not be held to the same standards when conducting "business as usual" in schools. Investigating unique methods to support intervention fidelity and promote training of new school counselors is essential. For example, future work might test the effectiveness of having experienced school personnel train others or using online training modules (Masia Warner et al., 2013).

In addition to possibly using technology to train school personnel, technology may be used as a vehicle to deliver SASS to students or to supplement SASS by providing accessible means of social skills practice and exposure to social fears. Preliminary data exist to support the benefit of web-based or computerized delivery of interventions for children and adolescents with mixed anxiety diagnoses (Kendall et al., 2012; Wuthrich et al., 2012) and specifically SAD (Tillfors et al., 2011). In addition, as a substitute for in-person skills practice, Wong Sarver, Beidel, and Spitalnick (2014) investigated the feasibility of using a virtual school environment in which socially anxious children interacted with avatars (e.g., peer, bully, teacher). Reports from children, parents, and clinicians indicated that the virtual environment was acceptable and credible (Wong Sarver et al., 2014). These findings are encouraging given the challenges of disseminating CBT to community settings and of providing real-life practice opportunities.

Extension of SASS across MTSS tiers

As mentioned previously, SASS is designed to fit into an MTSS framework within the school setting and can be adapted to address students' social anxiety across a range of severity, including youth with moderate (Tier 2) or severe (Tier 3) levels of SAD. Given the emphasis of SASS on social skills involved in building interpersonal relationships (e.g., conversing with others), assertiveness, and handling peer conflict, instruction and practice using these skills are beneficial for all students, not simply those experiencing social anxiety. Future work may consider extending the evidence-based strategies used to teach social skills in the small group format to reach a larger audience, as a Tier 1 intervention. This is an identified need in today's schools, as many states have implemented social-emotional learning standards (Zins & Elias, 2007) that focus on improving social strategies for all students in school. Carefully extending the SASS program to promote positive social behaviors in schools more universally may be an important area to explore in future work. For example, teachers could implement social skills training and role-play activities into their daily routines and support the development of skills related to interpersonal functioning. It is possible that exposure to SASS at a school-wide level may not only improve student skills across all tiers, but also enhance students' understanding of social anxiety and build empathy for those affected. Furthermore, extending SASS to all tiers may help to improve school climate, intervention acceptability, and the likelihood of sustained school adoption at higher levels of care. Future work may consider assessing these possibilities more specifically.

Use of peer support

Greater perceptions of social support from classmates have been associated with reduced social anxiety in school-based samples of middle- and high school-aged adolescents. Thus, it is important to explore interventions that develop unique and innovative methods to facilitate the development of supportive and positive peer relationships (Coyle et al., 2019; Coyle & Malecki, 2018; Rueger, Malecki, Pyun, Ayock, & Coyle, 2016). SASS specifically includes a component to promote the development of positive and supportive peer relationships through the incorporation of peer assistants and social events as part of the curriculum (Masia Warner et al., 2018). Using peers as agents to deliver the intervention and support students during distressing social events can help to encourage and facilitate the development of social support from classmates in school. Future research may consider whether this aspect of the treatment (e.g., social events) may improve adolescents' perceptions of social support and whether continued peer activities may be an effective way to maintain and generalize the effects of treatment outcomes. Furthermore, it may be worthwhile to measure changes in perceptions of classmate support in response to the social events and whether any improvements in perceived support may be linked with reduced symptoms of SAD. It is possible that decreasing concerns over whether peers will be receptive in social events and fostering social support from the larger peer context will increase school engagement of youth with social anxiety.

Multicultural considerations for future work

Lastly, although rates of SAD and other anxiety disorders are high among racial and ethnic minority adolescents (Beidas et al., 2012; Merikangas et al., 2010), mental health service utilization is low (Gudiño, Lau, Yeh, McCabe, & Hough, 2009). SASS may be particularly relevant as minority youth are more likely to receive mental health services in schools than in community clinics (Cummings, Ponce, & Mays, 2010; Jaycox et al., 2010). In addition, 75% of children from low-income communities receive mental health services at school (Burns et al., 1995). SASS should be evaluated with more racially, ethnically, and economically diverse youth. It is likely that some structural and cultural modifications to SASS will be necessary to enhance its relevance and fit within various communities. For Black American students, as an example, the potential for social anxiety to magnify internalized racism, or acceptance of negative beliefs about one's worth due to racism, poses a heightened risk (Graham, West, Martinez, & Roemer, 2016). Thus, Black American students with social anxiety may be particularly susceptible to the detrimental psychological and educational effects of racial discrimination and negative racial stereotypes, including lower academic engagement and performance (Chavous et al., 2003; Smalls, White, Chavous, & Sellers, 2007). It may be necessary to expand psychoeducation and cognitive strategies to address these issues. In addition, SASS social skills involve assertiveness, independence, and increased socialization away from the family, which may require revision based on cultural and social attributes.

Summary

SAD is highly prevalent among adolescents and causes significant social impairment. Research has consistently demonstrated that youth with SAD have deficits in their interpersonal relationships and are at great risk for victimization. These lead to negative social encounters that contribute to increased social anxiety and subsequent social avoidance, reducing opportunities to develop the social skills needed to overcome fears and improve relationships. Interventions focused on addressing social skills are imperative in the treatment of SAD. SASS is a group, school-based intervention focused on social skills training and behavioral exposures. It has been shown to be effective when implemented in schools by school counselors supporting broader school adoption. Future research should explore the use of technology to deliver SASS, as well as to train school counselors. Other promising areas involve extending SASS across service delivery levels of the MTSS framework in schools and addressing the unmet mental health needs of culturally, racially, and economically diverse populations.

References

Alfano, C. A., Beidel, D. C., & Turner, S. M. (2006). Cognitive correlates of social phobia among children and adolescents. *Journal of Abnormal Child Psychology*, *34*(2), 182–194.

American Psychiatric Association. (2013). *Diagnostic and statistical manual of mental disorders* (5th ed.). Arlington, VA: American Psychiatric Publishing.

Beidas, R. S., Suarez, L., Simpson, D., Read, K., Wei, C., Connolly, S., & Kendall, P. (2012). Contextual factors and anxiety in minority and European American youth presenting for treatment across two urban university clinics. *Assessment and Treatment of Anxiety Disorders in Ethnic Minority Adults and Children*, *26*(4), 544–554. https://doi.org/10.1016/j.janxdis.2012.02.008.

Beidel, D. C., Turner, S. M., & Morris, T. L. (1999). Psychopathology of childhood social phobia. *Journal of the American Academy of Child and Adolescent Psychiatry*, *38*(6), 643–650. https://doi.org/10.1097/00004583-199906000-00010.

Beidel, D. C., Turner, S. M., Young, B. J., Ammerman, R. T., Sallee, F. R., & Crosby, L. (2007). Psychopathology of adolescent social phobia. *Journal of Psychopathology and Behavioral Assessment*, *29*(1), 46–53.

Birmaher, B., Brent, D. A., Chiappetta, L., Bridge, J., Monga, S., & Baugher, M. (1999). Psychometric properties of the screen for child anxiety related emotional disorders (SCARED): A replication study. *Journal of the American Academy of Child and Adolescent Psychiatry*, *38*(10), 1230–1236.

Blöte, A. W., Miers, A. C., & Westenberg, P. M. (2015). The role of social performance and physical attractiveness in peer rejection of socially anxious adolescents. *Journal of Research on Adolescence*, *25*(1), 189–200. https://doi.org/10.1111/jora.12107.

Burns, B. J., Costello, E. J., Angold, A., Tweed, D., Stangl, D., Farmer, E. M. Z., & Erkanli, A. (1995). Children's mental health service use across service sectors. *Health Affairs*, *14*(3), 147–159. https://doi.org/10.1377/hlthaff.14.3.147.

Chavous, T. M., Bernat, D. H., Schmeelk-Cone, K., Caldwell, C. H., Kohn-Wood, L., & Zimmerman, M. A. (2003). Racial identity and academic attainment among African American adolescents. *Child Development*, *74*(4), 1076–1090.

Coelho, V. A., & Romão, A. M. (2018). The relation between social anxiety, social withdrawal and (cyber)bullying roles: A multilevel analysis. *Computers in Human Behavior*, *86*, 218–226. https://doi.org/10.1016/j.chb.2018.04.048.

Cohen, J. S., & Kendall, P. C. (2015). Peer victimization among children and adolescents with anxiety disorders. *Child Psychiatry and Human Development*, *46*, 393. https://doi.org/10.1007/s10578-014-0479-x.

Cook, C. R., Frye, M., Slemrod, T., Lyon, A. R., Renshaw, T. L., & Zhang, Y. (2015). An integrated approach to universal prevention: Independent and combined effects of PBIS and SEL on youths' mental health. *School Psychology Quarterly*, *30*(2), 166.

Coyle, S., & Malecki, C. M. (2018). The association between social anxiety and perceived frequency and value of classmate and close friend social support. *School Psychology Review*, *47*(3), 209–225. https://doi.org/10.17105/SPR-2017-0067.V47-3.

Coyle, S., Malecki, C. M., & Emmons, J. (2019). Keep your friends close: Exploring the associations of bullying, peer social support, and social anxiety. *Contemporary School Psychology*, 1–13.

Cummings, J. R., Ponce, N. A., & Mays, V. M. (2010). Comparing racial/ethnic differences in mental health service use among high-need subpopulations across clinical and school-based setting. *Journal of Adolescent Health*, *46*, 603–606.

Erath, S. A., Flanagan, K. S., & Bierman, K. L. (2007). Social anxiety and peer relations in early adolescence: Behavioral and cognitive factors. *Journal of Abnormal Child Psychology*, *35*, 405–416. https://doi.org/10.1007/s10801-007-9099-2.

Fox, J. K., Masia Warner, C., & Drew, M. (2018). School-based intervention for adolescents with impairing social anxiety. In A. Leschied, D. Saklosfske, & G. Flett (Eds.), *Handbook of school-based mental health promotion*. (pp. 411–427). https://doi.org/10.1007/978-3-319-89842-1_21.

Ginsburg, G. S., Kendall, P. C., Sakolsky, D., Compton, S. N., Piacentini, J., Albano, A. M., … March, J. (2011). Remission after acute treatment in children and adolescents with anxiety disorders: Findings from the CAMS. *Journal of Consulting and Clinical Psychology*, *79*, 806–813.

Graham, J. R., West, L. M., Martinez, J., & Roemer, L. (2016). The mediating role of internalized racism in the relationship between racist experiences and anxiety symptoms in a Black American sample. *Cultural Diversity and Ethnic Minority Psychology*, *22*(3), 369–376.

Greco, L. A., & Morris, T. L. (2005). Factors influencing the link between social anxiety and peer acceptance: Contributions of social skills and close friendships during middle childhood. *Behavior Therapy*, *36*(2), 197–205. https://doi.org/10.1016/S0005-7894(05)80068-1.

Gudiño, O. G., Lau, A. S., Yeh, M., McCabe, K. M., & Hough, R. L. (2009). Understanding racial/ethnic disparities in youth mental health services: Do disparities vary by problem type? *Journal of Emotional and Behavioral Disorders*, *17*(1), 3–16.

Hartup, W. W., & Stevens, N. (1999). Friendships and adaptation across the lifespan. *Current Directions in Psychological Science*, *8*(3), 76–79.

Inderbitzen-Nolan, H. M., Anderson, E. R., & Johnson, H. S. (2007). Subjective versus objective behavioral ratings following two analogue tasks: A comparison of socially phobic and non-anxious adolescents. *Journal of Anxiety Disorders*, *21*(1), 76–90. https://doi.org/10.1016/j.janxdis.2006.03.013.

Jaycox, L. H., Cohen, J. A., Mannarino, A. P., Walker, D. W., Langley, A. K., Gegenheimer, K. L., … Schonlau, M. (2010). Children's mental health care following Hurricane Katrina: A field trial of trauma-focused psychotherapies. *Journal of Traumatic Stress*, *23*(2), 223–231.

Kendall, P. C., Settipani, C. A., & Cummings, C. M. (2012). No need to worry: The promising future of child anxiety research. *Journal of Clinical Child and Adolescent Psychology, 41*, 103–115.

Kessler, R. C., Berglund, P., Demler, O., Jin, R., Merikangas, K. R., & Walters, E. E. (2005). Lifetime prevalence and age-of-onset distributions of DSM-IV disorders in the national comorbidity survey replication. *Archives of General Psychiatry, 62*(6), 593. https://doi.org/10.1001/archpsyc.62.6.593.

Kilgus, S. P., Reinke, W. M., & Jimerson, S. R. (2015). Understanding mental health intervention and assessment within a multi-tiered framework: Contemporary science, practice, and policy. *School Psychology Quarterly, 30*(2), 159–165. https://doi.org/10.1037/spq0000118.

Kowalski, R. M., Giumetti, G. W., Schroeder, A. N., & Lattanner, M. R. (2014). Bullying in the digital age: A critical review and meta-analysis of cyberbullying research among youth. *Psychological Bulletin, 140*(4), 1073–1137. https://doi.org/10.1037/a0035618.

La Greca, A. M., & Harrison, H. M. (2005). Adolescent peer relations, friendships, and romantic relationships: Do they predict social anxiety and depression? *Journal of Clinical Child and Adolescent Psychology, 34*, 49–61. https://doi.org/10.1207/s15374424jccp3401_5.

Masia, C. L., Klein, R. G., Storch, E. A., & Corda, B. (2001). School-based behavioral treatment for social anxiety disorder in adolescents: Results of a pilot study. *Journal of the American Academy of Child & Adolescent Psychiatry, 40*(7), 780–786.

Masia Warner, C., Brice, C., Esseling, P. G., Stewart, C. E., Mufson, L., & Herzig, K. (2013). Consultants' perceptions of school counselors' ability to implement an empirically-based intervention for adolescent social anxiety disorder. *Administration and Policy in Mental Health and Mental Health Services Research, 40*(6), 541–554.

Masia Warner, C., Colognori, D., Brice, C., Herzig, K., Mufson, L., Lynch, C., … Klein, R. G. (2016). Can school counselors deliver cognitive behavioral treatment for social anxiety effectively? A randomized controlled trial. *Journal of Child Psychology and Psychiatry, 57*(11), 1229–1238.

Masia Warner, C., Colognori, D., Kim, R. E., Reigada, L. C., Klein, R. G., Browner-Elhanan, K. J., … Benkov, K. (2011). Cognitive-behavioral treatment of persistent functional somatic complaints and pediatric anxiety: An initial controlled trial. *Depression and Anxiety, 28*(7), 551–559. https://doi.org/10.1002/da.20821.

Masia Warner, C., Colognori, D., & Lynch, C. (2018). *Helping students overcome social anxiety: Skills for academic and social success (SASS)*. New York: Guilford Publications.

Masia Warner, C., Fisher, P. H., Shrout, P. E., Rathor, S., & Klein, R. G. (2007). Treating adolescents with social anxiety disorder in school: An attention control trial. *Journal of Child Psychology and Psychiatry, 48*(7), 676–686.

Masia Warner, C., Klein, R. G., Dent, H. C., Fisher, P. H., Alvir, J., Albano, A. M., & Guardino, M. (2005). School-based intervention for adolescents with social anxiety disorder: Results of a controlled study. *Journal of Abnormal Child Psychology, 33*(6), 707–722.

Merikangas, K. R., He, J., Burstein, M., Swanson, S. A., Avenevoli, S., Cui, L., … Swendsen, J. (2010). Lifetime prevalence of mental disorders in U.S. adolescents: Results from the National Comorbidity Survey replication-adolescent supplement (NCS-A). *Journal of the American Academy of Child & Adolescent Psychiatry, 49*(10), 980–989. https://doi.org/10.1016/j.jaac.2010.05.017.

Miers, A. C., Blöte, A. W., de Rooij, M., Bokhorst, C. L., & Westenberg, P. M. (2013). Trajectories of social anxiety during adolescence and relations with cognition, social competence, and temperament. *Journal of Abnormal Child Psychology, 41*(1), 97–110. https://doi.org/10.1007/s10802-012-9651-6.

Miers, A. C., Blöte, A. W., & Westenberg, P. M. (2010). Peer perceptions of social skills in socially anxious and nonanxious adolescents. *Journal of Abnormal Child Psychology, 38*(1), 33–41. https://doi.org/10.1007/s10802-009-9345-x.

Navarro, R., Yubero, S., Larranaga, E., & Martinez, V. (2011). Children's cyberbullying victimization: Associations with social anxiety and social competence in a Spanish sample. *Child Indicators Research, 5*(2), 281–295.

Pabian, S., & Vandebosch, H. (2016). An investigation of short-term longitudinal associations between social anxiety and victimization and perpetration of traditional bullying and cyberbullying. *Journal of Youth and Adolescence, 45*(2), 328–339. https://doi.org/10.1007/s10964-015-0259-3.

Ranta, K., Kaltiala-Heino, R., Fröjd, S., & Marttunen, M. (2013). Peer victimization and social phobia: A follow-up study among adolescents. *Social Psychiatry and Psychiatric Epidemiology, 48*(4), 533–544. https://doi.org/10.1007/s00127-012-0583-9.

Rapee, R. M., Wignall, A., Spence, S. H., Cobham, V., & Lyneham, H. (2008). *Helping your anxious child: A step-by-step guide for parents*. Oakland, CA: New Harbinger Publications, Inc.

Rueger, Y. S., Malecki, C. K., Pyun, Y., Ayock, C., & Coyle, S. (2016). A meta-analytic review of the association between perceived social support and depression in childhood and adolescence. *Psychological Bulletin, 142*, 1017–1067.

Schneider, B. H. (2009). An observational study of the interactions of socially withdrawn/anxious early adolescents and their friends. *Journal of Child Psychology and Psychiatry, 50*(7), 799–806. https://doi.org/10.1111/j.1469-7610.2008.02056.x.

Schneider, B. W., & Turk, C. L. (2014). Examining the controversy surrounding social skills in social anxiety disorder: The state of the literature. In J. W. Weeks (Ed.), *The Wiley Blackwell handbook of social anxiety disorder* (pp. 366–391). Chichester, UK: John Wiley & Sons, Ltd.

Siegel, R. S., La Greca, A. M., & Harrison, H. M. (2009). Peer victimization and social anxiety in adolescents: Prospective and reciprocal relationships. *Journal of Youth and Adolescence, 38*, 1096–1109. https://doi.org/10.1007/s10964-009-9392-1.

Singh, P., & Bussey, K. (2011). Peer victimization and psychological maladjustment: The mediating role of coping self-efficacy. *Journal of Research on Adolescence, 21*(2), 420–433.

Smalls, C., White, R., Chavous, T., & Sellers, R. (2007). Racial ideological beliefs and racial discrimination experiences as predictors of academic engagement among African American adolescents. *Journal of Black Psychology, 33*(3), 299–330. https://doi.org/10.1177/0095798407302541.

Spence, S. H., Donovan, C., & Brechman-Toussaint, M. (1999). Social skills, social outcomes, and cognitive features of childhood social phobia. *Journal of Abnormal Psychology, 108*(2), 211–221. https://doi.org/10.1037/0021-843X.108.2.211.

Spence, S. H., & Rapee, R. M. (2016). The etiology of social anxiety disorder: An evidence-based model. *Behaviour Research and Therapy, 86*, 50–67. https://doi.org/10.1016/j.brat.2016.06.007.

Strein, W., Hoagwood, K., & Cohn, A. (2003). School psychology: A public health perspective. I. Prevention, populations, and systems change. *Journal of School Psychology, 41*(1), 23–38.

Sweeney, C., Warner, C. M., Brice, C., Stewart, C., Ryan, J., Loeb, K. L., & McGrath, R. E. (2015). Identification of social anxiety in schools: The utility of a two-step screening process. *Contemporary School Psychology, 19*(4), 268–275.

Tillfors, M., Andersson, G., Ekselius, L., Furmark, T., Lewenhaupt, S., Karlsson, A., & Carlbring, P. (2011). A randomized trial of internet-delivered treatment for social anxiety disorder in high school students. *Cognitive Behaviour Therapy, 40*(2), 147–157.

Tillfors, M., Persson, S., Willen, M., & Burk, W. J. (2012). Prospective links between social anxiety and adolescent peer relations. *Journal of Adolescence, 35*(5), 1255–1263.

Trompeter, N., Bussey, K., & Fitzpatrick, S. (2018). Cyber victimization and internalizing difficulties: The mediating roles of coping self-efficacy and emotion dysregulation. *Journal of Abnormal Child Psychology*, *46*(5), 1129–1139.

Van Zalk, N., Van Zalk, M., Kerr, M., & Stattin, H. (2011). Social anxiety as a basis for friendship selection and socialization in adolescents' social networks. *Journal of Personality*, *79*(3), 499–526.

Verduin, T. L., & Kendall, P. C. (2008). Peer perceptions and liking of children with anxiety disorders. *Journal of Abnormal Child Psychology*, *36*(4), 459–469. https://doi.org/10.1007/s10802-007-9192-6.

Vernberg, E. M., Abwender, D. A., Ewell, K. K., & Beery, S. H. (1992). Social anxiety and peer relationships in early adolescence: A prospective analysis. *Journal of Clinical Child Psychology*, *21*(2), 189–196.

Waite, P., & Creswell, C. (2014). Children and adolescents referred for treatment of anxiety disorders: Differences in clinical characteristics. *Journal of Affective Disorders*, *167*, 326–332. https://doi.org/10.1016/j.jad.2014.06.028.

Wong Sarver, N., Beidel, D. C., & Spitalnick, J. S. (2014). The feasibility and acceptability of virtual environments in the treatment of childhood social anxiety disorder. *Journal of Clinical Child & Adolescent Psychology*, *43*(1), 63–73.

Wuthrich, V. M., Rapee, R. M., Cunningham, M. J., Lyneham, H. J., Hudson, J. L., & Schniering, C. A. (2012). A randomized controlled trial of the Cool Teens CD-ROM computerized program for adolescent anxiety. *Journal of the American Academy of Child & Adolescent Psychiatry*, *51*(3), 261–270. https://doi.org/10.1016/j.jaac.2011.12.002.

Zins, J. E., & Elias, M. J. (2007). Social and emotional learning: Promoting the development of all students. *Journal of Educational and Psychological Consultation*, *17*(2–3), 233–255.

Chapter 13

The Program for the Education and Enrichment of Relational Skills (PEERS)

Emily Moulton and Elizabeth Laugeson
University of California, Los Angeles Semel Institute for Neuroscience and Human Behavior, Los Angeles, CA, United States

Autism Spectrum Disorder (ASD) is a neurodevelopmental disorder characterized by deficits in social communication accompanied by restricted, repetitive behaviors and interests (RRBIs; American Psychiatric Association [APA], 2013). While both core symptom domains (social communication and RRBIs) are impactful, deficits in social communication and associated poor social functioning are often considered to be defining features of the disorder. ASD is a spectrum disorder affecting those with varying degrees of intellectual abilities, but challenges with social skills exist for individuals with ASD at all functioning levels, regardless of cognitive or language abilities (Carter, Davis, Klin, & Volkmar, 2005).

The Centers for Disease Control and Prevention reports an overall prevalence rate for ASD of one in 59 in the United States, with boys affected at greater rates than girls (4:1; Baio et al., 2018). This reflects an approximately 15% increase in ASD diagnoses over the past 2 years, which is thought to be due to a number of factors. These include the broadening of the diagnostic criteria, an enhanced ability to differentiate ASD from intellectual disabilities, and an increased detection of ASD in traditionally lower-resourced populations (Baio et al., 2018). Additionally, ASD is now identified at higher rates in girls than it had been previously. This is likely due to improved detection of ASD in girls; however, research indicates that we likely continue to underidentify ASD in girls, for whom symptoms may present differently, and/or may be camouflaged with certain strengths. In turn, symptoms of ASD may go unnoticed by caregivers, teachers, and clinicians (Ratto et al., 2018). Research indicates that specific social challenges may vary by gender, with boys more likely to be socially excluded and girls more likely be overlooked rather than explicitly rejected

Social Skills Across the Life Span. https://doi.org/10.1016/B978-0-12-817752-5.00013-5

(Dean et al., 2014). With increased detection of ASD in girls, social skills interventions need to adequately address the needs of individuals of all genders.

For individuals with ASD, fundamental atypicalities in social communication are apparent from very early in development. By around 18–24 months, infants later diagnosed with ASD display delays in language development, poor eye contact, lack of joint attention (e.g., a lack of pointing to show), lack of response to name, and fewer overall communicative bids (Franchini et al., 2019; Mitchell, Brian, Roberts, & Bryson, 2006; Wetherby, Watt, Morgan, & Shumway, 2007; Zwaigenbaum et al., 2015). Preschool-age children with ASD often display atypicalities in play behaviors, including a lack of pretend play and a lack of reciprocal play with peers (Sigman, Dijamco, Gratier, & Rozga, 2004; Toth, Munson, Meltzoff, & Dawson, 2006). Weaknesses in core social skills, including poor recognition of critical social cues, often become increasingly apparent during the elementary school years (Bernier, Webb, & Dawson, 2006). Interfering behaviors such as restricted interests, repetitive behaviors, sensory sensitivities, and general rigidities may further negatively impact social relationships. Moreover, poor social functioning generally persists throughout the lifespan, often worsening as demands on social relationships increase during the late childhood, adolescent, and adult years (Reichow & Volkmar, 2010).

Although individuals with ASD often have a desire for social relationships and report having some friendships, the quality of their relationships is often poor. This includes lower ratings of companionship, security, and helpfulness (Bauminger & Kasari, 2000), as well as fewer mutual friendships (Dean et al., 2014). Well-documented consequences of poor social skills include peer rejection and/or victimization, poor social support, a lack of satisfying friendships, experiences of loneliness and isolation, academic and occupational difficulties, and the development of anxiety and mood disturbances (Bauminger & Kasari, 2000; Chamberlain, Kasari, & Rotheram-Fuller, 2007; Humphrey & Symes, 2010; Ratcliffe, Wong, Dossetor, & Hayes, 2015). To compound these difficulties, in addition to contending with the universal adolescent challenge of identity development, adolescents with ASD often have an emerging awareness of their social deficits, which one might argue makes this a particularly critical period for social skills intervention (Laugeson, 2013).

Social skills training needs for adolescents with Autism Spectrum Disorders

To improve the social relationships of adolescents with ASD, it is critical to recognize how specific social communication weaknesses may negatively interfere with making and keeping friends during this developmental period. Whereas preschool and elementary school-age children typically engage with their peers and develop friendships through play interactions, adolescent friendships are more often based in conversational exchange (Laugeson, Frankel, Mogil, & Dillon, 2009). Engagement in reciprocal conversations involves many skills, which socially adept individuals often employ without conscious thought. Critical communication skills include generating appropriate conversational topics, maintaining conversations, engaging in balanced, reciprocal turn taking, using appropriate tone and volume control, maintaining good body boundaries/physical spacing, utilizing appropriate and informative nonverbal behaviors when speaking (e.g., gestures, eye contact), as well as recognizing and understanding the nonverbal communicative behaviors of others (Laugeson & Frankel, 2010). Even verbally fluent individuals with ASD often have substantial difficulties engaging appropriately in reciprocal conversations, including challenges with many of the aforementioned component skills. In particular, individuals with ASD have a tendency to have one-sided conversations in which they may perseverate on personal interests, and have difficulty flexibly changing the conversational topic away from their personal interests (Elder, Caterino, Chao, Shacknai, & De Simone, 2006). Further, fundamental challenges with theory of mind have been linked to challenges recognizing important verbal and nonverbal cues in conversations, such as when a conversational partner is disinterested or even confused (Peterson, Garnett, Kelly, & Attwood, 2009). Difficulties with perspective taking and the use and understanding of nonverbal cues, such as facial expressions and body posturing, can also lead to confusion and misunderstandings in conversations (Peterson et al., 2009).

Global perspective-taking challenges, in combination with specific difficulties understanding nonliteral language and social tone (e.g., irony, sarcasm, deception, and metaphors), may also lead to challenges recognizing and understanding humor (Martin & McDonald, 2004; Persicke, Tarbox, Ranick, & St. Clair, 2013). For example, individuals with ASD may fail to recognize sarcasm, and therefore, may interpret a sarcastic statement incorrectly and concretely (e.g., misinterpreting "You're *so* funny" stated sarcastically to mean that their conversation partner believes that they are, in fact, funny). Despite frequent misunderstandings, many individuals with ASD enjoy and use humor, although they may not consistently use humor that is appropriate to context or to the age of their conversational partners (Van Bourgondien & Mesibov, 1987).

Difficulties with social communication are not limited to receptive language; they also often include expressive language. For example, poor speech prosody is common in ASD, with atypicalities in the rate, rhythm, and intonation of speech, which is often described as sounding robotic, flat, and monotone. Further, individuals with ASD may also demonstrate difficulty assessing the meaning of different speech characteristics used by others, including emotional intonations (Sharda et al., 2010).

These deficits in perspective taking, social-emotional reciprocity, and conversational skills can impede friendships in numerous ways. Challenges with reciprocal turn taking in conversations may result in individuals with ASD failing to trade information with conversational partners, not learning much about the other person, and, in turn, failing to identify common interests. This point is critical, as the first step in establishing whether someone may be a good prospective friend is to determine if there are shared interests and ideas (Laugeson et al., 2009). Further, atypicalities in communication of affect and/or humor may lead to confusion and potential conflict, which individuals with ASD are known to have difficulty navigating (Channon, Charman, Heap, Crawford, & Rios, 2001). Given a propensity for concrete, black-and-white thinking, individuals with ASD may tend to end friendships when conflicts or miscommunications arise rather than trying to maintain the relationship. While certain aspects of communication impairments may be addressed in speech-language therapy (e.g., speech prosody and volume, pragmatics), many areas of social communication can be better addressed through social skills training.

Existing social skills interventions

Given the pervasiveness of social deficits, it is not surprising that social skills interventions are becoming more prevalent, particularly for adolescents with ASD. Group instruction, including three or more students, is a common format for social skills instruction; yet, research indicates that these group-based programs are not particularly effective in improving adolescent's social skills outcomes (Rao, Beidel, & Murray, 2008). A recent meta-analysis of 19 randomized-controlled trials (RCTs) of social skills interventions for males and females (5–20 years of age) with a modest range of cognitive abilities (means ranging from 87.55 to 112.45) revealed moderate effects overall depending on who was completing pre- and postintervention ratings (Gates, Kang, & Lerner, 2017). Specifically, youth self-reports reflected an increase in knowledge of social skills but not in use of these social skills in day-to-day life. Task-based measures indicated medium effect sizes, and parent- and observer-reports indicated small effects. Teacher-reports generally reflected nonsignificant change. While the exact reason for these findings is unknown, it is possible that they may be due in part to variability in social behaviors exhibited across settings, and/or to differences in expectancy effects across raters. Sample sizes across these studies were small and not sufficient to investigate moderator analyses. Gates and colleagues (2017) did conduct an exploratory investigation of moderators of self-report findings and found that participant-level moderators (age, gender, overall cognitive ability, verbal ability, comorbidities, and medication) were not significant. Furthermore, intervention characteristics, including length of treatment (ranged from 5 to 97 sessions), and use of peer tutors, also did not significantly moderate effects.

In summary, while there has been an increase in the number of social skills interventions for youth with ASD and an increase in RCTs investigating their efficacy, there continues to be a need for thoroughly investigated, evidence-based social skills interventions that demonstrate positive impact on social competence across settings and raters.

The Program for the Education and Enrichment of Relational Skills (PEERS) for adolescents

The Program for the Education and Enrichment of Relational Skills (PEERS) is an evidence-based social skills program developed at the University of California, Los Angeles (UCLA). PEERS focuses on teaching the skills necessary for making and keeping friends and managing peer conflict and peer rejection for youth with ASD, including published manuals for adolescents (Laugeson, 2014; Laugeson & Frankel, 2010) and young adults (Laugeson, 2017). There is also a curriculum for early childhood (PEERS for Preschoolers) currently in development. The PEERS for Adolescents program is an evidence-based social skills intervention available in two formats, a 16-week, daily, school-based curriculum (Laugeson, 2014), and a 14-week, weekly, parent-assisted program (Laugeson & Frankel, 2010). At present, the program has been translated into over a dozen languages, is used internationally in over 70 countries, and is known to be efficacious for improving social skills and friendships through multiple rigorous clinical trials in the United States (e.g., Laugeson et al., 2009; Laugeson, Ellingsen, Sanderson, Tucci, & Bates, 2014; Laugeson, Frankel, Gantman, Dillon, & Mogil, 2012; Laugeson, Gantman, Kapp, Orenski, & Ellingsen, 2015) and outside of the United States (e.g., Shum et al., 2019; Yoo et al., 2014). Moreover, PEERS is one of only five existing manualized evidence-based programs for improving social functioning of children and adolescents with ASD (Hall, Leinert, & Jacquez, 2018).

Target population

The PEERS for Adolescents school-based program has been found to be effective for teens in middle and high school with ASD (Laugeson et al., 2014). The parent-assisted program has not only been validated for use with socially motivated teens with ASD (Chang et al., 2013; Laugeson et al., 2009, 2012; Mandelberg et al., 2014; Van Hecke et al., 2013) and also for adolescents with attention-deficit/hyperactivity-disorder (ADHD; Gardner, Gerdes, & Weinberger, 2015) and those with ASD and comorbid ADHD (Laugeson et al., 2012), social anxiety (Laugeson et al., 2012; McVey et al., 2016; Schohl et al., 2013), depression (Laugeson et al., 2012), and intellectual disabilities (Chang et al., 2013).

Adolescents are considered an appropriate fit for the program if they have identified difficulties making and keeping friends and/or handling conflict and rejection, and are intrinsically motivated to learn the skills needed to address these social challenges. Teens must be fully briefed on the contents, duration, and format of the program so that they can determine their own interest. During the intake process, a teen's motivation for program participation should be assessed, including their openness to attend 16 weekly group-based social skills training sessions, willingness to have a parent participate in concurrent social coaching sessions when relevant in order to help reinforce and generalize skills outside of the treatment setting, and readiness to complete weekly homework assignments to practice newly learned skills in natural social settings. Families are only included in the parent-mediated PEERS intervention if an identified caregiver whom the teen is comfortable having as a social coach is willing and able to participate in treatment. Adequate motivation to make friends and an openness to complete homework assignments and receive social coaching are thought to be essential components for success in treatment.

If teens are not intrinsically motivated to utilize the skills taught in PEERS, they may be resistant to completing homework assignments and to receiving social coaching. Further, a teen's lack of motivation may create a negative contagion in the group or create an unsafe environment in which motivated teens feel uncomfortable. Perhaps most important of all, teaching social skills to unwilling adolescents is not only unlikely to be effective, but it arguably may be unethical. To highlight this point in an atmosphere of neurodiversity, some individuals with ASD do not wish to learn the social rules used by neurotypical individuals. Forcing social skills on this group could be considered unethical. On the other hand, many adolescents with ASD desperately want to understand the rules and steps of social etiquette utilized by typically developing youth. In order to respect the individual wishes of this diverse group of individuals, it is critical to confirm intrinsic motivation and treatment motivation prior to initiating social skills treatment in PEERS.

Group composition and fit among the teens in the group are also important considerations prior to initiating treatment. According to White (2011), in order to increase group cohesion and to aid learning, it is important to limit the heterogeneity of functioning levels within the group as much as possible. Therefore, group composition is often determined by diagnosis and level of functioning, rather than just by age and gender alone. In particular, including youth with intellectual disabilities and/or language delays with youth without such delays may be problematic. For those with cognitive or language delays, the program may be perceived as too difficult to follow at the rate and speed typically delivered. For those without such delays, slowing down the intervention and simplifying the lessons (as is typically done for youth with intellectual disabilities and other cognitive delays) may be seen as too easy. It is therefore critical to consider level of functioning when determining group composition.

Ecologically valid social skills

The PEERS for Adolescents program includes a wide range of content areas related to friendship development and maintenance, and managing conflict and rejection, all of which seek to address the core deficits more commonly experienced by teens with ASD and other neurodevelopmental disorders. Rules and steps of social etiquette include *ecologically valid* social skills, which refers to behaviors that are exhibited by socially accepted same-aged individuals, rather than simply the social skills that are deemed appropriate by clinicians, teachers, and parents (Laugeson & Frankel, 2010). For example, adults may instruct children and teens to meet new peers by "just going up and saying 'hi' or introducing themselves." In reality, however, these strategies would likely be perceived as odd by socially accepted peers and may lead to rejection. A more ecologically valid strategy involves casually watching and listening from a distance while remaining engaged in another activity (e.g., looking at your phone), identifying a potential common interest (e.g., peer is wearing a t-shirt with your favorite band), approaching the peer, and mentioning the common interest (e.g., "Nice t-shirt. Have you heard their new album yet?"). If the interaction goes well, socially accepted teens then introduce themselves at the end of the conversation, rather than at the beginning (e.g., "By the way, my name is Melissa"). This is one of numerous examples that illustrate the importance of teaching ecologically valid skills if the goal is to improve social functioning within the dominant peer group. Each content area in the PEERS for Adolescents program includes ecologically valid skills, and rules discouraging common social errors often committed by those with ASD. Table 1 includes descriptions of each content area taught in the 16-session PEERS for Adolescents curriculum, including key PEERS rules and steps.

Effective methods of instruction and application in PEERS

Existing research indicates that there are numerous important components of effective cognitive behavioral treatment, which are likely critical to include in social skills interventions (Laugeson & Park, 2014). First, as described earlier, the content of the intervention must be ecologically valid, rather than simply the social skills adults believe teens should use. Second, in order to increase standardization of the intervention and enhance results, it is critical that evidence-based treatment manuals are utilized. At present, only a few evidence-based, publicly available treatment manuals exist (Frankel & Myatt, 2003; Laugeson, 2014, 2017; Laugeson & Frankel, 2010). Finally, effective interventions should utilize empirically supported methods of instruction, including the following.

Didactic instruction

Structured lesson plans with didactic instruction should be utilized. While more open, process-oriented frameworks are more common in group-based social skills treatment (e.g., "Tell the group how your week went"), the effects of process-oriented social skills groups are less known. However, the use of structured lesson plans with step-by-step rules has been shown to be effective in social skills training (White et al., 2010) and is likely a better fit for the information processing style of individuals with ASD (e.g., concrete, literal, rule driven). Because individuals with ASD tend to process information in a concrete and literal manner, and often are more comfortable with rules and structure than ambiguity, presenting rules and steps of social etiquette is a natural method for

TABLE 1 Overview of the 16-session PEERS® for adolescents curriculum

Session number	Didactic lesson	Key skills and information taught
1	Introduction and trading information	*Rules include asking the other person questions, answering your own question, finding common interests, sharing the conversation, don't be a conversation hog, don't be an interviewer, don't get too personal at first, and assess interest.*
2	Two-way conversations	*Rules include asking open-ended questions, asking follow-up questions, don't be repetitive, listen to your friend, don't police, don't tease, and use good volume control, body boundaries, and eye contact.*
3	Electronic communication	*Appropriate steps for exchanging contact information, steps for starting and ending phone calls, and leaving voicemails. General rules for electronic communication, and strategies for staying safe online.*
4	Choosing appropriate friends	*Identifying good qualities of friends, good sources of friends (based on common interests), and identifying signs of peers acceptance and rejection.*
5	Appropriate use of humor	*Rules include being a little more serious at first, identifying the right (and wrong) time for jokes, avoiding insult jokes and dirty jokes, avoiding repeating jokes with people who have heard them, paying attention to your humor feedback, and identifying important humor feedback cues.*
6	Starting and joining conversations	*Steps for starting individual conversations and steps for joining group conversations.*
7	Exiting conversations	*Steps for exiting conversations under different circumstances (including if you are not accepted, if you are initially accepted and then excluded, or if you are full accepted).*
8	Good sportsmanship	*Rules include praising your friend, sharing and taking turns, playing by the rules, helping and showing concern if someone is hurt, suggesting a change if you become bored, don't cheat, don't "referee" or "coach" friends, don't be overly competitive, and don't be a bad winner or a sore loser.*
9	Get-togethers	*Identify common get-together activities (based on common interests), steps for planning get-togethers, steps for starting and ending get-togethers when they are hosting, rules to follow during get-togethers (e.g., allowing guests to pick activities, not ignoring your friends, trading information at least 50% of the time, etc.).*

TABLE 1 Overview of the 16-session PEERS® for adolescents curriculum—cont'd

Session number	Didactic lesson	Key skills and information taught
10	Handling arguments	*Steps include keeping your cool, listening to the other person, repeating what the other person said so that they feel understood, explaining your side using "I statements," saying you are sorry, and trying to solve the problem.*
11	Changing reputations	*Steps include laying low, following the crowd (i.e., using the PEERS® skills and not performing the behavior that led to your the bad reputation), changing your look as a physical sign that you have changed, owning up to your previous reputation if asked about it, and finding a new, accepting social group.*
12	Handling teasing and embarrassing feedback	*Steps include acting as though what they said did not bother you, using effective verbal teasing comebacks from an established list (e.g., "whatever," "yeah, and?," "am I supposed to care?," "anyway…"), using nonverbal comebacks (e.g., eye roll, shoulder shrug), and removing yourself after using a few comebacks. Rules include not teasing back, not telling an adult right away, and not using teasing comebacks with people in authority positions or physically aggressive people.*
13	Handling physical bullying	*Rules include avoiding the bully if possible (e.g., through using strategies such as planning your route), laying low when the bully is round, not teasing, provoking, or policing the bully, hanging out with peers, or staying near an adult, when the bully is around, and getting help from an adult if your feel threatened or in danger.*
14	Handling cyber bullying	*Rules include not "feeding the trolls" (i.e., do not respond to negative comments), having friends stick up for you online, laying low online for a while, using privacy settings, blocking the cyber bully, saving the evidence in case you need to report the cyber bullying, and getting help from adults if needed.*
15	Minimizing rumors and gossip	*Rules include not trying to disprove the rumor, do not appear upset, do not confront the person spreading the gossip, avoid the rumor-spreader (i.e., appear neutral), and acting amazed anyone believes or cares about the gossip. Steps for spreading the rumor about yourself (to decrease the importance and believability of the rumor) include finding a supportive friend and an audience, acknowledging that the rumor exists, acting amazed anyone would believe or care about the rumor, and repeating the above steps several times.*
16	Graduation	*Graduation celebration, final review for social coaches, and discussion of where to go from here.*

teaching to their cognitive style. When complex social behaviors (e.g., starting conversations with unfamiliar peers) are broken down into concrete steps, they become more manageable for individuals with ASD, ADHD, and those with executive functioning deficits. Further, didactic instruction should avoid use of metaphors or overly figurative language, as this kind of language is often more difficult for individuals on the spectrum to understand (Martin & McDonald, 2004). In order to increase the adolescents' engagement, a Socratic method of teaching should be employed during didactic lessons, rather than lecturing. Socratic teaching is commonly utilized in cognitive-behavioral therapy, and has been shown to increase understanding and encoding of new information, as well as critical thinking (Zare & Mukundan, 2015). Additionally, it has been found to be useful in reducing confrontation or resistance from teens (Overholser, 1993).

Behavioral modeling and behavioral rehearsal

Given findings that social skills interventions often increase knowledge of skills without an improvement in day-to-day social behavior, an emphasis on role-play demonstrations and behavioral modeling must be included in effective social skills instruction. This makes the new rules more understandable and concrete (Cappadocia & Weiss, 2011; Moree & Thompson, 2010), and allows participants to see and hear the important verbal and nonverbal components of rules (e.g., what to say, how to say it, body language, gestures). Following behavioral modeling and role-playing demonstrations, in order to learn how to apply the skill, participants benefit from practicing the new skills themselves (i.e., behavioral rehearsal or participant modeling). It is critical that this initial practice occur within a safe environment, such as within a group treatment setting, and/or with parents/caregivers, rather than immediately with potential friends. This allows the teen to receive behavioral coaching and performance feedback, which will help them to trouble-shoot and correct any areas of difficulty before trying the skill in the "real world." Performance feedback is most effective for adolescents with ASD if feedback is direct, concrete, specific, and given immediately (Anderson & Morris, 2006; White et al., 2010).

Homework assignments and parent involvement

If practice of novel social skills only occurs during group treatment sessions, it is unlikely that skills will be effectively generalized to new social contexts (e.g., school, get-togethers, extra-curricular activities, home). Therefore, practice in between sessions and across multiple contexts (i.e., via homework assignments) is critical. Parents and caregivers can facilitate even greater individualization of the program to their child and can help support completion of between-session homework assignments. Involvement of parents and caregivers has been shown to increase treatment gains in interventions for children (Frankel & Myatt, 2003), adolescents, and adults (Laugeson, 2017; Laugeson & Frankel, 2010).

Application in PEERS

Critical components of effective group-based social skills interventions are incorporated into the PEERS program, including small group format (8–12 teens), didactic instruction using concrete rules and steps of ecologically valid social skills (see Table 1), a Socratic method of teaching, role-playing/modeling of newly learned skills, behavioral rehearsal exercises, parent assistance and social coaching with performance feedback, and in vivo homework assignments and homework review.

Within the PEERS program, role-play demonstrations include modeling of skills live by program staff/social coaches or via watching videos (i.e., video modeling). Skills are modeled both inappropriately and appropriately, to help participants recognize common social errors and how to correct them. Role-play demonstrations always incorporate perspective-taking questions about the thoughts and experiences of the individuals in the social interaction (e.g., "What was that like for Dan?" "What would Dan think of Melissa?" "Would Dan want to talk to Melissa again?"). This allows teens to identify which cues to attend to during social exchanges and how to understand and interpret positive and negative cues (Koning, Magill-Evans, Volden, & Dick, 2013).

To reinforce good behavior during treatment sessions, a token economy is utilized, whereby teens are reinforced for completing homework assignments, participating in the group didactic lesson, and in behavior rehearsal exercises through a "point" system. Teens earn points collectively to earn a "bigger and better" graduation party, which occurs during the final session of the group. Teen's individual point earnings determine the order in which they select graduation prizes during the final session. Teens *do not lose points*; points are solely utilized as a positive reward for participation.

Within the "social coaching" group, parents and caregivers are coached on strategies for using "teachable moments" in between lessons to provide social coaching with appropriate performance feedback. When giving feedback, social coaches are taught to give a "*praise sandwich*" by first providing specific positive praise for any correct use of the skills, or any attempts/approximations of the skills using the buzzwords of the program. This should then be followed by corrective feedback given as a calm and gentle reminder for any missed or misused social rules or steps utilizing the buzzwords. Corrective feedback is then followed by another brief praising comment. For example, if a teen successfully enters a group conversation by following the appropriate steps, but then begins to "hog" the conversation, a parent is encouraged to find a private moment soon after the conversation to state, "Great job joining the conversation by listening, waiting for a pause, and then mentioning the topic. Next time, let's be careful not to be a conversation hog, but great job!" These "social coaching" principles are based on basic reinforcement principles, as well as the cognitive style of individuals with ASD (Anderson & Morris, 2006; White et al., 2010).

In the 14-week, parent-assisted PEERS program (Laugeson & Frankel, 2010), teens and parents ("social coaches") attend weekly, 90-min concurrent but separate sessions. In brief, each session includes homework review, a didactic lesson, behavioral rehearsal for teens, and the assigning of new homework. Table 2 includes a description of the format, including time allotted to each component, for the teen and parent ("social coach") sessions.

Assessment of efficacy

The efficacy of the PEERS for Adolescents program has been carefully evaluated through multiple randomized clinical trials (RCTs), including comparing the intervention to a delayed treatment control (Laugeson et al., 2009, 2012) and to an active treatment control (Laugeson et al., 2014), in addition to numerous additional pre- and postintervention research designs, including examining biomarkers of treatment outcome (Van Hecke et al., 2013). The first two RCTs (Laugeson et al., 2009, 2012) evaluated the 14-week, parent-assisted PEERS for Adolescents program. Both studies included teens aged 12–17 years, with diagnoses of ASD and verbal cognitive abilities greater than 70 on the Kaufman Brief Intelligence Test—Second Edition (KBIT-2; Kaufman & Kaufman, 2005). For the treatment group (compared to the waitlist group) in both studies, there was a significant improvement in teen's knowledge of social skills taught during the intervention using the Test of Adolescent Social Skills Knowledge (TASSK; Laugeson & Frankel, 2010). Additionally, there was an increase in the quality of the teen's self-reported "best" friendship using the Friendship Qualities Scale (FQS; Bukowski, Hoza, & Boivin, 1994), and the frequency of get-togethers hosted by the teen using the Quality of Play Questionnaire (QPQ; Frankel & Mintz, 2011). Further, across both RCTs, there was an increase in parent-reported social skills on the Social Skills Rating Scale (SSRS; Gresham & Elliott, 1990). Within the second clinical trial (Laugeson et al., 2012), subdomain level analyses indicated that improvements were seen for the treatment group across the SSRS social skills subdomains of cooperation, assertion, and responsibility. Additionally, improvement was seen on the parent-reported Social Responsiveness Scale (SRS; Constantino, 2005), including both a decrease in the total score (reflecting social improvement), and a reduction in restricted, repetitive behaviors and interests.

Fourteen-week follow-up (Laugeson et al., 2012) and 1- to 5-year follow-up (Mandelberg et al., 2014) assessments were conducted to assess maintenance of treatment gains from the parent-assisted PEERS for Adolescents program over time. In both studies, treatment gains were maintained in teen knowledge of social skills on the TASSK, parent-reported SSRS Social Skills, parent-reported SRS total scores, and the number of monthly hosted get-togethers. New positive findings included significant reduction in parent-reported SSRS Problem Behaviors and teacher-reported SSRS Social Skills (14-week follow-up only).

TABLE 2 Teen and parent ("social coach") 90-min weekly session formats

Time allotted	Section	Brief description
Teen session format		
30 min	Homework review	*The prior week's assignments are reviewed. This allows for reinforcement of the importance of completing homework assignments, and repetition of instruction through review of the skills learned in the prior lessons.*
30 min	Didactic instruction	*Didactic instruction is provided about a targeted social skill using concrete rules and steps, role-play demonstrations with perspective taking questions, and a Socratic teaching method.*
20 min	Behavioral rehearsal	*Adolescents practice the newly learned skills and receive behavioral coaching and performance feedback from the treatment team.*
10 min	Reunification	*With social coaches and teens together, a brief review of the new skills is provided, homework is assigned for the coming week, and individual "check-outs" with members of the treatment team are conducted in order to establish a mutually agreed upon plan for homework completion.*
Parent ("social coach") session format		
50 min	Homework review	*It includes review of completed and uncompleted homework assignments from the prior week, discussion of problem-solving strategies to increase homework completion, discussion of ways for parents to help to expand their teen's social opportunities and social networks, and identification of "teachable moments" for social coaching.*
20 min	Didactic instruction	*Parents are taught the same didactic lessons as their teens to ensure that they are coaching utilizing ecologically valid social rules and steps of social etiquette.*
10 min	Reunification	*Same as in teen lesson above.*

A cluster randomized controlled trial was also conducted evaluating the school-based PEERS for Adolescents program (Laugeson et al., 2014) through comparing the PEERS curriculum to an active treatment control (Super Skills; Coucouvanis, 2005). Findings were similar to those for the parent-assisted program described earlier, with significantly greater gains for students in the PEERS condition (compared with "Super Skills") in the following domains: increase in teen's social skills knowledge on the TASSK, improvement in teacher-reported SRS total scores, and increase in hosted and invited get-togethers (on the QPQ). Additionally, parent ratings of teen social anxiety decreased on the Social Anxiety Scale for Adolescents (SAS-A; La Greca & López, 1998).

Numerous independent studies have been conducted exploring the efficacy of the PEERS for Adolescents program throughout the United States (Chang et al., 2013; Karst et al., 2014; Lordo et al., 2016; Mandelberg et al., 2014; Schohl et al., 2013), with positive findings across studies. Schohl and colleagues (2013) independently replicated the findings of prior studies, finding increases in teen's social skills knowledge, increases in positive social skills behaviors, increases in frequency of get-togethers, and decreases in social anxiety and problem behaviors. Research has additionally indicated that following the PEERS for Adolescents program, individuals have shown improvements in neuropsychological functioning, including decreased aggression, anxiety, and withdrawal; improvements in emotional responsiveness, adaptability, leadership, and daily living skills (Lordo et al., 2016), and improvements in family functioning overall, including reduced family chaos and increased parenting self-efficacy (Karst et al., 2014). Changes to neural functioning have also been found following the PEERS for Adolescents program (Van Hecke et al., 2013). Specifically, adolescents participating in the PEERS program shifted from right hemisphere EEG asymmetry before the program to left hemisphere EEG asymmetry after the program. These changes did not differ from typically developing peers and were associated with more social contacts, more social knowledge, and fewer symptoms of ASD (Van Hecke et al., 2013).

PEERS for Adolescents has also been studied internationally through implementation of carefully culturally and linguistically adapted versions of the program. Positive results supporting gains in social skills and increases in get-togethers have been found for a Canadian-adapted version (Marchica & D'Amico, 2016), a Korean-adapted version (Yoo et al., 2014), a Chinese (Hong-Kong) adapted version (Shum et al., 2019), a Dutch-adapted version (Jagersma, Idris, Jacobs, Van Pelt, & Greaves-Lord, 2018), and an Israel-adapted version (Rabin, Israel-Yaacov, Laugeson, Mor-Snir, & Golan, 2018) of PEERS for Adolescents.

In sum, PEERS for Adolescents addresses common social skills impairments in youth with ASD and incorporates effective instruction and application of new social skills. Research supports the efficacy of the PEERS for Adolescents program in improving social skills for teens with ASD across regions and cultures. The program addresses a critical need for teens on the spectrum through improving friendship, and, in turn, helping to foster positive overall mental health and well-being.

References

American Psychiatric Association (APA). (2013). *Diagnostic and statistical manual of mental disorders, fifth edition (DSM-5)*. Arlington, VA: American Psychiatric Publishing.

Anderson, S., & Morris, J. (2006). Cognitive behavior therapy for people with Asperger syndrome. *Behavioral and Cognitive Psychotherapy, 34*(3), 293–303.

Baio, J., Wiggins, L., Christensen, D. L., Maenner, M. J., Daniels, J., Warren, Z., … Dowling, N. F. (2018). Prevalence of autism spectrum disorder among children aged 8 years. Autism and Developmental Disabilities Monitoring Network, 11 sites, United States, 2014. *MMWR Surveillance Summary, 67*(SS-6), 1–23. https://doi.org/10.15585/mmwr.ss6706a1External.

Bauminger, N., & Kasari, C. (2000). Loneliness and friendship in high-functioning children with autism. *Child Development, 71*(2), 447–456.

Bernier, R., Webb, S. J., & Dawson, G. (2006). Understanding impairments in social engagement in autism. In P. J. Marshall & N. A. Fox (Eds.), *The development of social engagement: Neurobiological perspectives* (pp. 304–330). New York, NY: Oxford University Press.

Bukowski, W. M., Hoza, B., & Boivin, M. (1994). Measuring friendship quality during pre- and early adolescence: The development and psychometric properties of the Friendship Qualities Scale. *Journal of Social and Personal Relationships, 11*(3), 471–484. https://doi.org/10.1177/0265407594113011.

Cappadocia, M. C., & Weiss, J. A. (2011). Review of social skills training groups for youth with Asperger syndrome and high functioning autism. *Research in Autism Spectrum Disorder, 5*(1), 70–78.

Carter, A. S., Davis, N. O., Klin, A., & Volkmar, F. R. (2005). Social development in autism. In F. R. Volkmar, R. Paul, A. Klin, & D. Cohen (Eds.), Vol. 1. *Handbook of autism and pervasive developmental disorders, diagnosis, development, neurobiology, and behavior* (pp. 312–334). Hoboken, NJ: John Wiley & Sons.

Chamberlain, B., Kasari, C., & Rotheram-Fuller, E. (2007). Involvement or isolation? The social networks of children with autism in regular classrooms. *Journal of Autism and Developmental Disorders, 37*, 230–242. https://doi.org/10.1007/s10803-006-0164-4.

Chang, Y.-C., Laugeson, E. A., Gantman, A., Ellingsen, R., Frankel, F., & Dillon, A. R. (2013). Predicting treatment success in social skills training for adolescents with autism spectrum disorders: The UCLA Program for the Education and Enrichment of Relational Skills. *Autism, 18*(4), 467–470. https://doi.org/10.1177/1362361313478995.

Channon, S., Charman, T., Heap, J., Crawford, S., & Rios, P. (2001). Real-life-type problem-solving in Asperger's syndrome. *Journal of Autism and Developmental Disorders, 31*(5).

Constantino, J. N. (2005). *Social Responsiveness Scale*. Los Angeles: Western Psychological Services.

Coucouvanis, J. (2005). *Super skills: A social skills group program for children with Asperger syndrome, high-functioning autism and related challenges*. Shawnee Mission: Autism Asperger Publishing Company.

Dean, M., Kasari, C., Shih, W., Frankel, F., Whitney, R., Landa, R., … Harwood, R. (2014). The peer relationships of girls with ASD at school: Comparison to boys and girls with and without ASD. *Journal of Child Psychology and Psychiatry, 11*(55), 1218–1225. https://doi.org/10.1111/jcpp.12242.

Elder, L. M., Caterino, L. C., Chao, J., Shacknai, D., & De Simone, G. (2006). The efficacy of social skills treatment for children with Asperger syndrome. *Education and Treatment of Children, 29*(4), 635–663.

Franchini, M., Hamodat, T., Armstrong, V. L., Sacrey, L. R., Brian, J., Bryson, S. E., & Garon, N. (2019). Infants at risk for autism spectrum disorder: Frequency, quality, and variety of joint attention behaviors. *Journal of Abnormal Child Psychology, 47*(5), 907–920. https://doi.org/10.1007/s10802-018-0471-1.

Frankel, F., & Mintz, J. (2011). Maternal reports of play dates of clinic referred and community children. *Journal of Child and Family Studies*, 623–630. https://doi.org/10.1007/s10826-010-9437-9.

Frankel, F., & Myatt, R. (2003). *Children's friendship training*. New York, NY: Brunner-Routledge.

Gardner, D. M., Gerdes, A. C., & Weinberger, K. (2015). Examination of a parent-assisted, friendship-building program for adolescents with ADHD. *Journal of Attention Disorders*, 1–11. https://doi.org/10.1177/1087054715588188.

Gates, J. A., Kang, E., & Lerner, M. D. (2017). Efficacy of group social skills interventions for youth with autism spectrum disorder: A systematic review and meta-analysis. *Clinical Psychology Review, 52*, 164–181. https://doi.org/10.1016/j.cpr.2017.01.006.

Gresham, F. M., & Elliott, S. (1990). *The social skills rating system*. Minneapolis, MN: American Guidance Service.

Hall, L. J., Leinert, S., & Jacquez, J. (2018). A review of social skills manuals for adolescents with autism spectrum disorder. *Current Developmental Disorders Reports, 5*, 77–88.

Humphrey, N., & Symes, W. (2010). Perceptions of social support and experience of bullying among pupils with autistic spectrum disorders in mainstream secondary schools. *European Journal of Special Needs Education, 6257*(25), 77–91. https://doi.org/10.1080/08856250903450855.

Jagersma, G., Idris, S., Jacobs, S., Van Pelt, B. J., & Greaves-Lord, K. (2018). Nederlandse hertaling van de PEERS-training. *Wetenschappelijk Tijdschrift Autisme, 17*(3), 31–46.

Karst, J. S., Vaughan, A., Carson, A. M., Stevens, S., Schohl, K., & Dolan, B. (2014). Parent and family outcomes of PEERS: A social skills intervention for adolescents with autism spectrum disorder. *Journal of Autism and Developmental Disorders*, https://doi.org/10.1007/s10803-014-2231-6.

Kaufman, A. S., & Kaufman, N. L. (2005). *Kaufman Brief Intelligence Test* (2nd ed.). Circle Pines, MN: American Guidance Service.

Koning, C., Magill-Evans, J., Volden, J., & Dick, B. (2013). Efficacy of cognitive behavior therapy-based social skills intervention for school-aged boys with autism spectrum disorders. *Research in Autism Spectrum Disorders, 7*, 1282–1290.

La Greca, A. M., & López, N. (1998). Social anxiety among adolescents: Linkages with peer relations and friendships. *Journal of Abnormal Child Psychology, 26*, 83–94.

Laugeson, E. A. (2013). *The science of making friends: Helping socially challenges teens and young adults*. San Francisco, CA: Jossey-Base.

Laugeson, E. A. (2014). *The PEERS® curriculum for school-based professionals*. New York, NY: Routledge.

Laugeson, E. A. (2017). *PEERS® for young adults*. New York, NY: Routledge.

Laugeson, E. A., Ellingsen, R., Sanderson, J., Tucci, L., & Bates, S. (2014). The ABC's of teaching social skills to adolescents with autism spectrum disorder in the classroom: The UCLA PEERS program. *Journal of Autism and Developmental Disorders*, https://doi.org/10.1007/s10803-014-2108-8.

Laugeson, E. A., & Frankel, F. (2010). *Social skills for teenagers with developmental and autism spectrum disorders: The PEERS® treatment manual*. New York, NY: Routledge.

Laugeson, E. A., Frankel, F., Gantman, A., Dillon, A. R., & Mogil, C. (2012). Evidence-based social skills training for adolescents with autism spectrum disorders: The UCLA PEERS® program. *Journal of Autism and Developmental Disorders*, *42*, 1025–1036. https://doi.org/10.1007/s10803-011-1339-1.

Laugeson, E. A., Frankel, F., Mogil, C., & Dillon, A. R. (2009). Parent-assisted social skills training to improve friendships in teens with autism spectrum disorders. *Journal of Autism and Developmental Disorders*, *39*, 596–606. https://doi.org/10.1007/s10803-008-0664-5.

Laugeson, E. A., Gantman, A., Kapp, S. K., Orenski, K., & Ellingsen, R. (2015). A randomized controlled trial to improve social skills in young adults with autism spectrum disorder: The UCLA PEERS program. *Journal of Autism and Developmental Disorders*, https://doi.org/10.1007/s10803-015-2504-8.

Laugeson, E. A., & Park, M. N. (2014). Using a CBT approach to teach social skills to adolescents with autism spectrum disorder and other social challenges: The PEERS method. *Journal of Rational-Emotive and Cognitive Behavioral Therapy*, *32*, 84–97. https://doi.org/10.1007/s10942-014-0181-8.

Lordo, D. N., Bertolin, M., Sudikof, E. L., Keith, C., Braddock, B., & Kaufman, D. (2016). Parents perceive improvements in socio-emotional functioning in adolescents with ASD following social skills treatment. *Journal of Autism and Developmental Disorders*, https://doi.org/10.1007/s10803-016-2969-0.

Mandelberg, J., Laugeson, E. A., Cunningham, T. D., Ellingsen, R., Bates, S., & Frankel, F. (2014). Long-term treatment outcomes for parent-assisted social skills training for adolescents with autism spectrum disorders: The UCLA PEERS® program. *Journal of Mental Health Research in Intellectual Disabilities*, *7*(1), 45–73. https://doi.org/10.1080/19315864.2012.730600.

Marchica, L., & D'Amico, M. (2016). Examining the efficacy of an adapted version of the UCLA PEERS® program with Canadian adolescents. *Journal of Education & Social Policy*, *3*(4), 54–65.

Martin, I., & Mcdonald, S. (2004). An exploration of causes of non-literal language problems in individuals with Asperger syndrome. *Journal of Autism and Developmental Disorders*, *34*(3).

Mcvey, A. J., Dolan, B. K., Willar, K. S., Pleiss, S., Karst, J. S., Casnar, C. L., … Van Hecke, A. V. (2016). A replication and extension of the PEERS® for young adults social skills intervention: Examining effects on social skills and social anxiety in young adults with autism spectrum disorder. *Journal of Autism and Developmental Disorders*, https://doi.org/10.1007/s10803-016-2911-5.

Mitchell, S., Brian, J., Roberts, W., & Bryson, S. (2006). Early language and communication development of infants later diagnosed with autism spectrum disorder. *Developmental and Behavioral Pediatrics*, *27*(2).

Moree, B. N., & Thompson, E. D. (2010). Cognitive-behavioral therapy for anxiety in children diagnosed with autism spectrum disorders: Modification trends. *Research in Autism Spectrum Disorders*, *4*(3), 346–354.

Overholser, J. C. (1993). Elements of the Socratic method: Systematic questioning. *Psychotherapy: Theory, Research, and Practice*, *30*(1), 67–74.

Persicke, A., Tarbox, J., Ranick, J., & St. Clair, M. (2013). Teaching children with autism to detect and respond to sarcasm. *Research in Autism Spectrum Disorders*, *7*(1), 193–198. https://doi.org/10.1016/j.rasd.2012.08.005.

Peterson, C., Garnett, M., Kelly, A., & Attwood, T. (2009). Everyday social and conversation applications of theory-of-mind understanding by children with autism-spectrum disorders or typical development. *European Child & Adolescent Psychiatry*, *18*, 105–115. https://doi.org/10.1007/s00787-008-0711-y.

Rabin, S. J., Israel-Yaacov, S., Laugeson, E. A., Mor-Snir, I., & Golan, O. (2018). A randomized controlled trial evaluating the Hebrew adaptation of the PEERS intervention: Behavioral and questionnaire-based outcomes. *Autism Research*, 1–14. https://doi.org/10.1002/aur.1974.

Rao, P. A., Beidel, D. C., & Murray, M. J. (2008). Social skills interventions for children with Asperger's syndrome or high-functioning autism: A review and recommendations. *Journal of Autism and Developmental Disorders*, *38*, 353–361. https://doi.org/10.1007/s10803-007-0402-4.

Ratcliffe, B., Wong, M., Dossetor, D., & Hayes, S. (2015). The association between social skills and mental health in school-aged children with autism spectrum disorder, with and without intellectual disability. *Journal of Autism and Developmental Disorders*, *45*, 2487–2496. https://doi.org/10.1007/s10803-015-2411-z.

Ratto, A. B., Kenworthy, L., Yerys, B. E., Bascom, J., Trubanova, A., White, S. W., … Anthony, G. (2018). What about the girls? Sex-based differences in autistic traits and adaptive skills. *Journal of Autism and Developmental Disorders*, *48*(5), 1698–1711. https://doi.org/10.1007/s10803-017-3413-9.

Reichow, B., & Volkmar, F. R. (2010). Social skills interventions for individuals with autism: Evaluation for evidence-based practices within a best evidence synthesis framework. *Journal of Autism and Developmental Disorders*, *40*, 149–166. https://doi.org/10.1007/s10803-009-0842-0.

Schohl, K., Van Hecke, A., Meyer Carson, A., Dolan, B., Karst, J., & Stevens, S. (2013). A replication and extension of the PEERS® intervention: Examining effects on social skills and social anxiety in adolescents with autism spectrum disorders. *Journal of Autism and Developmental Disorders*, https://doi.org/10.1007/s10803-013-1900-1.

Sharda, M., Subhadra, T. P., Sahay, S., Nagaraja, C., Singh, L., Mishra, R., … Singh, N. C. (2010). Neuroscience letters sounds of melody: Pitch patterns of speech in autism. *Neuroscience Letters*, *478*(1), 42–45. https://doi.org/10.1016/j.neulet.2010.04.066.

Shum, K., Cho, W. K., Lourdes, M. O. L., Laugeson, E., Wong, W. S., & Law, L. (2019). Learning how to make friends for Chinese adolescents with autism spectrum disorder: A randomized controlled trial of the Hong Kong Chinese version of the PEERS® intervention. *Journal of Autism and Developmental Disorders*, *49*(2), 527–541. https://doi.org/10.1007/s10803-018-3728-1.

Sigman, M., Dijamco, A., Gratier, M., & Rozga, A. (2004). Early detection of core deficits in autism. *Mental Retardation and Developmental Disabilities Research Reviews*, *10*(November), 221–233. https://doi.org/10.1002/mrdd.20046.

Toth, K., Munson, J., Meltzoff, A. N., & Dawson, G. (2006). Early predictors of communication development in young children with autism spectrum disorder: Joint attention, imitation, and toy play. *Journal of Autism and Developmental Disorders*, *36*(8), 993–1005. https://doi.org/10.1007/s10803-006-0137-7.

Van Bourgondien, M. E., & Mesibov, G. B. (1987). Humor in high-functioning autistic adults. *Journal of Autism and Developmental Disorders*, *17*, 417–424.

Van Hecke, A. V., Stevens, S., Carson, A. M., Karst, J. S., Dolan, B., Schohl, K., … Brockman, S. (2013). Measuring the plasticity of social approach: A randomized controlled trial of the effects of the PEERS intervention on EEG asymmetry in adolescents with autism spectrum disorders. *Journal of Autism and Developmental Disorders*, https://doi.org/10.1007/s10803-013-1883-y.

Wetherby, A., Watt, N., Morgan, L., & Shumway, S. (2007). Social communication profiles of children with autism spectrum disorders late in the second year of life. *Journal of Autism and Developmental Disorders*, *37*, 960–975. https://doi.org/10.1007/s10803-006-0237-4.

White, S. W. (2011). *Social skills training for children with Asperger syndrome and high-functioning autism*. New York: Guilford Press.

White, S. W., Albano, A. M., Johnson, C. R., Kasari, C., Ollendick, T., Klin, A., ... Scahill, L. (2010). Developmental of a cognitive-behavioral intervention program to treat anxiety and social deficits in teens with high-functioning autism. *Clinical Child and Family Psychology Review*, *13*(1), 77–90.

Yoo, H., Bahn, G., Cho, I., Kim, E., Kim, J., Min, J., ... Laugeson, E. A. (2014). A randomized controlled trial of the Korean version of the PEERS® parent-assisted social skills training program for teens with ASD. *Autism Research*, 1–17. https://doi.org/10.1002/aur.1354.

Zare, P., & Mukundan, J. (2015). The use of Socratic method as a teaching/learning tool to develop students' critical thinking: A review of literature. *Language in India*, *15*(6), 256–265.

Zwaigenbaum, L., Bauman, M. L., Fein, D., Pierce, K., Buie, T., Davis, P. A., ... Wagner, S. (2015). Early screening of autism spectrum disorder: Recommendations for practice and research. *Pediatrics*, *136*, S41–S59.

Further reading

Steiner, A. M., Goldsmith, T. R., Snow, A. V., & Chawarska, K. (2012). Practitioner's guide to assessment of autism spectrum disorders in infants and toddlers. *Journal of Autism and Developmental Disorders*, *42*, 1183–1196. https://doi.org/10.1007/s10803-011-1376-9.

Section B

Adults

Chapter 14

Emotional and social competence (ESC) for adults: Keys for health, happiness, and success

Carol A. Kusché[a,b,c], Anna-Lisa Mackey[c,d], and Julian B.R. Kusché[c]
[a]*Seattle Psychoanalytic Society and Institute, Seattle, WA, United States,* [b]*University of Washington, Seattle, WA, United States,* [c]*Institute for Emotional & Social Competence (IESC), Seattle, WA, United States,* [d]*PATHS® Program LLC, Avondale, AZ, United States*

Thirty-five years ago, the terms "SEL" (social-emotional learning) and "emotional intelligence" had not yet been coined. CASEL (Collaborative for Academic, Social, and Emotional Learning, https://casel.org) did not yet exist. The idea of teaching emotional literacy and social understanding in the classroom was virtually unheard of, with most educators unaware of how badly it was needed. Now, 35 years later, "The debate over whether schools should attend to the social and emotional aspects of learning is increasingly settled" (Faria, Kendziora, Brown, O'Brien, & Osher, 2013, p. 1).

We believe that a situation comparable to the early 1980s is currently underway with regard to the lack of recognition of the importance of training in emotional and social competence (ESC) for adults. Universal ESC is badly needed, but for the most part, it remains a novel idea. That the present volume is unique in its coverage of social skills across the lifespan rather than just childhood is a tangible example of how overlooked this concept really is.

In this chapter, we will examine the crucial need for universal ESC instruction for all adults. While there are many applications for this type of social skills training (e.g., parenting, marriage, friendships), to limit the scope of the present chapter, we will focus primarily on the use of ESC in the workplace. We predict that 35 years from now (hopefully sooner), ESC for adults, like SEL for children, will be considered mainstream, with evidence-based documentation to support its importance and effectiveness.

Social Skills Across the Life Span. https://doi.org/10.1016/B978-0-12-817752-5.00014-7

What is ESC?

Among other things, people who are emotionally and socially competent are generally aware of their own feelings, as well as the feelings of others, are able to regulate their emotions, have good self-control over their behaviors, are able to relate well to others, and have well-developed problem-solving abilities. (There is considerable controversy with regard to the terms "feelings" and "emotions." In this chapter, we use these words interchangeably.)

ESC is sometimes referred to as emotional intelligence (EI). However, unlike the connotation attached to "intelligence," competence is something that can be taught and learned. In addition, EI often makes a distinction between emotional competence and social skills and focuses only on the former. ESC is also sometimes referred to as SEL, but almost all research and applications of SEL involve children, not adults. Nevertheless, the theory and concepts associated with SEL and EI can be applied to ESC. For example, expanding on the basic components of SEL delineated by CASEL, ESC includes the following six domains:

1. SELF AWARENESS—use of insight into oneself, both strengths and weaknesses; ability to recognize, label, and understand one's own feelings, beliefs, and values; positive self-esteem; able to adapt well to change.
2. SELF-MANAGEMENT—ability to maintain self-control over one's behavior and impulses; capacity to regulate emotions; good frustration tolerance; effective focus, attention, and concentration; resilience to stress; healthy defense mechanisms; healthy motivation.
3. SOCIAL AWARENESS—use of insight and perspective taking to understand social structures and cultures; empathy and compassion for others; awareness of one's role in and impact on the larger group; desire to support and improve the healthy functioning of society.
4. RELATIONSHIP SKILLS—ability to interact well with others; use of insight to understand the feelings, beliefs, and values of others; maintaining connectedness and harmonizing with others; strong communication skills; the ability to provide and utilize social support.
5. RESPONSIBLE DECISION-MAKING—capability to reason and analyze; ability to make healthy choices and life decisions; proficiency at setting and achieving goals; skill at organization and planning; capacity to problem solve ethically and effectively.
6. INTEGRITY—ethical and moral principles such as honesty, trustworthiness, and compassion necessary for an ethical society

Soft skills

In the business-related literature, ESC is frequently termed "soft skills" (as opposed to "hard skills" such as coding, welding, keyboarding, etc.). The term soft skills reportedly came from the military between 1968 and 1972, when it was observed that success with troops of soldiers was largely related to how the groups were led, not on military skills ("hard skills"). Since the military had not been teaching leadership skills at that time, they wanted to identify and then train the factors (or "soft skills") responsible for successful leadership (Wright, 2018).

There is no definitive list of domains encompassed by the term soft skills, but there is general consensus that they include social skills, interpersonal skills, emotional intelligence, communication skills, creativity, and leadership skills. Top business coaches from the Forbes Coaches Council (2019) recently listed 15 soft skills needed by professionals for success in the workplace as follows: relationship building, emotional intelligence, empathy, ability to influence peers, curiosity and positivity, active listening, humility, communication skills, creative problem solving, resilience, observation skills, ability to contextualize, willingness to ask questions, courage to make recommendations, and self-awareness.

A movement is currently underway to relabel the term "soft skills" because for some people, "soft" implies that these skills are optional, unimportant, and cannot be taught, none of which is true. On the contrary, the Global Talent Trends 2019 report from LinkedIn put soft skills at the top of their list of major trends "fueling the future of the workplace" (Blaschka, 2019). The report noted that 92% of talent professionals reported that soft skills mattered as much or more than hard skills during the hiring process, while 80% believed they are increasingly important for company success. According to the Forbes Coaches Council (2019), soft skills are necessary in the current workplace, and while they are not often taught, they can be learned.

Why is ESC needed in the workplace?

ESC is crucial for health, happiness, and success in all aspects of life, including in the workplace. Social interactions and communication with coworkers, vendors, and customers are pervasive with almost all employment, whether writing memos, networking, attracting clients, making presentations, or collaborating on a project. These skills promote organization, cohesion, and productivity. Understanding oneself and others can also be extremely valuable for individual achievement and happiness, as well as for business success.

In 1999, the Secretary's Commission on Achieving Necessary Skills (SCANS) was appointed by the Secretary of Labor to determine the skills young people would need to succeed in the U.S. workforce, primarily with regard to high-skill, high-wage employment. In the Commission's report (U.S. Department of Labor, 1999), half of the 16 workplace skills considered essential for life success were social and emotional in nature. These skill categories included self-esteem, integrity, self-management, sociability, responsibility, listening, decision making, and problem solving.

According to Gratton and Scott (2016), most individuals will have multiple jobs over the course of their lives. The vast majority of these jobs will involve working with other people (e.g., coworkers, managers, customers). As the SCANS report suggested, emotional understanding and aptitude in relationship skills will be even more important in the work world than they have been in the past. "Yet most organizations don't get 'social' right....Given what we know now about the social brain, creating the right social environment in our places of work should be a top priority" (Lieberman, 2013, pp. 257–258).

When companies are interested in ESC training, it is usually because they believe it will improve efficiency, productivity, employee morale, and profits. Businesses want to attract top talent, increase productivity, decrease absenteeism, and lower rates of employee turnover. Leaders also want to improve their own skills and knowledge. ESC can help promote these goals in many different ways while simultaneously improving the workplace environment and personal growth for employees. Some of these domains are summarized here.

Leadership

Research has shown that social skills play a significant role in leadership success and can even be more important than cognitive ability: "The best bosses understand and care about the social motivations of all the members of the team" (Lieberman, 2013, p. 273). Many managers, however, could benefit from training in better leadership skills. For example, an online Harris Poll survey of 616 managers found that 69% reported that they are frequently uncomfortable communicating with employees (Soloman, 2016). Many managers also reported feeling uncomfortable with such things as giving clear instructions, speaking face to face, and recognizing achievements. These types of social skills are all teachable, beneficial elements of ESC.

Teamwork

Rock (2009) introduced the SCARF model (status, certainty, autonomy, relatedness, and fairness) to describe motivational factors in the workplace, which all relate to our strong need for interpersonal connection and our desire to harmonize with other members of our group. It has been found that most people will work hard when they feel that they belong to a group that values them, but lack this motivation when they do not feel a sense of belonging or of being value by others. Moreover, oxytocin, which modifies dopaminergic processes to promote preference toward members of "liked" groups (i.e., "us"), also facilitates hostility toward members of "disliked" groups (i.e., "them;" Lieberman, 2013). Instead of merely assigning people to teams, socially skilled managers understand the importance of using strategies to promote group cohesion, fairness, and recognition.

Our world is increasingly global, and employees from very different cultures often work in the same workspace. Although all humans have the same feelings, they often feel differently about many important things (e.g., time, personal space, respect). In addition, cultures and subcultures have different beliefs, values, and display rules (i.e., cultural norms regarding how one is expected to act).

While we cannot know all of the rules for every subculture, we can use cross-cultural intelligence to observe and recognize when others are responding and interacting differently from what we normally expect, and if we want to do so, we can do research to delve into it further. These are social skills that everyone can learn.

For example, one large corporation asked us to do a series of workshops with computer experts who had recently arrived from India. While they were brilliant with their computer skills, they were having difficulty interacting with American customers and coworkers. This is not to say that these kinds of problems occur only with individuals from other countries. Cultural ignorance can be equally problematic for Americans working in foreign countries. And certainly subcultural differences between individuals from the same country can benefit from intervention.

Another example of cultural (and subcultural) differences involves complimenting, which is generally considered a positive behavior in the US (although complimenting women has recently become more complicated due to the potential perceptions of sexual harassment). In many Eastern countries (e.g., Pakistan, Japan), complimenting is considered a negative social interaction, and when used, is reserved primarily for behaviors or achievement (Inam, Tariq, & Zaman, 2015). Critchley (2019) reported that Indian bosses tend to focus on shortcomings and rarely give compliments to employees because a compliment is likely to be interpreted by employees to mean that they are doing "too good" of a job and should take a break.

One does not need to go to foreign countries, however, to find these types of cultural differences. Subgroups within the same area can have very different values and beliefs (e.g., generational, racial, political, religious, gender, sexual orientation) that can result in misunderstandings between employees. Moreover, people can unconsciously project feelings from the past onto coworkers or can experience transference based on past relationships. Practicing social awareness, empathy, perspective taking, and communication skills can help to create a more comfortable and safe environment for everyone in the company.

Bullying

Most people know that bullying is a huge problem in schools, but relatively few realize that bullying in the workplace is also a "pervasive and detrimental social problem" (Nielsen & Einarsen, 2018). Lutgen-Sandvik, Tracy, and Alberts (2007) found that between 35% and 50% of US workers reported one negative act at least weekly, while nearly 30% reported at least two. A Joint Position Statement on Workplace Violence and Bullying from The Canadian Nurses Association (CNA) and the Canadian Federation of Nurses Unions (CFNU) (2014) reported a significant increase in bullying in recent years that now affects more than half of all nurses, as well as nursing students. According to Niedhammer, Chastang, Sultan-Taieb, Vermeylen, and Parent-Thirion (2013), bullying is now considered to be "one of the most detrimental stressors in contemporary working life" (p. 79).

Different definitions have been given with regard to bullying, but a commonly accepted definition is: "A situation in which one or more individuals encountered in a repetitive manner a number of negative acts from the part of one or more of their coworkers, supervisors or subordinates, in a situation which makes the person defenceless [sic]" (Chirilă & Constantin, 2013, p. 1178). According to Nielsen and Einarsen (2018), bullying involves incessant, recurring harassment that results in the victim feeling tormented and helpless, which distinguishes it from other forms of workplace aggression.

Bullying negatively affects everyone in the workgroup. Karabulut (2016) reported that victims experience chronic stress and evidence serious outcomes such as severe health problems (emotional disorders, physical symptoms, and psychosomatic illnesses), despair, burnout, low job satisfaction, decreased morale, and earlier retirement. Organizational problems include such things as decreased job performance, increased absenteeism, lost production time, increased job turnover, and poorer financial outcomes. Coworkers witnessing bullying show significantly more general stress and mental distress reactions compared to nonexposed workers (Vartia, 2001, p. 65). In spite of these pervasive and serious consequences, according to the Washington State Department of Labor and Industries (2013), bullying is not illegal in the US unless it involves discrimination.

Given the ubiquitous nature of workplace bullying and the serious consequences involved, effective prevention and intervention are badly needed for everyone affected (victim, bully, bystanders). Unfortunately, most antibullying interventions have been largely ineffective (Nielsen & Einarsen, 2018). Lutgen-Sandvik et al. (2007) argue that successful programs will need to address the larger, structural issues that allow bullying to continue.

Rapid change

The world is changing rapidly at an unprecedented rate to which we all need to adapt. Artificial Intelligence, for example, may result in 40% of today's jobs becoming obsolete over the next 15–25 years (Reisinger, 2019). New jobs will be created, which will require employees to adjust to a changing workforce. ESC, such as social skills, communication skills, team building, and problem solving, is expected to become even more crucial for future employment as hard skills become increasingly taken over by automation. Deming (2017) found that between 1980 and 2012, social skills-intensive occupations increased by nearly 12%, and wages for these jobs grew more rapidly than for other types of employment. In addition, predictions for the future include individuals having multiple jobs and ongoing education throughout life, rather than college/initial training and a lifelong career. Employees will need help to prepare for and adapt to these new ways of working and relating. According to Gratton and Scott (2016):

> *We are in the midst of an extraordinary transition that few of us are prepared for... Much will change and this process of transformation is already underway. You need to be prepared for this and adapt accordingly... The same holds true for the*

companies you work for and the society in which you live (p. 1)... In a way that past generations simply didn't have to do, each one of us will have to think about who we are and how we construct our life and how this reflects our identity and values (pp. 20–21).

IESC (Institute for Emotional and Social Competence)

We established IESC after having worked in the field of SEL for over three decades. "It's not just children who need this type of instruction," teachers would tell us. "We need it too!" When we receive a request for ESC training, we begin with a needs assessment. We work with each organization to define their specific reasons for contacting us. If problems are described, we try to determine why those issues might be occurring. We utilize our 12-step problem solving model with clients to work through the process for each problem identified, while concentrating on the organization's goals (i.e., what are they looking for from training?). Surveys and/or evaluations are conducted if more data are needed. We also review other considerations such as identifying who will receive training, time needed to achieve competencies, benefits that are likely to be achieved, and potential obstacles. In addition, we inquire about the organization's interest in research or documenting effectiveness (e.g., with the trainees, for the organization).

Once the problem and goals are well understood, we offer potential solutions and work with management to articulate a specific plan. When the focus involves an individual (e.g., Leadership Training), we choose a coach who we believe is a good match. The agenda is then set between the individual and the trainer, with input from the organization if needed. For groups that need training, we usually recommend onsite workshops with one of our trainers in combination with online e-learning activities. In general, training requires more than one workshop, but we remain flexible to try to accommodate individual needs. We offer different options from which the organization can choose, as well as assistance with how to introduce these workshops to employees to minimize resistance.

As a hypothetical example, suppose a large organization tells us that due to recent difficulties, they want to improve their overall workplace atmosphere and promote more introspection and self-reliance among employees. In exploring this further, the organization tells us that they want better cooperation between employees, especially with regard to teamwork, greater acceptance of diversity, improvement in communication skills, more empathy, improved self-confidence, and better problem-solving skills. They are also concerned about workplace stress and the potential for workplace violence, opioid addiction, and bullying. They want to start with a department with which they have experienced an especially high level of problems, but given the results, they might want additional training for other departments. Based on this and other input, we would recommend our resilience set of monthly workshops (listed later).

Each training is conducted over 1 day through an in-person, onsite workshop, which includes didactics, discussions, role plays, video clips, and activities. The material emphasizes personal applications (e.g., a self-assessment for sensitivity), as well as ways in which concepts pertain to the participants' workplace. Each topic builds on previous learning and reviews are periodically interspersed. As can be seen with the topics listed (with each domain involving a separate 1-day training each month), our workshops include an integration of social skills training, emotional intelligence, and psychodynamic learning (i.e., skillset and mindset), in addition to other models, as we believe that insight and understanding greatly facilitate ability and willingness to engage in and internalize behavioral change. Additional online activities and practice between workshops (e.g., keeping a journal) are assigned for follow-up between workshops.

Month 1. *Introduction to ESC.* Why is ESC Important? The Nervous System & the Brain; Pain & Sensitivity; The Emotional System; Emotional (Mental) Health vs. Emotional (Mental) Disorder; Happiness & Health; Immune System; Epigenetics; Group Cohesion.

Month 2. *Emotional Literacy*. What are Feelings? Why Do We Have Them? Feelings vs. Behaviors; Display Rules; Some Core Concepts Regarding Emotions; Conscious Awareness vs. Unconscious Processing of Emotions; Defenses & Coping Mechanisms; Empathy, Compassion, & the Brain; Labeling Feelings & Brain Integration; Perspective Taking; Recognizing Feelings in Others; Recognizing Feelings in Ourselves.

Month 3. *Self-Control: Anger & Frustration*. What are Anger & Frustration?; Gender Differences; Reactivity & Frustration Tolerance; Internal Conflict; Emotional Hijacking; Prefrontal Cortical Control over Amygdala; Polyvagal Theory; Anger: Using it Productively; Impulse Control; Delayed Gratification; Insight & Self-Reflection; Hedonic Adaptation; Achieving True Happiness; Resilience & Adaptability.

Month 4. *Self-Regulation*. Stress & Stress Management. What is Stress? Consequences of Chronic Stress; Chronic Stress in the Workplace; Examples of Stress; Metabolic Syndrome; Prevention & Intervention; Stress & Rapid Change; Coping Strategies & Defense Mechanisms; Balancing Work & Home; Eating Well; "Hangry"; Sleep Deprivation; Getting Enough Sleep.

Month 5. *Self-Esteem, Self-Confidence, & Attributions*. Primary vs. Secondary Self-Esteem; Confidence vs. Competence; Internal vs. External Locus of Control; Attributions for Success & Failure; Improving Self-Esteem & Self-Confidence; Complimenting.

Month 6. *Attachment, Relationships, & Happiness*. Relationships & Happiness; Reaching Out & Relating to Others; Social Support; Repairing Relationships; Leaders, Thinkers, & Followers; Individual vs. Group Think; Social (Group) Affiliations; Work Identity; Belonging, Rejection, & Exclusion; Peer/Group Pressure; Teamwork & Trust; Hierarchies; Cooperation & Competition; Sharing; Setting Boundaries; Respecting Boundaries;

Transference; Regression; Ego & Power; Healthy Pride vs. Narcissism; Empathy & Altruism; Gratitude; Tit for Tat.

Month 7. *Problem Solving & Decision Making*. Insight, Analytic Thinking, & Logical Reasoning; Organization & Setting Priorities; Ethical Considerations; Everyone Has Problems (Fair vs. Unfair); Problems are not Punishments; Learning from Our Problems & Mistakes; Responsibility; Prosocial Decision Making; 12 Step Problem-Solving Model; Group Problem Solving; Applications; Healthy Conflict Resolution; Internal Conflict Resolution; Creativity & Innovation.

Month 8. *Attention, Concentration, & Motivation*. Attention & Pain (physical & emotional); Attention & the Brain; Conscious vs. Unconscious Processing; Filtering Distractions; Improving Attention & Concentration; Memory; Types of Motivation; Motivation & Your Job; Improving Motivation.

Month 9. *Communication Skills*. Verbal vs. Nonverbal Communication; Written Communication; Choice of Communication Medium (e.g., phone, email, text, in person); Speaking Clearly & Concisely; Tone of Voice; Delivering Difficult Information; Active/Intentional Listening; Responding, Clarifying, & Demonstrating Understanding; Defensiveness vs. Openness; Giving Feedback; Handling Resentment; Committees & Teamwork; Mobile Devices at Work.

Month 10. *Personality, Individual Differences, & Diversity*. Beliefs, Morals, & Values; Personal Strengths & Weaknesses; Five Personality Traits (Openness, Conscientiousness, Agreeableness, Extraversion/Introversion, Neuroticism); Optimism vs. Pessimism; Dependence vs. Independence; Patience & Persistence; Diversity; Unconscious Bias; Crosscultural Intelligence.

Month 11. *Mental Health & Addiction*. Neurotic vs. Psychotic vs. Personality Disorders; Anxiety Disorders; Clinical Depression & Suicide; Somatoform Disorders vs. Hypochondriasis vs. Malingering; Brain in the Gut; Personality Disorders (e.g., Avoidant, Narcissism, Masochistic, Sadistic; Sociopathic); Addictions & Substance Abuse (e.g., Alcohol, Drugs, Gambling, Social Media); Psychosocial Risk Factors; Prevention; Treatment Options.

Month 12. *Bullying in the Workplace*. Aggression & Abuse in the Workplace; What Does Bullying in the Workplace Look Like?; Incidence of Workplace Bullying; Consequences of Bullying; Violence in the Workplace; PTSD; Prevention & Intervention; Workplace Support; Respect and Empathy for Self and Others.

Throughout the year, the trainer maintains contact with the liaison and/or management to provide support, assess progress, answer questions, and address any problems that might arise. At the end of the series of workshops, we reassess the original problems and goals and evaluate the success of the program. Follow-up or training with other employees, if desired, is then discussed.

An example of one workshop topic is problem solving (Workshop 7 above), which involves our Twelve-Step Problem-Solving Model. In the workshop, we describe and review each step (note that Step #1 was already covered in

Workshop 3, while Step #2 was covered in Workshop 2). To provide actual practice, the group works together to solve a real problem. The trainer also explains how this model can be used to solve problems and conflicts between individuals, as well as internal conflicts within oneself.

Twelve-step problem-solving model

1. Stop and calm down.
2. Identify emotions (your own and other people's).
3. Identify the problem(s).
4. Determine your goal(s).
5. Strategize and generate potential solutions.
6. Envision potential consequences.
7. Select the most effective and advantageous solution.
8. Consider potential obstacles.
9. Develop an effective plan.
10. Institute your plan.
11. Evaluate the outcome.
12. If you are dissatisfied with the results, create another plan, select another solution, or revise your goal. If your outcome was successful, reward yourself for a job well done.

Another example of a domain covered during the resilience workshop involves defenses and coping mechanisms, which many people think of as bad, when they are actually crucial for protecting the psyche from being overwhelmed by powerful feelings (similar to the immune system's role with the body). We describe the development of defense mechanisms over the course of childhood from infantile defenses to those of a mature adult. The goals are to help participants improve their defense repertoires and to practice using the best defenses for different situations. While defense mechanisms are not generally considered social skills, the important role that they play in social interactions is underappreciated. For example, passive-aggressiveness frequently escalates interpersonal conflicts, but most people are unaware of and do not recognize the undercurrents involved. Understanding the dynamics allows for more conscious control.

These are just two of many topics that can be included in a workshop or series of workshops. Humans are extremely complicated, as are emotions and social skills, so a comprehensive program needs to address a wide variety of topics.

Research in ESC

Over the last decade, interventions to improve adults' ESC have multiplied rapidly, but very few have been scientifically tested. When research has been done, it has usually involved a quasiexperimental design (e.g., no random assignment, no control groups). Moreover, with programs designed for use in the workplace, other than in the world of academia, there is generally little interest in rigorous research design or whether or not a program is evidence-based. So it seems likely that there has been little incentive to conduct this research, but as the field matures, that should be changing. Nevertheless, there are several questions that can be answered based on the research that has already been reported.

Does research confirm that ESC is important in the workplace?

Google: Project oxygen & project Aristotle

If anyone has data, it's Google, and they have been active in using it. Founded by two computer scientists, Sergey Brin and Larry Page, Google originally set its hiring algorithms to select computer science students from elite universities based on the belief that technology was best understood by technologists (Davidson, 2017). To test this hypothesis, Google commenced Project Oxygen in which all of their data for hiring, firing, and promoting of managers between 1998 and 2013 were examined. More than 10,000 observations were correlated with measures of team success.

Results showed that these founders were quite wrong in their original hypothesis; the top seven characteristics of Google's most successful managers were all related to ESC: Being a good coach; empowering the team rather than micromanaging; showing interest in employees' lives, well-being, and success; being results-oriented and productive; having good communicating and listening skills; supporting career development of employees; and having a clear strategy and vision for the team. Expertise in technical skills was in eighth (and last) place (Davidson, 2017). Two additional factors were later added: Collaborating across the organization and decision-making skills (Stillman, 2018).

Data also showed that employees appreciated having an even-keeled boss: The greatest factor affecting how employees felt about their jobs, as well as on how they performed, was their manager. Google found that the biggest reason given for leaving the company was having a terrible boss. The best managers, on the other hand, had the happiest and best-performing teams, as well as the greatest employee retention. Google concluded that quality management was causal with regard to better outcomes for both employees and the company. (Note that these findings are similar to those observed by the military when the term "soft skills" was originally coined.) Google subsequently changed its hiring practices and offered in-house coaching for its worst-performing managers (Bryant, 2011).

In another major investigation, Project Aristotle, Google studied 180 Google teams to determine the key characteristics of its most innovative and productive teams (Davidson, 2017). The researchers at Google were surprised to find that the company's most important new ideas came from their B-teams (as opposed to the A teams that included the smartest people). The top five qualities for successful teams were dependability, structure and clarity, meaning, impact, and psychological safety (e.g., no bullying!). Tools for improving management skills that are based on the results of their studies are available from Google free of charge. Links can be found at https://www.inc.com/jessica-stillman/google-is-giving-away-its-best-tools-for-managers-.html (Stillman, 2017).

Additional studies

In a review of 380 worldwide resources, researchers found five critical skills that were most likely to increase the chances for success in the workforce for individuals aged 15–29 years: social skills; communication skills; higher-order thinking skills (including critical thinking, decision making, and problem solving); self-control; and positive self-concept (Lippman, Ryberg, Carney, & Moore, 2015). In a survey involving 260 large and small businesses conducted by the National Association of Colleges and Employers, communication skills were ranked as one of the most sought-after qualities by job recruiters. In a study of 81 aircrew and maintenance teams ($N=349$), Koman and Wolff (2008) found that the EI of the team leader was significantly related to the presence of emotionally competent group norms. Analyzing data from 215 employees, their subordinates, and supervisors in 66 organizations in Israel, Carmeli and Josman (2006) found that appraisal and expression of emotions, regulation of emotions, utilization of emotions, altruism, and compliance were all related to task performance.

Are most people skilled in ESC?

Surprisingly little research seems to have been done in this regard, but Kannaiah and Shanthi (2015) collected data with structured questionnaires from 150 individuals who were randomly sampled from the same organization. Categories covered in the questionnaire included leadership, responsibility, team building, relationships, adaptability, initiative, optimism, emotional competence, and empathy. Results showed that most of the individuals scored as average in these categories of emotional competencies. The authors concluded that emotional competence training sessions should be held regularly in the workplace to improve emotional intelligence, with weekly sessions in every department to problem solve, understand employees' viewpoints, and create innovative ideas.

Can ESC be effectively taught in the workplace?

It used to be assumed that ESC or soft skills could not be taught, but that was confused with the fact that they were not being taught. Although few well-designed studies have been published, there are enough to be able to answer the question: Yes they can! Implementations that have been studied have generally been short, but even then, significant results have been found.

A metaanalysis

To investigate whether EI can be taught to adults, Mattingly and Kraiger (2019) conducted a metaanalysis of 58 published and unpublished studies with an EI training program and either a pre-post or a treatment-control design. Using Cohen's d to estimate the effect of training on EI scores, these researchers found a moderate positive effect for training (similar to effect sizes typically reported in metaanalytic studies of training programs for competency). This finding held for both genders and was not affected by treatment design.

Two studies with 18h of training

Using a pre-, post-, follow-up design with matched control group for Study 1, and a pre-post design with two control groups for Study 2, Nelis et al. (2011) found significant improvement in adult emotional competencies (EC) with 18h of training (three 6-h or six 3-h sessions) in a set of two experimental studies. The first study included 58 volunteer undergraduate students with 29 each in the experimental and control groups. The second study included 92 undergraduates: 34 in the training group, 31 in a drama improvisation group, and 27 in the control group. Four EC measures were used in Study 1, while nine measures were used in Study 2. All measures were completed three times: before and after the intervention and at 6-month follow-up. Study 2 also included an informant report of emotional competence and an assessment of the probability of being hired by a future employer.

EC intervention was the same for both studies and focused on understanding emotions, identifying one's own emotions, identifying the emotions of others, emotion regulation, regulating others' emotions, and fostering well-being through the use of short lectures, discussions, work in dyads, and role-playing games. Two e-mails were sent to participants each week to promote follow-up transfer to daily life, and participants kept personal diaries between sessions. Study 1 included a no-treatment control group, while two control groups were used in Study 2 (no-treatment and improvisation training).

Results for Study 1 showed significant pre-post increases for the treatment group for global EC, emotion regulation, emotion understanding, and extraversion. Changes in neuroticism and agreeableness were not significant. All significant findings remained stable at 6-month follow-up. In addition, after 6months, the treatment group reported significantly lower neuroticism and higher agreeableness, which suggests that emotional competences kept improving after training. The control group showed no significant differences, with the exception of lower global EC and openness scores pre-follow-up.

Pre-post results for Study 2 showed significant increases for the EC group for global EC, emotion regulation, happiness, life satisfaction, global social functioning, informant-report global EC, and employability. Significant decreases were found for somatic complaints and mental disorders. The improvisation group showed significant increases in happiness and global social functioning, a marginal increase in life satisfaction, and marginally significant reductions of somatic complaints and mental disorders. No significant differences were found for global EC, emotion regulation, informant-report global EC, or employability. The no-treatment control group showed no significant differences between Time 1 and Time 2. The fact that EC did not increase in either the improvisation or no-treatment control groups, but did improve with the treatment group, suggests that the EC improvements were specific to EC training. The authors concluded that "emotional abilities and habits may be effectively improved, even using a relatively short training…[and] could be fruitfully included in programs that aim to raise people's employability" (pp. 360–361).

Medical residents and 4h of training

In a study with 31 medical resident volunteers, Shahid, Stirling, and Adams (2018) tested a 4-h EI workshop that focused on social skills, self-awareness, social awareness, and self-management with a pre-posttest design. Prior to intervention, residents completed a self-report survey online (the Bar-On Emotional Quotient Inventory 2.0, EQi 2.0, 2004). After completing their surveys, residents received a detailed report of EI level with suggestions for areas of improvement. The workshop consisted of two separate two-hour sessions (total of 4h) and was conducted by the principal investigator with didactics, discussion, and video examples. The first workshop focused on improving self-awareness and self-management skills, while the second workshop provided strategies to improve social awareness and social skills. Participants took the same EQi 2.0 online 2 months after the intervention. A significant increase was found for overall EI scores as well as self-regard, independence, self-expression, decision making, stress management, stress tolerance, optimism, flexibility, and overall wellness score. No gender differences were found for any score.

Improving customer service

A leading hotel chain recently launched a new training program, Dare to Connect, to increase the emotional awareness of hotel employees in 98 European hotels to promote better attunement to the needs of their guests (Press Release, 2017). The program focused on six main EI skills: connection, vulnerability, self-belief, authenticity, anticipation, and perseverance with training implemented by department heads at each hotel. Trainees learned such skills as anticipating emotional needs of travelers and ways in which to alleviate anxiety of guests. A pilot study in four hotels in the UK showed that overall service scores increased by 4%, while overall experience scores grew by 5%. There was also an increase in positive guest reviews.

Is new research in the pipeline?

New research from Yale

In 2017, the Yale Center for Emotional Intelligence announced plans for a ground-breaking study called the Emotion Revolution in the Workplace. In partnership with the Faas Foundation, this study seeks to discover how workplace culture affects the psychological well-being and health of employees. Researchers will explore such issues as how employees feel at work and why and the impact that employees' emotions may be having on mental and physical health, as well as on performance. These findings will then be used to promote psychologically healthy, safe, and fair workplaces. Because research-based measures of workplace culture are currently scarce, one of the goals of this project will be to develop evidence-based assessment tools to quantify such topics as the impact of emotions and motivational factors. Data collection will then guide the development of evidence-based, quantifiable solutions to reduce stress, increase motivation, and improve productivity in the workplace.

Research from IESC

As previously noted, much of our program is informed by our decades of experience with SEL implementation, where effectiveness has been well documented by a substantial body of peer-reviewed, published research. However, at this point, we are still in the planning stages with regard to our research at IESC with adults. Our research will focus on the effects of comprehensive ESC training with adults in the workplace on several levels: Did participants learn what we were trying to teach them? If so, are they applying their learning and using it in the workplace? How has the training impacted the participants (e.g., happiness, job satisfaction)? How has training impacted the larger organization (e.g., productivity, profits, employee turnover)? The field of ESC training for adults is still in its infancy, and there are numerous research questions waiting to be answered.

Conclusion

Despite its crucial importance, most adults have received little to no education in ESC. While some components might be learned at home during childhood, most parents lack the knowledge needed to adequately instruct their children. Schools have recently started teaching SEL, but most of today's adults have never had that instruction. Sadly, most people are on their own when it comes to navigating these domains, and in their naiveté, they often ricochet through life like rebounding pachinko balls. But the world is changing rapidly and becoming more complex, so while bouncing fortuitously may have been a more or less adequate way to live in the past, it will likely be handicapping in the future. Developing and improving evidence-based ESC programs for the workplace and for other facets of adult life will be important contributions both in the present and for the future.

References

Bar-On, R. (2004). *Emotional quotient inventory 2.0 user's handbook.* Toronto, Canada: Multi-Health Systems.

Blaschka, A. (2019). *Five hard truths about soft skills that might surprise you.* Forbes. Retrieved from: https://www.forbes.com/sites/amyblaschka/2019/04/11/five-surprisingly-hard-truths-about-soft-skills/#3bc4dcdd6238.

Bryant, A. (2011, March 12). *Google's quest to build a better boss*. The New York Times, Business Day, BU1. Retrieved from: https://www.nytimes.com/2011/03/13/business/13hire.html.

Carmeli, A., & Josman, Z. E. (2006). The relationship among emotional intelligence, task performance, and organizational citizenship behaviors. *Human Performance*, *19*(4), 403–419. https://doi.org/10.1207/s15327043hup1904_5.

Chirilă, T., & Constantin, T. (2013). Understanding workplace bullying phenomenon through its concepts: A literature review. *Social and Behavioral Sciences*, *84*, 1175–1179.

Critchley, O. (2019). *Importance of compliments in India*. Jagaha. Retrieved from: https://www.jagaha.com/blog/2019/01/importance-of-compliments-in-india/.

Davidson, C. N. (2017). *Reported by Valerie Strauss. The surprising thing Google learned about its employees—And what it means for today's students*. Washington Post. Retrieved from: https://www.washingtonpost.com/news/answer-sheet/wp/2017/12/20/the-surprising-thing-google-learned-about-its-employees-and-what-it-means-for-todays-students/.

Deming, D. (2017). The growing importance of social skills. NBER Working Paper No. 21473. *The Quarterly Journal of Economics*, *132*(4), 1593–1640.

Faria, A.-M., Kendziora, K., Brown, L., O'Brien, B., & Osher, D. (2013). *PATHS implementation and outcome study in the Cleveland Metropolitan School District: Final report*. American Institutes for Research: Education division. Retrieved 7/27/19 from: https://www.air.org/sites/default/files/downloads/report/Evaluation_of_PATHS_in_CMSD_final_report_6_2413_0.pdf.

Forbes Coaches Council. (2019). *15 soft skills you need to succeed when entering the workforce*. Forbes. Retrieved from: https://www.forbes.com/sites/forbescoachescouncil/2019/01/22/15-soft-skills-you-need-to-succeed-when-entering-the-workforce/#26404e6410ae.

Gratton, L., & Scott, A. (2016). *The 100-year life: Living and working in an age of longevity*. London: Bloomsbury Publishing.

Inam, A., Tariq, P. N., & Zaman, S. (2015). Cultural adaptation of preschool PATHS (promoting alternative thinking strategies) curriculum for Pakistani children. *International Journal of Psychology*, *50*(3), 232–239.

Kannaiah, D., & Shanthi, R. (2015). A study on emotional intelligence at work place. *European Journal of Business and Management*, *7*(24), 147–154.

Karabulut, A. T. (2016). Bullying: Harmful and hidden behavior in organizations. *Social and Behavioral Sciences*, *229*, 4–11.

Koman, E., & Wolff, S. (2008). Emotional intelligence competencies in the team and team leader: A multi-level examination of the impact of emotional intelligence on team performance. *Journal of Management Development*, *27*, 55–75.

Lieberman, M. D. (2013). *Social: Why our brains are wired to connect*. NY: Broadway Books.

Lippman, L. H., Ryberg, R., Carney, R., & Moore, K. A. (2015). *Workforce connections: Key "soft skills" that foster youth workforce success: Toward a consensus across fields. Executive Summary*. Child Trends. Retrieved from: https://www.usaid.gov/sites/default/files/documents/1865/KeySoftSksills.pdf.

Lutgen-Sandvik, P., Tracy, S. J., & Alberts, J. K. (2007). Burned by bullying in the American workplace: Prevalence, perception, degree and impact. *Journal of Management Studies*, *44*(6), 837–862.

Mattingly, V., & Kraiger, K. (2019). Can emotional intelligence be trained? A meta-analytical investigation. *Human Resource Management Review*, *29*, 140–155.

Nelis, D., Kotsou, I., Quoidbach, J., Hansenne, M., Weytens, F., Dupuis, P., & Mikolajczak, M. (2011). Increasing emotional competence improves psychological and physical well-being, social relationships, and employability. *Emotion*, *11*, 354–366.

Niedhammer, I., Chastang, J. F., Sultan-Taieb, H., Vermeylen, G., & Parent-Thirion, A. (2013). Psychosocial work factors and sickness absence in 31 countries in Europe. *European Journal of Public Health, 23*(4), 622–629.

Nielsen, M. B., & Einarsen, S. V. (2018). What we know, what we do not know, and what we should and could have known about workplace bullying: An overview of the literature and agenda for future research. *Aggression and Violent Behavior, 42*, 71–83.

Press Release. (2017). *Crowne plaza and the school of life to offer an emotionally intelligent hotel experience*. Hospitality Net. Retrieved from: https://www.hospitalitynet.org/nees/4091277.html.

Reisinger, D. (2019). *A.I. expert says automation could replace 40% of jobs in 15 years*. Fortune. Retrieved from: https://fortune.com/2019/01/10/automation-replace-jobs/.

Rock, D. (2009). Managing with the brain in mind. *Strategy + Business, 56*, 58–67.

Shahid, R., Stirling, J., & Adams, W. (2018). Promoting wellness and stress management in residents through emotional intelligence training. *Advances in Medical Education and Practice, 9*, 681–686.

Soloman, J. (2016). *Two-thirds of managers are uncomfortable communicating with employees*. Harvard Business Review. Retrieved from: https://hbr.org/2016/03/two-thirds-of-managers-are-uncomfortable-communicating-with-employees.

Stillman, J. (2017). *Google is giving away its best tools for managers absolutely free*. Inc. Magazine. Retrieved from: https://www.inc.com/jessica-stillman/google-is-giving-away-its-best-tools-for-managers-.html.

Stillman, J. (2018). *New Google research: The highest performing teams all have managers with these 2 skills*. Inc. Retrieved from: https://www.inc.com/jessica-stillman/google-has-just-discovered-2-more-key-skills-all-great-managers-must-have.html.

The Canadian Nurses Association (CNA) and the Canadian Federation of Nurses Unions (CFNU). (2014). *Joint position statement: Workplace violence and bullying*. Retrieved from: https://cna-aiic.ca/~/media/cna/page-content/pdf-en/Workplace-Violence-and-Bullying_joint-position-statement.pdf.

U.S. Department of Labor. (1999). *Secretary's commission on achieving necessary skills (SCANS) report: What work requires of schools*. Retrieved from:http://wdr.doleta.gov/scans.

Vartia, M. (2001). Consequences of workplace bullying with respect to the well-being of its targets and the observers of bullying. *Scandinavian Journal of Work, Environment and Health, 27*, 63–69.

Washington State Department of Labor and Industries. (2013). *What everyone needs to know about workplace bullying* Retrieved from: https://www.lni.wa.gov/Safety/Research/Files/FY13-204SHARPBullyingFactsheet.pdf.

Wright, J. (2018). *The origin of soft skills*. JoeJag. Retrieved from: https://code.joejag.com/2018/the-origin-of-soft-skills.html.

Chapter 15

Charisma™: A virtual reality training to promote Social BrainHealth in adults

Tandra T. Allen, Lara Ashmore, Shelly Gordon, Aaron Tate, Lori G. Cook, and Sandra Bond Chapman
Center for BrainHealth®, The University of Texas at Dallas, Dallas, TX, United States

Imagine practicing making a friend without fear, embarrassment, shame, or stigma. Imagine interviewing for a job and saying something wrong. Instead of being passed over for the next candidate, you interview again and get a second chance to improve your responses. Imagine learning to stand up for yourself when someone insults or excludes you. Through newly learned strategies and tactics, you navigate conversations across a variety of people and contexts, expressing your views while showing empathy toward others' feelings and perspectives. Such a world does exist. It is a parallel "virtual reality" (VR) set in a computerized game-based technology, called Charisma.

In this chapter, we illustrate with Charisma how advanced VR technology offers promising venues to promote social health and well-being for adults. The goal is for clinicians and clients everywhere to become aware of the opportunities to advance social skill training from emerging technological developments and to learn ways to access the user-friendly capabilities of virtual environments and protocols, such as Charisma.

Characterizing Social BrainHealth

Social-cognitive skills and related outcomes

Now and well into the future, our social-cognitive abilities are essential to successfully interact with others and are becoming increasingly important to succeed in life. We label this competence in using one's social abilities to engage, direct, and influence the world around them as **Social BrainHealth.** According to the World Economic Forum's Future of Jobs Report (2016), effective use of one's social intellect is among the top 10 recently identified skills that will be needed to succeed in the upcoming decades. Social BrainHealth

Social Skills Across the Life Span. https://doi.org/10.1016/B978-0-12-817752-5.00015-9

reflects this notion of social-emotional intelligence, which entails developing and expanding one's understanding of what others are feeling and thinking, recognizing and regulating one's own responses, managing and impacting relationships, as well as making healthy social decisions (Mayer, Salovey, Caruso, & Cherkasskiy, 2011). Equally integral to Social BrainHealth is how well an individual socially thrives in their day-to-day life, using their social abilities to establish meaningful relationships and navigate everyday social challenges. Essentially, Social BrainHealth accounts for the social-cognitive brain networks that support recognizing, processing, and integrating social information, as well as one's ability to actively engage social strategies to drive positive social interactions.

More specifically, the social-cognitive skills underlying Social BrainHealth include: (1) recognizing key social information, including the emotions and intentions of others, (2) integrating that knowledge into one's own thinking in order to decide how best to respond, and (3) considering how to be assertive, proactive, and problem solve. These social-perception and social-processing abilities help inform proactive social responses when actively engaged in a continual feedback recognition and response loop. Social behaviors that enhance social connections include initiating conversation, maintaining appropriate topic focus, displaying positive social cues that indicate one's attention and interest in the conversation, and taking turns. While these social behaviors can be easily observed and tracked, effective use of social-cognitive abilities can be more challenging to measure. However, both are vital social features that together influence how engaged or disengaged someone can become in their relationships.

Brain plasticity for social abilities in adults

Based on principles of neuroplasticity, the majority of humans retain the ability to improve performance and modify their brain through repeated experience and increased cognitive challenges at any age across a wide range of domains, including social (Denes, 2016). This principle applies to Social BrainHealth, where a range of latent capabilities exists that can be improved, rather than social ability being simply a positive, negative, or absent trait. Regardless of whether a previous social impairment has been diagnosed as a child, upon entering adulthood and transitioning beyond high school, individuals can experience social decline due to an increase in life responsibilities and demands (Reblin & Uchino, 2008). As such, one can experience a range of social skill abilities affecting their quality of Social BrainHealth that is contingent on real-world demands and stressors. When at a suboptimal level, a person may experience social isolation and withdraw from meaningful relationships, perhaps due to anxiety, sense of failure, or social-skill inadequacies. When at an optimal level, this continuum of Social BrainHealth can positively influence one's social actions to achieve a desired functional outcome.

Potential of technology to advance Social BrainHealth

Clinical approach with VR

We propose that vibrant Social BrainHealth is manifested in higher-quality social engagements. Two key questions we ask are inter-related. First, can we help people increase their Social BrainHealth at any age, becoming more socially adept in sustainable ways? This line of clinical research is vital given that social relations may act as a buffer for stress and anxiety, and that we live in a time when social isolation and loneliness are growing (Tomaka, Thompson, & Palacios, 2006). Second, what is the role of technology in offering a promising platform to enhance this cognitive domain? Whereas technology provides a solution, it may also contribute to the problem when used in a negative way.

Technology can be both a contributor to greater social difficulty, as well as a source of scaffolding to expand Social BrainHealth. Evidence shows that the capacity to flourish in social settings is compromised by over-reliance on technology and technical distractions such as mobile phones, tablets, and computers (Waytz & Gray, 2018). Social difficulties and challenges may be more prevalent in those with disrupted social abilities, such as those diagnosed with autism spectrum disorder (ASD). However, neurotypical individuals can also experience social struggles in daily interactions or the workplace. The detrimental aspect may arise from the constant distractions away from meaningful conversation leading to isolation and overall decreased social engagement. As such, clinical research efforts need to take into account the implications of modifying an individual's behavior using technology. Paradoxically, technology also offers a compelling medium to explore and enhance critical life skills when incorporated into a deliberate and holistic clinical training program. Moreover, the latest cutting-edge technology has a novelty effect and has potential to advance development of assessment and training programs for social abilities.

Today, new approaches to improve social-cognitive competencies are rapidly emerging and transforming health care. These approaches are breaking new ground by taking advantage of innovative technological developments that can be adapted to harness the brain's neuroplasticity. Interactive, game-based technology can provide dynamic, lifelike practice that changes the brain (Iakimova et al., 2013), with recent findings demonstrating enhanced social brain networks linked to improved social skills (Yang et al., 2018). The key to success is that these technologies must be driven by trained clinicians. Classic therapies that target improvement in social skills outside of a natural social context can be slow to make progress and generalize to real-world interactions. For example, traditional role-play scenarios require a suspension of belief that is not likely to transfer to face-to-face conversations (Krasny, Williams, Provencal, & Ozonoff, 2003). The brain rarely gets stronger by simply learning the rules of social behavior. Instead, it is through meaningful practice incorporating real emotional responses and timely reinforcement that cognitive growth is facilitated. VR leverages the impact of training by facilitating an immersive (i.e., psychological sensation of being in another place) and embodied presence (i.e., physical sense that one's body is in an environment; Riva, Wiederhold, & Mantovani, 2019). This new approach provides clinicians with the tools necessary to enhance the social health and well-being of their adult clients.

Design features of VR as a training platform

Research involving VR training platforms, such as computer-based simulations of reality, cite several beneficial factors that promote social learning. In their design, VR environments are customizable, allowing flexibility to meet the social and cognitive needs of a wide range of individuals, including both children and adults. VR technology allows the user to be removed from a real-life experience long enough to provide a nonthreatening context to practice life-like social interactions that might otherwise provoke fear or anxiety (Maskey, Lowry, Rodgers, McConachie, & Parr, 2014; Parsons & Mitchell, 2002; Wainer & Ingersoll, 2011).

Once placed in this simulated environment, game-based components facilitate "engaged learning" and elicit targeted attention to practice any type of situation that may be encountered in everyday life, especially ones that can be challenging yet pivotal to navigating relationships (Kriz, 2003; Miller & Bugnariu, 2016). This motivation to improve performance is achieved specifically by features of the VR that: (1) present a focused goal that is challenging to achieve but able to be conquered given effort, (2) offer an environment that has protection from real-world adverse consequences, (3) provide timely encouragement when performance has been successful, (4) have enough novelty and variety to stave boredom, (5) control the amount of environmental structure including sensory input and distractions, and (6) allow the individual to make independent choices within the environment (Jones, Valdez, Norakowski, & Rasmussen, 1994). Game design can be harnessed to encourage users to analyze, synthesize, and use critical reasoning skills in order to play and execute game objectives (Dickey, 2005). Collectively, these factors suggest that VR offers an effective training platform to promote cognitive and social skill learning, with implications for generalization of abilities to enhance everyday social function (Gena, Krantz, McClannahan, & Poulson, 1996; Hwang & Hughes, 2000).

Charisma: Virtual reality social cognition training

VR platform and clinical training

In this section, we outline Charisma as an evidence-based VR training focused on enhancing social-cognitive function through a strategic learning approach (Didehbani, Allen, Kandalaft, Krawczyk, & Chapman, 2016; Kandalaft, Didehbani, Krawczyk, Allen, & Chapman, 2013; Yang et al., 2018). Charisma is one of the few research-validated training programs for adults, bridging the gap of services in adulthood to build social skills and enhance social well-being and life engagement. Charisma offers the flexibility to train individuals aged 8 years through adulthood and can be modified for a wide range of social abilities and needs. As further described, we offer clinical guidelines and rationale as to how our clinicians utilize and test the virtual environments of Charisma to improve adult Social BrainHealth. A similar approach could be adopted with other emerging interactive VR programs.

Over the past 10 years, the Center for BrainHealth at the University of Texas at Dallas has developed various iterations of Charisma, continually upgrading and further customizing the technology platform as the clinical training needs evolved. Today, Charisma consists of two elements: (1) the clinical training and (2) the technology platform. Together, they target building specific Social BrainHealth skills to recognize others' emotions and intentions, respond appropriately, and apply self-assertion. Within the technology platform of an online 3D virtual world, clinicians and their participants practice live, real-time conversations using personalized avatars or digital characters to engage with one another.

Charisma's initial training platform utilized Second Life (Linden Lab, 2003), and training has since been adapted for use in Center for BrainHealth's customized proprietary platform to allow clinicians added flexibility in training delivery. At present, our interdisciplinary team of clinicians, game designers, programmers, and biometric and technology experts continue to work collaboratively, advancing delivery and scalability of Charisma to meet the needs of those with social challenges. Our current iteration of Charisma is built on Unreal Engine 4 and packaged for Windows 10. To run Charisma, users need a computer built at least within the last 5–10 years and high-speed internet. A typical user can access Charisma by direct download of an installer from a web link or a web interface that can stream the program through a virtual cloud-based machine. To interact within the program and verbally communicate, an individual can use a standard computer microphone and speakers, or can elect for a headset with a built-in microphone for their training (see Fig. 1). Users have the option to use a standard keyboard to control their avatars' movement within the game or utilize a regular game controller. MovphVox (Screaming Bee, 2005) software is utilized by clinicians during the training for their audio voice manipulation.

Clinician-driven training

For the clinical training of Charisma, each session is led by a coach clinician and a confederate clinician who serves as the conversational partner with the client. All training conversations and feedback discussions between clients and clinicians take place in the virtual environment through avatars, while each person physically resides in separate rooms. To enhance the realism and immersion of the client within the social practice, the confederate utilizes the voice changing software and changes her avatar's appearance within the VR platform to match the character profile being represented (e.g., a friendly male neighbor,

FIG. 1 Charisma set-up with headphones and computer.

a preoccupied female coffee clerk, an aloof male coworker). Multiple practice scenarios with different conversational partners, varying in personality and gender, are presented in each session. Providing a variety of conversations and social relationships is necessary and made possible by the VR platform, so the client can adopt a flexible social response style instead of rote or patterned responses.

The training begins with the coach orienting the client to the technology platform itself, which includes creating a customized avatar in the likeness of the client and instructing the client how to navigate their avatar within the VR. This can be done either physically in-person (outside of the VR) or remotely online via video-conferencing software to sync visual and audio connection between locations. Once the client is independently navigating the virtual world, the clinician will begin the session through their personal avatar within Charisma. The client and clinicians have independent use of their own computer to drive their own avatar within the session. The remainder of the training is completed entirely within the VR using the audio connection of the video-conferencing system to verbally communicate through the avatars.

Each session begins with a coach virtually greeting the client in the Charisma platform through their avatars (see Fig. 2). The coach verbally instructs the client, reviewing the strategy objective and conversation focus of the session (e.g., self-assertion in job interviews). The coach says a social prompt, for example with an adult, "You are attending a job fair today, go and talk with each representative to find out more about what jobs are available" (see Figs. 3 and 4). The client is then directed to start and build a conversation using the strategies that have been discussed. The coach's avatar remains in close proximity to the client's avatar throughout the conversational practice to be a support if needed. A confederate, using their avatar and audio connection, then begins to interact

FIG. 2 Charisma in-session with client and coach.

FIG. 3 Practice interview conversation in Charisma.

FIG. 4 Practice conversation in Charisma's coffee shop.

with the client providing a real-time response with loosely scripted conversation targets and personality characteristics utilizing vocal tone inflection, spatial orientation of their avatar within the game, and verbal responses to indicate an engaged or disengaged reaction to the client. The confederate follows the lead of the client, providing naturalistic (in character) social cues in the context of their conversation to alert the client as to whether their response is appropriate or off-target. In the event a participant is struggling in the interaction (e.g., lack of initiation, unsuccessful reciprocal conversation building), the coach provides feedback in-the-moment, through their avatar, and gives a second opportunity to repeat the conversation to improve the outcome.

Feedback, reinforcement, and skill progression

The process for clinicians providing feedback to their client during a Charisma session is outlined in Table 1. Once a coach provides the initial social prompt to begin the conversation practice, the coach continually monitors and evaluates in real time during the session how well the client is using their Social BrainHealth abilities to achieve the goal of the interaction. Following the conversation practice, the client is given the opportunity to initially self-rate their performance and indicate if the conversation was an overall success (a gain that moved the relationship forward in some way), a maintain (the relationship level remained at the same connection level), or a loss (the relationship was hurt or decreased in some way). The clinician and client's independent ratings become discussion points during the breaks between each practiced scenario.

Once independent ratings are complete, the coach provides feedback questions to reinforce insight and self-reflection for skill development, including: (1) What did you notice? (2) What did you experience/think? (3) What did you do? (4) What was the impact of your response on the relationship? (5) What are ways you could improve your exchange in the next interaction? Based upon the client's responses, the coach can follow-up with additional questions to identify the client's thoughts and/or experiences. The questions provide "cognitive scaffolding" or support for the client to improve and refine their metacognitive abilities to apply Social BrainHealth strategies. Based upon the client's level of comprehension, insight, and success from the practiced scenario, the coach can increase or decrease complexity for the next practiced conversational practice within the session. This occurs by modifying the confederate responses to make their social cues and emotional reactions more subtle or overt. Complexity can also be altered with additional external cues provided by the coach jumping into the conversation to provide a verbal reminder to use a strategy.

Assessments for social skills and real-world function

To capture a baseline of social-cognitive skill function and change related to training, a specialized assessment battery has been developed for the Charisma training. As shown in Table 2, specific to the adult population, a core assessment,

TABLE 1 Process for clinicians providing feedback during a Charisma session.

Charisma—Clinician feedback guide			
Clinician probe questions	**Social BrainHealth observations**	**Structure/cueing from coach**	**Outcome**
Clinician asks the following immediately following a practice scenario:	*Clinician asks follow-up questions to help identify if the client understood the following objectives*:	*What did you have to do as clinician to help the client achive understanding/insight?*	*What action did you take as a clinican to carry over to next practice scenario?*
What did you notice?	Did the client notice all emotional cues or just relevant (important) cues?	Did the clinician point out observations that the client missed or incorrectly interpreted?	Was complexity increased or decreased for next scenario?
What did you think?	Did the client recognize the objective/goal of the other person as well as their own personal goal/objective?	Did the clinician provide alternative suggestions instead of the client generating on their own?	Was scenario repeated?
What did you do?	Was the client's message clear/concise? Did the client recognize the impact of their words?	List any other structure that was provided	Was objective achieved?
Was the relationship connection a gain, maintain, or loss?	Did the client recognize different perspectives of opinion to consider?		Describe any revised goal/ objective for client
What are ways you can improve the next conversation?	Did the client recognize different approaches/ responses that could be considered?		
	Did the client recall any past experiences or personal insight that helped to inform their response? Did the client respond in a way that was rote or novel? Did the relationship grow or deepen?		

TABLE 2 Social BrainHealth assessment and training.

Components and measurements of Social BrainHealth		
Social BrainHealth skill	**Social assessment**	**Charisma integration targets**
Social perception: 1. Recognize emotions 2. Recognize intentions	ACS-SP; The social attribution test	*Client asked to identify in context of a social scenario*: 1. What is someone feeling 2. What is someone thinking
Social responses: 1. Prioritize social efforts (initiate conversation, relationship building) 2. Anticipate consequences (plan and show appropriate social communication and social cues) 3. Social adaptability (topic maintenance, turn-taking)	Social BrainHealth scale	*Client asked to initiate & respond across many types of situations to achieve a positive outcome with the goals to*: 1. Identify what relationships are important to them 2. Plan a proactive approach and potential responses 3. Self-correct & repair responses in-the-moment of a conversation 4. Follow-up or repeat conversations to improve performance and outcome
Self-assertion: 1. Healthy decision making 2. Social engagement	Birchwood social functioning scale; Social skills rating form; Social interaction anxiety scale; Social BrainHealth scale	*Following a conversation practice, client asked to decide*: 1. What's the overall impact of the conversation long-term on self and others? 2. Did the interaction lead to relationship gain, maintain, or loss?

Note. ACS-SP Advanced Clinical Solutions Social Perception Subtest (WAIS-IV & WMS IV) (Pearson, 2009); The Social Attribution Task, Triangles Task (Abell, Happe, & Frith, 2000); Social BrainHealth Scale (Developed at Center for BrainHealth); Birchwood Social Functioning Scale (Birchwood, Smith, Cochrane, Wtton & Copestake, 1990); Social Skills Rating Form (Developed at Center for BrainHealth); Social Interaction Anxiety Scale (Mattick & Clarke, 1998).

The Advanced Clinical Solutions for WAIS-IV and WMS-IV Social Perception Subtest Social Perception Subtest (ACS-SP), measures emotion recognition abilities (Pearson, 2009). A second core measure is *The Social Attribution Task*, also known as the triangles task, to evaluate theory-of-mind and understanding of intentions of others (Abell et al., 2000). In the first pilot study by Kandalaft et al. (2013), to capture real-world social abilities and daily life function, the *Social Skills Performance Assessment, Version 3.2(2)* (Patterson, Moscona, McKibbin, Davidson, & Jeste, 2001) was utilized to measure conversational skills and a *Follow-Up Survey* developed at Center for BrainHealth was conducted to capture change in real-world social functioning. Currently, our social-cognitive battery includes the *Birchwood Social Functioning Scale* (Birchwood, Smith, Cochrane, Wetton, & Copestake, 1990), *Social Interaction Anxiety Scale* (Mattick & Clarke, 1998), *Social Skill Rating Measure* developed at Center for BrainHealth, and the *Social BrainHealth Scale*, a measure in development to capture a holistic view of someone's social abilities.

These assessments, when completed before training, serve as a guide to the clinician for treatment planning and promote the client participating as an active decision-maker in the goal setting. The test battery provides a comprehensive overview of strengths and limitations, as well as a protocol to continuously monitor changes in social functioning over one's lifetime. Additionally, within the context of Charisma training, these social assessments can help monitor changes in Social BrainHealth skills when coupled with real-time clinician ratings and observations during the social training scenarios.

Evaluation of Charisma

Charisma was first published in two initial research studies completed in a young adult (Kandalaft et al., 2013) and pediatric population (Didehbani et al., 2016), where recruitment was targeted to individuals with a diagnosis of high-functioning ASD. Specific to the adult study, the aim was to improve social-cognitive abilities and real-world social functioning (Kandalaft et al., 2013). Delivered in 10h over a 5-week training period, eight participants aged 18–26 years engaged in practice of different social scenarios that were functional in nature and appropriate to their social daily life. Scenarios included opportunities to practice meeting a roommate, interviewing for a job, managing conflict with coworkers, and going on a blind date. Following training, as reflected in two previously described social-cognitive assessments (i.e., ACS-SP and The Social Attribution Task), the adult participants improved in emotion recognition and recognition of intentions with theory-of-mind. Participants additionally self-reported improvement in real-life social functioning and social engagement, as demonstrated through the Follow-Up Survey (Kandalaft et al., 2013). While no control group was utilized, this pilot study provided initial results suggesting that VR is a promising mechanism to improve social abilities in adults.

Neuroplasticity: Facilitating enhanced brain networks

Following the initial pilot study, the next progression was to evaluate the impact of Charisma on social-cognitive neural networks that support social learning. To evaluate the brain-level mechanisms related to changes after training, the Center for BrainHealth partnered with Yale Child Study Center (YCSC) to recruit adults with a diagnosis of ASD to take part in a Phase 1 trial study (Yang et al., 2018). Seventeen participants aged 18–31 years, recruited at both Center for BrainHealth and YCSC, completed in-person pre- and posttraining social behavioral assessments that measured social skills specific to emotion recognition, recognizing intentions, and social functioning using the social-cognitive measures outlined in Table 2. Additionally, functional brain imaging was completed at each site using a well-validated biological/social versus scrambled/nonsocial motion neuroimaging task that has been previously shown to activate regions within the social brain networks. All training was delivered via the virtual platform, with the coach remotely delivering Charisma from the Center for BrainHealth in Dallas, while participants logged in remotely from a designated location at each center in Texas or Connecticut. Behavioral assessment results from this study replicated similar findings to the original research showing improvements in emotion recognition and recognizing intentions with theory-of-mind following training. Overall, the neural networks identified as impacted by training suggested correlation with the measured behavioral improvements in theory-of-mind and emotion recognition.

To understand the neural mechanisms related to the measured behavioral changes, individual- and group-level brain changes were tracked. At the individual level, the right posterior superior temporal sulcus increased in brain activation to social versus nonsocial stimuli for individuals who made the most gains on a theory-of-mind measure. Also identified at the individual level was the left inferior frontal gyrus, which decreased in activation to social versus nonsocial stimuli in individuals who made the most improvement behaviorally on a measure of emotion recognition. At the group level, change in mean brain activations before and after training suggested that the left superior lobule decreased in activation to nonsocial versus social stimuli. At the global level of brain response, findings suggest a neural mechanism by which all participants learned to enhance how they process social information. Specifically, following training, participants were showing more cognitive attention to socially relevant stimuli vs. unimportant stimuli. This has particular implications for real-world social function in that findings suggest an improved social perceptual ability to attend to important social information and block irrelevant social distractions that can therefore influence improved social responses. Similar to the initial pilot studies, interpretation of these findings is limited by lack of a control group and thus only suggests that brain activation results are a correlate of behavioral change.

Charisma as a clinical service

The next advancement of Charisma extended the program as a clinical service to adults on a larger scale through a feasibility study. The goals were to extend training to a wider audience of individuals, increase the number of participants served within a single session, and track real-world social changes. This expansion translated the original research findings in a scalable fashion to offer Charisma broadly to those with or without a social diagnosis or confirmed impairment, while continuing to collect research validation on real-world social functioning.

Charisma was offered across three locations, including the Center for BrainHealth, a college campus at The University of Texas at Dallas, and a post-secondary education institute at nonPareil Institute (Gordon, Allen, Faso, & Chapman, 2019). Recruitment criteria did not require an individual to have a formal diagnosis, only a self-identified social difficulty. Individuals recruited through nonPareil Institute did have a diagnosis of ASD, as that was a requirement to attend the Institute. Forty-two adults (aged 18–45 years) completed the 10-h training across a span of 5 weeks. They were seen in groups of two or three, and matched according to level of social ability. Following training, significant social-cognitive improvements were found using the previously mentioned core assessments (as shown in Table 2) of emotion recognition, theory-of-mind, and self-reported social functioning skills. In addition, participants exhibited a significant decrease in self-reported social anxiety. While no control group was utilized in this preliminary feasibility study, results suggest that Charisma is an effective social skill training program that can decrease social anxiety, which may contribute to overall improved social well-being. A similar program in a VR platform like that of Charisma might induce comparable change in daily social function and overall Social BrainHealth.

Conclusions

In looking to the future, VR platforms offer promising opportunities to increase access and quality of training to adults. VR-based social trainings, such as Charisma, are becoming increasingly intriguing for a wide range of users who want to improve their social adeptness and perhaps increase their "charisma," neither of which is innate. Rather, social astuteness or ability to relate to others with differing perspectives is a learned and highly modifiable trait. Research with Charisma illustrates how technology provides a promising vehicle for clinicians to assess and train social abilities in a nonthreatening, safe environment. The features of VR environments offer an almost infinite flexibility to meet the social demands and needs of adults at various phases of their career and life productivity, where social contexts are constantly changing and presenting with new challenges. Charisma leverages technology's unique features to improve social brain function and ultimately enhance one's quality of Social BrainHealth and overall well-being. Future research is needed to further explore the full-scale capabilities of technology with programs such as Charisma and others, as well as to enhance efforts in training clinicians to take advantage of this type of technology platform.

Our next challenge at BrainHealth, and as clinicians, is to continue to grow our vision of improving social capabilities and learn more about how this enhanced dimension serves to elevate overall psychological well-being, cognitive growth, and life productivity. Another future goal is to measure sustainability of gains long-term over the life span and to regularly monitor, through technology, any setbacks with a focus on proactively addressing them before losses and isolation grow. We propose that as VR interactive programs become readily accessible and scalable, they can be utilized to optimize one of the most important dimensions of human brain health; social cognition or, as termed herein, Social BrainHealth. The mission to optimize Social BrainHealth from a health perspective is a bold challenge, worthy of serious focus and large-scale efforts of investment from many transdisciplinary teams working around the globe.

References

Abell, F., Happe, F., & Frith, U. (2000). Do triangles play tricks? Attribution of mental states to animated shapes in normal and abnormal development. *Cognitive Development*, *15*, 1–16.

Birchwood, M., Smith, J., Cochrane, R., Wetton, S., & Copestake, S. (1990). The social functioning scale: The development and validation of a new scale of social adjustment for use in family intervention programmes with schizophrenic patients. *The British Journal of Psychiatry*, *157*, 853–859. https://doi.org/10.1192/bjp.157.6.853.

Denes, G. (2016). *Neural plasticity across the lifespan: How the brain can change*. New York, NY: Routledge/Taylor & Francis Group.

Dickey, M. D. (2005). Engaging by design: How engagement strategies in popular computer and video games can inform instructional design. *Educational Technology Research & Development*, *53*(2), 67–83. https://doi.org/10.1007/BF02504866.

Didehbani, N., Allen, T., Kandalaft, M., Krawczyk, D., & Chapman, S. (2016). Virtual reality social cognition training for children with high functioning autism. *Computers in Human Behavior*, *62*, 703–711. https://doi.org/10.1016/j.chb.2016.04.033.

Gena, A., Krantz, P. J., McClannahan, L. E., & Poulson, C. L. (1996). Training and generalization of affective behavior displayed by youth with autism. *Journal of Applied Behavior Analysis*, *29*(3), 291–304. https://doi.org/10.1901/jaba.1996.29-291.

Gordon, S., Allen, T., Faso, D., & Chapman, S. (2019). *Transition to adulthood with Charisma: Generalization of virtual-reality social cognition training on adults with autism*. In: *Technical presentation presented at American speech-language and hearing association annual convention, Orlando, FL*.

Hwang, B., & Hughes, C. (2000). The effects of social interactive training on early social communicative skills of children with autism. *Journal of Autism and Developmental Disorders*, *30*(4), 331–343.

Iakimova, G., Mardaga, S., Couvreux, M., Hun, S., Serret, S., & Askenazy, F. (2013). Can a training with video game of social cognition enhance neurocognitive processes of emotional perception in autism spectrum? Insights of event-related potentials. *European Psychiatry*, *28*, 1. https://doi.org/10.1016/S0924-9338(13)77126-8.

Jones, B., Valdez, G., Norakowski, J., & Rasmussen, C. (1994). *Designing learning and technology for educational reform*. North Central Regional Educational Laboratory. Retrieved from: https://files.eric.ed.gov/fulltext/ED378940.pdf.

Kandalaft, M. R., Didehbani, N., Krawczyk, D. C., Allen, T. T., & Chapman, S. B. (2013). Virtual reality social cognition training for young adults with high-functioning autism. *Journal of Autism and Developmental Disorders*, *43*, 34–44. https://doi.org/10.1007/s10803-012-1544-6.

Krasny, L., Williams, B. J., Provencal, S., & Ozonoff, S. (2003). Social skills interventions for the autism spectrum: Essential ingredients and a model curriculum. *Child and Adolescent Psychiatric Clinics of North America*, *12*(1), 107–122.

Kriz, W. C. (2003). Creating effective learning environments and learning organizations through gaming simulation design. *Simulation & Gaming*, *34*(4), 495–511.

Linden Lab. (2003). *Second life (version 2.1) [software]*. Available from: http://secondlife.com/.

Maskey, M., Lowry, J., Rodgers, J., McConachie, H., & Parr, J. R. (2014). Reducing specific phobia/fear in young people with autism spectrum disorders (ASDs) through a virtual reality environment intervention. *PLoS One*, *9*(7), e100374. https://doi.org/10.1371/journal.pone.0100374o.

Mattick, R. P., & Clarke, J. C. (1998). Development and validation of measures of social phobia scrutiny fear and social interaction anxiety. *Behaviour Research and Therapy*, *36*, 455–470. https://doi.org/10.1016/S0005-7967(97)10031-6.

Mayer, J. D., Salovey, P., Caruso, D. R., & Cherkasskiy, L. (2011). Emotional intelligence. In R. J. Sternberg & S. B. Kaufman (Eds.), *The Cambridge handbook of intelligence* (pp. 528–549). New York, NY: Cambridge University Press. https://doi.org/10.1017/CBO9780511977244.027.

Miller, H. L., & Bugnariu, N. L. (2016). Level of immersion in virtual environments impacts the ability to assess and teach social skills in autism spectrum disorder. *Cyberpsychology, Behavior and Social Networking*, *19*(4), 246–256. https://doi.org/10.1089/cyber.2014.0682.

Parsons, S., & Mitchell, P. (2002). The potential of virtual reality in social skills training for people with autistic spectrum disorders. *Journal of Intellectual Disability Research*, *46*(5), 430–443.

Patterson, T. L., Moscona, S., McKibbin, C. L., Davidson, K., & Jeste, D. V. (2001). Social skills performance assessment among older patients with schizophrenia. *Schizophrenia Research*, *48*(2), 351–360.

Pearson. (2009). *Advanced clinical soultions (ACS) for the WAIS-IV and WMS-IV*. San Antonio, TX: Pearson.

Reblin, M., & Uchino, B. N. (2008). Social and emotional support and its implication for health. *Current Opinion in Psychiatry*, *21*(2), 201–205. https://doi.org/10.1097/YCO.0b013e3282f3ad89.

Riva, G., Wiederhold, B. K., & Mantovani, F. (2019). Neuroscience of virtual reality: From virtual exposure to embodied medicine. *Cyberpsychology, Behavior and Social Networking*, *22*(1), 82–96. https://doi.org/10.1089/cyber.2017.29099.gri.

Screaming Bee. (2005). *MorphVox, 3.4.18 ed*. Available from: http://www.screamingbee.com/product/MorphVOX.aspx.

Tomaka, J., Thompson, S., & Palacios, R. (2006). The relation of social isolation, loneliness, and social support to disease outcomes among the elderly. *Journal of Aging and Health*, *18*(3), 359–384. https://doi.org/10.1177/0898264305280993.

Wainer, A., & Ingersoll, B. R. (2011). The use of innovative computer technology for teaching social communication to individuals with autism spectrum disorders. *Research in Autism Spectrum Disorders*, *5*(1), 96–107.

Waytz, A., & Gray, K. (2018). Does online technology make us more or less sociable? A preliminary review and call for research. *Perspectives on Psychological Science*, *13*(4), 473–491. https://doi.org/10.1177/1745691617746509.

World Economic Forum. (2016, January). *The future of jobs: Employment, skills and workforce strategy for the fourth industrial revolution*. Cologny/Geneva, Switzerland: World Economic Forum.

Yang, Y. J. D., Allen, T., Abdullahi, S. M., Pelphrey, K. A., Volkmar, F. R., & Chapman, S. B. (2018). Neural mechanisms of behavioral change in young adults with high-functioning autism receiving virtual reality social cognition training: A pilot study. *Autism Research*, *11*(5), 713–725. https://doi.org/10.1002/aur.1941.

Chapter 16

PREP4Work: A social skills intervention to prepare adults with autism spectrum disorder and intellectual disabilities to access the workplace

Jennifer Holloway, Helena Lydon, and Edith Walsh
National University of Ireland Galway, Galway, Ireland

Failure to develop adequate social skills is often a defining characteristic of autism spectrum disorder (ASD), and it can prohibit full participation and integration within the community. Social skills do not readily develop in children with ASD and often require specific interventions to promote positive outcomes. During infancy, individuals with ASD often exhibit fewer nonverbal social gestures—such as pointing, showing, and giving behaviors—as well as less looking at people and orientating to their names (Osterling & Dawson, 1994; Osterling, Dawson, & Munson, 2002; Rohlfing, Grimminger, & Luke, 2017). Such social skills deficits, if left untreated, persist over time, and children with ASD often present with similar deficits in eye contact, joint attention, social smiling, imitation, and interest in other children (Frye, 2018). Other notable deficits include deficits in initiating social interaction, reciprocating conversation, perspective taking, and shared enjoyment (Bellini, Peters, Benner, & Hopf, 2007).

With advancing age, deficits in social skills become more apparent as social environments become more complex, and these deficits can impact an individual's ability to integrate in social contexts and develop friendships (Koegel, Kim, & Koegel, 2013). The development of social skills may also be curtailed by limited exposure to opportunities for social interactions. Jennes-Coussens, Magill-Evans, and Koning (2006) report that individuals with ASD are more likely to engage in solitary activities (i.e., watching television, playing video games) and are less likely to participate in community-based recreational and leisure activities; moreover, one-third of individuals with ASD report no involvement in social activities.

Social Skills Across the Life Span. https://doi.org/10.1016/B978-0-12-817752-5.00016-0

Failure to engage in social activities affords individuals with ASD fewer opportunities to develop friendships (Orsmond, Krauss, & Seltzer, 2004).

In adulthood, for many, the goal of securing employment is an important life transition, which ensures continued community and social integration. For individuals with ASD, obtaining employment is seen as a step toward independence and is associated with a number of positive outcomes such as increased cognitive functioning (García-Villamisar & Hughes, 2007), higher quality of life (García-Villamisar, Wehman, & Navarro, 2002), and improved mental health (Hiller, Fish, Siegel, & Beversdorf, 2011). Even though the positive outcomes of being employed are highlighted within the literature, employment rates for individuals with ASD are among the poorest when compared to individuals with other developmental disabilities (Roux et al., 2013). It has been documented that only 10%–50% of individuals with ASD obtain employment upon school completion (Barneveld, Swabb, Fagel, van Engeland, & de Sonneville, 2014; Shattuck et al., 2012). Furthermore, of those who gain employment, many are underemployed (i.e., obtaining fewer working hours), earn less than typically developing peers (Burgess & Cimera, 2014), or do not obtain employment, which adequately reflects their abilities or qualifications (Marriage, Wolverton, & Marriage, 2009). Being unemployed or underemployed further curtails opportunities for social engagement.

Deficits in social skills are often considered the primary barrier for individuals with ASD in obtaining and maintaining employment (Baldwin, Costley, & Warren, 2014; Chiang, Cheung, Li, & Tsai, 2013) rather than an ability to complete job specific skills. Failure to develop adequate social skills exacerbates the risk of social withdrawal and isolation for individuals with ASD (Koegel, Frea, & Surratt, 1994) and limits the formation of social relationships and friendships with colleagues. Deficits in social skills are evident and become more pronounced across the lifespan. Such deficits are unlikely to ameliorate without targeted intervention, even for individuals without cognitive impairments (Gresham, Sugai, & Horner, 2001). Therefore, to ensure that individuals with ASD can access employment within their community and to avoid social isolation, it is essential that appropriate interventions to remediate these social skills deficits are readily available. Furthermore, as individuals with ASD are a heterogeneous group, interventions to address social skills deficits often require modifications based on individual needs, such as level of intellectual and social functioning.

When an individual with ASD is successful in securing employment, their employer may have expectations with regard to social competencies and may expect that they will have the relevant social skills to interact with coworkers and supervisors. Such skills may include listening, working as part of a team, acknowledging instructions by making confirming statements, notifying a supervisor when a task is complete, asking for help when needed, offering help to a colleague when appropriate, responding to corrective feedback appropriately, and dealing with conflict. Many of these skills may be challenging for individuals with ASD (Baldwin et al., 2014; Krieger, Kinébanian, Prodinger, & Heigl, 2012; Lerman, White, Grob, & Laudont, 2017). In addition, more subtle social skills may be required in order to integrate into the work setting by engaging in effective communication and maintaining rapport with colleagues. For example, it may be necessary to differentiating between acquaintances, friends, peers, colleagues, an employer, or a superior in order to select suitable topics of conversations at work. Additional goals relevant to more subtle aspects of socializing may include tempering the use of loudness and duration of speech (Bernstein et al., 1977), matching facial affect to the context (Szatmari, Bartolucci, Bremner, Bond, & Rich, 1989), and being appropriately assertive conversation, while also displaying emotional empathy by responding appropriately to a colleague who is stressed (Bellesi, Jameel, Vyas, Crawford, & Channon, 2016). Underlying these is having an awareness of others perspectives.

Social skills instruction and workplace inclusion

Early research on employment for individuals with ASD primarily focused on job skills such as completion of specific tasks and remaining on task (Kellems & Morningstar, 2012; Montgomery, Storey, Post, & Lemley, 2011). Even for individuals who excel at specific job related tasks, however, retention is often challenging due to difficulties in social integration. A shortcoming of the research base to date is that the focus has been primarily on individuals with higher functioning ASD. This limits the generalizability of findings to practice, as it is estimated that many individuals with ASD also present with intellectual disability and other comorbid diagnosis.

Social skills interventions support adults with ASD to integrate successfully into the workplace and to avoid termination of employment and subsequent unemployment. There exists a number of curricula designed to improve social skills for individuals with ASD. Examples include the social cognition and interaction training adapted for ASD (SCIT-A; Turner-Brown, Perry, Dichter, Bodfish, & Penn, 2008), the Interpersonal Problem-Solving for Workplace Adaptation Programme (Bonete, Calero, & Fernandez-Parra, 2015), a nonmanualized social skills group based in London (Howlin & Yates, 1999), the program for the education and enrichment of relational skills (PEERS) for adults with ASD without ID (Laugeson, Frankel, Gantman, Dillon, & Mogil, 2012), and an adapted version of the walker social skills curriculum called the adolescent curriculum for communication and effective social skills program (ACCESS; Walker, Todis, Holmes, & Horton, 1988; Walsh, Holloway, & Lydon, 2018; Walsh, Holloway, Lydon, McGrath, & Cunningham, 2019). Social skills curricula target a range of social behaviors that may be helpful in navigating a variety of employment settings. Social skills targeted are typically taught sequentially and grouped according to stages of social development. Many programs are delivered through applied behavior analysis (ABA), with scientific principles applied to ensure evidence-based practices are in operation. On review of the components of successful curriculum-based interventions, a number of commonalities, and variations of implementation exist, which may provide valuable information for future research and clinical practice.

Curriculum-based interventions

With respect to social skills curricula, most interventions deliver an entire curriculum, taught in sequence, and which follow a set of instructional guidelines (Laugeson, Gantman, Kapp, Orenski, & Elingsen, 2015). The majority of interventions have delivered social skills instruction within small group settings as opposed to one-to-one instruction, with group size varying from 4 to 6 (Bonete et al., 2015; Turner-Brown et al., 2008), 6–7 (Walsh et al., 2018), and up to 10 participants (Howlin & Yates, 1999; McVey et al., 2016). Interventions are delivered by trained facilitators or certified instructors (Bonete et al., 2015; McVey et al., 2016). Some interventions include additional staff, often referred to as assistants or coaches. The intensity of intervention delivery carries from: monthly sessions (2.5 h per month across a year; Howlin & Yates, 1999) to weekly sessions (50 min in duration over an 18-week period; Turner-Brown et al., 2008). The most common structures being two 75-min sessions a week over 10 weeks (Bonete et al., 2015), 90-min weekly sessions over 16 weeks (McVey et al., 2016), and 90-min weekly sessions across 20 weeks (Walsh et al., 2018). From the research to date, it appears that longer and more frequent intervention sessions are required for individuals with ASD and ID (Walsh et al., 2018).

The mode of instruction primarily revolves around behavioral skills training (BST) involving, instruction, modeling, practice, and feedback (Dib & Sturmey, 2012). Instruction is presented in didactic lessons (McVey et al., 2016), with instructors explaining each skill, providing a rationale for its use, and describing how to use the skill correctly. Modeling is a core feature of all interventions. However, there are some variations, including the use of in vivo and video modeling. In vivo modeling involves role plays enacted by instructors and including up to three examples (i.e., multiple exemplars) of appropriate and inappropriate social behaviors (McVey et al., 2016). Other research has evaluated video models incorporating multiple exemplars (Walsh et al., 2018). Subsequently, a discussion is typically used to problem-solve social situations, identify critical features of a skill, and assess whether these critical skill features were shown or not within the session (Bonete et al., 2015; Walsh et al., 2018). Following the modeling phase, individuals typically have an opportunity to practice (role play) the social skills with the instructors (e.g., McVey et al., 2016).

Highlighting context and particular considerations

As discussed, identifying effective interventions to ameliorate social impairments should be a primary concern for researchers and practitioners. However, assessing social skills and designing social skills interventions for adults with

ASD and ID is complex. In adulthood, the appraisal of social communication skills can be more arbitrary when compared to earlier developmental stages, with cultural factors and environments playing an important influential role (Lai & Baron-Cohen, 2015). Within the literature and in practice, it is challenging to identify a common definition of social skills and what is meant by social competency. As such, many researchers interpret the repertoire in different ways. It is important for researchers and clinicians to avoid these challenges by employing clear operational definitions of social skills (e.g., Ryan, Brady, Holloway, & Lydon, 2018) to ensure interventions are accurately designed and it is apparent when target skills have been mastered. Utilizing direct observational methods in addition to indirect assessment methods [e.g., Social Responsiveness Scale-Second Edition (SRS-2); Constantino & Gruber, 2012] can help serve to evaluate program outcomes for the individual.

When considering assessments, there are limited standardized rating scales and observational measures of social skills that exist for adults with ASD. This presents difficulties in terms of assessing social functioning and providing sensitive measures to evaluate treatment effects. For example, the social skills improvement system (SSIS; Gresham & Elliott, 2008) was designed to assess social behaviors in individuals aged 3–18 years. Previous research examining social skills interventions in adulthood have utilized the SSIS as a dependent measure of social skills due to the current lack of standardized assessments available for this population (Laugeson et al., 2015; Walsh et al., 2018). More research is needed to identify assessment methods that explicitly assess social skills deficits in adults with ASD. Lerman et al. (2017) recommend that when assessing job-related social skills, it is essential that direct methods of assessment are combined with indirect assessments in order to identify each individual's skills deficits. They recommend that evocative situations (ES) be used to assess an individual's readiness for employment or to identify the supports needed for success within existing employment settings.

Second, the acquisition of "camouflaging" strategies in adults with ASD may present challenges in terms of identifying and supporting individuals in need of intervention. Through long-term societal pressures, some adults with ASD may develop "camouflaging" or coping strategies for use within social situations (Kopp & Gillberg, 2011; Lai et al., 2011). These strategies may include concealing specific behaviors or using specific strategies and techniques to navigate or avoid social situations. For example, some adults might learn to look at their conversational partner in the eye when talking, copy facial expressions, or use specific learnt phrases during a conversation (Lai & Baron-Cohen, 2015). However, research shows that "camouflaging" may adversely impact on ASD diagnosis and quality of life (Hull et al., 2017).

Third, adults with ASD are not a homogeneous group. A high frequency of co-occurring disorders exists for this population with 70% of individuals with ASD presenting with a coexisting medical, developmental, and/or psychiatric conditions (Simonoff et al., 2008). The spectrum nature of ASD symptoms and the current lack of evidence-based social skills interventions existing for this group (Ledford, King, Harbin, & Zimmerman, 2018; Reichow & Volkmar, 2010), presents challenges in terms of identifying what works for whom, and under what conditions. Ledford et al. (2018) reviewed 113 peer-reviewed articles, including 263 studies with 409 total participants, examining the effects of social skills interventions for individuals with ASD. Results showed that only four participants were 18 years of age or older. Interestingly, intellectual ability was only reported for 24% of all participants. Of the 24%, just under half were identified as having an intellectual disability (Ledford et al., 2018). As social functioning is challenging for all adults with ASD, more research must be conducted to better understand what interventions are effective across cognitive functioning ranges.

Fourth, the use of technology in intervention and instruction for individuals with ASD is increasing (Odom et al., 2015; Walsh, Holloway, McCoy, & Lydon, 2016). Technology-aided interventions can be a resource efficient tool and used in conjunction with other teaching strategies to optimize services within clinical settings (DiGennaro Reed, Hyman, & Hirst, 2011). A variety of technologies have been explored in the literature including, video modeling, audio-cueing, video prompting, and the use of iPad applications to teach employment skills (Alexander, Ayres, Smith, Shepley, & Mataras, 2013; Allen, Burke, Howard, Wallace, & Bowen, 2012; Bereznak, Ayres, Mechling, & Alexander, 2012; Hill, Belcher, Brigman, Renner, & Stephens, 2013). More recently, video modeling was successfully integrated into an intervention to increase social skills for adults with ASD and ID preparing for employment (Walsh et al., 2018). Results showed significant improvements in social skills following completion of the intervention, with evidence of generalization and maintenance.

Other important components to consider when implementing a social skills intervention include (a) the number of social skills targeted, (b) delivery agents (e.g., peer, social skill facilitator, parent, technology, combination), (c) format of delivery (e.g., individual, group [size, format]), (d) intervention density, (e) programming for generalization and maintenance, (f) procedure fidelity, (g) social validity outcomes, and (h) caregiver involvement.

PREP4Work

PREP4Work is a technology-based intervention package designed to target socially significant skills to support meaningful community and workplace inclusion for individuals with ASD and co-occurring ID. The intervention is delivered within a classroom environment with additional opportunities to practice skills in the real-world context. PREP4Work represents the culmination of a number of empirical studies, which have aimed to evaluate the role of technology within social skills interventions (Ryan et al., 2018; Walsh et al., 2016, 2018; Walsh, Holloway, et al., 2019; Walsh, Lydon, & Holloway, 2019). Overall, the intervention employs curriculum content from The walker social skills curriculum:

ACCESS program (Walker et al., 1988), technology (i.e., video modeling), and current evidence-based practices (i.e., programmed generalization), to target a range of meaningful social skills necessary for inclusion. PREP4Work is guided by the principles of ABA. This section will outline the procedural elements of the intervention.

The PREP4Work intervention is designed to meet the needs of young adults with ASD and co-occurring mild-to-moderate ID. Young adults who might benefit from the intervention present with the following prerequisite skills: (a) observational learning skills, such that the learner would benefit from practices that employ role play and video modeling, (b) language skills, including listening and following simple directions, as well as the ability to communicate using vocal verbal behavior, and (c) a behavioral repertoire that allows for satisfactory academic engagement (i.e., attending and following simple directions within a group). While PREP4Work employs behavior support strategies (e.g., behavioral contracts and differential reinforcement schedules), it is not designed to target extreme levels of challenging behaviors (e.g., aggression toward others, self-injury, extreme property damage).

PREP4Work is a treatment package, employing the content of The ACCESS Curriculum (Walker et al., 1988). This curriculum targets 31 social behaviors, divided across three domains, (1) peer-related social skills (e.g., listening to others, greetings, joining in with other people, having conversations, showing a sense of humor, negotiation, expressing anger), (2) adult-related social skills (e.g., responding to requests from employers, doing quality work, developing good work habits), and (3) self-related social skills [e.g., being organized, taking pride in your appearance, feeling good about yourself, accepting consequences of own actions; see Walsh et al. (2018) and Walker et al. (1988) for full details]. Within PREP4Work, the target skills are operationally defined (Ryan et al., 2018) and critical features of the social skills are clearly outlined for intervention delivery. The curriculum also provides a 10-step instructional procedure, role-play cards, behavioral contracts, teaching scripts for each lesson, and a placement test to identify target skills.

Prior to intervention, classroom rules are established to promote positive classroom behavior. In PREP4Work, three classroom rules—namely (1) paying attention, (2) participation during intervention sessions, and (3) raising one's hand to speak—are targeted during the intervention. Each rule is written in positive language with accompanying visual supports to clearly specify the target skill. An interdependent group contingency is employed to reinforce rule following. Each 90-min session is divided into 5-min intervals, with reinforcement (i.e., tokens) delivered contingent upon each member of the group following the classroom rules, during each interval. Following each intervention session and pending 80% success on the contingency, learners access back-up reinforcers from the reinforcer bank (e.g., board games, iPad, photographs of favorite music group). Assessment of potential reinforcers is conducted with learners prior to starting the intervention to ascertain their specific interests. Further assessments are conducted throughout the intervention to ensure the correct reinforcers are identified and used within the intervention. In this manner, the back-up reinforcer lists for use within the token economy and group contingencies are updated regularly (i.e., every 3–4 weeks).

In addition to the group contingency for rule following and participation on the program, an individual reinforcement schedule is also used with the some of the learners, as required. The token economy, whereby learners receive tokens on a variable ratio schedule for active engagement, is used during the intervention sessions. Furthermore, a progress chart is used as part of the intervention, whereby the learners receive a star to indicate the lesson has been completed and that the homework activity has been finished. These various reinforcement schedules support high levels of learner engagement and motivation.

A variety of materials are used to support delivery of the PREP4Work intervention. Technological aspects include video models and myPref App (KV Adaptive, 2016). Other materials included posters depicting the target social skills, folders of worksheets for in-class and homework sessions, and banks of reinforcers.

Video modeling, as described in Walsh et al. (2018), is employed to depict the target social skills and the supported employment options available for selection. A total of 158 video models were created for use within the intervention. The video models are relatively short (ranging from approximately 30–120 s) and portray similar-aged peers demonstrating the target social behaviors. The video models depict the scripted examples included in the ACCESS curriculum; for example, one model shows a young adult demonstrating the skill of listening when a friend has problem they want to share. Video models are also used to depict the different supported employment options available and to support learners to select job preferences (Walsh, Holloway, et al., 2019; Walsh, Lydon, et al., 2019). Again, same-aged adult models demonstrate each of the available jobs. For example, another model shows a young adult stocking milk on shelves in a local supermarket to demonstrate the tasks required for that employment setting. A total of 12 video models were created to illustrate the 12 supported employment opportunities available.

The iPad application "myPref" (KV Adaptive, 2016) assesses learners' job preferences. An image, depicting an adult model engaging in the job and/or items required for the job, is uploaded to the app. Images are presented on the myPref as a paired-choice preference assessment across six items to determine job preferences. The myPref app presents 30 trials with each item presented against every other option. In this method of presenting representations of possible job opportunities, it is possible to record the learner's choice of preferred job. This allows the program team to create a hierarchy of preferred job options, and it thereby aims to match learner preferences to learner strengths and skill sets. This is a unique feature of the intervention, as it is common practice within disability services to match learners to jobs available rather than preferred jobs. It also provides the team with an opportunity to explore job opportunities within related professional categories to allow learners to sample similar jobs. For example, if a learner indicates a preference for working at a pet store as they enjoy animals and have good skills in caring for and knowledge of animals, then roles such as dog walker/pet minder, veterinary nurse, and/or farm worker could be explored.

PREP4Work procedural elements include (1) intensive initial and ongoing social skills facilitators' training sessions, (2) initial and ongoing program evaluation, (3) employing evidence-based practices to target sequenced social skills, (4) embedding generalization promotion strategies, (5) behavioral contracts, and (6) parent/caregiver involvement. The intervention is delivered within a social skills group; thus, multiple further learning opportunities to practice social behaviors are created. In addition to group-based instruction, sessions within the community are also run to provide opportunities both to train skills in situ, as well as offer opportunities to test for skill transfer to real-world settings.

Social skills facilitators' and coaches' training

The social skills facilitators and coaches are trained using BST prior to the onset of intervention. The BST training consists of instruction, modeling, practice, and feedback. Written instructions and summaries of the instructional steps are provided to the facilitators and coaches. During training there are opportunities to ask questions. The 10-step instructional sequence of PREP4Work is outlined as a task analysis checklist and used as a method of assessing fidelity of intervention delivery. The fidelity checks are conducted periodically across the duration of intervention. Corrective feedback is provided during training sessions, with a clear explanation on how the skill is performed and recorded if incorrect. Each facilitator and coach is required to obtain a score of 100% during training to progress to intervention delivery. The facilitators are tasked with teaching the social skills within the intervention sessions, whereas the coaches are required to oversee the behavior support strategies and deliver the in situ practice sessions within the community.

Direct measures and indirect standardized assessments are used to evaluate learners' performance before and after intervention (Walsh et al., 2018; Walsh, Holloway, et al., 2019; Walsh, Lydon, et al., 2019). Direct measures of performance, prior to intervention, are taken at baseline and again post intervention within the learner's typical environment. As such, the assessor aims to create an ES for each of the target skills, whereby the environment is set up in such a way as to establish the opportunities for the learner to emit the target social skills. For example, when greeting your employer or job coach has been positively reinforced by social attention, deprivation of the employer's/job coaches attention (e.g., as a result of a weekend off work) would increase the effectiveness of such attention as a reinforcer on Monday morning upon returning to work (establishing operations). Similarly, when conversing with a colleague has been positively reinforced by peer attention, satiation as a result of working with that person in a 1:1 setting for an entire day would decrease the effectiveness of such attention as a reinforcer (abolishing operation). A further example might include when the target skills of "joining in with others" have been mastered within the group instructional sessions, the coach may create an ES, whereby the learner goes for coffee with a group of peers to provide the opportunity to practice "joining in with others" during typical conversations outside of the instructional sessions. No feedback is given during these sessions, and the coach records data on the independent performance of the learner within this real-world scenario. Should the skill not be demonstrated within this session, the team will review the target and can decide to provide further in situ training opportunities or more group exercises within the instructional sessions. In the PREP4Work intervention, each of the 30 target social skills is operationally defined and tested across the natural environment pre- and postintervention.

Indirect assessments include measures taken with the learner and significant others. The SRS-2 (Constantino & Gruber, 2012) and SSIS (Gresham & Elliott, 2008) are used to evaluate the impact of social skills intervention. The ACCESS placement assessment is used to assess outcomes post intervention. Such a mix of assessments provide researchers and clinicians with the opportunity to evaluate the overall impact of the intervention for the individual. In essence, the standardized assessments provide an evaluation of the overall impact of the PREP4Work intervention. The direct assessments provide a more individualized assessment of each learner's performance, as well as the opportunity to make specific changes (e.g., provide more learning opportunities or include more visual supports for a given lesson) when evaluating the learning patterns. This is achieved by assessing each learner on the target social skills preintervention and ongoing throughout the intervention. For example, the direct skills preassessment provides specific information on the skill deficits of the learner, then the ongoing monitoring of learner performance gives information on the rate of acquisition, as well as the number of criteria achieved. This learning pattern can be unique to the individual and when analyzed provides information to the intervention team on when to progress to the next target skill, when additional learning opportunities are required, or when/if any additional supports would benefit the learner. There is a further test of performance conducted in the community (e.g., coffee shop) outside of the classroom setting. This assessment is taken during typical social exchanges and in the absence of corrective feedback from the facilitators or coaches. The information gathered gives an indication of the skill learned within the structured teaching environment has transferred to real-world situations. This assessment for skill transfer (i.e., generalization) can also be conducted by employing peers (blind to the procedural elements) to role play a series of social exchanges that are representative of real-world scenarios.

The intervention is delivered within a small group setting (i.e., 6–7 learners). This allows for adequate opportunities to respond, paired dyad work, individualization where needed (e.g., creation of additional learning opportunities), and implementation of appropriate schedules of reinforcement. The intervention is delivered for two sessions per week (1.5 h per session) across a period of 20 weeks or approximately 5 months.

The same lesson sequence delivery is employed for each social skills group. At the outset of a lesson, the social skills facilitator reviews the previous lesson and behavior contracts (Step 1) and then introduces the new target social skill (Step 2). Visual supports depicting the social rules are displayed and used to facilitate learning. Following this, video models depicting incorrect and correct examples of the target skills are presented (Steps 3 and 4). The facilitator then discusses the critical features of the target skill to aid the learners to identify the important aspects of the target skill (Step 5) and central message (Step 6). An assessment of the learners' accuracy in identifying the presence or absence of critical skill features takes place in Step 7, through the presentation of further novel video models and a series of prescripted questions. Step 8 involves role plays, whereby learners are provided with social scenarios and opportunities to role play the target skills with a peer. As part of the social skills training, learners are provided with situational role-play cards during each session. The role plays are used to practice new skills. The facilitators incorporate examples of familiar social situations that learners are likely to encounter when using the target skills in their natural settings. During role-play sessions, feedback is delivered immediately in the form of praise for correct responses or describing incorrect elements following an incorrect response, which typically follows the discrete trial instruction model. Learners are required to pass a criterion of 100% correct across two role plays to progress. A test of knowledge is also taken, whereby learners are asked two open-ended questions to assess knowledge (i.e., describe the target skill and identify critical features). Step 9 involves a discussion around the application of the target skill in the natural environment and learners are required to complete a generalization plan. This plan sets out an agreement to practice the skill across the learner's typical routines (Step 10).

PREP4Work intervention incorporates strategies to promote generalization, to enhance treatment outcomes. PREP4Work aims to: (1) employ training in the natural setting; (2) establish naturally occurring reinforcement contingencies; (3) utilize multiple exemplars during instruction; and (4) incorporate materials and social scenarios from the naturally occurring setting. Training in the learner's natural setting is an important part of the intervention and is delivered in two ways. In the first instance, the coaches create real-life ES within the learner's workplace or community setting. The coach provides feedback on whether the learner responds correctly under the ES. These in situ training sessions provide the learner with direct learning opportunities of naturally occurring ES. Furthermore, as these opportunities are typically present in the learner's environment, it is likely that multiple further opportunities are created when the coach is not directly present.

Generalization planning is also discussed prior to the learner finishing each group session. This involves the learner working with the facilitator to identify the naturally occurring ES within their own work and community settings to practice the skills. The facilitator supports the learner to write a "contract to practice." This involves the learner providing examples of when it was likely for the skill to be warranted and with whom it could be practiced, as well as a description of the target skill to be emitted by the learner, and then the naturally occurring reinforcer that might be expected (e.g., smile). In this way, the learner can identify their own naturally occurring ES for a given skill and outline how they would practice the skill. Both the learner and facilitator sign the document, and the facilitator checks this agreement at the beginning of each new session, delivering reinforcement contingent upon meeting the agreement terms (i.e., progress chart). In addition, these sessions provide learners with the opportunities to discuss any particular barriers for practice, and the facilitator can support the individual to problem solve potential solutions to overcome the identified barriers.

Within the social skills group, learners are provided with multiple opportunities to practice the target skills and those already mastered from previous lessons. The facilitator also provides reinforcement for naturally occurring social exchanges within the group. Reinforcement is delivered in the form of social attention, social nonverbal behavior (e.g., smile, laugh, attention), and social vocal behavior (e.g., "That's great, thank you"). The reinforcers selected are chosen to reflect the naturally occurring contingencies (i.e., attention/praise/response) typically observed within the community. The schedule by which the reinforcement is delivered is also mirrored upon the typical social contingencies within the community. Furthermore, staff within the community or workplace settings are appraised of the target skills mastered and those in acquisition. This is achieved by publically posting target social skills. In this way, further social skills practice opportunities are created by other members in the environment. Parents/caregivers also receive workshops on the program and are notified of the skills mastered and those in acquisition. Parents are given opportunities to discuss the skills, identify opportunities to practice, methods of reinforcer delivery, error correction procedures, and to problem solve barriers to skill acquisition.

Concluding reflections

The elements of PREP4Work were assessed across a number of studies (Walsh et al., 2018; Walsh, Holloway, et al., 2019; Walsh, Lydon, et al., 2019). Overall, the research outcomes demonstrated a positive impact for the intervention across indirect and direct measures. In Walsh et al. (2018), the results showed a significant improvement in overall social skills on the SSIS rating scale and the ACCESS placement test. Furthermore, problem behaviors, as measured by the SSIS, decreased significantly following the social skills training. In a follow-up study, a similar pattern of performances was observed in participants (Walsh, Holloway, et al., 2019; Walsh, Lydon, et al., 2019), showing increases in scores

TABLE 1 Reflections for practice.

1. It is important to consider using curricula, which present an array of social skills that are necessary to navigate a range of employment environments
2. Curriculum placement tests and assessments of typically occurring evocative situations help ascertain individual needs
3. Social skills groups can capitalize on the use of peers as role-play partners, peers as models of social behavior, and mediators of performance feedback, which can enrich outcomes. The group format also provides individuals with multiple opportunities to practice the target skills in both contrived (e.g., role plays) and uncontrived social situations (i.e., naturally occurring social interactions between peers)
4. Video modeling allows for the repeated presentation of an array of stimuli and depictions of the real-world scenarios that may not be immediately accessible in within the target setting (e.g., how to use the skill of joining in with others in a café). Additionally, video modeling provides a medium in which to create multiple exemplars of social skills being taught, a key strategy to support the generalization of skills
5. Classroom behavior management strategies (e.g., structuring the environment, classroom rules/expectations, visual schedules, reinforcement, group contingencies) are helpful in supporting appropriate learning environments to optimize intervention delivery (e.g., attention, staying on task)
6. Programming for generalization requires systematic planning and should occur prior to the onset of intervention
7. Contract for generalization is a helpful tool in guiding individuals to identify environments in which newly acquired skills could be practiced and applied. Individuals are also committing to practice the skill
8. Caregivers, staff, and significant others should be aware of the weekly target social skills. This helps create awareness, allowing staff and others to reinforce newly acquired skills and create further opportunities to practice (i.e., increasing learning opportunities)
9. Behavior skills training is effective in training staff to become social skills facilitators and supporting successful implementation of the intervention

on the SSIS, SRS-2, and baseline placement assessment. This study explored the generalization planning element of the intervention and successfully demonstrated that the target skills were also observed in untrained setting and across novel instructors.

The evaluation helped to broaden an understanding of social skills interventions and the importance of increasing social competencies in adults with ASD and complex needs. Table 1 provides some tips for intervention delivery and reflections for practice from evaluations of the intervention.

References

Alexander, J. L., Ayres, K. M., Smith, K. A., Shepley, S. B., & Mataras, T. K. (2013). Using video modelling on an iPad to teach generalized matching on a sorting mail task to adolescents with autism. *Research in Autism Spectrum Disorder*, *7*, 1346–1357. https://doi.org/10.1016/2013.07.021.

Allen, K. D., Burke, R. V., Howard, M. R., Wallace, D. P., & Bowen, S. L. (2012). Use of audio cuing to expand employment opportunities for adolescents with autism spectrum disorders and intellectual disabilities. *Journal of Autism and Developmental Disorders*, *42*(11), 2410–2419. https://doi.org/10.1007/s10803-012-1519-7.

Baldwin, S., Costley, D., & Warren, A. (2014). Employment activities and experiences of adults with high-functioning autism and Asperger's disorder. *Journal of Autism and Developmental Disorders*, *44*, 2440–2449. https://doi.org/10.1007/s10803-014-2112-z.

Barneveld, P. S., Swabb, H., Fagel, S., van Engeland, H., & de Sonneville, L. M. J. (2014). Quality of life: A case-controlled long-term follow-up study, comparing young high-functioning adults with autism spectrum disorder with adults with other psychiatric disorders diagnosed in childhood. *Comprehensive Psychiatry*, *55*, 302–310. https://doi.org/10.1016/j.comppsych.2013.08.001.

Bellesi, G., Jameel, L., Vyas, K., Crawford, S., & Channon, S. (2016). Using and reasoning about social strategies in autism spectrum disorder in everyday situations. *Research in Autism Spectrum Disorders*, *25*, 112–121.

Bellini, S., Peters, J. K., Benner, L., & Hopf, A. (2007). A meta-analysis of school-based social skills interventions for children with autism spectrum disorders. *Remedial and Special Education*, *28*(3), 153–162. https://doi.org/10.1177/07419325070280030401.

Bereznak, S., Ayres, K. M., Mechling, L. C., & Alexander, J. L. (2012). Video self-prompting and mobile technology to increase daily living and vocational independence for students with autism spectrum disorder. *Journal of Developmental Physical Disabilities*, *24*, 269–285. https://doi.org/10.1007/s10882-012-9270-8.

Bernstein, F. C., Koetzle, T. F., Williams, G. J., Meyer, E. F., Jr., Brice, M. D., Rodgers, J. R., … Tasumi, M. (1977). The protein data bank: A computer-based archival file for macromolecular structures. *Journal of Molecular Biology*, *112*(3), 535–542. https://doi.org/10.1016/s0022-2836(77)80200-3.

Bonete, S., Calero, M. D., & Fernandez-Parra, A. (2015). Group training in interpersonal problem-solving skills for workplace adaptation of adolescents and adults with Asperger syndrome: A preliminary study. *Autism*, *19*(4), 409–420. https://doi.org/10.1177/1362361314522354.

Burgess, S., & Cimera, R. E. (2014). Employment outcomes of transition-aged adults with autism Spectrum disorders: A state of the states report. *American Journal on Intellectual and Developmental Disabilities*, *119*(1), 64–83. https://doi.org/10.1352/1944-7558-119.1.64.

Chiang, H., Cheung, Y. K., Li, H., & Tsai, L. Y. (2013). Factors associated with participation in employment for high school leavers with autism. *Journal of Autism and Developmental Disorders*, *43*, 1832–1842. https://doi.org/10.1007/s10803-012-1734-2.

Constantino, J. N., & Gruber, C. P. (2012). *Social responsiveness scale-second edition (SRS-2)*. Torrance, CA: Western Psychological Services.https://doi.org/10.1177/0734282913517525.

Dib, N., & Sturmey, P. (2012). Behavioral skills training and skill learning. In N. M. Seel (Ed.), *Encyclopedia of the sciences of learning*. (pp. 437–438). Boston: Springer. https://doi.org/10.1007/978-1-4419-1428-6_644.

DiGennaro Reed, F. D., Hyman, S. R., & Hirst, J. M. (2011). Applications of technology to teach social skills to children with autism. *Research in Autism Spectrum Disorders*, *5*, 1003–1010. https://doi.org/10.1016/j.rasd.2011.01.022.

Frye, R. E. (2018). Social skills deficits in autism spectrum disorder: Potential biological origins and progress in developing therapeutic agents. *CNS Drugs*, *32*(8), 713–734. https://doi.org/10.1007/s40263-018-0556-y.

García-Villamisar, D., & Hughes, C. (2007). Supported employment improves cognitive performance in adults with autism. *Journal of Intellectual Disability Research*, *51*(2), 142–150. https://doi.org/10.1111/j.1365-2788.2006.00854.x.

García-Villamisar, D., Wehman, P., & Navarro, M. D. (2002). Changes in the quality of autistic people's life that work in supported and sheltered employment. A 5-year follow-up study. *Journal of Vocational Rehabilitation*, *17*(4), 309–312.

Gresham, F. M., & Elliott, S. N. (2008). *Social skills improvement system-rating scales*. Minneapolis, MN: Pearson Assessments.https://doi.org/10.1177/0734282910385806.

Gresham, F. M., Sugai, G., & Horner, R. H. (2001). Interpreting outcomes of social skills training for students with high-incidence disabilities. *Exceptional Children*, *67*(3), 331–344. https://doi.org/10.1177/001440290106700303.

Hill, D. A., Belcher, L., Brigman, H. E., Renner, S., & Stephens, B. (2013). The Apple iPad as an innovative employment support for young adults with autism spectrum disorder and other developmental disabilities. *Journal of Applied Rehabilitation Counselling*, *44*(1), 28–37.

Hiller, A. J., Fish, T., Siegel, J. H., & Beversdorf, D. Q. (2011). Social and vocational skills training reduces self-reported anxiety and depression among young adults on the autism spectrum. *Journal of Developmental and Physical Disabilities*, *23*, 267–276. https://doi.org/10.1007/s10882-011-9226-4.

Howlin, P., & Yates, P. (1999). The potential effectiveness of social skills groups for adults with autism. *Autism*, *3*(3), 299–307. https://doi.org/10.1177/1362361399003003007.

Hull, L., Petrides, K. V., Allison, C., Smith, P., Baron-Cohen, S., Lai, M.-C., & Mandy, W. (2017). "Putting on my best normal": Social camouflaging in adults with autism Spectrum conditions. *Journal of Autism and Developmental Disorders*, *47*(8), 2519–2534. https://doi.org/10.1007/s10803-017-3166-5.

Jennes-Coussens, M., Magill-Evans, J., & Koning, C. (2006). The quality of life of young men with Asperger syndrome: A brief report. *Autism*, *10*(4), 403–414. https://doi.org/10.1177/1362361306064432.

Koegel, R. L., Frea, W. D., & Surratt, A. V. (1994). Self-management of problematic social behavior. In E. Schopler & G. B. Mesibov (Eds.), *Behavioral issues in autism (current issues in autism)*. Boston, MA: Springer.

Koegel, R., Kim, S., & Koegel, L. (2013). Improving socialization for high school students with ASD by using their preferred interests. *Journal of Autism and Developmental Disorders*, *43*(9), 2121–2134. https://doi.org/10.1007/s10803-013-1765-3.

Kopp, S., & Gillberg, C. (2011). The autism spectrum screening questionnaire (ASSQ)-revised extended version (ASSQ-REV): An instrument for better capturing the autism phenotype in girls? A preliminary study involving 191 clinical cases and community controls. *Research in Developmental Disabilities*, *32*(6), 2875–2888. https://doi.org/10.1016/j.ridd.2011.05.017.

Krieger, B., Kinébanian, A., Prodinger, B., & Heigl, F. (2012). Becoming a member of the work force: Perceptions of adults with Asperger syndrome. *Work*, *43*, 141–157. https://doi.org/10.3233/WOR-2012-1392.

KV Adaptive. (2016). *myPref (Version 2.1)* [Mobile application software]. Retrieved from https://itunes.apple.com/us/app/mypref/id1091815522?mt=8.

Lai, M. C., & Baron-Cohen, S. (2015). Identifying the lost generation of adults with autism spectrum disorder conditions. *The Lancet Psychiatry*, *2*(10), 13–27. https://doi.org/10.1016/s2215-0366(15)00277-1.

Lai, M.-C., Lombardo, M. V., Pasco, G., Ruigrok, A. N. V., Wheelwright, S. J., … Sadek, S. A. (2011). A behavioral comparison of male and female adults with high functioning autism spectrum conditions. *PLoS One*, *6*(6), e20835https://doi.org/10.1371/journal.pone.0020835.

Laugeson, E. A., Frankel, F., Gantman, A., Dillon, A. R., & Mogil, C. (2012). Evidence-based social skills training for adolescents with autism spectrum disorders: The UCLA PEERS program. *Journal of Autism Developmental Disorders*, *42*, 1025–1036. https://doi.org/10.1007/s10803-011-1339-1.

Laugeson, E. A., Gantman, A., Kapp, S. K., Orenski, K., & Elingsen, R. (2015). A randomized controlled trial to improve social skills in young adults with autism spectrum disorder: The UCLA PEERS program. *Journal of Autism and Developmental Disorders*, *45*, 3978–3989. https://doi.org/10.1007/s10803-015-2504-8.

Ledford, J. R., King, S., Harbin, E. R., & Zimmerman, K. N. (2018). Antecedent social skills interventions for individuals with ASD: What works, for whom, and under what conditions? *Focus on Autism and Other Developmental Disabilities*, *33*(1), 3–13. https://doi.org/10.1177/1088357616634024.

Lerman, D. C., White, B., Grob, C., & Laudont, C. (2017). A clinic-based assessment for evaluating job-related social skills in adolescents and adults with autism. *Behavior Analysis in Practice*, *10*(4), 323–336. https://doi.org/10.1007/s40617-017-0177-9.

Kellems, R. O., & Morningstar, M. E. (2012). Using video modeling delivered through iPods to teach vocational tasks to young adults with autism spectrum disorders. *Career Development and Transition for Exceptional Individuals*, *35*(3), 155–167. https://doi.org/10.1177/0885728812443082.

Marriage, S., Wolverton, A., & Marriage, K. (2009). Autism spectrum disorder grown up: A chart review of adult functioning. *Journal of Canadian Academy of Child and Adolescent Psychiatry*, *18*(4), 322–328. 19881941.

McVey, A. J., Dolan, B. K., Willar, K. S., Pleiss, S., Karst, J. S., Carson, C. L., … Vaughan Van Hecke, A. (2016). A replication and extension of the PEERS for young adults social skills intervention: Examining effects on social skills and social anxiety in young adults with autism spectrum disorder. *Journal of Autism and Developmental Disorders*, *46*(12), 3739–3754. https://doi.org/10.1007/s10803-016-2911-5.

Montgomery, J., Storey, K., Post, M., & Lemley, J. (2011). The use of auditory prompting systems for increasing independent performance of students with autism in employment training. *International Journal of Rehabilitation Research*, *34*(4), 330–335. https://doi.org/10.1097/MRR.0b013e32834a8fa8.

Odom, S. L., Thompson, J. L., Hedges, S., Boyd, B. A., Dykstra, J. R., Duda, M. A., … Bord, A. (2015). Technology-aided interventions and instruction for adolescents with autism spectrum disorder. *Journal of Autism and Developmental Disorders*, *45*, 3805–3819. https://doi.org/10.1007/s10803-014-2320-6.

Orsmond, G. I., Krauss, M. W., & Seltzer, M. M. (2004). Peer relationships and social and recreational activities among adolescents and adults with autism. *Journal of Autism and Developmental Disorders*, *34*(3), 245–256. https://doi.org/10.1023/B:JADD.0000029547.96610.df.

Osterling, J., & Dawson, G. (1994). Early recognition of children with autism: A study of first birthday home videotapes. *Journal of Autism and Developmental Disorders*, *24*(3), 247–257. https://doi.org/10.1007/bf02172225.

Osterling, J. A., Dawson, G., & Munson, J. A. (2002). Early recognition of 1-year-old infants with autism spectrum disorder versus mental retardation. *Development and Psychopathology*, *14*(2), 239–251. https://doi.org/10.1017/S0954579402002031.

Reichow, B., & Volkmar, F. R. (2010). Social skills interventions for individuals with autism: Evaluation for evidence-based practices within a best evidence synthesis framework. *Journal of Autism and Development Disorders*, *40*, 149–166. https://doi.org/10.1007/s10803-009-0842-0.

Rohlfing, K. J., Grimminger, A., & Luke, C. (2017). An interactive view on the development of deictic pointing in infancy. *Frontiers in Psychology*, *8*, 1319. https://doi.org/10.3389/fpsyg.2017.01319.

Roux, A. M., Shattuck, P. T., Cooper, B. P., Anderson, K. A., Wagner, M., & Narendorf, S. C. (2013). Postsecondary employment experiences among young adults with an autism spectrum disorder. *Journal of the American Academy of Child & Adolescent Psychiatry*, *52*(9), 931–939. https://doi.org/10.1016/j.jaac.2013.05.019.

Ryan, G., Brady, S., Holloway, J., & Lydon, H. (2018). Increasing appropriate conversation social skills using a behavioral skills training package with adults with intellectual disability and autism spectrum disorder. *Journal of Intellectual Disabilities*, https://doi.org/10.1177/1744629517750744.

Shattuck, P. T., Narendorf, S. C., Cooper, B., Sterzing, P. R., Wagner, M., & Taylor, J. L. (2012). Postsecondary education and employment among youth with an autism spectrum disorder. *Pediatrics*, *129*(6), 1042–1049. https://doi.org/10.1542/peds.2011-2864.

Simonoff, E., Pickles, A., Charman, T., Chandler, S., Loucas, T., & Baird, G. (2008). Psychiatric disorders in children with autism spectrum disorders: Prevalence, comorbidity, and associated factors in a population-derived sample. *Journal of the American Academy of Child & Adolescent Psychiatry*, *47*, 921–929.

Szatmari, P., Bartolucci, G., Bremner, R., Bond, S., & Rich, S. (1989). A follow-up study of high-functioning autistic children. *Journal of Autism and Developmental Disorders*, *19*(2), 213–225. https://doi.org/10.1007/BF02211842.

Turner-Brown, L., Perry, T., Dichter, G., Bodfish, J., & Penn, D. (2008). Brief report: Feasibility of social cognition and interaction training for adults with high functioning autism. *Journal of Autism and Developmental Disorders*, *38*(9), 1777–1784. https://doi.org/10.1007/s10803-008-0545-y.

Walker, J., Todis, B., Holmes, D., & Horton, G. (1988). *The Walker social skills curriculum: The ACCESS program (adolescent curriculum for communication and effective social skills)*. Austin, TX: Pro-Ed.

Walsh, E., Lydon, H., & Holloway, J. (2019). An evaluation of assistive technology in determining job specific preference for adults with autism and intellectual disabilities. *Behavior Analysis in Practice*, 1–11. https://doi.org/10.1007/s40617-019-00380-3.

Walsh, E., Holloway, J., & Lydon, H. (2018). An evaluation of a social skills intervention for adults with autism spectrum disorder and intellectual disabilities preparing for employment in Ireland: A pilot study. *Journal of Autism and Developmental Disorders*, *48*(5), 1727–1741. https://doi.org/10.1007/s10803-017-341-5.

Walsh, E., Holloway, J., McCoy, A., & Lydon, H. (2016). Technology-aided interventions for employment skills in adults with autism spectrum disorder: A systematic review. *Review Journal of Autism and Developmental Disorders*, https://doi.org/10.1007/s40489-016-0093-x.

Walsh, E., Holloway, J., Lydon, H., McGrath, A., & Cunningham, T. (2019). An exploration of the performance and generalization outcomes of a social skills intervention for adults with autism and intellectual disabilities. *Advances in Neurodevelopmental Disorders*, 1–14.

Further reading

Gantman, A., Kapp, S. K., Orenski, K., & Laugeson, E. A. (2012). Social skills training for young adults with autism spectrum disorders: A randomized controlled pilot. *Journal of Autism and Developmental Disorders*, *42*(6), 1094–1103. https://doi.org/10.1007/s10803-011-1350-6.

Orsmond, G. I., Shattuck, P. T., Cooper, B. P., Sterzing, P. R., & Anderson, K. A. (2013). Social participation among young sdults with an autism spectrum disorder. *Journal of Autism and Developmental Disorders*, *43*(11), 2710–2719. https://doi.org/10.1007/s10803-013-1833-8.

Chapter 17

Social skills training for persons with schizophrenia

Julia Browne[a,b], Kim T. Mueser[c], and Sarah I. Pratt[d]
[a]*Center of Excellence for Psychosocial and Systemic Research, Massachusetts General Hospital, Boston, MA, United States,* [b]*Harvard Medical School, Boston, MA, United States,* [c]*Center for Psychiatric Rehabilitation, Boston University, Boston, MA, United States,* [d]*The Geisel School of Medicine at Dartmouth, Concord, NH, United States*

Schizophrenia is a serious mental illness (SMI) that usually develops in late adolescence or early adulthood and frequently persists over the lifetime. It is characterized by the presence of positive and/or negative symptoms, functional impairment, and other associated problems. Positive (or psychotic) symptoms include hallucinations (e.g., hearing voices), delusions (e.g., strongly held beliefs despite disconfirming evidence), disorganized speech (e.g., tangentiality or incoherence), and disorganized or catatonic behavior (e.g., limited movement, rigidity). Negative symptoms include affective flattening (e.g., constricted emotional expression), anhedonia (lack of pleasure), alogia (poverty of speech), and avolition (lack of motivation). To meet diagnostic criteria for schizophrenia, two or more of these symptoms, at least one of which must be delusions, hallucinations, or disorganized speech, need to be present for at least 1 month, or less if successfully treated. Functioning must be impaired in one or more important domains such as work, interpersonal relationships, or self-care, and the total duration of disturbance must be at least 6 months (American Psychiatric Association, 2013).

While the diagnosis of schizophrenia is primarily based on the presence of positive and negative symptoms combined with impaired psychosocial functioning, other symptoms and impairments are common. Schizophrenia is associated with a decline in cognitive functioning that begins before the onset of psychotic symptoms (Meier et al., 2014). Depressive symptoms are common, including a 5%–7% risk of suicide, comparable to the risk associated with major mood disorders (Gale, Skegg, Mullen, Patterson, & Gray, 2012).

Social Skills Across the Life Span. https://doi.org/10.1016/B978-0-12-817752-5.00017-2

Comorbid substance use disorders are also common, with a lifetime prevalence of 50% (Thoma & Daum, 2013).

Despite advances in treatments over the past several decades, schizophrenia remains one of the most disabling and economically burdensome illnesses. The annual costs of schizophrenia in the United States were reported to be as high as $155.7 billion in 2013 (Cloutier et al., 2016). Indirect costs (e.g., unemployment) rather than direct costs (e.g., clinical care) account for the majority of the burden associated with schizophrenia, underscoring the need for interventions that improve functioning in this population.

Impairments in functioning among persons with schizophrenia result from a variety of factors, most notably deficits in neurocognition and social cognition and the presence of negative symptoms (Green, 2016; Milev, Ho, Arndt, & Andreasen, 2005). With regard to neurocognition, schizophrenia is associated with poor working memory, attention, processing speed, verbal learning, visual learning, reasoning, and problem solving (Green, 2006). In terms of social cognition, schizophrenia is associated with low ability to recognize emotions, facial expressions, and voice tone, poor grasp of social context and unwritten rules of social behavior, and impaired understanding of others' feelings, motives, and perspectives (i.e., theory of mind; Pinkham, 2014; Pinkham, Harvey, & Penn, 2017). In addition, the presence of negative symptoms, including lowered motivation, reduced emotional expressiveness, and social withdrawal, significantly reduce the capacity of individuals with schizophrenia to fully engage in the community. Taken together, approaches that target these domains are important for promoting recovery and improving functioning in this population.

Context and particular considerations

The most effective treatment for persons with schizophrenia includes a combination of pharmacotherapy, psychosocial intervention, and case management. Though individual treatment characteristics vary, a combination of medications, psychotherapy (e.g., cognitive-behavioral therapy, social skills training, training in illness self-management) are most effective in promoting recovery and improved functioning (Kane & McGlashan, 1995). People with schizophrenia receive treatment in both inpatient and outpatient settings, with the former occurring during periods of higher symptom acuity that present potential safety concerns. In addition to medication and psychotherapy, programs that provide practical supports and community-based assistance can help individuals obtain work (e.g., supported employment; Drake, Bond, Goldman, Hogan, & Karakus, 2016) and live stably in the community (e.g., Assertive Community Treatment; Bond & Drake, 2015). Furthermore, peer support (e.g., provided by a person with lived experience of mental health challenges; Davidson, Chinman, Sells, & Rowe, 2006; Lloyd-Evans et al., 2014) can play an important role in improving quality of life and functioning. Moreover, group-based interventions can be valuable aspects of treatment as they promote social interaction and mutual support as well as learning and discussion of useful information and skills.

Social skills training approach

Social skills training (SST; Bellack, Mueser, Gingerich, & Agresta, 2013) is a therapeutic approach that is especially effective for people with schizophrenia for several important reasons. First, SST methods are typically direct and straightforward, thereby minimizing the cognitive abilities required to participate in the intervention. Second, SST addresses social cognitive deficits through discussion of contextual (e.g., setting), nonverbal (e.g., body language), and paralinguistic (e.g., voice tone) aspects of interpersonal interactions. Third, persons receiving SST are actively involved in the intervention (e.g., through role playing, providing feedback to others, taking community trips), which can promote engagement, even in the face of significant negative symptoms. Fourth, SST can be tailored to various functional domains (e.g., social relationships, community living), which is valuable given that challenges often span multiple life areas. Finally, SST can be delivered flexibly, in a variety of different formats based on the setting and client needs (e.g., inpatient or outpatient, individually or in a group).

Broadly based on theories of social learning theory and operant conditioning, the SST approach was initially developed in the 1950s to help persons overcome experiences of anxiety and depression. In fact, clinicians began to incorporate some of the SST methods in the 1950s and 1960s into therapeutic approaches for the treatment of social anxiety. For example, Wolpe (1958) hypothesized that social anxiety could be overcome through counterconditioning. Specifically, he posited that acting in a socially assertive manner during interactions with others would inhibit (and reduce) social anxiety. In the early 1960s, Bandura's research on social learning (Bandura, Ross, & Ross, 1961) demonstrated the role of modeling (i.e., demonstrating) in learning social behaviors, which was subsequently incorporated into SST teaching methods. It was later during the 1960s that various components of SST were systematically integrated into a cohesive approach to teaching effective social behaviors, and clinical applications of SST became more widespread (Mueser, Drake, & Bond, 2016). Many early applications of SST focused on assertiveness skills aimed at teaching persons how to "stand up for themselves" (Mueser et al., 2016, p. 244). Assertiveness training programs then began to incorporate other social skills into the training curriculum (e.g., expressing positive feelings), leading to exploratory efforts to evaluate whether SST methods could be used to improve social skills in individuals with profound impairment in their social functioning, such as persons with schizophrenia. SST is now widely used to help persons with schizophrenia and other severe mental illnesses improve their interpersonal interactions and psychosocial functioning (Bellack et al., 2013), as well as in other populations with pronounced social impairment, such as autism spectrum disorders (White, 2011).

SST can readily be delivered within the context of standard treatment for persons with schizophrenia (Bellack et al., 2013; Liberman, DeRisi, & Mueser, 1989). SST can be provided in a variety of formats, in groups or individually, in inpatient and outpatient settings, and for varied lengths of time (e.g., weeks to years). SST can be delivered in closed groups (i.e., with the same group of people for the length of program) or open groups (i.e., members can join and terminate throughout the length of the program). Whereas pharmacology is focused primarily on symptom reduction, SST can be designed to focus on a variety of goals (e.g., close interpersonal relationships, leisure and recreational activities, interacting with healthcare providers). Attending to these unmet needs can improve functioning, goal-oriented behavior, working alliance with treatment providers, and adherence to recommended treatments. The teaching methods and content of SST can also be adapted to meet the specific needs of individuals to address the acuity of their symptoms, level of cognitive functioning, and degree of psychosocial impairment.

SST is based on five principles: (1) modeling (i.e., demonstrating the skill), (2) reinforcement (i.e., positive consequences promote recurrence of a positive behavior or skill), (3) shaping (i.e., reinforcing successive approximations of a desired behavior or skill), (4) overlearning (i.e., practicing a behavior or skill repeatedly until it becomes effortless), and (5) generalization (i.e., transferring a behavior or skill from one context to another, such as from the training session to the community). These five principles are infused within SST sessions to facilitate acquisition, practice, and generalization of new skills. SST sessions follow a structured teaching format, which includes the following 10 steps: (1) establish the rationale for the skill, (2) discuss the steps of the skill, (3) model the skill in a role play and review the role play with the group members, (4) engage a group member in a role play, (5) provide positive feedback, (6) provide corrective feedback, (7) engage the group member in another role play, (8) provide additional feedback, (9) engage other group members in role plays and provide feedback, as in steps 4–8, and (10) collaboratively develop home assignments for participants to practice the skill on their own.

The first three steps focus on the group leaders' description and modeling of the skills as well as providing feedback on social skills, whereas the subsequent six steps more actively engage group members in behavioral rehearsal and shaping effective skills through successive role plays. The tenth and final step promotes generalization of skills by collaboratively developing a home practice assignment for each group member that allows for real-world practice of the skill from the session. Each step is described in more detail in the following sections.

Eliciting the rationale for the skill (Step 1) generates buy-in from group members about the relevance of the skill to their lives. Specifically, it is helpful to elicit input from the group regarding their thoughts about how the skill is important to them and could contribute to achieving their goals. Reviewing the steps of the skill (Step 2) helps group members better understand the components of the skill. Steps of the skill often contain nonverbal (e.g., maintaining eye contact), paralinguistic (e.g., voice volume, intonation, and clarity), and verbal content (e.g., applicability to specified topic) components, as well as interactive balance (e.g., response latency; Mueser, Gottlieb, & Gingerich, 2014). Group leaders invite group members to share their thoughts about each step of the skill and further tailor the descriptions to cognitive level and comprehension. Next, group leaders model the skill with each other in a brief role play and elicit feedback from group members (Step 3). Prior to beginning the role play, leaders remind group members to pay close attention to how well the steps of the skill are followed (outlined in Step 2). Feedback on role play performance always begins with brief, specific positive comments (e.g., "What did group leader X do well in that role play?"). The emphasis on providing positive feedback first facilitates participants' willingness and effort to engage in role plays. Following positive feedback, a limited number of specific, brief suggestions for improved performance can be elicited from group members (e.g., "How could group leader X have been even more effective?").

During Steps 4–9, each group member is engaged in at least two role plays with group leaders who elicit and provide feedback after each role play as described earlier. Specifically, one group member completes a role play with a volunteer from the group while the rest of the group members observe (Step 4). At the completion of the role play, the group members are asked for positive feedback (Step 5) followed by corrective feedback (Step 6). The group member is then encouraged to make recommended changes (e.g., "What could make it even better is if you…") in another role play of the same situation (Step 7), with additional feedback from the members (Step 8). It can be valuable to repeat the same role play with the same group member more than once, successively providing feedback to enable adequate opportunities for practicing the skills. Following role plays, group members are encouraged to make a plan for a home practice to use the skill in furtherance of recovery-oriented goals before the next session. Group leaders assist with developing the plans for home practice, encouraging members to specify important details like when, where, and with whom the behavioral plan will be enacted. The home practice not only allows for rehearsal of the skill but also promotes generalization of the skill from one situation (e.g., the group session) to another (e.g., work environment).

Though the types of skills taught during sessions can vary, Bellack and colleagues (2013) recommend first focusing on four basic social skills (Listening to Others, Making Requests, Expressing Positive Feelings, and Expressing Unpleasant Feelings). After teaching these initial skills, there are a variety of other skills that can be taught, including those related to conversation, assertiveness, conflict management, communal living, friendship and dating, health maintenance, vocational/work, and skills for coping with drug and alcohol use. Group leaders can choose the specific skill areas to target based on the needs of the group members and/or can elicit suggestions from group members. Each skill is broken down into small steps and can be applied to a variety of situations. An example SST session demonstrating the skill of "Making a Request" is outlined in Table 1.

TABLE 1 Sample SST session for "Making a Request."

SST session step	Description and sample script
Step 1. Establish the rationale for the skill	Group leaders provide introduction to the "Making a Request" skill and offer a brief rationale for why it is important (e.g., "It can help us get our needs met"). Group leaders then elicit thoughts from group members about why they think the skill is relevant in their lives (e.g., "Why else might this skill be useful in your lives?") and discuss any experiences with it previously (e.g., "What experiences have you had with making requests?")
Step 2. Review the steps of the skill	Group leaders write the steps of the skill on a whiteboard or on handouts for group members: 1. *Look at the person* 2. *Say exactly what you would like the person to do* 3. *Tell the person how it would make you feel if they did what you requested* Group leaders pause after each step and ask group members why that particular step is important to the overall skill
Step 3. Model the skill in a role play and review the role play with the group members	Group leaders demonstrate the skill effectively for the group members. They first setup the role play (e.g., "I am going to ask my coleader for help carrying my groceries up the stairs at my apartment"). Then, they ask the group members to observe how well the group leader demonstrates the steps of the skill After the role play is complete, the group leaders ask the group members for positive feedback and suggested improvements. It can be helpful to ask for feedback specifically about each step (e.g., "How well did I do Step 1?") to emphasize the importance of using each step. Moreover, group leaders are encouraged to role play the skill effectively to demonstrate a model for how it can be done well. Asking for tips to improve performance emphasizes that everyone can enhance their social skills
Step 4. Engage a group member in a role play using the same situation	Group leaders complete a role play (as in Step 3) with a group member. They review the specifics of the role play and encourage the rest of the group members to observe in preparation for providing feedback
Step 5. Provide/elicit positive feedback	Group leaders provide and elicit positive feedback about the role play from the group members. They can ask a general question to begin (e.g., "What did the group member do well?") and then follow up with questions regarding specifics about each step (e.g., "How did the group member do well with Step 1?")

TABLE 1 Sample SST session for "Making a Request."—cont'd

SST session step	Description and sample script
Step 6. Provide/elicit corrective feedback	Group leaders provide and elicit one or a few suggestions for improving the person's performance in the role play from the group members. Requests for feedback can be made in a positive tone to maintain the supportive environment, including general questions such as "What could the group member do next time that would make the role play even better?" and more specific questions such as "What could the group member do to improve Step 1?"
Step 7. Engage the group member in another role play using the same situation	The group leaders engage the member in another role play of the same situation. Next, the group leaders summarize feedback from Steps 5–6 and provide a specific piece of the corrective feedback for the group member to focus on in repeating the role play (We are going to do the same role play again. This time see if you can keep your eye contact with me while you make the request)
Step 8. Provide additional feedback	Group leaders provide and elicit feedback on the role play. Feedback can focus on how this role play was better than the previous role play (e.g., "How did the group member improve Step 1 during this role play as compared to the first role play?"). Group leaders can elicit suggestions for improvements for the group member if there will be another (e.g., third or fourth) role play. If not, suggestions for improvements can be skipped for the last role play in order to end on a positive note
Step 9. Engage other group members in role plays and provide feedback, as in steps 4–8	Group leaders engage other group members in role plays that are relevant to their lives. They aim to have all group members participate in a role play twice (or three times) in order to allow for sufficient practice of the skill. Group members provide and elicit positive feedback and suggestions at the end of each role play
Step 10. Assign homework that will be reviewed at the beginning of the next session	Group leaders collaborate with group members to identify ways that they can practice the skill in the community before the next session. Group leaders develop homework assignments that are individualized to each member and specific (e.g., where and when skill will be practiced). Possible obstacles to practicing the skill are elicited (e.g., forgetting) and solutions are identified to address them (e.g., setting a reminder on one's cell phone)

Notes: Example skill (Making a Request) is from Bellack et al. (2013). A detailed list of example skills, sample scripts, and associated scenarios can be found in Mueser et al. (2014) and Bellack et al. (2013).

Research support for SST

Turner et al. (2018) completed the most recent review and meta-analysis of the effect of SST on outcomes for those with schizophrenia. The review includes 27 randomized controlled trials that collectively enrolled 1437 participants and examined the effect of SST as compared to a control condition [treatment as usual (TAU), active controls, or supportive counseling]. In terms of its overall effects on symptoms, SST was found to be superior to TAU but not to active controls. SST was no more effective than any comparison condition in treating positive symptoms; however, it was significantly more effective than all control conditions for treating negative symptoms. SST was also superior to TAU for treating general symptoms (e.g., anxiety, depression). In terms of social functioning, SST had superior effects to all comparison conditions combined; however, it was not found to be more effective than active controls or TAU when each was examined separately. In light of the significant differences between SST and all the control groups in improving social functioning, the lack of significant differences between SST and specific types of control conditions is likely due to the smaller number of studies in these particular comparisons, resulting in reduced statistical power to detect significant differences between groups. Thus, the findings of this meta-analysis highlight that the most substantive benefits of SST are in treating negative symptoms and improving social functioning, with some evidence for its impact on total and general symptoms as well (Turner et al., 2018).

As illustrated by the research evidence, SST is an effective approach for persons with schizophrenia. An important strength of SST is its potential applicability to a variety of impairments and functional domains. Three evidence-based SST programs, Social and Independent Living Skills (SILS; Liberman, 2007), Cognitive Behavioral Social Skills Training (CBSST; Granholm, McQuaid, & Holden, 2016), and Helping Older People Experience Success (HOPES; Pratt, Bartels, Mueser, & Forester, 2008), are described in the following section, along with a brief summary of the research supporting their effectiveness.

Social and independent living skills (SILS)

The SILS program was designed to improve illness management, interpersonal relationships, and functioning among persons with SMI (Liberman, 2007). SILS comprises eight modules that cover different skill domains: (1) Medication Management, (2) Symptom Management, (3) Substance Abuse Management, (4) Community Re-entry, (5) Recreation for Leisure, (6) Basic Conversation, (7) Friendship and Intimacy, and (8) Workplace Fundamentals. Skills are taught using principal elements of SST such as focused instruction, modeling, role-play practice, feedback, and home assignments. SILS also uses videos as a teaching and modeling tool. Further, SILS incorporates problem solving into the program to address barriers to practicing and using skills as well as to achieving personally meaningful goals. For example, teaching resource management involves using problem solving to identify the types of resources (e.g., people, money, time) that get in the way of executing skills. Group members are provided with workbooks with practice exercises as well as forms to monitor their progress. This comprehensive program is delivered in a structured format such that sessions include: (1) introduction to the skill (along with strategies to enhance motivation), (2) video of skill demonstration and opportunity to ask and answer questions, (3) in-session role plays, (4) resource management to identify potential obstacles to practicing the skill in the community, (5) problem solving to identify solutions to relevant barriers, (6) planning of in vivo exercises that allow for practice of the skill in the community, and (7) homework assignments that allow for practice of the skill in furtherance of personally meaningful goals.

The SILS program not only has been evaluated in controlled research studies but also has been widely implemented in more than 30 countries. Several controlled trials have demonstrated the benefits of SILS for persons with SMI in facilitating improved functioning (e.g., Glynn et al., 2002; Kopelowicz, Zarate, Gonzalez-Smith, Mintz, & Liberman, 2003; Rossotto, Wirshing, & Liberman, 2004). The SILS modules were created to facilitate use without the need for lengthy training or monitoring of clinicians. Each module has a comprehensive but accessible manual that is easy to use even by persons with limited formal training in SST. Further, the SILS modules can be used in a broad range of treatment settings (e.g., inpatient, outpatient, forensic), and combined with other evidence-based programs (e.g., Supported Employment; Drake & Becker, 1995; Mueser et al., 2005), facilitating its successful and widespread implementation (Liberman, 2007).

Helping older people experience success (HOPES)

The HOPES program is a standardized, manual-based intervention that was originally designed to train older persons with schizophrenia in social skills and skills needed to function maximally in the community (Pratt et al., 2008), but it is also applicable and effective when used with younger adults. HOPES includes two primary components: (1) psychosocial rehabilitation and (2) training in health management skills. The social rehabilitation component is delivered through skills classes and community practice trips following a curriculum that includes seven modules: (1) Communicating Effectively, (2) Making and Keeping Friends, (3) Making the Most of Leisure Time, (4) Healthy Living, (5) Using Medications Effectively, (6) Living Independently in the Community, and (7) Making the Most of a Health Care Visit. Skills classes follow procedures from SST, including modeling, role playing, feedback, and home assignments. Community practice trips serve as opportunities to practice the relevant skill in a real-world setting and are collaboratively planned by the group members and group leaders. The health management component consists of training on skills required for managing chronic health conditions as well as education on recommended preventive health care.

Bartels et al. (2004) compared HOPES with nurse health management (i.e., individual meetings with a psychiatric nurse to address health care needs) in a group of 24 persons with SMI. HOPES was associated with greater improvements in social functioning and independent living skills compared to the health management group. Both groups increased their receipt of preventive health care (Bartels et al., 2004). A randomized controlled trial (RCT) compared HOPES to TAU in a sample of 183 persons with schizophrenia or serious mood disorder (Mueser et al., 2010). In this study, HOPES was delivered over a two-year period with the first year serving as an intensive phase (i.e., weekly skills classes, twice monthly community practice trips, and monthly individual meetings with a nurse) and the second as a maintenance phase (i.e., monthly skills classes, community practice trips, and meetings with a nurse). Results included significantly greater improvements for HOPES versus TAU participants in social skills, psychosocial and community functioning, negative symptoms, and self-efficacy (Mueser et al., 2010). HOPES participants also received significantly more preventive health treatment, including more frequent eye exams, visual acuity tests, hearing tests, mammographs, and pap smears (Bartels et al., 2014). Moreover, improvements in community living skills persisted at the three-year follow-up for persons who received HOPES, highlighting the long-term effects of this skills-based intervention (Bartels et al., 2014). An individually tailored version of HOPES (HOPES-I) also demonstrated superiority compared with TAU (Pratt, Mueser, Santos, Wolfe, & Bartels, 2017).

Cognitive behavioral social skills training (CBSST)

CBSST is a manual-based intervention that combines cognitive behavioral therapy with social skills training to improve functioning and reduce negative symptoms in persons with schizophrenia (Granholm et al., 2016). It comprises three modules that teach: (1) cognitive skills, (2) social skills, and (3) problem solving. The cognitive skills module focuses on teaching people how to challenge beliefs that can interfere with functioning (also known as defeatist beliefs) by using the "3C's": Catch It, Check It, Change It. This strategy is based on the general principles of cognitive behavioral therapy and cognitive restructuring. The social skills component of CBSST uses social skills training methods (e.g., modeling, role playing, etc.) to improve communication skills such as active listening, expressing positive feelings, and expressing negative feelings. Cognitive skills (using the 3C's) are also applied during role plays when defeatist thoughts arise. Finally, the problem-solving component is aimed at learning a structured way for addressing issues that interfere with functioning. Problem solving is taught using SCALE, an acronym that stands for *S*pecify, *C*onsider all possible solutions, *A*ssess the best solution, *L*ay out a plan, and *E*xecute and evaluate the outcome.

CBSST has been shown to improve functioning in samples of middle-aged and older-aged adults (Granholm et al., 2005; Granholm, Holden, Link,

McQuaid, & Jeste, 2013), as well as in younger persons with schizophrenia (Granholm, Holden, Link, & McQuaid, 2014). Granholm et al. (2005) first evaluated CBSST in comparison to TAU in 76 middle-aged and older (*M* age = 54 years) persons with schizophrenia or schizoaffective disorder over 24 weeks. Persons assigned to CBSST experienced greater improvements in social functioning than persons assigned to TAU, which were maintained at one-year follow-up (Granholm et al., 2007). Subsequently, Granholm et al. (2013) tested weekly CBSST against an active control condition, goal-focused supportive contact (GFSC), in 64 middle-aged and older (*M* age = 55 years) persons with schizophrenia or schizoaffective disorder. Results included greater effects of CBSST over GFSC in improving functioning. In order to evaluate the potential benefits of the intervention in a more representative sample, Granholm et al. (2014) conducted a large RCT comparing weekly CBSST to GFSC in a sample of 149 older and younger adults (*M* age = 41 years) with schizophrenia or schizoaffective disorder over nine months. Results of this large RCT demonstrated the superiority of CBSST over GFSC for improving functioning and negative symptoms.

Summary and conclusion

SST is an evidence-based approach that has been shown to improve functioning and negative symptoms in persons with schizophrenia. It is based on principles of social learning theory and operant conditioning, whereby modeling and feedback are critically important. SST involves education, role plays, providing/eliciting feedback, and home practice assignments. Though SST is often provided in a group setting, it can be delivered individually and can also be tailored to meet the specific needs of group members (e.g., setting, cognitive ability level). In addition to the flexibility in how it is delivered, the content foci can be adjusted so that they address salient life domains for given persons (e.g., improving general conversation skills or improving skills to talk with potential employers). Several specific programs based on SST principles have been developed and evaluated with persons with schizophrenia (e.g., SILS, HOPES, CBSST). The SST approach, including these interventions, has substantial evidence demonstrating its capacity to improve important outcomes in people with schizophrenia.

References

American Psychiatric Association. (2013). *Diagnostic and statistical manual of mental disorders* (5th ed.). Arlington, VA: Author.

Bandura, A., Ross, D., & Ross, S. A. (1961). Transmission of aggression through the imitation of aggressive models. *Journal of Abnormal and Social Psychology*, *63*, 575–582.

Bartels, S. J., Forester, B., Mueser, K. T., Miles, K. M., Dums, A. R., Pratt, S. I., & Perkins, L. (2004). Enhanced skills training and health care management for older persons with severe mental illness. *Community Mental Health Journal*, *40*(1), 75–90.

Bartels, S. J., Pratt, S. I., Mueser, K. T., Forester, B. P., Wolfe, R., Cather, C., & Naslund, J. A. (2014). Long-term outcomes of a randomized trial of integrated skills training and preventive healthcare for older adults with serious mental illness. *The American Journal of Geriatric Psychiatry*, *22*(11), 1251–1261. https://doi.org/10.1016/j.jagp.2013.04.013.

Bellack, A. S., Mueser, K. T., Gingerich, S., & Agresta, J. (2013). *Social skills training for schizophrenia: A step-by-step guide*. New York: Guilford Press.

Bond, G. R., & Drake, R. E. (2015). The critical ingredients of assertive community treatment. *World Psychiatry*, *14*, 240–242. https://doi.org/10.1002/wps.20234.

Cloutier, M., Aigbogun, M. S., Guerin, A., Nitulescu, R., Ramanakumar, A. V., Kamat, S. A., & François, C. (2016). The economic burden of schizophrenia in the United States in 2013. *The Journal of Clinical Psychiatry*, *77*(6), 764–771. https://doi.org/10.4088/jcp.15m10278.

Davidson, L., Chinman, M., Sells, D., & Rowe, M. (2006). Peer support among adults with serious mental illness: A report from the field. *Schizophrenia Bulletin*, *32*(3), 443–450. https://doi.org/10.1093/schbul/sbj043.

Drake, R. E., & Becker, D. R. (1995). The individual placement and support model of supported employment. *Psychiatric Services*, *47*, 473–475. https://doi.org/10.1176/ps.47.5.473.

Drake, R. E., Bond, G. R., Goldman, H. H., Hogan, M. F., & Karakus, M. (2016). Individual placement and support services boost employment for people with serious mental illnesses, but funding is lacking. *Health Affairs*, *35*, 1098–1105. https://doi.org/10.1377/hlthaff.2016.0001.

Gale, C., Skegg, K., Mullen, R., Patterson, T., & Gray, A. (2012). Thoughts of suicide and stage of recovery in patients with schizophrenia in community mental health care. *Australasian Psychiatry*, *20*(4), 313–317. https://doi.org/10.1177/1039856212449669.

Glynn, S. M., Marder, S. R., Liberman, R. P., Blain, K., Wirshing, W. C., Wirshing, D. A., et al. (2002). Supplementing clinic-based skills training for schizophrenia with manual-based, community support. *American Journal of Psychiatry*, *159*, 829–837.

Granholm, E., Holden, J., Link, P. C., & McQuaid, J. R. (2014). Randomized clinical trial of cognitive behavioral social skills training for schizophrenia: Improvement in functioning and experiential negative symptoms. *Journal of Consulting and Clinical Psychology*, *82*(6), 1173–1185. https://doi.org/10.1037/a0037098.

Granholm, E., Holden, J., Link, P. C., McQuaid, J. R., & Jeste, D. V. (2013). Randomized controlled trial of cognitive behavioral social skills training for older consumers with schizophrenia: Defeatist performance attitudes and functional outcome. *The American Journal of Geriatric Psychiatry*, *21*(3), 251–262. https://doi.org/10.1016/j.jagp.2012.10.014.

Granholm, E. L., McQuaid, J. R., & Holden, J. L. (2016). *Cognitive-behavioral social skills training for schizophrenia: A practical treatment guide*. New York: Guilford Press.

Granholm, E., McQuaid, J. R., McClure, F. S., Auslander, L. A., Perivoliotis, D., Pedrelli, P., & Jeste, D. V. (2005). A randomized, controlled trial of cognitive behavioral social skills training for middle-aged and older outpatients with chronic schizophrenia. *American Journal of Psychiatry*, *162*(3), 520–529. https://doi.org/10.1176/appi.ajp.162.3.520.

Granholm, E., McQuaid, J. R., McClure, F. S., Link, P. C., Perivoliotis, D., Gottlieb, J. D., & Jeste, D. V. (2007). Randomized controlled trial of cognitive behavioral social skills training for older people with schizophrenia: 12-month follow-up. *The Journal of Clinical Psychiatry*, *68*(5), 730–737. https://doi.org/10.4088/JCP.v68n0510.

Green, M. F. (2006). Cognitive impairment and functional outcome in schizophrenia and bipolar disorder. *The Journal of Clinical Psychiatry*, *67*, 3–8.

Green, M. F. (2016). Impact of cognitive and social cognitive impairment on functional outcomes in patients with schizophrenia. *The Journal of Clinical Psychiatry*, *77*, 8–11. https://doi.org/10.4088/jcp.14074su1c.02.

Kane, J. M., & McGlashan, T. H. (1995). Treatment of schizophrenia. *The Lancet, 346*(8978), 820–825.

Kopelowicz, A., Zarate, R., Gonzalez-Smith, V., Mintz, J., & Liberman, R. P. (2003). Disease management in Latinos with schizophrenia: A family-assisted, skills training approach. *Schizophrenia Bulletin, 29*, 211–228. https://doi.org/10.1093/oxfordjournals.schbul.a006999.

Liberman, R. P. (2007). Dissemination and adoption of social skills training: Social validation of an evidence-based treatment for the mentally disabled. *Journal of Mental Health, 16*, 595–623. https://doi.org/10.1080/09638230701494902.

Liberman, R. P., DeRisi, W. J., & Mueser, K. T. (1989). *Social skills training for psychiatric patients*. New York: Pergamon Press.

Lloyd-Evans, B., Mayo-Wilson, E., Harrison, B., Istead, H., Brown, E., Pilling, S., … Kendall, T. (2014). A systematic review and meta-analysis of randomised controlled trials of peer support for people with severe mental illness. *BMC Psychiatry, 14*, 39. https://doi.org/10.1186/1471-244X-14-39.

Meier, M. H., Caspi, A., Reichenberg, A., Keefe, R. S., Fisher, H. L., Harrington, H., … Moffitt, T. E. (2014). Neuropsychological decline in schizophrenia from the premorbid to the postonset period: Evidence from a population-representative longitudinal study. *American Journal of Psychiatry, 171*, 91–101.

Milev, P., Ho, B. C., Arndt, S., & Andreasen, N. C. (2005). Predictive values of neurocognition and negative symptoms on functional outcome in schizophrenia: A longitudinal first-episode study with 7-year follow-up. *American Journal of Psychiatry, 162*(3), 495–506. https://doi.org/10.1176/appi.ajp.162.3.495.

Mueser, K. T., Aalto, S., Becker, D. R., Ogden, J., Wolfe, R., Schiavo, D., … Xie, H. (2005). The effectiveness of skills training for improving outcomes in supported employment. *Psychiatric Services, 56*, 1254–1260. https://doi.org/10.1176/appi.ps.56.10.1254.

Mueser, K. T., Drake, R. E., & Bond, G. R. (2016). Recent advances in supported employment for people with serious mental illness. *Current Opinion in Psychiatry, 29*(3), 196–201. https://doi.org/10.1097/YCO.0000000000000247.

Mueser, K. T., Gottlieb, J. D., & Gingerich, S. (2014). Social skills and problem solving training. In S. G. Hoffman (Ed.), *Vol. I. Wiley handbook of cognitive behavioral therapy* (pp. 243–271). New York: Wiley.

Mueser, K. T., Pratt, S. I., Bartels, S. J., Swain, K., Forester, B., Cather, C., & Feldman, J. (2010). Randomized trial of social rehabilitation and integrated health care for older people with severe mental illness. *Journal of Consulting and Clinical Psychology, 78*(4), 561–573. https://doi.org/10.1037/a0019629.

Pinkham, A. E. (2014). Social cognition in schizophrenia. *The Journal of Clinical Psychiatry, 75*(Suppl 2), 14–19. https://doi.org/10.4088/JCP.13065su1.04.

Pinkham, A. E., Harvey, P. D., & Penn, D. L. (2017). Social cognition psychometric evaluation: Results of the final validation study. *Schizophrenia Bulletin, 44*(4), 737–748. https://doi.org/10.1093/schbul/sbx117.

Pratt, S. I., Bartels, S. J., Mueser, K. T., & Forester, B. (2008). Helping Older People Experience Success (HOPES): An integrated model of psychosocial rehabilitation and health care management for older adults with serious mental illness. *American Journal of Psychiatric Rehabilitation, 11*, 41–60.

Pratt, S. I., Mueser, K. T., Santos, M. M., Wolfe, R., & Bartels, S. J. (2017). One size doesn't fit all: A trial of individually tailored skills training. *Psychiatric Rehabilitation Journal, 40*, 380–386. https://doi.org/10.1037/prj0000261. PMID: 2860415.

Rossotto, E., Wirshing, D. A., & Liberman, R. P. (2004). Enhancing treatment adherence among persons with schizophrenia by teaching community re-integration skills. *Psychiatric Services, 55*, 26–27.

Thoma, P., & Daum, I. (2013). Comorbid substance use disorder in schizophrenia: A selective overview of neurobiological and cognitive underpinnings. *Psychiatry and Clinical Neurosciences, 67*(6), 367–383. https://doi.org/10.1111/pcn.12072.

Turner, D. T., McGlanaghy, E., Cuijpers, P., van der Gaag, M., Karyotaki, E., & MacBeth, A. (2018). A meta-analysis of social skills training and related interventions for psychosis. *Schizophrenia Bulletin, 44*(3), 475–491. https://doi.org/10.1093/schbul/sbx146.

White, S. W. (2011). *Social skills training for children with Asperger syndrome and high-functioning autism*. New York: Guilford Press.

Wolpe, J. (1958). *Psychotherapy by reciprocal inhibition*. Stanford, CA: Stanford University Press.

Index

Note: Page numbers followed by *f* indicate figures and *t* indicate tables.

T

U

V

W

Y

Z